Multimedia Encryption and Authentication Techniques and Applications

OTHER TELECOMMUNICATIONS BOOKS FROM AUERBACH

Chaos Applications in Telecommunications
Peter Stavroulakis
ISBN: 0-8493-3832-8

Fundamentals of DSL Technology
Philip Golden; Herve Dedieu; Krista S Jacobsen
ISBN: 0-8493-1913-7

IP Multimedia Subsystem: Service Infrastructure to Converge NGN, 3G and the Internet
Rebecca Copeland
ISBN: 0-8493-9250-0

Mobile Middleware
Paolo Bellavista and Antonio Corradi
ISBN: 0-8493-3833-6

MPLS for Metropolitan Area Networks
Nam-Kee Tan
ISBN: 0-8493-2212-X

Network Security Technologies, Second Edition
Kwok T Fung
ISBN: 0-8493-3027-0

Performance Modeling and Analysis of Bluetooth Networks: Polling, Scheduling, and Traffic Control
Jelena Misic and Vojislav B Misic
ISBN: 0-8493-3157-9

Performance Optimization of Digital Communications Systems
Vladimir Mitlin
ISBN: 0-8493-6896-0

A Practical Guide to Content Delivery Networks
Gilbert Held
ISBN: 0-8493-3649-X

Resource, Mobility and Security Management in Wireless Networks and Mobile Communications
Yan Zhang, Honglin Hu, and Masayuki Fujise
ISBN: 0-8493-8036-7

Service-Oriented Architectures in Telecommunications
Vijay K Gurbani; Xian-He Sun
ISBN: 0-8493-9567-4

Testing Integrated QoS of VoIP: Packets to Perceptual Voice Quality
Vlatko Lipovac
ISBN: 0-8493-3521-3

Traffic Management in IP-Based Communications
Trinh Anh Tuan
ISBN: 0-8493-9577-1

Understanding Broadband over Power Line
Gilbert Held
ISBN: 0-8493-9846-0

WiMAX: A Wireless Technology Revolution
G.S.V. Radha Krishna Rao; G. Radhamani
ISBN: 0-8493-7059-0

WiMAX: Taking Wireless to the MAX
Deepak Pareek
ISBN: 0-8493-7186-4

Wireless Mesh Networks
Gilbert Held
ISBN: 0-8493-2960-4

Wireless Security Handbook
Aaron E Earle
ISBN: 0-8493-3378-4

Multimedia Encryption and Authentication Techniques and Applications

Editors-in-Chief and Authors

Borko Furht
Darko Kirovski

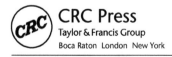

CRC Press
Taylor & Francis Group
Boca Raton London New York

CRC Press is an imprint of the
Taylor & Francis Group, an **informa** business
AN AUERBACH BOOK

The material was previously published in *Multimedia Security Handbook.* © Taylor & Francis Group, LLC 2005.

First published 2006 by Auerbach Pblications

Published 2019 by CRC Press
Taylor & Francis Group
6000 Broken Sound Parkway NW, Suite 300
Boca Raton, FL 33487-2742

© 2006 by Taylor & Francis Group, LLC
CRC Press is an imprint of Taylor & Francis Group, an Informa business

First issued in paperback 2019

No claim to original U.S. Government works

ISBN-13: 978-0-367-45363-3 (pbk)
ISBN-13: 978-0-8493-7212-4 (hbk)

Visit the Taylor & Francis Web site at
http://www.taylorandfrancis.com

and the CRC Press Web site at
http://www.crcpress.com

Library of Congress Cataloging-in-Publication Data

Multimedia encryption and authentication techniques and applications / edited by Borko Furht, Darko Kirovski.
    p. cm.
  Includes bibliographical references and index.
  ISBN 0-8493-7212-7 (alk. paper)
  1. Multimedia systems--Security measures. 2. Data encryption (Computer science) I. Furht, Borivoje. II. Kirovski, Darko.

QA76.575.M83185 2006
005.8'2--dc22   2005058037

Library of Congress Card Number 2005058037

Preface

Recent advances in digital communications and storage technologies have brought major changes for consumers. High-capacity hard disks and DVDs can store large amounts of audiovisual data. In addition, faster Internet connection speeds and the emerging high bitrate DSL connections provide sufficient bandwidth for entertainment networks. These improvements in computers and communication networks are radically changing the economics of intellectual property reproduction and distribution. Intellectual property owners must exploit new ways of reproducing, distributing, and marketing their intellectual property. However, a major problem with current digital distribution and storage technologies is the great threat of piracy.

This book is carefully edited — authors are worldwide experts in the field of multimedia encryption and authentication. Our goal is to cover all current and future trends in designing modern systems for multimedia encryption and authentication.

The technical level of the book is between an intermediate and high level. The book is primarily intended for researchers and practitioners in the field. However, some chapters are less technical than others and can be beneficial to those readers who need a broad understanding of multimedia security. The key points of the book can be summarized as follows:

- The book describes and evaluates the current state-of-the-art in multimedia encryption and authentication techniques and related technologies, architectures, standards, and applications.
- The book also presents future trends and developments in this area.
- Advanced topics, such as chaotic video encryption techniques and streaming media encryption, are also covered.
- Contributors to the book are the leading researchers from academia and practitioners from industry.

With the dramatic growth of *digital entertainment* and *Internet applications*, this book can be the definitive resource for persons working in this field as researchers, scientists, programmers, and engineers. This book can also be beneficial for business managers, entrepreneurs, and investors.

We would like to thank the authors, who are world experts in the field, for their contributions of individual chapters. Without their expertise and effort, this book would never have come to fruition. The Auerbach Publications editors and staff also deserve our sincere recognition for their support throughout the project.

Borko Furht and Darko Kirovski

Editors-in-Chief and Authors

Borko Furht is a professor and chairman of the Department of Computer Science and Engineering at Florida Atlantic University (FAU) in Boca Raton, Florida. Before joining FAU, he was a vice president of research and a senior director of development at Modcomp (Ft. Lauderdale), a computer company of Daimler Benz, Germany, and a professor at the University of Miami in Coral Gables, Florida. Professor Furht received Ph.D. degrees in electrical and computer engineering from the University of Belgrade. His current research is in multimedia systems, video coding and compression, video databases, wireless multimedia, and Internet computing. He is currently Principal Investigator and Co-PI of two multiyear, multimillion dollar projects — on Coastline Security Technologies, funded by the Department of Navy, and One Pass to Production, funded by Motorola. He is the author of numerous books and articles in the areas of multimedia, computer architecture, real-time computing, and operating systems. He is a founder and editor-in-chief of *The Journal of Multimedia Tools and Applications* (Kluwer Academic Publishers). He has received several technical and publishing awards, and has consulted for many high-tech companies, including IBM, Hewlett-Packard,

Xerox, General Electric, JPL, NASA, Honeywell and RCA. He has also served as a consultant to various colleges and universities. He has given many invited talks, keynote lectures, seminars, and tutorials.

Darko Kirovski received his Ph.D. degree in computer science from the University of California, Los Angeles, in 2001. Since April 2000, he has been a researcher at Microsoft Research. His research interests include certificates of authenticity, system security, multimedia processing, biometric identity authentication, and embedded system design and debugging. He received the 1999 Microsoft Graduate Research Fellowship, the 2000 ACM/IEEE Design Automation Conference Graduate Scholarship, the 2001 ACM Outstanding Ph.D. Dissertation Award in Electronic Design Automation, and the Best Paper Award at ACM Multimedia 2002.

List of Contributors

Rolf Blom, Ericsson Research, Communications Security Laboratory, Ericsson AB, Sweden

Elisabetta Carrara, Ericsson Research, Communications Security Laboratory, Ericsson AB, Sweden

Shih-Fu Chang, Department of Electrical Engineering, Columbia University, New York, New York

Guanrong Chen, Department of Electronic Engineering, City University of Hong Kong, Hong Kong SAR, China

Mohamed Daoudi, MIIRE Group, LIFL/INT ENIC-Telecom Lille1, Cité Scientifique, Villeneuve d'Ascq, France

Edward J. Delp, Video and Image Processing Laboratory (*VIPER*), School of Electrical and Computer Engineering, Purdue University, West Lafayette, Indiana

Chabane Djeraba, MIIRE Group, LIFL/INT ENIC-Telecom Lille1, Cité Scientifique, Villeneuve d'Ascq, France

Sabu Emmanuel, Nanyang Technological University, Singapore

Ahmet M. Eskicioglu, Department of Computer and Information Science, Brooklyn College, The City University of New York, Brooklyn, New York

Borko Furht, Department of Computer Science and Engineering, Florida Atlantic University, Boca Raton, Florida

Mohan S. Kankanhalli, National University of Singapore, Singapore

Deepa Kundur, Texas A&M University, Department of Electrical Engineering, College Station, Texas

Shujun Li, Department of Electronic Engineering, City University of Hong Kong, Hong Kong SAR, China

Fredrik Lindholm, Ericsson Research, Communications Security Laboratory, Ericsson AB, Sweden

Jeffrey Lotspiech, Henderson, Nevada

William Luh, Texas A&M University, Department of Electrical Engineering, College Station, Texas

Mohamed F. Mansour, Texas Instruments Inc., Dallas, Texas

Mats Näslund, Ericsson Research, Communications Security Laboratory, Ericsson AB, Sweden

Karl Norrman, Ericsson Research, Communications Security Laboratory, Ericsson AB, Sweden

Dimitrios Skraparlis, Toshiba Research Europe Limited, Telecommunications Research Laboratory, Bristol, United Kingdom

Daniel Socek, Department of Computer Science and Engineering, Florida Atlantic University, Boca Raton, Florida

Qibin Sun, Institute for Infocomm Research, Singapore 119613

Ahmed H. Tewfik, Department of Electrical and Computer Engineering, University of Minnesota, Minneapolis, Minnesota

Christophe Tombelle, MIIRE Group, LIFL/INT ENIC-Telecom Lille1, Cité Scientifique, Villeneuve d'Ascq, France

Heather Yu, Panasonic Digital Networking Laboratory, Princeton, New Jersey

Huicheng Zheng, MIIRE Group, LIFL/INT ENIC-Telecom Lille1, Cité Scientifique, Villeneuve d'Ascq, France

Xuan Zheng, Department of Electrical and Computer Engineering, University of Virginia, Charlottesville, Virginia

Contents

1
Protection of Multimedia Content in Distribution Networks

Ahmet M. Eskicioglu and Edward J. Delp

INTRODUCTION

In recent years, advances in digital technologies have created significant changes in the way we reproduce, distribute, and market intellectual property (IP). Digital media can now be exploited by IP owners to develop new and innovative business models for their products and services. The lowered cost of reproduction, storage, and distribution, however, also invites much motivation for large-scale commercial infringement. In a world where piracy is a growing potential threat, the rights of the IP owners can be protected using three complementary weapons: technology, legislation, and business models. Because of the diversity of IP (ranging from e-books to songs and movies) created by copyright industries, no single solution is applicable to the protection of multi-media products in distribution networks.

Intellectual property is created as a result of intellectual activities in the industrial, scientific, literary, and artistic fields [1]. It is divided into two general categories:

1. *Industrial property*. This includes inventions (patents), trademarks, industrial designs, and geographic indications of source. A *patent* is an exclusive right granted for an invention, which is a product or a process that provides either a new way of doing something or a new technical solution to a problem. A *trademark* is a distinctive sign that identifies certain goods or services as those produced or provided by a specific person or enterprise. It provides protection to the owner by ensuring the exclusive right to use it to identify goods or services or to authorize another to use it in return for payment. An *industrial design* is the ornamental or aesthetic aspect of an article. The design may consist of three-dimensional features (such as the shape or surface of an article) or of two-dimensional features (such as patterns, lines, or color). A *geographical indication* is a sign used on goods that have a specific geographical origin and possess qualities or a reputation that are due to that place of origin. In general, a geographical indication is associated with the name of the place of origin of the goods. Typically, agricultural products have qualities that derive from their place of production identified by specific local factors such as climate and soil.

2. *Copyright*. This includes literary and artistic works such as novels, poems and plays, films, musical works, artistic works such as drawings, paintings, photographs, and sculptures, and architectural designs. As many creative works protected by copyright require mass distribution, communication, and financial investment for their dissemination (e.g., publications, sound recordings, and films), creators usually sell the rights to their works to individuals or companies with a potential to market the works in return for payment. Copyright and its related rights are essential to human creativity, providing creators incentives in the form of recognition and fair economic rewards and assurance that their works can be disseminated without fear of unauthorized copying or piracy.

To understand the increasing importance of copyrighted content protection, we should apprehend the essential difference between old and new technologies for distribution and storage. Prior to the development of digital technologies, content was created, distributed, stored, and displayed by analog means. The popular video cassette recorders (VCRs) of the 1980s introduced a revolutionary way of viewing audiovisual (A/V) content but, ironically, allowed unauthorized copying, risking the investments made in IP. The inherent characteristics of analog recording, however, prevented piracy efforts from reaching alarming proportions. If taped content is copied on a VCR, the visual quality of the new (i.e., the first generation) copy is relatively reduced. Further generational copies result in noticeably reduced quality, decreasing the commercial value of the content. Today, reasonably efficient analog copy protection methods exist and have recently been made mandatory in consumer electronics devices to further discourage illegal analog copying.

With the advent of digital technologies, new tools have emerged for making perfect copies of the original content. We will briefly review digital representation of data to reveal why generational copies do not lose their quality. A text, an image, or a video is represented as a stream of bits (0s and 1s) that can be conveniently stored on magnetic or optical media. Because digital recording is a process whereby each bit in the source stream is read and copied to the new medium, an exact replica of the content is obtained. Such a capability becomes even more threatening with the ever-increasing availability of the Internet, an immense and boundless digital distribution mechanism. Protection of digital multimedia content therefore appears to be a crucial problem for which immediate solutions are needed.

Recent inventions in digital communications and storage technologies have resulted in a number of major changes in the distribution of multimedia content to consumers:

- Magnetic and optical storage capacity is much higher today. Even the basic configuration of personal computers comes with 40 GB of magnetic hard disk storage. Although a DVD (digital versatile disk) is the same physical size as a CD, it has a much higher optical storage capacity for audiovisual data. Depending on the type of DVD, the capacity ranges between 4 and 17 GB (2 to 8 h of video).
- The speed of the Internet connection has grown rapidly in recent years. Currently, cable modems and Asymmetric Digital Subscriber Line (ADSL) are the two technologies that dominate the industry. The emerging VDSL (very high bitrate DSL) connection with speeds up to 52 Mbps will provide sufficient bandwidth for entertainment networks.

End-to-end security is the most critical requirement for the creation of new digital markets where copyrighted content is a major product. In this chapter, we present an overview of copyright and copyright industries and examine how the technological, legal, and business solutions help maintain the incentive to supply the lifeblood of the markets.

WHAT IS COPYRIGHT?

To guide the discussion into the proper context, we will begin with the definition of "copyright" and summarize the important aspects of copyright law. Copyright is a *form of protection provided by the laws of the United States (Title 17, U.S. Code) to the authors of "original works of authorship," including literary, dramatic, musical, artistic, and certain other intellectual works* [2]. Although copyright literally means "right to copy," the term is now used to cover a number of exclusive rights granted to the authors for the protection of their work. According to Section 106 of the 1976 Copyright Act [3], the owner of copyright is given the exclusive right to do, and to authorize others to do, any of the following:

- To *reproduce the copyrighted work* in copies or phonorecords
- To prepare *derivative works* based on the copyrighted work
- To *distribute copies or phonorecords* of the copyrighted work to the public by sale or other transfer of ownership, or by rental, lease, or lending
- To *perform the copyrighted work publicly*, in the case of literary, musical, dramatic, and choreographic works, pantomimes, and motion pictures and other audiovisual works
- To *display the copyrighted work publicly*, in the case of literary, musical, dramatic, and choreographic works, pantomimes, and pictorial, graphic, or sculptural works, including the individual images of a motion picture or other audiovisual work
- To *perform the copyrighted work publicly* by means of a digital audio transmission, in the case of sound recordings

It is illegal to violate the rights provided by the copyright law to the owner of the copyright. There are, however, limitations on these rights as established in several sections of the 1976 Copyright Act. One important limitation, the doctrine of "fair use," has been the subject of a major discussion on content protection. Section 107 states that the use of a copyrighted work by reproduction in copies or phonorecords or by any other means specified by the law, for purposes such as criticism, comment, news reporting, teaching (including multiple copies for classroom use), scholarship, or research, is not an infringement of copyright. In any particular case, the following criteria, among others, may be considered in determining whether fair use applies or not:

1. The purpose and character of the use, including whether such use is of a commercial nature or is for nonprofit educational purposes
2. The nature of the copyrighted work
3. The amount and substantiality of the portion used in relation to the copyrighted work as a whole
4. The effect of the use upon the potential market for, or value of, the copyrighted work

For copyright protection, the original work of authorship should be fixed in a tangible medium of expression from which it can be perceived, reproduced, or otherwise communicated, either directly or with the aid of a machine or device. This language incorporates three fundamental concepts [4] of the law: fixation, originality, and expression. *Fixation* (i.e., the act of rendering a creation in some tangible form) may be achieved in a number of ways, depending on the category of the work. *Originality* is a necessary (but not a sufficient) condition for a work produced by the human mind to be copyrightable. Scientific discoveries, for example, are not copyrightable, as they are regarded as the common property of all people (however, an inventor can apply for a patent, which is another form of protection). Finally, it is the *expression* of an idea, and not idea itself, that is copyrightable. Ideas, like facts, are in the public domain without a need for protection. Nevertheless, the separation of an idea from an expression is not always clear and can only be studied on a case-by-case basis. When the three basic requirements of fixation, originality, and expression are met, the law provides for highly broad protection. Table 1.1 summarizes the range of copyrightable works.

It is interesting to note that copyright is secured as soon as the work is created by the author in some fixed form. No action, including publication and registration, is needed in the Copyright Office. *Publication* is the distribution of copies or phonorecords of a work to the public by sale or other transfer of ownership or by rental, lease, or lending. *Registration* is a legal process to create a public record of the basic facts of a particular copyright. Although neither publication nor registration is a requirement for protection, they provide certain advantages to the copyright owner.

The copyright law has different clauses for the protection of published and unpublished works. All unpublished works are subject to protection, regardless of the nationality or domicile of the author. The published works are protected if certain conditions are met regarding the type of work, citizenship, residency, and publication date and place.

TABLE 1.1. Main Categories of Copyrightable and Not Copyrightable Items

Copyrightable	Not Copyrightable
Literary works	Works that have not been fixed in a
Musical works (including any	tangible form of expression
accompanying words)	Titles, names, short phrases, and
Dramatic works (including	slogans; familiar symbols or
any accompanying music)	designs; mere variations of
Pantomimes and choreographic works	typographic ornamentation,
Pictorial, graphic, and sculptural works	lettering, or coloring; mere
Motion pictures and other audiovisual	listings of ingredients or contents
works	Ideas, procedures, methods,
Sound recordings	systems, processes, concepts,
Architectural works	principles, discoveries, or devices,
	as distinguished from a description,
	explanation, or illustration
	Works consisting entirely of
	information that is common
	property and containing
	no original authorship

International copyright laws do not exist for the protection of works throughout the entire world. The national laws of individual countries may include different measures to prevent unauthorized use of copyrighted works. Fortunately, many countries offer protection to foreign works under certain conditions through membership in international treaties and conventions. Two important international conventions are the Berne Convention and the Universal Copyright Convention [3].

A work created on or after January 1, 1978, is given copyright protection that endures 70 years after the author's death. If more than one author is involved in the creation, the term ends 70 years after the last surviving author's death. For works predating January 1, 1978, the duration of copyright depends on whether the work was published or registered by that date.

A law enacted by the U.S. Congress in 1870 centralized the copyright system in the Library of Congress. Today, the U.S. Copyright Office is a major service unit of the Library, providing services to the Congress and other institutions in the United States and abroad. It administers the copyright law, creates and maintains public records, and serves as a resource to the domestic and international copyright communities. Table 1.2 lists some of the copyright milestones in the United States for the past two centuries [5–7].

TABLE 1.2. Notable Dates in the U.S. History of Copyright

Date	Event
May 31, 1790	First copyright law, derived from the English copyright law (Statute of Anne) and common law, enacted under the new constitution
April 29, 1802	Prints added to protected works
February 3, 1831	First general revision of the copyright law
August 18, 1856	Dramatic compositions added to protected works
March 3, 1865	Photographs added to protected works
July 8, 1870	Second general revision of the copyright law
January 6, 1897	Music protected against unauthorized public performance
July 1, 1909	Third general revision of the copyright law
August 24, 1912	Motion pictures, previously registered as photographs, added to classes of protected works
July 30, 1947	Copyright law codified as Title 17 of the U.S. Code
October 19, 1976	Fourth general revision of the copyright law
December 12, 1980	Copyright law amended regarding computer programs
March 1, 1989	United States joined the Berne Convention
December 1, 1990	Copyright protection extended to architectural works
October 28, 1992	Digital Audio Home Recording Act required serial copy management systems in digital audio recorders
October 28, 1998	The Digital Millennium Copyright Act (DMCA) signed into law

U.S. COPYRIGHT INDUSTRIES

The primary domestic source of marketable content is the U.S. copyright industries [8], which produce and distribute materials protected by national and international copyright laws. The products include the following categories:

1. All types of computer software (including business applications and entertainment software)
2. Motion pictures, TV programs, home videocassettes, and DVDs
3. Music, records, audio cassettes, audio DVDs and CDs
4. Textbooks, tradebooks, and other publications (both in print and electronic media)

Depending on the type of activity, U.S. copyright industries can be studied in two groups: "core" and "total." The core industries are those that create copyrighted works as their primary product. The total copyright industries include the core industries and portions of many other industries that create, distribute, or depend on copyrighted works. Examples are retail trade (with sales of video, audio, books, and software) and the toy industry.

The International Intellectual Property Alliance (IIPA) [8] is a private-sector coalition that represents U.S. copyright-based industries in bilateral and multilateral efforts to improve international protection of copyrighted materials. Formed in 1984, the IIPA is comprised of six trade associations, each representing a different section of the U.S. copyright industry. The member associations are:

Association of American Publishers (AAP): the principal trade association of the book publishing industry

American Film Marketing Association (AFMA): a trade association whose members produce, distribute, and license the international rights to independent English language films, TV programs, and home videos

Business Software Alliance (BSA): an international organization representing leading commercial software industry and its hardware partners

Entertainment Software Association (ESA): the U.S. association of the companies publishing interactive games for video game consoles, handheld devices, personal computers, and the Internet

Motion Picture Association of America (MPAA): the MPAA, along with its international counterpart, the Motion Picture Association (MPA), serve as the voice and advocate of seven of the largest producers and distributors of filmed entertainment

Recording Industry Association of America (RIAA): a trade association that represents companies that create, manufacture, and/or distribute approximately 90% of all legitimate sound recordings in the United States.

"Copyright Industries in the U.S. Economy: The 2002 Report," which updates eight prior studies, details the importance of the copyright industries to the U.S. economy based on three economic indicators: value added to GDP, share of national employment, and revenues generated from foreign sales and exports. This report gives an indication of the significance of the copyright industries to the U.S. economy:

- In 2001, the U.S. core copyright industries accounted for 5.24% ($535.1 billion) of the U.S. Gross Domestic Product (GDP). Between 1977 and 2001, their share of the GDP grew more than twice as fast as the remainder of the U.S. economy (7% vs. 3%).

- Between 1977 and 2001, employment in the U.S. core copyright industries grew from 1.6% (1.5 million workers) to 3.5% (4.7 million workers) of the U.S. workforce. Average annual employment growth was more than three times as fast as the remainder of the U.S. economy (5% vs. 1.5%).

- In 2001, the U.S. core copyright industries estimated foreign sales and exports was $88.97 billion, leading all major industry sectors (chemical and allied products; motor vehicles, equipment and parts; aircraft and aircraft parts; electronic components and accessories; computers and peripherals).

Special 301, an annual review, requires the U.S. Trade Representative (USTR) to identify those countries that deny adequate and effective protection for intellectual property rights or deny fair and equitable market access for persons who rely on intellectual property protection. It was created by the U.S. Congress when it passed the Omnibus Trade and Competitive Act of 1988, which amended the Trade Act of 1974. According to IIPA's 2003 Special 301 Report on Global Copyright Protection and Enforcement, the U.S. copyright industries suffered estimated trade losses due to piracy of nearly $9.2 billion in 2002 as a result of the deficiencies in the copyright regimes of 56 countries. The losses for the five copyright-based industry sectors are given in Table 1.3. In USTR 2003 "Special 301" Decisions on Intellectual Property, this data is updated for 49 countries to be almost $9.8 billion. The annual losses due to piracy of U.S. copyrighted materials around the world are estimated to be $20 to 22 billion (not including Internet piracy) [8].

A major study titled "The Digital Dilemma — Intellectual Property in the Information Age" [9] was initiated by the Computer Science and Telecommunications Board (CSTB) to assess issues related to the nature, evolution, and use of the Internet and other networks and to the generation, distribution, and protection of content accessed through networks. The study committee convened by the CSTB included experts from industry, academia, and the library and information science community. The work was carried out through the expert deliberations of the committee and by soliciting input and discussion from a wide range

TABLE 1.3. Estimated Trade Losses due to Copyright Piracy in 56 Selected Countries in 2002 (in millions of U.S. dollars)

Industry	Estimated Losses
Motion pictures	1322.3
Records and music	2142.3
Business software applications	3539.0
Entertainment software	1690.0
Books	514.5
Total	**9208.1**

of institutions and individuals. An important contribution of the study is a detailed review of the mechanisms for protecting IP. After a careful analysis of the technical tools and business models, the report concludes that

> There is great diversity in the kinds of digital intellectual property, business models, legal mechanisms, and technical protection services possible, making a one-size-fits-all solution too rigid. Currently, a wide variety of new models and mechanisms are being created, tried out, and in some cases discarded, at a furious pace. This process should be supported and encouraged, to allow all parties to find models and mechanisms well suited to their needs.

In the above study, the reliability of the figures attempting to measure the size of the economic impact of piracy was found questionable for two reasons:

1. The IIPA reports may imply that the copyrights industries' contribution to the GDP depends on copyright policy and protection measures, pointing to a need for greater levels of protection in the digital world. However, from an economics viewpoint, the specific relation between the level of protection and revenue of a business in the copyright industries is not clear.
2. The accuracy of the estimates of the cost of piracy is problematic.

At any rate, there is evidence of illegal copying, and we need to have a better understanding of its complex economic and social implications.

TECHNICAL SOLUTIONS

Figure 1.1 shows a "universe" of digital content distribution systems with five primary means of delivery to consumers: satellite, cable, terrestrial, Internet, and prerecorded media (optical and magnetic).

This universe is commonly used for distributing and storing entertainment content that is protected by copyright. The basic requirements for end-to-end security from the source to the final destination include:

- *Secure distribution of content and access keys.* In secure multimedia content distribution, the audiovisual stream is compressed, packetized, and encrypted. Encryption is the process of transforming an intelligible message (called the plaintext) into a representation (called the ciphertext) that cannot be understood by unauthorized parties [10,11]. In *symmetric key* ciphers, the enciphering and deciphering keys are the same or can be easily determined from each other. In *asymmetric (public) key* cipher, the enciphering and deciphering keys differ in such a way that at least one key is computationally infeasible to determine from the other.

Figure 1.1. The universe of digital systems.

Symmetric key ciphers are commonly used for the protection of content, whereas the decryption keys sent to the consumers may be protected by public key ciphers (the protection of the decryption keys is normally privately defined for security reasons).

- *Authentication of source and sink consumer devices in home networks.* In a digital home network, copyrighted content can be moved from one digital device to another. Before this transfer can take place, the source and sink devices are normally engaged in mutual authentication to provide evidence that they are manufactured with the licensed protection technology. If a device is not able to produce that evidence, depending on its role, it cannot receive or transmit content.

- *Association of digital rights with content.* For the association of the digital rights with multimedia content, two approaches have been proposed: using metadata or watermarks. In the past few years, rights expression languages (RELs) have become an essential component of digital rights management systems. RELs are a means of expressing the rights of a party to certain assets, and they serve as standardized exchange formats for rights expressions. In the market, there are competing proposals that need to be standardized:

  - Started in 2001, the Open Digital Rights Language (ODRL) Initiative is an international effort aimed at developing an open standard and promoting the language at numerous standards bodies. The ODRL specification supports an extensible language and vocabulary (data dictionary) for the expression of terms and conditions over any content, including permissions, constraints, obligations, conditions, and offers and

11

agreements with rights holders. The Open Mobile Alliance (OMA) has adopted the ODRL as the rights commerce standard for mobile content.

– The eXtensible rights Markup Language (XrML) is a general-purpose, XML-based specification grammar for expressing rights and conditions associated with digital content, services, or any digital resource. The goal of XrML is to expand the usefulness of digital content, resources, and Web services to rights holders, technology developers, service providers, and users by providing a flexible, extensible, and interoperable industry-standard language that is platform, media, and format independent. XrML was selected as the basis for MPEG-21 Rights Expression Language (MPEG-21 REL), which is a Final Draft International Standard. XrML is also the choice of the Open eBook Rights and Rules Working Group (RRWG) as the rights expression language for its Rights Grammar specification.

- *Renewability of content protection systems.* Most of the content protection systems define renewability as device revocation. If a licensed device's secret information (keys, etc.) is compromised by the hacker, he can use the same secret information in devices that do not use the licensed protection technology. When such pirated devices appear on the black market in large numbers and are identified by law enforcement agencies, the technology provider adds the hacked device's ID to a revocation list that is distributed to all licensed devices with proper cryptographic methods. When the new revocation list reaches the authorized devices, any pirated device will fail the authentication process and be unable to process protected content.

There are three industries with vested interest in the digital content protection arena: motion picture, consumer electronics, and information technology. Table 1.4 lists some of the key players that represent companies ranging from content owners to device manufacturers and service providers.

In the past two decades, several protection systems have been proposed and implemented in commonly used digital distribution networks. These include:

- Conditional access (CA) systems for satellite, cable, and terrestrial distribution
- Digital Rights Management (DRM) systems (unicast-based and multicast-based) for Internet distribution
- Copy protection (CP) systems for distribution within digital home networks

TABLE 1.4. Key Players in Multimedia Content Protection

Player	Brief Information
ATSC [12]	ATSC (Advanced Television Systems Committee) Inc. is an international, nonprofit organization developing voluntary standards for digital television. Currently, there are approximately 140 members representing the broadcast, broadcast equipment, motion picture, consumer electronics, computer, cable, satellite, and semiconductor industries. ATSC incorporated on January 3, 2002.
CEA [13]	CEA (Consumer Electronics Association) represents more than 1000 companies within the U.S. consumer technology industry. The Board of Directors meets three times annually to review the state of the industry and determine CEA strategic goals to assist the industry and members. The Board of Directors elects the Officers of CEA (Executive Board members, including division chairs) and EIA Board of Governors representatives. CEA produces the International CES, the world's largest consumer technology event.
CPTWG [14]	CPTWG (Copy Protection Technical Working Group) was formed in early 1996 with the initial focus of protecting linear motion picture content on DVD. Supported by the motion picture, consumer electronics, information technology, and computer software industries, the scope of CPTWG now covers a range of issues from digital watermarking to protection of digital television.
DVD Forum [15]	DVD Forum is an international association of hardware manufacturers, software firms, and other users of DVDs. Originally known as the DVD Consortium, the Forum was created in 1995 for the purpose of exchanging and disseminating ideas and information about the DVD format and its technical capabilities, improvements, and innovations. The ten companies that founded the organization are Hitachi, Ltd., Matsushita Electric Industrial Co. Ltd., Mitsubishi Electric Corporation, Pioneer Electronic Corporation, Royal Philips Electronics N.V., Sony Corporation, Thomson, Time Warner Inc., Toshiba Corporation, and Victor Company of Japan, Ltd.

(Continued)

TABLE 1.4. Continued

Player	Brief Information
SCTE [16]	SCTE (Society of Cable Telecommunications Engineers) is a nonprofit professional organization committed to advancing the careers of cable telecommunications professionals and serving the industry through excellence in professional development, information, and standards. Currently, SCTE has almost 15,000 members from the United States and 70 countries worldwide and offers a variety of programs and services for the industry's educational benefit.
MPAA [17]	MPAA (Motion Picture Association of America) and its international counterpart, the Motion Picture Association (MPA), represent the American motion picture, home video, and television industries, domestically through the MPAA and internationally through the MPA. Founded in 1922 as the trade association of the American film industry, the MPAA has broadened its mandate over the years to reflect the diversity of an expanding industry. The MPA was formed in 1945 in the aftermath of World War II to reestablish American films in the world market and to respond to the rising tide of protectionism resulting in barriers aimed at restricting the importation of American films.
RIAA [18]	RIAA (Recording Industries Association of America) is the trade group that represents the U.S. recording industry. Its mission is to foster a business and legal climate that supports and promotes the members' creative and financial vitality. The trade group's more than 350 member companies create, manufacture, and distribute approximately 90% of all legitimate sound recordings produced and sold in the United States.
IETF [19]	IETF (Internet Engineering Task Force) is a large, open international community of network designers, operators, vendors, and researchers concerned with the evolution of the Internet architecture and the smooth operation of the Internet. The IETF working groups are grouped into areas and are managed by Area Directors (ADs). The ADs are members of the Internet Engineering Steering Group (IESG). Architectural oversight is provided by the Internet Architecture Board, (IAB). The IAB and IESG are chartered by the Internet Society (ISOC) for these purposes. The General Area Director also serves as the chair of the IESG and of the IETF and is an ex-officio member of the IAB.

(Continued)

TABLE 1.4. Continued

Player	Brief Information
MPEG [20]	MPEG (Moving Pictures Expert Group) is originally the name given to the group of experts that developed a family of international standards used for coding audiovisual information in a digital compressed format. Established in 1988, the MPEG Working Group (formally known as ISO/IEC JTC1/SC29/WG11) is part of JTC1, the Joint ISO/IEC Technical Committee on Information Technology. The MPEG family of standards includes MPEG-1, MPEG-2, and MPEG-4, formally known as ISO/IEC-11172, ISO/IEC-13818, and ISO/IEC-14496, respectively.
DVB [21]	DVB (Digital Video Broadcasting) Project is an industry-led consortium of over 300 broadcasters, manufacturers, network operators, software developers, regulatory bodies, and others in over 35 countries committed to designing global standards for the global delivery of digital television and data services. The General Assembly is the highest body in the DVB Project. The Steering Board sets the overall policy direction for the DVB Project and handles its coordination, priority setting and, management, aided by three Ad Hoc Groups on Rules & Procedures, Budget, and Regulatory issues. The DVB Project is divided in four main Modules, each covering a specific element of the work undertaken. The Commercial Module and Technical Module are the driving force behind the development of the DVB specifications, with the Intellectual Property Rights Module addressing IPR issues and the Promotion and Communications Module dealing with the promotion of DVB around the globe.

Many problems, some of which are controversial, are still open and challenge the motion picture, consumer electronics, and information technology industries.

In an end-to-end protection system, a fundamental problem is to determine whether the consumer is authorized to access the requested content. The traditional concept of controlling physical access to places (e.g., cities, buildings, rooms, highways) has been extended to the digital world in order to deal with information in binary form. A familiar example is the access control mechanism used in computer operating systems to manage data, programs, and other system resources. Such systems can be effective in "bounded" communities [9] (e.g., a corporation or a college campus), where the emphasis is placed on the original access to information rather than how the information is used once it is in the possession of the user. In contrast, the conditional access systems for digital content in "open" communities need to provide reliable services for long periods of time (up to several decades) and be capable of controlling the use of content after access.

We will look at three approaches for restricting access to content. The first approach has been used by the satellite and terrestrial broadcasters and cable operators in the past few decades (for both analog and digital content). The second approach is adopted by the developers of emerging technologies for protecting Internet content. In the third approach, we have a collection of copy protection systems for optical and magnetic storage and two major digital interfaces.

Security in CA Systems for Satellite, Cable, and Terrestrial Distribution

A CA system [22–30] allows access to services based on payment or other requirements such as identification, authorization, authentication, registration, or a combination of these. Using satellite, terrestrial, or cable transmissions, the service providers deliver different types of multimedia content, ranging from free-access programs to services such as PayTV, Pay-Per-View, and Video-on-Demand.

Conditional access systems are developed by companies, commonly called the CA providers, that specialize in the protection of audio visual (A/V) signals and secure processing environments. A typical architecture of a CA system and its major components are shown in Figure 1.2. The common activities in this general model are:

1. Digital content (called an "event" or a "program") is compressed to minimize bandwidth requirements. MPEG-2 is a well-known industry standard for coding A/V streams. More recent MPEG alternatives (MPEG-4, MPEG-7, and MPEG-21) are being considered for new applications.

2. The program is sent to the CA head-end to be protected and packaged with entitlements indicating the access conditions.

3. The A/V stream is scrambled[1] and multiplexed with the entitlement messages. There are two types of entitlement message [31] associated with each program: The Entitlement Control Messages (ECMs) carry the decryption keys (called the "control words") and a short description of the program (number, title, date, time, price, rating, etc.), whereas the Entitlement Management Messages

---

[1]In the context of CA systems, *scrambling* is the process of content encryption. This term is inherited from the analog protection systems where the analog video was manipulated using methods such as line shuffling. It is now being used to distinguish the process from the protection of *descrambling* keys.

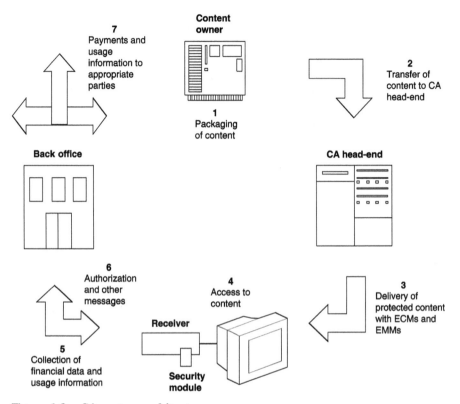

Figure 1.2. CA system architecture.

(EMMs) specify the authorization levels related to services. In most CA systems, the EMMs can also be sent via other means such as telephone networks. The services are usually encrypted using a symmetric cipher such as the Data Encryption Standard (DES) or any other public-domain or private algorithm. The lifetime and the length of the scrambling keys are two important system parameters. For security reasons, the protection of the ECMs is often privately defined by the CA providers, but public key cryptography and one-way functions are useful tools for secure key delivery.

4. If the customer has received authorization to watch the protected program,[2] the A/V stream is descrambled by the receiver (also called a "decoder"), and sent to the display unit for viewing. A removable security module (e.g., a smartcard) provides a safe environment for the processing of ECMs, EMMs, and other sensitive functions such as user authorization and temporary storage of purchase records.

---

[2]The program may come directly from the head-end or a local storage device. Protection of local storage (such as a hard disk) is a current research area.

5. The back office is an essential component of every CA system, handling billings and payments, transmission of EMMs, and interactive TV applications. A one-to-one link is established between the back office and the decoder (or the removable security module, if it exists) using a "return channel," which is basically a telephone connection via a modem. As with other details of the CA system, the security of this channel may be privately defined by the CA providers. At certain times, the back office collects the purchase history and other usage information for processing.

6. Authorizations (e.g., EMMs) and other messages (system and security updates, etc.) are delivered to the customer's receiver.

7. Payments and usage information are sent to the appropriate parties (content providers, service operators, CA providers, etc.).

In today's CA systems, the security module is assigned the critical task of recovering the descrambling keys. These keys are then passed to the receiver for decrypting the A/V streams. The workload is, therefore, shared between the security module and its host. Recently, two separate standards have evolved to remove all of the security functionality from navigation devices. In the United States, the National Renewable Security Standard (NRSS) [32] defines a renewable and replaceable security element for use in consumer electronics devices such as digital set-top boxes and digital TVs. In Europe, the DVB project has specified a standard for a common interface (CI) between a host device and a security module.

The CA systems currently in operation support several purchase methods, including subscription, pay-per-view, and impulsive pay-per-view. Other models are also being considered to provide more user convenience and to facilitate payments. One such model uses prepaid "cash cards" to store credits that can be obtained from authorized dealers or ATM-like machines.

Note that the model described in Figure 1.2 has been traditionally used to provide conditional access for viewing purposes. Recording control depends on the type of the signal output from the receiver. If the device has NTSC, PAL, or SECAM output (which is the case for some devices in the field today), protection can be provided by a Macrovision [33] system, which modifies the video in such a way that it does not appreciably distort the display quality of the video but results in noticeable degradation in recording. For higher-definition analog or digital outputs, however, the model is drastically changing, requiring solutions that are more complex and relatively more expensive.

The DVB Project has envisaged two basic CA approaches: "Simul-crypt" and "Multicrypt" [27,34]:

1. *Simulcrypt.* Each program is transmitted with the entitlement messages for multiple CA systems, enabling different CA decoders to receive and correctly descramble the program.
2. *Multicrypt.* Each decoder is built with a common interface for multiple CA systems. Security modules from different CA system operators can be plugged into different slots in the same decoder to allow switching between CA systems.

These architectures can be used for satellite, cable, and terrestrial transmission of digital television. The ATSC [35] has adopted the Simulcrypt approach.

A recent major discussion item on the agenda for content owners and broadcasters has been the broadcast flag [36]. Also known as the ATSC flag, the broadcast flag is a sequence of digital bits sent with a television program that signals that the program must be protected from unauthorized redistribution. It is argued that implementation of this broadcast flag will allow digital TV (DTV) stations to obtain high-value content and assure consumers a continued source of attractive, free, over-the-air programming without limiting the consumer's ability to make personal copies. The suitability of the broadcast flag for protecting DTV content was evaluated by the Broadcast Protection Discussion Group (BPDG) that was comprised of a large number of content providers, television broadcasters, consumer electronics manufacturers, information technology companies, interested individuals, and consumer activists. The group completed its mission with the release of the BPDG Report. The broadcast flag can be successfully implemented once the suppliers of computer and electronics systems that receive broadcast television signals incorporate the technical requirements of the flag into their products. Undoubtedly, full implementation requires a legislative or regulatory mandate. In November 2003, the Federal Communications Commission (FCC) adopted a broadcast flag mandate rule, despite the objections of thousands of individuals and dozens of organizations [37].

Security in DRM Systems for Internet Distribution

DRM refers to the protection, distribution, modification and enforcement of the rights associated with the use of digital content. In general, the primary responsibilities of a DRM system are:

- Packaging of content
- Secure delivery and storage of content
- Prevention of unauthorized access
- Enforcement of usage rules
- Monitoring the use of content

Although such systems can, in principle, be deployed for any type of distribution media, the present discussions weigh heavily on the Internet.

The unprecedented explosion of the Internet has opened potentially limitless distribution channels for the electronic commerce of content. Selling goods directly to consumers over an open and public network, without the presence of a clerk at the point of sale, has significant advantages. It allows the businesses to expand their market reach, reduce operating costs, and enhance customer satisfaction by offering personalized experience. Although inspiring new business opportunities, this electronic delivery model raises challenging questions about the traditional models of ownership. The lessons learned from the MP3 phenomenon, combined with the lack of reliable payment mechanisms, have shown the need for protecting the ownership rights of copyrighted digital material.

A DRM system uses cryptography (symmetric key ciphers, public-key ciphers, and digital signatures) as the centerpiece for security-related functions, which generally include secure delivery of content, secure delivery of the content key and the usage rights, and client authentication.

Figure 1.3 shows the fundamentals of an electronic delivery system with DRM: a publisher, a server (streaming or Web), a client device, and a financial clearing house. The communication between the server and the customer is assumed to be unicast (i.e., point-to-point). Although details may vary among DRM systems, the following steps summarize typical activities in a DRM-supported e-commerce system:

1. The publisher packages the media file (i.e., the content) and encrypts it with a symmetric cipher. The package may include information about the content provider, retailer, or the Web address to contact for the rights.
2. The protected media file is placed on a server for downloading or streaming. It can be located with a search engine using the proper content index.
3. The customer requests the media file from the server.
4. The file is sent after the client device is authenticated. The customer may also be required to complete a purchase transaction. Authentication based on public-key certificates is commonly used for this purpose. Depending on the DRM system, the usage rules and the key to unlock the file may either be attached to the file or need to be separately obtained (e.g., in the form of a license) from the clearinghouse or any other registration server. The attachment or the license are protected in such a way that only

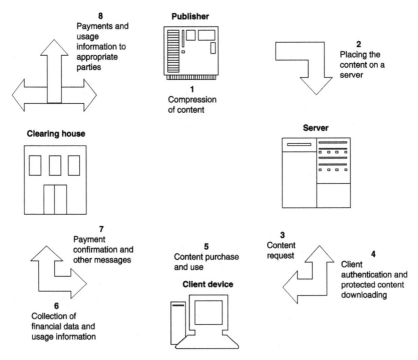

Figure 1.3. DRM system architecture.

the client is able to retrieve the information. Public-key ciphers are appropriately used here.

5. The customer purchases the content and uses it according to the rights and rules.

6. At certain times, the clearinghouse collects financial records and usage information from the clients.

7. Payment confirmation and other messages (system and security updates, etc.) are delivered to the client.

8. Payments and usage information are sent to the appropriate parties (content providers, publishers, distributors, authors, artists, etc.).

Renewability is achieved by upgrading DRM system components and preventing the compromised devices from receiving content. New security software may be released as a regular enhancement or in response to a threat or hack. Revocation lists allow the servers to refuse service to revoked clients (multimedia applications software can also be revoked if it can be authenticated by the DRM component that resides in the client).

A DRM enables the content owners to specify their own business models in managing the use of content. A wide range of sales models can be supported, including subscription, pay-per-use, and superdistribution. Time-limited reading of an e-book, multiple viewings of a movie, and transfer of a song to a portable music player are all possible scenarios.

Superdistribution is a relatively new concept for redistributing content across the Internet. It is a process that allows the consumers to forward a content that they have acquired to other consumers (friends, relatives, and associates) in the market. The content forwarded to a potential buyer cannot be accessed until the new rights are obtained. This approach has important advantages and drawbacks:

- It is an efficient way of using a DRM-supported e-commerce system because repeated content downloads are avoided.
- From an economic point of view, superdistribution may help widen the market penetration. Once a particular content is downloaded to a client, the customer, with sufficient encouragement, can act as an agent of the retailer with minimal effort and cost.
- From a security point of view, if the content, encrypted with a particular key, becomes available in the market in large quantities, it may increase the likelihood of the key being compromised. For increased security, different copies of a media file need to be encrypted with different keys. This, of course, requires new downloads from the server.

The unicast-based model in Figure 1.3 can be extended to multicast networks where the data can be efficiently delivered from a source to multiple receivers. In the past few years, there has been a substantial amount of research in group key management [38].

A number of organizations are in the process of standardizing Internet-based DRM systems for handling different types of content. The major efforts led by MPEG, Open eBook Forum, and IRTF are summarized in Table 1.5.

Security in Multicast Systems for Internet Distribution

The traditional mechanism to support multicast communications is IP multicast [44]. It uses the notion of a group of members identified with a given group address. When a sender sends a message to this group address, the network uses a multicast routing protocol to optimally replicate the message and forward copies to group members located throughout the network.

Although the Internet community began discussing architectural issues in the mid-1980s using Internet Engineering Task Force (IETF) Request for Comments (RFCs), significant activity in multicast IP did not

TABLE 1.5. DRM-Related Activities

Organization	Recent Efforts
MPEG (Moving Picture Experts Group) [39] is a working group of ISO/IEC developing a family of standards used for coding audiovisual information in a digital compressed format.	MPEG-4: Latest compression standard designed specially for low-bandwidth (less than 1.5 Mbps *bitrate*) video/audio encoding purposes. As a universal language for a range of multimedia applications, it will provide additional functionality such as bitrate scalability, object-based representation, and intellectual property management and protection. MPEG-4 IPMP (version 1) is a simple "hook" DRM architecture standardized in 1999. As each application may have different requirements for the protection of multimedia data, MPEG-4 allows the application developers to design domain-specific IPMP systems (IPMP-S). MPEG-4 standardizes only the MPEG-4 IPMP interface with IPMP Descriptors (IPMP-Ds) and IPMP Elementary Streams (IPMP-ES), providing a communication mechanism between IPMP systems and the MPEG-4 terminal. MPEG-7: Formally named "Multimedia Content Description Interface," the MPEG-7 standard provides a set of standardized tools to describe multimedia content. The main elements of the standard are description tools (Descriptors [D] and Description Schemes [DS]), a Description Definition Language (DDL) based on the XML Schema Language, and system tools. The DDL defines the syntax of the Description Tools and allows the creation of new Description Schemes and Descriptors as well as the extension and modification of existing Description Schemes. System tools enable the deployment of descriptions, supporting binary-coded representation for efficient storage and transmission, transmission mechanisms, multiplexing of descriptions, synchronization of descriptions with content, and management and protection of intellectual property in MPEG-7 descriptions.

(Continued)

TABLE 1.5. Continued

Organization	Recent Efforts
	MPEG-21: MPEG-21 defines a normative open framework for multimedia delivery and consumption that can be used by content creators, producers, distributors, and service providers in the delivery and consumption chain. The framework is based on two essential concepts: the definition of a fundamental unit of distribution and transaction (the Digital Item) and the concept of Users interacting with Digital Items. Development of an interoperable framework for Intellectual Property Management and Protection (IPMP) is an ongoing effort that will become a part of the MPEG-21 standard.
	IPMP-X (Intellectual Property Management and Protection Extension) [40] is a DRM architecture that provides a normative framework to support many of the requirements of DRM solution (renewability, secure communications, verification of trust, granular and flexible governance at well-defined points in the processing chain, etc.). IPMP-X comes in two flavors: MPEG-2 IPMP-X (applicable to MPEG-2 based systems) and MPEG-4 IPMP-X (applicable to MPEG-4 based systems). The MPEG-4 IPMP extensions were standardized in 2002 as an extension to MPEG-4 IPMP "hooks." IPMP Tools are modules that perform IPMP functions such as authentication, decryption, and watermarking. In addition to specifying syntax to signal and trigger various IPMP Tools, IPMP-X specifies the architecture to plug the IPMP Tools seamlessly into IPMP-X terminal.
	MPEG LA, LLC [41] provides one-stop technology platform patent licensing with a portfolio of essential patents for the international digital video compression standard known as MPEG-2. In addition to MPEG-2, MPEG LA licenses portfolios of essential patents for the IEEE 1394 Standard, the DVB-T Standard, the MPEG-4 Visual Standard, and the MPEG-4 Systems Standard. In October 2003, MPEG LA, LLC, issued a call for patents that are essential to digital rights management technology (DRM) as described in DRM Reference Model v 1.0. The DRM Reference Model does not define a standard for interoperability among DRM devices, systems, or methods, or provide a specification of commercial products. It is an effort to provide users with convenient, fair, reasonable, nondiscriminatory access to a portfolio of essential worldwide patent rights under a single license.

Open eBook Forum (OeBF) [42] is an international trade and standards organization for the electronic publishing industries.	Its members consist of hardware and software companies, print and digital publishers, retailers, libraries, accessibility advocates, authors, and related organizations. The OeBF engages in standards and trade activities through the operation of Working Groups and Special Interest Groups. The Working Groups are authorized to produce official OeBF documents (such as specifications and process documents (such as policies and procedures, position papers, etc.). In the current organization, there are five Working groups: Metadata & Identifiers WG, Publication Structure WG, Requirements WG, Rights & Rules WG, and Systems WG. The mission of the Rights & Rules Working Group is to create an open and commercially viable standard for interoperability of digital rights management (DRM) systems.
The Internet Research Task Force (IRTF) [43] is composed of a number of small Research Groups working on topics related to Internet protocols, applications, architecture, and technology.	Internet Digital Rights Management (IDRM) was an IRTF Research Group formed to research issue and technologies relating to Digital Rights Management (DRM) on the Internet. The IRTF is a sister organization of the Internet Engineering Task Force (IETF). There were three IRTF drafts, formally submitted through IDRM, that carried the IRTF title. The IDRM group is now closed.

occur until the creation of the Mbone in 1992. The Mbone is a set of multicast-enabled subnetworks connected by IP tunnels. Tunneling is a technique that allows multicast traffic to traverse parts of the network by encapsulating multicast datagrams within unicast datagrams.

In IPv4, multicast IP addresses are defined by Class D, which differs from Classes A, B, and C that are used for point-to-point communications. The multicast address space, assigned by the Internet Assigned Numbers Authority (IANA), covers the range (224.0.0.0 – 239.255.255.255). IPv6 has 128 bits of address space compared with 32 bits in IPv4.

The Internet Group Management Protocol (IGMP) defines a protocol for multicast-enabled hosts and routers to manage group membership information. Developed by the Defense Advance Research Projects Agency (DARPA), the Transmission Control Protocol/Internet Protocol (TCP/IP) connects networks designed by different vendors into a network of networks (i.e., the Internet). It has two transport layers for the applications: the Transport Control Protocol (TCP) and the User Datagram Protocol (UDP). Currently, UDP is the only protocol for IP multicast, providing minimal services such as port multiplexing and error detection. Any host can send a UDP packet to a multicast address, and the multicast routing mechanism will deliver the packet to all members of the multicast group. TCP provides a higher level of service with packet ordering, port multiplexing, and error-free data delivery. It is a *connection-oriented* protocol (unlike UDP, which is *connectionless*) and does not support multicast applications.

MSEC is a Working Group (WG) in the Internet Engineering Task Force (IETF). Its purpose is to "standardize protocols for securing group communication over internets, and in particular over the global Internet." The initial primary focus of the MSEC WG will be on scalable solutions for groups with a single source and a very large number of recipients. The standard will be developed with the assumption that each group has a single trusted entity (i.e., the Group Controller) that sets the security policy and controls the group membership. It will attempt to guarantee at least the following two basic security features:

1. Only legitimate group members will have access to current group communication. (This includes groups with highly dynamic membership.)
2. Legitimate group members will be able to authenticate the source and contents of the group communication. (This includes cases in which group members do not trust each other.)

We will look at the recent developments in key management, authentication, and watermarking for secure group communications in wired and wireless networks. The proposed methods provide solutions to address three different issues of secure multimedia data distribution:

1. Controlling access to multimedia data among group members
2. Assuring the identity of participating group members (senders or receivers)
3. Providing copyright protection

Some of the challenging questions regarding these issues include the following:

1. How does a group manager, if it exists, accept members to the group?
2. How is the group key generated and distributed to members?
3. How is multimedia data source authenticated by the receivers?
4. How is the group key changed when a member joins or leaves a group?
5. How does multicast multimedia data received by a member have a unique watermark?

Secure multicast communications in a computer network involves efficient packet delivery from one or more sources to a large group of receivers having the same security attributes. The four major issues of IP multicast security are [45]:

1. *Multicast data confidentiality.* As the data traverses the public Internet, a mechanism is needed to prevent unauthorized access to data. Encryption is commonly used for data confidentiality.
2. *Multicast group key management.* The security of the data packets is made possible using a group key shared by the members that belong to the group. This key needs to change every time a member joins (leaves) the group for backward access control (forward access control). In some applications, there is also a need to change the group key periodically. Encryption is commonly used to control access to the group key.
3. *Multicast data source authentication.* An assurance of the identity of the data source is provided using cryptographic means. This type of authentication also includes evidence of data integrity. Digital signatures and Message Authentication Codes (MACs) are common authentication tools.
4. *Multicast security policies.* The correct definition, implementation, and maintenance of policies governing the various mechanisms of multicast security is a critical factor. The two general categories are the policies governing group membership and the policies regarding security enforcement.

In multicast communications, a session is defined as the time period in which data is exchanged among the group members. The type of member participation characterizes the nature of a session. In a *one-to-many* application, data are multicast from a single source to multiple receivers. Pay-per-view, news feeds, and real-time delivery of stock market information are a few examples. A *many-to-many* application involves multiple senders and multiple receivers. Applications such as teleconferencing, white boarding, and interactive simulation allow each member of the multicast group to send data as part of group communications.

Wired Network Security

Key Management Schemes for Wired Networks. Many multicast key management schemes have been proposed in the last 10 to 15 years. Four classifications from the literature are:

1. *Nonscalable* and *scalable* schemes [46]. The scalable schemes are, in turn, divided into three groups: hierarchical key management (node-based and key-based), centralized flat key management, and distributed flat key management.

2. *Flat* schemes, *clustered* schemes, *tree-based* schemes, and other schemes [47].

3. *Centralized* schemes, *decentralized* schemes, and *distributed* schemes [48].

4. *Key tree-based* schemes, *contributory key agreement* schemes, *computational number theoretic* schemes, and *secure multicast framework* schemes [49].

It may be possible to have a new classification using two criteria: the entity who exercises the control and whether the scheme is scalable or not — *centralized group control, subgroup control, and member control*:

1. *Centralized group control.* A single entity controls all the members in the group. It is responsible for the generation, distribution, and replacement of the group key. Because the controlling server is the single point of failure, the entire group is affected as a result of a malfunction.

2. *Subgroup control.* The multicast group is divided into smaller subgroups, and each subgroup is assigned a different controller. Although decentralization substantially reduces the risk of total system failure, it relies on trusted servers, weakening the overall system security.

3. *Member control.* With no group or subgroup controllers, each member of the multicast group is trusted with access control and contributes to the generation of the group key.

Each of the above classes is further divided into *scalable* and *nonscalable* schemes. In the context of multicast key management, scalability refers to the ability to handle a larger group of members without considerable performance deterioration. A scalable scheme is able to manage a large group over a wide geographical area with highly dynamic membership. If the computation and communication costs at the sender increase linearly with the size of the multicast group, then the scheme is considered nonscalable. Table 1.6 lists the key management schemes according to the new criteria.

Hierarchical key distribution trees form an efficient group of proposals for scalable secure multicasting. They can be classified into two groups: *hierarchical key-based* schemes and *hierarchical node-based* schemes.

Table 1.6. Classification of Key Management Schemes

	Scalable	Nonscalable
Centralized group control	Wong et al., 1997 [50]	Chiou and Chen, 1989 [63]
	Caronni et al., 1998 [51]	Gong and Shacham, 1994 [64]
	Balenson et al., 1999 [52]	Harney and Muckenhirn, 1997 [65]
	Canetti et al., 1999 [53]	
	Chang et al., 1999 [54]	Dunigan and Cao, 1998 [66]
	Wallner et al., 1999 [55]	Blundo et al., 1998 [67]
	Waldvogel et al., 1999 [56]	Poovendran et al., 1998 [68]
	Banerjee and Bhattacharjee, 2001 [57]	Chu et al., 1999 [69]
		Wallner et al., 1999 [55]
	Eskicioglu and Eskicioglu, 2002 [58]	Scheikl et al., 2002 [70]
	Selcuk and Sidhu, 2002 [59]	
	Zhu and Setia, 2003 [60]	
	Huang and Mishra, 2003 [61]	
	Trappe et al., 2003 [62]	
Subgroup control	Mittra, 1997 [71]	Ballardie, 1996 [76]
	Dondeti et al., 1999 [72]	Briscoe, 1999 [77]
	Molva and Pannetrat, 1999 [73]	
	Setia et al., 2000 [74]	
	Hardjono et al., 2000 [75]	
Member control	Dondeti et al., 1999 [78]	Boyd, 1997 [82]
	Perrig, 1999 [79]	Steiner et al., 1997 [83]
	Waldvogel et al., 1999 [56]	Becker and Willie, 1998 [84]
	Rodeh et al., 2000 [80]	
	Kim et al., 2000 [81]	

A hierarchical key-based scheme assigns a set of keys to each member, depending on the location of the member in the tree. Hierarchical node-based schemes define internal tree nodes that assume the role of subgroup managers in key distribution.

Among the schemes listed in Table 1.6, three hierarchical schemes, namely the Centralized Tree-Based Key Management (CTKM), Iolus, and DEP, are compared through simulation using real-life multicast group membership traces [85]. The performance metrics used in this comparison are (1) the encryption cost at the sender and (2) encryption and decryption cost at the members and subgroup managers. It is shown that hierarchical node-based approaches perform better than hierarchical key-based approaches, in general. Furthermore, the performance gain of hierarchical node-based approaches increases with the multicast group size.

An Internet Draft generated by the MSEC WG presents a common architecture for MSEC group key management protocols that support a variety of application, transport, and internetwork security protocols. The document includes the framework and guidelines to allow for a modular and flexible design of group key management protocols in order to accommodate applications with diverse requirements [86].

Periodic Batch Rekeying. Despite the efficiency of the tree-based scalable schemes for one-to-many applications, changing the group key after each join or leave (i.e., individual *rekeying*) has two major drawbacks:

1. *Synchronization problem.* If the group is rekeyed after each join or leave, synchronization will be difficult to maintain because of the interdependencies among rekey messages and also between rekey and data messages. If the delay in rekey message delivery is high and the join or leave requests are frequent, a member may need to have memory space for a large number of rekey and data messages that cannot be decrypted.
2. *Inefficiency.* For authentication, each rekey message may be digitally signed by the sender. Generation of digital signatures is a costly process in terms of computation and communication. A high rate of join or leave requests may result in a performance degradation.

One particular study attempts to minimize these problems with *periodic batch rekeying* [87]. In this approach, join or leave requests are collected during a rekey interval and are rekeyed in a batch. The out-of-sync problems are alleviated by delaying the use of a new group key until the next rekey interval. Batch processing also leads to a definite performance advantage. For example, if digital signatures are used for data source authentication, the number of signing operations for J join and L leave requests is reduced from $J+L$ to 1.

Periodic batch rekeying provides a trade-off between performance improvement and delayed group access control. A new member has to wait longer to join the group, and a leaving member can stay longer with the group. The period of the batch rekeying is, thus, a design parameter that can be adjusted according to security requirements. To accommodate different application needs, three modes of operation are suggested:

1. *Periodic batch rekeying.* The key server processes both join and leave requests periodically in a batch.

2. *Periodic batch leave rekeying.* The key server processes each join request immediately to reduce the delay for a new member to access group communications but processes leave requests in a batch.

3. *Periodic batch join rekeying.* The key server processes each leave request immediately to reduce the exposure to members who have left but processes join requests in a batch.

A *marking algorithm* is proposed to update the key tree and to generate a rekey subtree at the end of each rekey interval with a collection of J join and L leave requests. A rekey subtree is formed using multiple paths corresponding to multiple requests. The objectives of the marking algorithm are to reduce the number of encrypted keys, to maintain the balance of the updated key tree, and to make it efficient for the users to identify the encrypted keys they need. To meet these objectives, the server uses the following steps:

1. Update the tree by processing join and leave requests in a batch. If $J \leq L$, J of the departed members with the smallest IDs are replaced with the J newly joined members. If $J > L$, L departed members are replaced with L of the newly joined members. For the insertion of the remaining $J-L$ new members, three strategies have been investigated [88,89].

2. Mark the key nodes with one of the following states: Unchanged, Join, Leave, and Replace.

3. Prune the tree to obtain the rekey subtree.

4. Traverse the rekey subtree, generate new keys, and construct the rekey message.

Balanced Key Trees. The efficiency of a tree-based key management scheme depends highly on how well the tree remains balanced. In this context, a tree is balanced if the difference between the distances from the root node to any two leaf nodes does not exceed 1 [90]. For a balanced binary tree with n leaves, the distance from the root to any leaf is $\log_2 n$. The issue of maintaining trees in a balanced manner is critical for any real implementation of a key management tree. Several techniques, based on the scheme described by Wallner et al., are introduced to maintain a balanced tree in the presence of arbitrary group membership updates [90]. Although we have complete control over how the tree is edited for new member additions, there is no way to predict the locations in the tree at which the deletions will occur. Hence, it is possible to imagine extreme cases leading to costs that have linear order in the size of the group. Two simple tree rebalancing schemes have been proposed to avoid this cost increase [90]. The first is a modification of the deletion algorithm; the other allows the tree to become imbalanced after a sequence of key updates and periodically invokes a tree rebalancing algorithm to bring the tree back to a balanced state.

A recent work presents the design and analysis of three scalable online algorithms for maintaining multicast key distribution trees [91]. To minimize worst-case costs and to have good average-case performance, there was a trade-off between tree structures with worst-case bounds and the restructuring costs required to maintain those trees. Simulations showed that the height-balanced algorithm performed better than the weight-balanced algorithm.

Authentication. In multicast architectures, group membership control, dictated by security policies, allows access to a secure multicast group. *Member authentication* involves methods ranging from the use of access control lists and capability certificates [92] to mutual authentication [93] between the sender and the receiver.

- *Access control lists.* The sender maintains a list of hosts who are either authorized to join the multicast group or excluded from it. When a host sends a join request, the sender checks its identity against the access control list to determine if membership is permitted. The maintenance of the list is an important issue, as the list may be changing dynamically based on new authorizations or exclusions.
- *Capability certificates.* Issued by a designated Certificate Authority, a capability certificate contains information about the identity of the host and the set of rights associated with the host. It is used to authenticate the user and to allow group membership.
- *Mutual authentication.* The sender and the host authenticate each other via cryptographic means. Symmetric or public-key schemes can be used for this purpose.

A challenging problem in secure group communications is *data source authentication* (i.e., providing assurance of the identity of the sender and the integrity of the data). Depending on the type of multicast application and the computational resources available to the group members, three levels of data source authentication can be used [94]:

1. *Group authentication*: provides assurance that the packet was sent by a registered group member (a registered sender or a registered receiver)
2. *Source authentication*: provides assurance that the packet was sent by a registered sender (not by a registered receiver)
3. *Individual sender authentication*: provides assurance of the identity of the registered sender of the packet

In a naive approach, each data packet can be digitally signed by the sender. For group (source) authentication, all members, sender or receiver (all senders), can share a private key to generate the same signature on the packets. Individual sender authentication, however, requires each sender to have a unique private key. Although digital signature-based authentication per packet is desirable as a reliable tool, it exhibits poor performance because of lengthy keys and computational overhead for signature generation and verification.

Recent research has led to more efficient authentication methods, including:

*   *Multiple Message Authentication Codes (MACs)* [53]
*   *Stream signing* [95]
*   *Authentication tree-based signatures* [96]
*   *Hybrid signatures* [97]
*   *TESLA, EMSS, and BiBa* [98–100]
*   *Augmented chain* [101]
*   *Piggybacking* [102]
*   *Multicast packet authentication with signature amortization* [103]
*   *Multicast packet authentication* [104]

A Message Authentication Code (MAC) is a keyed hash function used for data source authentication in communication between two parties (sender and receiver). At the source, the message is input to a MAC algorithm that computes the MAC using a key K shared by both parties. The sender then appends the MAC to the message and sends the pair {message|MAC} to the receiver. In an analysis of the generalization of MACs to multicast communications, it is shown that a short and efficient collusion-resistant multicast MAC (MMAC) cannot be constructed without a new advance in digital signature design [105].

Watermarking. Watermarking (data hiding) [106–108] is the process of embedding data into a multimedia element such as image, audio, or video. This embedded data can later be extracted from, or detected in, the multimedia for security purposes. A watermarking algorithm consists of the watermark structure, an embedding algorithm, and an extraction, or a detection, algorithm. Watermarks can be embedded in the pixel domain or a transform domain. In multimedia applications, embedded watermarks should be invisible, robust, and have a high capacity [109]. Invisibility refers to the degree of distortion introduced by the watermark and its effect on the viewers or listeners. Robustness is the resistance of an embedded watermark against intentional attacks and normal A/V processes such as noise, filtering (blurring, sharpening, etc.), resampling, scaling, rotation, cropping, and lossy compression. Capacity is the amount of data that can be represented by an embedded watermark. The approaches used in watermarking still images include least significant bit encoding, basic M-sequence, transform techniques, and image-adaptive techniques [110]. Because video watermarking possesses additional requirements, development of more sophisticated models for the encoding of video sequences is currently being investigated.

Typical uses of watermarks include *copyright protection (identification of the origin of content, tracing illegally distributed copies) and disabling unauthorized access to content*. Requirements and characteristics for the digital watermarks in these scenarios are different, in general. Identification of the origin of content requires the embedding of a single watermark into the content at the source of distribution. To trace illegal copies, a unique watermark is needed based on the location or identity of the recipient in the multimedia network. In both of these applications, watermark extraction or detection needs to take place only when there is a dispute regarding the ownership of content. For access control, the watermark should be checked in every authorized consumer device used to receive the content. Note that the cost of a watermarking system will depend on the intended use and may vary considerably.

The *copyright protection* problem in a multicast architecture raises a challenging issue. All receivers in a multicast group receive the same watermarked content. If a copy of this content is illegally distributed to the public, it may be difficult to find the parties responsible for this criminal act. Such a problem can be eliminated in a unicast environment by embedding a unique watermark for each receiver. To achieve uniqueness for multicast data, two distinct approaches are feasible:

1. Multiple copies of content, each with a different watermark, are created to allow the selection of appropriate packets in distribution.
2. A single copy of unwatermarked content is created to allow the insertion of appropriate watermarks in distribution.

The following proposals are variations of these two approaches:

- *A different version of video for each group member* [69]. For a given multicast video, the sender applies two different watermark functions to generate two different watermarked frames, $d_{i,w0}$ and $d_{i,w1}$, for every frame i in the stream. The designated group leader assigns a randomly generated bit stream to each group member. The length of the bit string is equal to the number of video frames in the stream. For the ith watermarked frame in stream j, $j = 0$, 1, a different key $K_{i,j}$ is used to encrypt it. The random bit stream determines whether the member will be given K_{i0} or K_{i1} for decryption. If there is only one leaking member, its identification is made possible with the collaboration of the sender who can read the watermarks to produce the bit stream and the group leader who has the bit streams of all members. The minimum length of the retrieved stream to guarantee a c-collusion detection, where c is the number of collaborators, is not known. An important drawback of the proposal is that it is not scalable and two copies of the video stream need to be watermarked, encrypted, and transmitted.

- *Distributed watermarking (watercasting)* [111]. For a multicast distribution tree with maximum depth d, the source generates a total of n differently watermarked copies of each packet such that $n \geq d$. Each group of n alternate packets is called a transmission group. On receiving a transmission group, a router forwards all but one of those packets to each downstream interface on which there are receivers. Each last-hop router in the distribution tree will receive $n - d_r$ packets from each transmission group, where d_r is the depth of the route to this router. Exactly one of these packets will be forwarded onto the subnet with receivers. The goal of this filtering process is to provide a stream for each receiver with a unique sequence of watermarked packets. The information about the entire tree topology needs to be stored by the server to trace an illegal copy. A major potential problem with watercasting is the support required from the network routers. The network providers may not be willing to provide a security-related functionality unless video delivery is a promising business for them.

- *Watermarking with a hierarchy of intermediaries* [112]. WHIM Backbone (WHIM-BB) introduces a hierarchy of intermediaries into the network and forms an overlay network between them. Each intermediary has a unique ID used to define the path from the source to the intermediary on the overlay network. The Path ID is embedded into the content to identify the path it has traveled. Each intermediary embeds its portion of the Path ID into the content before it forwards the content through the network. A watermark embedded by a WHIM-BB identifies the domain of a receiver.

WHIM-Last Hop (WHIM-LH) allows the intermediaries to mark the content uniquely for any child receivers they may have. Multiple watermarks can be embedded using modified versions of existing algorithms. The above two "fingerprinting" schemes [69,111] require a certain number of video frames in order to deduce sufficient information about the recipient, whereas WMIN requires only one frame because the entire trace is embedded into each frame. A serious overhead for this scheme, however, is the hierarchy of intermediaries needed for creating and embedding the fingerprint.

Finally, the two techniques described below appear to be viable approaches for copyright protection and access control, respectively.

- *Hierarchical tagging and bulk tagging* [113]. Hierarchical tagging allows an artist to insert a different watermark for each of his distributors. Similarly, each distributor can insert a watermark for several subdistributors. This process can continue until the individual customers receive tagged content identifying the artist and all the distributors in the chain. In practice, however, more than a few layers of watermarks may reduce the visual quality to an unacceptable level. With bulk tagging, the distributor creates multiple, tagged versions of the data. The contents are hidden using cryptographic techniques and distributed as a single dataset. Each customer receives the same dataset, performs some preprocessing, and retrieves only the tagged data prepared for him. A simple approach is described to show the feasibility of bulk-tagging for images. It requires registration with the producer and the delivery of keys to decrypt the consumer's individually tagged copy. The preprocessing required by the client device creates a weakness in system security, as the individual tag is used for access control only. If the decryption keys are recovered for one consumer, the content would become available in-the-clear and there would be no trace to the illegal distributor.

Wireless Network Security. Key management in wireless networks is a more complicated problem because of the mobility of group members [114,115]. When a member joins or leaves a session, the group key needs to change for backward access control and forward access control. Because secure data cannot be communicated during the rekeying process, an important requirement for a key management scheme is to minimize the interruption in secure data communications. Mobility also allows the members to move to other networks without leaving the session. The existence of a member whose position changes with time adds another dimension of complexity to the design of rekeying algorithms.

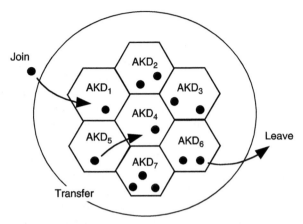

DKD: domain key distributor, AKD: area key distributor

Figure 1.4. Mobility framework.

A common approach in designing a scalable multicast service is to use a hierarchical structure in group key distribution. The hierarchical key management schemes fall into two major groups [92]: *logical* hierarchy of keys and *physical* hierarchy of servers. These schemes divide the key management domain into smaller areas in order to distribute the processing workload. Members of the multicast group belong to a key distribution tree having a root at the sender. In *hierarchical key-based* schemes, the set of keys kept by a member is determined by the location of the member in the tree. In *hierarchical node-based* schemes, internal tree nodes assume the role of subgroup managers in key distribution. For mobile members, the latter approach is more appropriate.

Consider the mobility framework in Figure 1.4. All the members in the group belong to a "domain," denoted by the collection of pentagons, managed by a *Domain Key Distributor* (DKD). The domain is divided into several independent "areas," each managed by an *Area Key Distributor*. An area is defined in such a way that member movement within an area does not require any rekeying, and a join or leave is handled locally by an *intra-area* rekeying algorithm. When a member moves between the areas, *interarea* rekeying algorithms provide the coordination for the transfer of security relationships.

The DKD generates the *data encryption key* (DEK) for the session and distributes it to all AKDs. Each AKD is responsible for distributing the DEK to its members. As the distribution of the DEK must be secure, it is protected by a local *key encryption key* (KEK). For intra-area rekeying, several approaches, including the hierarchical key-based schemes, can be used.

We will now summarize the three operations: join, leave, and transfer [116].

1. *Joining the group via area i.* When a member joins the group via area i, it sends a signaling message to AKD_i to notify AKD_i of its arrival. AKD_i creates a new KEK_i and securely distributes it to area i existing members and the new member. Once the new KEK_i is in place, the new DEK can be securely multicast among the AKDs and then from each AKD to area members.

2. *Leaving the group via area i.* When a member leaves the group via area i, all AKDs, j, for which the departing member holds a valid key KEK_j must be notified. A new KEK_j is created and securely distributed to remaining members for all areas, j, for which the departing member holds a valid key KEK_j. Once the new KEK_js are in place, the new DEK can be securely multicast among the AKDs and then from each AKD to area members.

3. *Transfer from area i to area j.* For member transfer from one area to another, three interarea rekeying algorithms have been defined:

   a. *Baseline rekeying (BR).* The member first leaves the group via area i and then rejoins the group via area j. The data transmission is halted during the distribution of the KEKs and the DEK. In BR, when a member leaves the group, a notification is sent to its current AKD.

   b. *Immediate rekeying (IR).* The member initiates a transfer by sending one notification to AKD_i and one notification to AKD_j. Area i performs a KEK_i rekey and area j performs a KEK_j rekey. The only KEK held by a group member is for the area in which it currently resides. Unlike the baseline algorithm, no DEK is generated and data transmission continues uninterrupted. In IR, when a member leaves the group, a notification is sent to its current AKD.

   c. *Delayed rekeying (DR).* The member sends one notification to AKD_i and one notification to AKD_j. Area j performs a KEK_j rekey, but area i does not perform a KEK_i rekey. AKD_i adds the member to the Extra Key Owner List (EKOL). The EKOL is reset whenever a local rekey occurs. A member accumulates KEKs as it visits different areas. If the entering member has previously visited area j, no KEK_j rekey occurs for j. If the member is entering area j for the first time, a KEK_j rekey occurs for j. To limit the maximum amount of time that KEK_i can be held by a member outside area i, each AKD_i maintains a timer. At $t = T_i$ (a threshold value), the KEK_i is updated and the timer is set to zero. At this point, no group member outside of area i has a valid KEK$_i$. In DR, when a member leaves the group, a notification is sent to all the AKDs.

Two studies that compare the above algorithms show that delayed rekeying, with reduced communication load and rekeying rate, can improve the performance of key management [114,116]. The first study uses messaging overhead, the KEK rekey rate, and the number of KEKs held by a member as the performance metrics. The second study employs rekeying rates, mean number of extra keys, and percentage of off-line time to compare the interarea rekeying algorithms.

Security in Digital Home Networks

A digital home network (DHN) is a cluster of digital A/V devices, including set-top boxes, TVs, VCRs, DVD players, and general-purpose computing devices such as personal computers [117]. The problem of content protection in home networks has the following dimensions:

- Protection of content across digital interfaces
- Protection of content on storage media
- Management of rights associated with content

This problem, it is believed, turns out to be the most difficult problem to solve for a number of technical, legal, and economic reasons:

1. Private CA systems are, by definition, proprietary and can be defined and operated using the strictest possible security means and methods. In comparison, the protection systems needed for the devices and interfaces in home networks must be developed with a consensus among the stakeholders, making the determination of requirements very difficult.

2. Renewability of a protection system must be properly defined and implemented. Important parameters are the cost, user convenience, and liabilities resulting from copyright infringements.

3. The new copyright legislation introduces controversial prohibitions subject to different interpretations.

4. The payer of the bill for the cost of protection in home networks is unclear. Several business models are under consideration.

Two groups of technologies are believed to be useful in designing technical solutions: encryption based and watermark based. The potential value of these technologies has been the subject of prolonged discussions in the past decade. Because each group presents strengths and weaknesses, some are of the opinion that both types of solution should be implemented to increase the robustness to possible attacks.

Encryption and watermarking each provide a different "line of defense" in protecting content. The former, the *first line of defense*, makes the content unintelligible through a reversible mathematical transformation based on a secret key. The latter, the *second line of defense*, inserts data directly into the content at the expense of imperceptible degradation in quality. The theoretical level of security provided by encryption depends on the cipher strength and key length. Other factors such as tamper-resistant hardware or software also play an important role in implementations. Watermarking has several useful applications that dictate how and where the watermark is placed. For content protection purposes, the watermark should be embedded in such a way that it is imperceptible to the human eye and robust against attacks. Its real value comes from the fact that the information it represents remains with the content in both analog and digital domains.

The technical solutions developed in the past several years are listed in Table 1.7. They represent the major components of a comprehensive framework called the Content Protection System Architecture (CPSA) [118]. Using 11 axioms, this architecture describes how compliant devices manage copy control information (CCI), playback, and recording.

In the CSS system, each manufacturer is assigned a distinct master key. If a particular master key is compromised, it is replaced by a key that is used in the subsequent manufacturing of DVD players. With the new key assignment, future releases of DVDs cannot be played on the players manufactured with the compromised key. The CSS system was hacked in 1999 because a company neglected to protect its master key during the software implementation for a DVD drive. The software utility created by a group of hackers is commonly referred to as DeCSS. A computer that has the DeCSS utility can make illegal copies of decrypted DVD content on blank DVDs for distribution on the Internet.

In the rest of the protection systems, renewability is defined as device revocation as well. When a pirated device is found in the consumer market, its ID is added to the next version of the revocation list. Updated versions of the revocation lists are distributed on new prerecorded media or through external connections (Internet, cable, satellite, and terrestrial). Some examples are:

- DVD players can receive updates from newer releases of prerecorded DVDs or other compliant devices.
- Set-top boxes (digital cable transmission receivers or digital satellite broadcast receivers) can receive updates from content streams or other compliant devices.
- Digital TVs can receive updates from content streams or other compliant devices.
- Recording devices can receive updates from content streams, if they are equipped with a tuner or other compliant devices.

Table 1.7. Content Protection in Digital Home Networks

	Solution	What is Protected?	Brief Description
Optical media	CSS [119]	Video on DVD-ROM	CSS-protected video is decrypted during playback on the compliant DVD player or drive.
	CPPM [120]	Audio on DVD-ROM	CPPM-protected audio is decrypted during playback on the compliant DVD player or drive.
	CPRM [121]	Video or audio on DVD-R/RW/RAM	A/V content is re-encrypted before recording on a DVD recordable disc. During playback, the compliant player derives the decryption key.
	4C/Verance Watermark [122]	Audio on DVD-ROM	Inaudible watermarks are embedded into the audio content. The compliant playback or recording device detects the CCI represented by the watermark and responds accordingly.
	To be determined	Video on DVD-ROM/ R/RW/RAM	Invisible watermarks are embedded into the video content. The compliant playback or recording device detects the CCI represented by the watermark and responds accordingly. If a copy is authorized, the compliant recorder creates and embeds a new watermark to represent "no-more-copies."
Magnetic media	HDCP [123]	Video on digital tape	Similar in function to the Content Scrambling System (CSS).

(Continued)

41

Table 1.7. Continued

	Solution	What is Protected?	Brief Description
Digital interfaces	DTCP [124]	IEEE 1394 serial bus	The source device and the sink device authenticate each other, and establish shared secrets. A/V content is encrypted across the interface. The encryption key is renewed periodically.
	HDCP [125]	Digital Visual Interface (DVI) and High-Definition Multimedia Interface (HDMI)	Video transmitter authenticates the receiver and establishes shared secrets with it. A/V content is encrypted across the interface. The encryption key is renewed frequently.

- Personal computers (PCs) can receive updates from Internet servers.

Each solution in Table 1.7 defines a means of associating the CCI with the digital content it protects. The CCI communicates the conditions under which a consumer is authorized to make a copy. An important subset of CCI is the two Copy Generation Management System (CGMS) bits for digital copy control: "11" (copy-never), "10" (copy-once), "01" (no-more-copies), and "00" (copy-free). The integrity of the CCI should be ensured to prevent unauthorized modification. The CCI can be associated with the content in two ways: (1) the CCI is included in a designated field in the A/V stream and (2) the CCI is embedded as a watermark into the A/V stream.

A CPRM-compliant recording device refuses to make a copy of content labeled as "copy-never" or "no-more-copies." It is authorized to create a copy of "copy-once" content and label the new copy as "no-more-copies." The DTCP carries the CGMS bits in the isochronous packet header defined by the interface specification. A sink device that receives content from a DTCP-protected interface is obliged to check the CGMS bits and respond accordingly. As the DVI is an interface between a content source and a display device, no CCI transmission is involved.

In addition to those listed in Table 1.7, private DRM systems may also be considered to be content protection solutions in home networks. However, interoperability of devices supporting different DRM systems is an unresolved issue today.

There are other efforts addressing security in home networking environments. Two notable projects are being discussed by the Video Electronics Standards Association (VESA) [126] and the Universal Plug and Play (UPnP) [127] Forum. VESA is an international nonprofit organization that develops and supports industrywide interface standards for the PC and other computing environments. The VESA and the Consumer Electronics Association (CEA) have entered a memo of understanding that allowed the CEA to assume all administration of the VESA Home Network Committee. The UPnP Forum is an industry initiative designed to enable easy and robust connectivity among stand-alone devices and PCs from many different vendors.

In Europe, the work of the DVB Project is shared by its Modules and Working Groups. The Commercial Module discusses the commercial issues around a DVB work item, leading to a consensus embodied in a set of "Commercial Requirements" governing each and every DVB specification. Proving technical expertise, the Technical Module works according to requirements determined by the Commercial Module and delivers specifications for standards via the Steering Board to the recognized standards setting entities, notably the EBU/ETSI/CENELEC Joint Technical Committee. The IPR Module is responsible for making recommendations concerning the DVB's IPR policy, overseeing the functioning of the IPR policy, dealing with IPR related issues in other areas of the DVB's work, and making recommendations on antipiracy policies. The Promotions and Communications Module handles the external relations of the DVB Project. It is responsible for trade shows, conferences, DVB & Multimedia Home Platform (MHP) Web sites, and press releases. The Copy Protection Technologies (CPT) subgroup of the Technical Module was set up in March 2001 to develop a specification for a DVB Content Protection & Copy Management (CPCM) system based upon the Commercial Requirements produced by the Copy Protection subgroup of the Commercial Module and ratified by the Steering Board. The CPT subgroup is working to define a CPCM system to provide interoperable, end-to-end copy protection in a DVB environment [128].

Finally, we summarize in Table 1.8 the technical protection solutions for all the architectures we have discussed in this chapter.

LEGAL SOLUTIONS

Intellectual property plays an important role in all areas of science and technology as well as literature and the arts. The World Intellectual Property Organization (WIPO) is an intergovernmental organization responsible for the promotion of the protection of intellectual property throughout the world through cooperation among member states and for the administration of various multilateral treaties dealing with the legal

Table 1.8. Protection Systems in the Digital Universe

Media Protected		Protection Type	Device Authentication	Association of Digital Rights	Licensed Technology	System Renewability
Prerecorded media	Video on DVD-ROM	Encryption	Mutual between DVD drive and PC	Metadata	CSS [119]	Device revocation
	Audio on DVD-ROM	Encryption	Mutual between DVD drive and PC	Metadata	CPPM [120]	Device revocation
		Watermarking	na	Watermark	4C/Verance Watermark [122]	na
	Video or audio on DVD-R/RW/RAM	Encryption	Mutual between DVD drive and PC	Metadata	CPRM [121]	Device revocation
		Watermarking	na	Watermark	tbd	na
	Video on digital tape	Encryption	na	Metadata	High-Definition Copy Protection (HDCP) [123]	Device revocation

Category	Technology					
Digital interface	IEEE 1394	Encryption	Mutual between source and sink	Metadata	DTCP [124]	Device revocation
	Digital Visual Interface (DVI) and High-Definition Multimedia Interface (HDMI)	Encryption	Mutual between source and sink	Metadata	HDCP [125]	Device revocation
	NRSS interface	Encryption	Mutual between host device and removable security device	Metadata	Open standards [129,130,131]	Service revocation
Broadcasting	Satellite transmission (privately defined by service providers and CA vendors)	Encryption	None	Metadata	Conditional access system [132,133] privately defined by service providers	Smartcard revocation
	Terrestrial transmission	Encryption	None	Metadata	Conditional access system [131] framework defined by ATSC	Smartcard revocation
Cable transmission		Encryption	None	Metadata	Conditional access system [134] privately defined by OpenCable	Smartcard revocation

(Continued)

Table 1.8. Continued

Media Protected		Protection Type	Device Authentication	Association of Digital Rights	Licensed Technology	System Renewability
Internet	Unicast-based DRM systems are privately defined, and hence are not interoperable	Encryption	Receiver	Metadata	DRM [135,136]	Software update
	Multicast-based DRM systems are yet to appear in the market. An Internet Draft defines a common architecture for MSEC group key management protocols that support a variety of application, transport, and internetwork security protocols. A few watermarking schemes have been proposed for multicast data.	Encryption	Sender and receiver (depends on the authentication type)	Metadata	Group key management [137] Watermarking proposals [38]	tbd

and administrative aspects of intellectual property. With headquarters in Geneva, Switzerland, it is 1 of the 16 specialized agencies of the United Nations system of organizations. WIPO has currently 179 member states, including the Unites States, China, and the Russian Federation.

The legal means of protecting copyrighted digital content can be classified into two categories:

1. National laws (copyright laws and contract laws)
2. International treaties and conventions

Two WIPO treaties — the WIPO Copyright Treaty and the WIPO Performances and Phonograms Treaty — obligate the member states to prohibit circumvention of technological measures used by copyright owners to protect their works and to prevent the removal or alteration of copyright management information.

The international conventions that have been signed for the worldwide protection of copyrighted works include [1,138]:

- The Berne Convention, formally the International Convention for the Protection of Literary and Artistic Works (1886)
- The Universal Copyright Convention (1952)
- Rome Convention for the Protection of Performers, Producers of Phonograms and Broadcasting Organizations (1961)
- The Geneva Convention for the Protection of Producers of Phonograms against Unauthorized Duplication of Their Phonograms (1971)
- Brussels Convention Relating to the Distribution of Programme-Carrying Signals Transmitted by Satellite (1974)
- TRIPS Agreement (1995)

Since the end of the 1990s, we have seen important efforts to provide legal solutions regarding copyright protection and management of digital rights in the United States.

The most important legislative development in the recent years was the Digital Millennium Copyright Act (DMCA). Signed into a law on October 28, 1998, this Act implements the WIPO Copyright Treaty and the WIPO Performances and Phonograms Treaty. Section 103 of the DMCA amends Title 17 of the U.S. Code by adding a new chapter 12. Section 1201 makes it illegal to circumvent technological measures that prevent unauthorized access and copying, and Section 1202 introduces prohibitions to ensure the integrity of copyright management information. The DMCA has received earnest criticism with regard to the ambiguity and inconsistency in expressing the anticircumvention provisions [9,139]

The second major attempt by the U.S. Congress to strike a balance between the U.S. laws and technology came with the Consumer Broadband and Digital Television Promotion Act (CBDTPA). Introduced by Senator Fritz Hollings on March 21, 2002, the Act intends "to regulate interstate commerce in certain devices by providing for private sector development of technological protection measures to be implemented and enforced by Federal regulations to protect digital content and promote broadband as well as the transition to digital television, and for other purposes." In establishing open security system standards that will provide effective security for copyrighted works, the bill specifies the standard security technologies to be reliable, renewable, resistant to attacks, readily implementable, modular, applicable to multiple technology platforms, extensible, upgradable, not cost prohibitive, and based on open source code (software portions).

Recently, a draft legislation was introduced by Senator Sam Brownback. Known as the "Consumers, Schools, and Libraries Digital Rights Management Awareness Act of 2003," the bill seeks to "to provide for consumer, educational institution, and library awareness about digital rights management technologies included in the digital media products they purchase, and for other purposes." With several important provisions, the bill prevents copyright holders from compelling an Internet service provider (ISP) to disclose the names or other identifying information of its subscribers prior to the filing of a civil lawsuit, requires conspicuous labeling of all digital media products that limits consumer uses with access or redistribution restrictions, imposes strict limits on the Federal Communication Commission's ability to impose federal regulations on digital technologies, and preserves the right to donate digital media products to libraries and schools.

In every country, legally binding agreements between parties would also be effective in copyright protection. All technological measures, without any exception, must include IP (mostly protected by patents) to be licensable. Before a particular technology is implemented in A/V devices, the licensee signs an agreement with the owner of the technology agreeing with the terms and conditions of the license. Contract laws deal with the violations of the license agreements in the event of litigations.

BUSINESS MODELS

In addition to technical and legal means, owners of digital copyrighted content can also make use of new, creative ways to bring their works to the market. A good understanding of the complexity and cost of
48

protection is probably a prerequisite to be on the right track. With the wide availability of digital A/V devices and networks in the near future, it will become increasingly difficult to control individual behavior and detect infringements of copyright. Would it then be possible to develop business models that are not closely tied to the inherent qualities of digital content? The current business models, old and new, for selling copyrighted works are summarized in Table 1.9 [9]. Some of these models are relevant for the marketing of digital copyrighted content. In general, the selection of a business model depends on a number of factors, including:

- Type of content
- Duration of the economic value of content
- Fixation method
- Distribution channel
- Purchase mechanism
- Technology available for protection
- Extent of related legislation

A good case study to explore the opportunities in a digital market is superdistribution. Figure 1.5 shows the players in a DRM-supported e-commerce system: a content owner, a clearinghouse, several retailers, and many customers. Suppose that the media files requested by the customers are hosted by the content owner or the retailers, and the licenses are downloaded from the clearinghouse. The following are a few of the possible ideas for encouraging file sharing and creating a competitive market [140]:

Promotions. The media file can be integrated with one or more promotions for retail offerings. Examples are a bonus track or a concert ticket for the purchase of an album or a discount coupon for the local music store. Attractive promotions may result in more file sharing.

Packaged media with a unique retailer ID. During the packaging of the media file, a unique retailer ID is added. The file is shared among customers. When a customer in the distribution chain is directed to the clearinghouse to get his license, the clearinghouse credits the original retailer. This may be an incentive for a retailer to offer the best possible deal for a content.

Packaged media with a unique customer ID. During the packaging of the media file, a unique customer ID is added. The file is shared among customers. When a customer in the distribution chain is directed to the clearinghouse to get his license, the clearinghouse credits the customer who initiated the distribution. This may be a good motivation for a customer to be the "first" in the chain.

Table 1.9. Business Models for Copyrighted Works

	Traditional	
Type	**Examples**	**Relevance to Copyright Protection**
Models based on fees for products and services		
Single transaction purchase	Books, videos, CDs, photocopies	
Subscription purchase	Newsletter and journal subscriptions	
Single transaction license	Software	
		High sensitivity to unauthorized use
Serial transaction license	Electronic subscription to a single title	
Site license	Software for a whole company	
Payment per electronic use	Information resource paid per article	
Models relying on advertising		
Combined subscription and advertising	Web sites for newspapers	Low sensitivity to unauthorized access
Advertising only	Web sites	Concern for reproduction and framing
Models with free distribution		
Free distribution	Scholarly papers on preprint servers	
Free samples	Demo version of a software	
Free goods with purchases	Free browser software to increase traffic on an income-producing Web site	Low concern for reproduction Sensitivity for information integrity
Information in the public domain	Standards, regulations	
Recent		
Give away the product and sell an auxiliary product or service	Free distribution of music because it enhances the market for concerts, t-shirts, posters, etc.	Services or products not subject to replication difficulties of the digital content
Give away the product and sell upgrades	Antivirus software	Products have short shelf life

(Continued)

Table 1.9. Continued

Traditional		
Type	**Examples**	**Relevance to Copyright Protection**
Extreme customization of the product	Personalized CDs	No demand from other people
Provide a large product in small pieces	Online databases	Difficulty in copying
Give away digital content to increase the demand for the actual product	Full text of a book online to increase demand for hard copies	
Give away one piece of digital content to create a market for another	Adobe's Acrobat Reader	Need for protecting the actual product sold
Allow free distribution of the product but request payment	Shareware	
Position the product for low-priced, mass market distribution	Microsoft XP	Cost of buying converges with cost of stealing

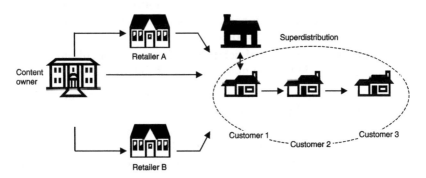

Figure 1.5. E-commerce with superdistribution.

SUMMARY

We presented an overview of the complex problem of copyrighted multimedia content protection in digital distribution networks. After an introduction to copyright and copyright industries, we examined the

51

technical, legal, and business solutions for multimedia security in commonly used satellite, cable, terrestrial, and Internet-based architectures as well as digital home networks. Our analysis can be summarized as follows:

- End-to-end security is a key requirement for the growth of digital markets. Digital copyrighted content must be protected in every stage of its life cycle in order to prevent piracy losses and encourage continued supply of products and services.

- The copyright industries, a segment of the U.S. economy with a high growth rate, are the primary source of marketable digital content. A better estimate of the economic impact of piracy on these industries is needed. Appropriate copyright policies can only be developed by understanding the complex social, cultural, legal, and ethical factors that influence the consumer behavior.

- Digital media offers certain advantages:

  - *Perfect reproduction.* Copies produced are indistinguishable from the original.

  - *Reduced costs for storage and distribution.* Because of efficient compression methods, high-quality content can be stored on lower-capacity media and transmitted through lower-band-width channels.

  - *New business models.* Content owners (artists, authors, musicians, etc.) can have direct access to consumers, specify and dynamically change their business rules, and regularly obtain customer information. Superdistribution appears to be a promising model for quick and inexpensive distribution of products and promotions.

- Irrespective of the model used, the following elements interact in a commerce cycle for the management of digital rights:

  - *Content owner* (or its agent) packages content according to established business rules.

  - *Content distributor* makes content available to consumers through retail stores or other delivery channels.

  - *Customer* (with a compliant receiver) purchases and consumes content according to usage rules.

  - *Clearinghouse* keeps track of financial information and collects usage information.

- Encryption and watermarking are two groups of technology used in developing technical solutions for the copy protection problem in DHNs [117,141–143]. Encryption, the first line of defense, is the most effective way to achieve multimedia security. Ciphers can be classified into two major categories: symmetric key ciphers and asymmetric key ciphers. Watermarking, the second line of defense, is the process of embedding a signal into multimedia content (images, video, audio, etc.). Depending on the purpose of the embedded watermark, there is an essential difference between the functionalities of the consumer electronics devices:

– *Copyright protection.* The open literature on watermarking has so far focused on copyright protection for which the receiver does not have to assume an active role in responding to the watermark. When a dispute arises regarding the ownership of content, the watermark must be detected or extracted by authorized entities such as the legal institutions.

– *Access control.* The use of watermarking for content protection has been the subject of prolonged discussions at the Copy Protection Technical Working Group (CPTWG) meetings in California in the last few years. The three industries (information technology, consumer electronics, and motion picture) supporting the CPTWG have agreed in principle to implement a watermarking system in DVD playback and recording devices. According to a set of principles, the playback and recording devices will detect and respond to watermarks representing the CGMS bits ("11" [copy-never], "10" [copy-once], "01" [no-more-copies], and "00" [copy-free]). If an unauthorized copy is detected, the playback device will prevent the playback of the copy and the recording device will refuse to make a next-generation copy. Despite several years of research and testing, the Interim Board of Directors of the DVD Copy Control Association (DVD CCA) decided not to select a watermarking system for copy protection before ending its term in the summer of 2002.[3] The new board has inherited the task of determining the next steps in the selection process.

• In every type of content protection system based on secrets (conditional access, digital rights management [unicast and multicast], and copy protection), key management (i.e., generation, distribution, and maintenance of keys) is a critical issue. System renewability should be defined with the right balance among economic, social, and legal factors.

• The U.S. copyright law has been evolving in the past 200 years in response to technological developments. The recent obligations introduced by the DMCA will most likely need future revision for clarity and consistency. Additional legislative efforts are underway

---

[3]The DVD CCA is a not-for-profit corporation with responsibility for licensing CSS (Content Scramble System) to manufacturers of DVD hardware, disks, and related products.

both in the United States and in other countries to update national laws in response to technological developments.

- Worldwide coordination for copyright protection is a challenging task. Despite international treaties, there are significant differences among countries, making it difficult to track national laws and enforcement policies.

- To complement the technical and legal solutions, content owners are also developing new business models for marketing digital multimedia content. The important factors used in selecting a business model include type of content, duration of the economic value of content, fixation method, distribution channel, purchase mechanism, technology available for protection, and extent of related legislation.

ACKNOWLEDGMENTS

The authors would like to acknowledge the permission granted by Springer-Verlag, Elsevier, the Institute of Electrical and Electronics Engineers (IEEE), the International Association of Science and Technology for Development (IASTED), and the International Society for Optical Engineering (SPIE) for partial use of the authors' following research material published by them:

- Eskicioglu, A.M. and Delp, E.J., Overview of Multimedia Content Protection in Consumer Electronics Devices, in *Proceedings of SPIE Security and Watermarking of Multimedia Content II*, 2000, San Jose, CA, Vol. 3971, pp. 246–263.

- Eskicioglu, A.M. and Delp, E.J., Overview of multimedia content protection in consumer electronics devices, *Signal Process.: Image Commun.*, 16(7), 681–699, 2001.

- Eskicioglu, A.M., Town J., and Delp, E.J., Security of Digital Entertainment Content from Creation to Consumption, in *Proceedings of SPIE Applications of Digital Image Processing XXIV*, San Diego, CA, 2001, Vol. 4472, pp. 187–211.

- Eskicioglu, A.M., Multimedia Security in Group Communications: Recent Progress in Wired and Wireless Networks, in *Proceedings of the IASTED International Conference on Communications and Computer Networks*, Cambridge, MA, 2002, pp. 125–133.

- Eskicioglu, A.M., Town, J., and Delp, E.J., Security of digital entertainment content from creation to consumption, *Signal Process.: Image Commun.*, 18(4), 237–262, 2003.

- Eskicioglu, A.M., Multimedia security in group communications: recent progress in key management, authentication, and watermarking, *Multimedia Syst. J.*, 239–248, 2003.

- Eskicioglu, A.M., Protecting intellectual property in digital multimedia networks, *IEEE Computer*, 39–45, 2003.
- Lin, E.T., Eskicioglu, A.M., Lagendijk, R.L., and Delp, E.J., Advances in digital video content protection, *Proc. IEEE*, 2004.

REFERENCES

1. http://www.wipo.org.
2. http://www.loc.gov/copyright/circs/circ1.html.
3. http://www.loc.gov/copyright/title17/92chap1.html#106.
4. Strong, W.S., *The Copyright Book*, MIT Press, Cambridge, MA, 1999.
5. http://www.loc.gov/copyright/docs/circ1a.html.
6. http://arl.cni.org/info/frn/copy/timeline.html.
7. Goldstein, P., *Copyright's Highway*, Hill and Wang, 1994.
8. http://www.iipa.com.
9. National Research Council, *The Digital Dilemma: Intellectual Property in the Information Age*, National Academy Press, Washington, D.C., 2000.
10. Menezes, J., van Oorschot, P.C., and Vanstone, S.A., *Handbook of Applied Cryptography*, CRC Press, Boca Raton, FL, 1997.
11. Schneier, B., *Applied Cryptography*, John Wiley & Sons, 1996.
12. Advanced Television Systems Committee, available at http://www.atsc.org.
13. Consumers Electronics Association, available at http://www.ce.org.
14. Copy Protection Technical Working Group, available at http://www.cptwg.org.
15. DVD Forum, available at http://www.dvdforum.org.
16. Society of Cable Telecommunications Engineers, available at http://www.scte.org.
17. Motion Picture Association of America, available at http://www.mpaa.org.
18. Recording Industries Association of America, available at http://www.riaa.org.
19. Internet Engineering Task Force, available at http://www.ietf.org/overview.html.
20. Moving Pictures Expert Group, available at http://mpeg.telecomitalialab.com.
21. Digital Video Broadcasting Project, available at http://www.dvb.org.
22. de Bruin, R. and Smits, J., *Digital Video Broadcasting: Technology, Standards and Regulations*, Artech House, 1999.
23. Benoit, H., *Digital Television: MPEG-1, MPEG-2 and Principles of the DVB System*, Arnold, London, 1997.
24. Guillou, L.C. and Giachetti, J.L., Encipherment and conditional access, *SMPTE J.*, 103(6), 398–406, 1994.
25. Mooij, W. Conditional Access Systems for Digital Television, International Broadcasting Convention, IEE Conference Publication, 397, 1994, pp. 489–491.
26. Macq, B.M. and Quisquater, J.J., Cryptology for digital TV broadcasting, *Proc. IEEE*, 83(6), 1995.
27. Rossi, G., Conditional access to television broadcast programs: Technical solutions, *ABU Tech. Rev.* 166, 3–12, September–October 1996.
28. Cutts, D., DVB conditional access, *Electron. Commn., Engi. J.*, 9(1), 21–27, 1997.
29. Mooij, W., Advances in Conditional Access Technology, *International Broadcasting Convention*, IEE Conference Publication, 447, 1997, pp. 461–464.
30. Eskicioglu, A.M., A Key Transport Protocol for Conditional Access Systems, in *Proceedings of the SPIE Conference on Security and Watermarking of Multimedia Contents III*, San Jose, CA, 2001, pp. 139–148.
31. International Standard ISO-IEC 13818-1 Information Technology — Generic Coding of Moving Pictures and Associated Audio Information: Systems, first edition, 1996.
32. EIA-679B National Renewable Security Standard, September 1998.

33. http://www.macrovision.com.
34. EBU Project Group B/CA, Functional model of a conditional access system, *EBU Techn. Rev.*, 266, Winter 1995–1996.
35. http://www.atsc.org/standards/a_70_with_amendment.pdf.
36. http://www.mpaa.org/Press/broadcast_flag_qa.htm.
37. Federal Communications Commission, Report and Order and Further Notice of Proposed Rulemaking, November 4, 2003.
38. Eskicioglu, A.M., Multimedia security in group communications: recent progress in key management, authentication, and watermarking, *Multimedia Syst. J.*, 239–248, September 2003.
39. http://www.chiariglione.org/mpeg/faq/mp4-sys/sys-faq-ipmp-x.htm.
40. http://www.chiariglione.org/mpeg.
41. MPEG LA, LLC, available at http://www.mpegla.com.
42. Open eBook Forum, available at http://www.openebook.org.
43. http://www.irtf.org.
44. Miller, C.K., *Multicast Networking and Applications*, Addison-Wesley Longman, Reading, MA, 1999.
45. Hardjono, T. and Tsudik, G., IP Multicast security: Issues and directions, *Ann. Telecom*, 324–334, July–August 2000.
46. Dondeti, L.R., Mukherjee, S., and Samal, A., Survey and Comparison of Secure Group Communication Protocols, Technical Report, University of Nebraska–Lincoln, 1999.
47. Bruschi, D. and Rosti, E., Secure multicast in wireless networks of mobile hosts and protocols and issues, *ACM Baltzer MONET J.*, 7(6), 503–511, 2002.
48. Rafaeli, S. and Hutchison, D., A survey of key management for secure group communication, *ACM Computing Surv.*, 35(3), 309–329, 2003.
49. Chan, K.-C. and Chan, S.-H.G., Key management approaches to offer data confidentiality for secure multicast, *IEEE Network*, 30–39, September/October 2003.
50. Wong, C.K., Gouda, M.G., and Lam, S.S., Secure Group Communications Using Key Graphs, Technical Report TR-97-23, Department of Computer Sciences, The University of Texas at Austin, July 1997.
51. Caronni, G., Waldvogel, M., Sun, D., and Plattner, B., Efficient Security for Large and Dynamic Groups, Technical Report No. 41, Computer Engineering and Networks Laboratory, Swiss Federal Institute of Technology, February 1998.
52. Balenson, D., McGrew, D., and Sherman, A., Key Management for Large Dynamic Groups: One-Way Function Trees and Amortized Initialization, Internet Draft (work in progress), February 26, 1999.
53. Canetti, R., Garay, J., Itkis, G., Micciancio, D., Naor, M., and Pinkas, B., Multicast Security: A Taxonomy and Some Efficient Constructions, in *Proceedings of IEEE INFOCOM*, Vol. 2, New York, March 1999, pp. 708–716.
54. Chang, I., Engel, R., Kandlur, D., Pendakaris, D., and Saha, D., Key Management for Secure Internet Multicast Using Boolean Function Minimization Techniques, in *Proceedings of IEEE INFOCOM*, Vol. 2, New York, March 1999, pp. 689–698.
55. Wallner, D., Harder, E., and Agee, R., Key Management for Multicast: Issues and Architectures, RFC 2627, June 1999.
56. Waldvogel, M., Caronni, G., Sun, D., Weiler, N., and Plattner, B., The VersaKey framework: versatile group key management, *JSAC*, Special Issue on Middleware, 17(8), 1614–1631, 1999.
57. Banerjee, S. and Bhattacharjee, B., Scalable Secure Group Communication over IP Multicast, presented at *International Conference on Network Protocols*, Riverside, CA, November 10–14, 2001.
58. Eskicioglu, A.M. and Eskicioglu, M.R., Multicast Security Using Key Graphs and Secret Sharing, in *Proceedings of the Joint International Conference on Wireless LANs and Home Networks and Networking*, Atlanta, GA, August 26–29, 2002, pp. 228–241.

59. Selcuk, A.A. and Sidhu, D., Probabilistic optimization techniques for multicast key management, *Computer Networks*, 40(2), 219–234, 2002.

60. Zhu, S., and Setia, S., Performance Optimizations for Group Key Management Schemes, presented at *23rd International Conference on Distributed Computing Systems*, Providence, RI, May 19–22, 2003.

61. Huang, J.-H. and Mishra, S., Mykil: A Highly Scalable Key Distribution Protocol for Large Group Multicast, presented at *IEEE 2003 Global Communications Conference*, San Francisco, CA, December 1–5, 2003.

62. Trappe, W., Song, J., Poovendran, R., and Liu, K.J.R., Key management and distribution for secure multimedia multicast, *IEEE Trans. Multimedia*, 5(4), 544–557, 2003.

63. Chiou, G.H. and Chen, W.T., Secure broadcast using the secure lock, *IEEE Trans. on Software Engi.*, 15(8), 929–934, 1989.

64. Gong, L. and Shacham, N., Elements of Trusted Multicasting, in *Proceedings of the IEEE International Conference on Network Protocols*, Boston, MA, October 1994, pp. 23–30.

65. Harney, H., and Muckenhirn, C., Group Key Management Protocol (GKMP) Architecture, RFC 2094, July 1997.

66. Dunigan, T. and Cao, C., *Group Key Management*, Oak Ridge National Laboratory, Mathematical Sciences Section, Computer Science and Mathematics Division, ORNL/TM-13470, 1998.

67. Blundo, C., De Santis, A., Herzberg, A., Kutten, S., Vaccaro, U., and Yung, M., Perfectly-secure key distribution for dynamic conferences, *Inform. Comput.*, 146(1), 1–23, 1998.

68. Poovendran, R., Ahmed, S., Corson, S., and Baras, J., A Scalable Extension of Group Key Management Protocol, Technical Report TR 98-14, Institute for Systems Research, 1998.

69. Chu, H., Qiao, L., and Nahrstedt, K., A Secure Multicast Protocol with Copyright Protection, in *Proceedings of IS&T/SPIE Symposium on Electronic Imaging: Science and Technology*, January 1999, pp. 460–471.

70. Scheikl, O., Lane, J., Boyer, R., and Eltoweissy, M., Multi-level Secure Multicast: The Rethinking of Secure Locks, in *Proceedings of the 2002 ICPP Workshops on Trusted Computer Paradigms*, Vancouver, BC, Canada, August 18–21, 2002, pp. 17–24.

71. Mittra, S., Iolus: A Framework for Scalable Secure Multicasting, in *Proceedings of the ACM SIGCOMM '97*, Cannes, France, September 1997, pp. 277–288.

72. Dondeti, L.R., Mukherjee, S., and Samal, A., A Dual Encryption Protocol for Scalable Secure Multicasting, presented at *Fourth IEEE Symposium on Computers and Communications*, Red Sea, Egypt, July 6–8, 1999.

73. Molva, R. and Pannetrat, A., Scalable Multicast Security in Dynamic Groups, in *Proceedings of the 6th ACM Conference on Computer and Communications Security*, Singapore, November 1999, pp. 101–112.

74. Setia, S., Koussih, S., and Jajodia, S., Kronos: A Scalable Group Re-keying Approach for Secure Multicast, presented at *IEEE Symposium on Security and Privacy 2000*, Oakland, CA, May 14–17, 2000.

75. Hardjono, T., Cain, B., and Doraswamy, N., A Framework for Group Key Management for Multicast Security, Internet Draft (work in progress), August 2000.

76. Ballardie, A., Scalable Multicast Key Distribution, RFC 1949, May 1996.

77. Briscoe, B., MARKS: Multicast Key Management Using Arbitrarily Revealed Key Sequences, presented at *First International Workshop on Networked Group Communication*, Pisa, Italy, November 17–20, 1999.

78. Dondeti, L.R., Mukherjee, S., and Samal, A., A Distributed Group Key Management Scheme for Secure Many-to-Many Communication, Technical Report, PINTL-TR-207-99, Department of Computer Science, University of Maryland, 1999.

79. Perrig, A., Efficient Collaborative Key Management Protocols for Secure Autonomous Group Communication, presented at *International Workshop on Cryptographic Techniques and E-Commerce (CrypTEC '99)*, 1999, pp. 192–202.
80. Rodeh, O., Birman, K., and Dolev, D., Optimized Group Rekey for Group Communication Systems, presented at *Network and Distributed System Security Symposium*, San Diego, CA, February 3–4, 2000.
81. Kim, Y., Perrig, A., and Tsudik, G., Simple and Fault-Tolerant Key Agreement for Dynamic Collaborative Groups, in *Proceedings of the 7th ACM Conference on Computer and Communications Security*, November 2000, pp. 235–241.
82. Boyd, C., On Key Agreement and Conference Key Agreement, in *Proceedings of Second Australasian Conference on Information Security and Privacy*, in Second Australasian Conference, ACISP'97, Sydney, NSW, Australia, July 7–9, 1997, pp. 294–302.
83. Steiner, M., Tsudik, G., and Waidner, M., Cliques: A New Approach to Group Key Agreement, Technical Report RZ 2984, IBM Research, December 1997.
84. Becker, C. and Willie, U., Communication Complexity of Group Key Distribution, presented at *5th ACM Conference on Computer and Communications Security*, San Francisco, CA, November 1998.
85. Dondeti, L.R., Mukherjee, S., and Samal, A., Comparison of Hierarchical Key Distribution Schemes, in *Proceedings of IEEE Globecom Global Internet Symposium*, Rio de Janeiro, Brazil, 1999.
86. Bauer, M., Canetti, R., Dondeti, L., and Lindholm, F., MSEC Group Key Management Architecture, Internet Draft, IETF MSEC WG, September 8, 2003.
87. Yang, Y.R., Li, X.S., Zhang, X.B., and Lam, S.S., Reliable Group Rekeying: A Performance Analysis, in *Proceedings of the ACM SIGCOMM '01*, San Diego, CA, 2001, pp. 27–38.
88. Li, X.S., Yang, Y.R., Gouda, M.G., and Lam, S.S., Batch Rekeying for Secure Group Communications, in *Proceedings of 10th International WWW Conference*, Hong Kong, 2001, pp. 525–534.
89. Zhang, X.B., Lam, S.S., Lee, D.Y., and Yang, Y.R., Protocol Design for Scalable and Reliable Group Rekeying, in *Proceedings of SPIE Conference on Scalability and Traffic Control in IP Networks*, Vol. 4526, Denver, CO, 2001.
90. Moyer, M.J., Rao, J.R., and Rohatgi, P., Maintaining Balanced Key Trees for Secure Multicast, Internet Draft, June 1999.
91. Goshi, J. and Ladner, R.E., Algorithms for Dynamic Multicast Key Distribution Trees, presented at *22nd ACM Symposium on Principles of Distributed Computing (PODC '03)*, Boston, MA, 2003.
92. Dondeti, L.R., Mukherjee, S., and Samal, A., Survey and Comparison of Secure Group Communication Protocols, Technical Report, University of Nebraska–Lincoln, 1999.
93. Menezes, J., van Oorschot, P.C., and Vanstone, S.A., *Handbook of Applied Cryptography*, CRC Press, Boca Raton, FL, 1997.
94. Moyer, M.J., Rao, J.R., and Rohatgi, P., A survey of security issues in multicast communications, *IEEE Network*, 12–23, November/December 1999.
95. Gennaro, R. and Rohatgi, P., How to Sign Digital Streams, in *Advances in Cryptology — CRYPTO '97*, 1997, pp. 180–197.
96. Wong, C.K. and Lam, S.S., Digital Signatures for Flows and Multicasts, in *Proceedings of 6th IEEE International Conference on Network Protocols (ICNP '98)*, Austin, TX, 1998.
97. Rohatgi, P., A Compact and Fast Hybrid Signature Scheme for Multicast Packets, in *Proceedings of 6th ACM Conference on Computer and Communications Security*, Singapore, 1999.
98. Perrig, A., Canetti, R., Tygar, J.D., and Song, D., Efficient Authentication and Signing of Multicast Streams over Lossy Channels, in *Proceedings of IEEE Symposium on Security and Privacy 2000*, Oakland, CA, 2000.

99. Perrig, A., Canetti, R., Song, D., and Tygar, J.D., Efficient and Secure Source Authentication for Multicast, in *Proceedings of Network and Distributed System Security Symposium*, San Diego, CA, 2001.

100. Perrig, A., The BiBa One-Time Signature and Broadcast Authentication Protocol, in *Proceedings of the 8th ACM Conference on Computer and Communications Security*, Philadelphia, 2001.

101. Golle, P. and Modadugu, N., Authenticating Streamed Data in the Presence of Random Packet Loss, presented at *Network and Distributed System Security Symposium Conference*, 2001.

102. Miner, S. and Staddon, J., Graph-Based Authentication of Digital Streams, in *Proceedings of the IEEE Symposium on Research in Security and Privacy*, Oakland, CA, 2001, pp. 232–246.

103. Park, J.M., Chong, E.K.P., and Siegel, H.J., Efficient multicast stream authentication using erasure codes, *ACM Trans. Inform. Syst. Security*, 6(2), 258–285, 2003.

104. Pannetrat, A. and Molva, R., Efficient Multicast Packet Authentication, presented at *10th Annual Network and Distributed System Security Symposium*, San Diego, CA, 2003.

105. Boneh, D., Durfee, G., and Franklin, M., Lower Bounds for Multicast Message Authentication, in *Proceedings of Eurocrypt 2001*, Lecture Notes in Computer Science Vol. 2045, Springer-Verlag, New York, 2001, pp. 437–452.

106. Podilchuk, C.I. and Delp, E.J., Digital watermarking: Algorithms and applications, *IEEE Signal Process. Mag.*, 33–46, July 2001.

107. Cox, I.J., Miller, M.L., and Bloom, J.A., *Digital Watermarking*, Morgan Kaufmann, 2002.

108. Lin, E.T., Eskicioglu, A.M., Lagendijk, R.L., and Delp, E.J., Advances in digital video content protection, *Proc. IEEE*, 93(1), 171–183, 2005.

109. Hartung, F. and Kutter, M., Multimedia watermarking techniques, *Proc. IEEE*, 87(7), 1079–1107, 1999.

110. Wolfgang, R.B., Podilchuk, C.I., and Delp, E.J., Perceptual watermarks for digital images and video, *Proc. IEEE*, 87(7), 1108–1126, 1999.

111. Brown, I., Perkins, C., and Crowcroft, J., Watercasting: Distributed Watermarking of Multicast Media, presented at *First International Workshop on Networked Group Communication (NGC '99)*, Pisa, 1999.

112. Judge, P. and Ammar, M., WHIM: Watermarking Multicast Video with a Hierarchy of Intermediaries, presented at *10th International Workshop on Network and Operation System Support for Digital Audio and Video*, Chapel Hill, NC, 2000.

113. Caronni, G. and Schuba, C., Enabling Hierarchical and Bulk-Distribution for Watermarked Content, presented at *17th Annual Computer Security Applications Conference*, New Orleans, LA, 2001.

114. DeCleene, B.T., Dondeti, L.R., Griffin, S.P., Hardjono, T., Kiwior, D., Kurose, J., Towsley, D., Vasudevan, S., and Zhang, C., Secure Group Communications for Wireless Networks, in *Proceedings of IEEE MILCOM 2001*, McLean, VA, 2001.

115. Griffin, S.P., DeCleene, B.T., Dondeti, L.R., Flynn, R.M., Kiwior, D., and Olbert, A., Hierarchical Key Management for Mobile Multicast Members, Technical Report, Northrop Grumman Information Technology, 2002.

116. Zhang, C., DeCleene, B.T., Kurose, J., and Towsley, D., Comparison of Inter-Area Rekeying Algorithms for Secure Wireless Group Communications, presented at *IFIP WG7.3 International Symposium on Computer Performance Modeling, Measurement and Evaluation*, Rome, 2002.

117. Eskicioglu, A.M. and Delp, E.J., Overview of multimedia content protection in consumer electronics devices, *Signal Process.: Image Commun.*, 16(7), 681–699, 2001.

118. CPSA: A Comprehensive Framework for Content Protection, available at http://www.4Centity.com.

119. Content Scramble System, available at http://www.dvdcca.org.

120. Content Protection for Prerecorded Media, available at http://www.4Centity.com.
121. Content Protection for Recordable Media, available at http://www.4Centity.com.
122. 4C/Verance Watermark, available at http://www.verance.com.
123. High Definition Copy Protection, available at http://www.wired.com/news/tech nology/0,1282,41045,00.html.
124. Digital Transmission Content Protection, available at http://www.dtcp.com.
125. High-bandwidth Digital Content Protection, available at http://www.digital-CP.com.
126. http://www.vesa.org.
127. http://www.upnp.org.
128. Vevers, R. and Hibbert, C., Copy Protection and Content Management in the DVB, presented at *IBC 2002 Conference*, Amsterdam, 2002.
129. EIA-679B National Renewable Security Standard, September 1998.
130. OpenCable CableCARD Copy Protection System Interface Specification, available at http://www.opencable.com.
131. ATSC Standard A/70: Conditional Access System for Terrestrial Broadcast, available at http://www.atsc.org.
132. Proprietary conditional access system for DirecTV, http://www.directv.com.
133. Proprietary conditional access system for Dish Network, http://www.dishnetwork. com.
134. OpenCable System Security Specification, available at http://www.opencable.com.
135. Microsoft Windows Media DRM, available at http://www.microsoft.com/windows/ windowsmedia/drm.aspx.
136. Helix DRM, available at http://www.realnetworks.com/products/drm/index.html.
137. http://www.securemulticast.org.
138. http://www.wto.org.
139. Samuelson, P., Intellectual property and the digital economy: why the anti-circumvention regulations need to be revised, *Berkeley Technol. Law J.*, 14, 1999.
140. Windows Media Rights Manager, available at http://msdn.microsoft.com.
141. Bell, A., The dynamic digital disk, *IEEE Spectrum*, 36(10), 28–35, 1999.
142. Bloom, J.A., Cox, I.J., Kalker, T., Linnartz, J.P.M.G., Miller, M.L., and Traw, C.B.S., Copy protection for DVD video, *Proc. IEEE*, 87(7), 1267–1276, 1999.
143. Eskicioglu, A.M., Town, J., and Delp, E.J., Security of digital entertainment content from creation to consumption, *Signal Process.: Image Commun.*, 18(4), 237–262, 2003.

2

Vulnerabilities of Multimedia Protection Schemes

Mohamed F. Mansour and Ahmed H. Tewfik

INTRODUCTION

The deployment of multimedia protection algorithms to practical systems has moved to the standardization and implementation phase. In the near future, it will be common to have audio and video players that employ a watermarking mechanism to check the integrity of the played media. The publicity of the detectors introduces new challenges for current multimedia security.

The detection of copyright watermarks is a binary hypothesis test with the decision boundary determined by the underlying test statistic. The amount of signal modification that can be tolerated defines a distortion hyperellipsoid around the representation of the signal in the appropriate multidimensional space. The decision boundary implemented by the watermark detector necessarily passes through that hyperellipsoid because the distortion between the original and watermarked signals is either undetectable or acceptable. Once the attacker knows the decision region, she can simply modify the signal within the acceptable limits and move it to the other side of the decision boundary.

The exact structure of the watermark is not important for our analysis because we focus on watermark detection rather than interpretation. What is important is the structure and operation of the detector. In many cases, especially for copyright protection purposes, the detection is based on thresholding the correlation coefficient between the test signal and the watermark. This detector is optimal if the host signal has a Gaussian distribution. The decision boundary in this case is a hyperplane, which can be estimated with a sufficient number of watermarked items.

The above scheme belongs to the class of *symmetric watermarking*, where the decoder uses the same parameters used in embedding. These parameters are usually generated using a *secret key* that is securely transmitted to the decoder. In contrast, *asymmetric watermarking* [1] employs different keys for encoding and decoding the watermark. In Reference 2, a unified decoding approach is introduced for different asymmetric watermarking schemes. The decoder uses a test statistic in quadratic form. Although the decision boundary is more complicated, it is still parametric and can be estimated using, for example, least square techniques.

Another important watermarking class is the quantization-based schemes. In this class, two or more codebooks are used to quantize the host signal. Each codebook represents an embedded symbol. The decision boundary in this case, although more complicated, is parameterized by the entries of each codebook. This boundary can be estimated using simple statistical analysis of the watermarked signal.

In this chapter, we propose a generic attack for removing the watermark *with minimum distortion* if the detector is publicly available. In this attack, the decision boundary is first estimated; then, the watermarked signal is projected onto the estimated boundary to remove the watermark with minimum distortion. We give implementations of the generic attack for the different watermarking schemes. Next, we propose a new structure for a watermark public detector that resists this attack. The structure is based on using a nonparametric decision boundary so that it cannot be estimated with unlimited access to the detector. The robustness degradation after this detector is minor and can be tolerated.

This chapter is organized as follows. In section "Vulnerability of Current Detection Algorithms," we describe the pitfalls of the current detectors when the detector is publicly available. In section "The Generic Attack," we introduce the generic attack, which aims at removing the watermark with minimum distortion. We propose possible implementations of the attack for the correlator and quantization-based detectors. In section "Secure Detector Structure," we describe the new detector structure with a fractal decision boundary and provide a practical implementation of it. Also, we give an overview of the results that show that the distortion is essentially similar to the original detector.

VULNERABILITY OF CURRENT DETECTION ALGORITHMS

In this section, we analyze the security of the current watermark detection schemes. As mentioned earlier, all schemes share the common feature that the decision boundary is *parametric* (i.e., it can be fully specified by a finite set of parameters). The estimation of the parameters is possible in theory. For example, least square techniques can be applied efficiently if sufficient samples (points on the decision boundary) are available. In this section, we will review common detector schemes and describe their security gaps.

We will use the following notations in the remainder of the chapter. $\underline{U}$ is the original (nonwatermarked) signal, $\underline{W}$ is the watermark, $\underline{X}$ is the watermarked signal, and $\underline{R}$ is the signal under investigation (at the detector). The individual components will be written in lowercase letters and referenced by the discrete index n, where n is a two-element vector in the case of image (e.g., samples of the watermark will be denoted by $w[n]$), L will denote the signal length, and in the case of images, M and N will denote the numbers of rows and columns, respectively, and in this case $L = M \times N$. γ will denote the detection threshold, which is usually selected using the Neyman–Pearson theorem for optimal detection [3, chap. 3].

Correlation-Based Detectors

This detector is the most common and it is optimum for the class of additive watermark with white Gaussian probability density function (pdf) of the underlying signal. It is of fundamental importance; hence, it will be considered in detail. First, assume that the correlation is performed in the signal domain. The detector can be formulated as a binary hypothesis test:

$$H_0: \underline{X} = \underline{U}$$

$$H_1: \underline{X} = \underline{U} + \underline{W}$$

(2.1)

Without loss of generality, we assume that the detector removes the signal mean prior to detection. The log-likelihood test statistic is reduced, after removing the common terms, to

$$l(\underline{R}) = \underline{R}^* \cdot \underline{W} = (1/L) \sum_n r^*[n] \cdot w[n]$$

(2.2)

63

where the asterisk denotes the conjugate transpose of the matrix. H_1 is decided if $l(\underline{R}) > \gamma$, and H_0 is decided otherwise. For this detector, the probability distribution of $l(\underline{R})$ is approximately Gaussian if L is large by invoking the central limit theorem. If we assume that the watermark and the underlying signal are uncorrelated, then the mean and the variance of $l(\underline{R})$ are

$$E\{l(\underline{R})|H_0\} = 0$$
$$E\{l(\underline{R})|H_1\} = (1/L) \sum_n (w[n])^2$$
$$\text{Var}\{l(\underline{R})\} = (1/L^2) \sum_n \sum_m E(x^*[n]x[m])w^*[n] \cdot w[m], \qquad \text{under } H_0 \text{ and } H_1$$

Furthermore, if the signal samples are assumed independent, then

$$\text{Var}\{l(\underline{R})\} = (1/L^2) \sum_n E\{|x[n]|^2\} \cdot (w[n])^2, \qquad \text{under } H_0 \text{ and } H_1 \qquad (2.3)$$

If the watermark $\underline{W}_c$ is embedded in the transform coefficients and if $\underline{R}_c$ is the transform of the test signal and T is the transformation matrix, then the correlation in the transform domain is

$$l_c(\underline{R}) = \underline{R}_c^* \cdot \underline{W}_c = (T \cdot \underline{R})^* \cdot TW = R^* \cdot T^* T \cdot \underline{W}$$

If the transformation is orthogonal (which is usually the case), then $T^*T = I$ and

$$l_c(\underline{R}) = \underline{R}^* \cdot \underline{W}$$

where $\underline{W}$ is the inverse transform of the embedded watermark. Therefore, even if the watermark is embedded in the transform coefficients, the correlation in Equation 2.1 is still applicable. However, the watermark $\underline{W}$ will have arbitrary values in the time domain even if $\underline{W}_c$ has binary values.

For this detector, the decision boundary is a hyperplane in the multi-dimensional space R^L. It is completely parameterized by a single orthogonal vector (of length L), which can be estimated by L independent points on the hyperplane. The displacement of the hyperplane is equivalent to the threshold γ. Therefore, it is not important in estimating the watermark, as it will only lead to a uniform scaling of the amplitude of each component of the watermark. As we shall see below, the proposed attack sequentially removes an adaptively scaled version of the estimated watermark from the signal. Hence, the exact value of the scale factor is not important in the attack.

If more points are available, a least square minimization can be applied to estimate the watermark. In the next section, we will provide techniques for estimating this boundary using the simple LMS algorithm.

Some variations of the basic correlator detector were discussed in Reference 5. However, the decision boundary of the modified detectors becomes a composite of hyperplanes. This new decision boundary, although more complicated, is still parametric and inherits the same security problem.

Asymmetric Detector

Asymmetric detectors were suggested to make the problem of estimating the secret key for unauthorized parties more difficult. In Reference 2, four asymmetric techniques were reviewed and a unified form for the detector was introduced. The general form of the test statistic is

$$l(\underline{R}) = \underline{R}^T \cdot A \cdot \underline{R} = \sum_{n,m} a_{n,m} r[n] \cdot r[m] \tag{2.4}$$

The decision boundary in this case is a multidimensional quadratic surface. This is more complicated than the hyperplane but still can be completely specified using a finite number of parameters, namely $\{a_{n,m}\}_{n,m=1:L}$. However, in this case, we will need at least L^2 samples to estimate the boundary rather than L.

Quantization-Based Detector

Techniques for data embedding using quantization are based on using two or more codebooks to represent the different symbols to be embedded. These codebooks can be simply scalar quantization with odd and even quantization indices. The most common schemes for quantization-based watermarking are quantized index modulation (QIM) and quantized projection, which will be discussed in the following subsections.

Quantized Index Modulation. In this class, multiple codebooks are used for embedding [6]. The data is embedded by mapping segments of the host signal to the cluster region of two or more codebooks. Each codebook represents a data symbol. The decoding is done by measuring the quantization errors between each segment and all codebooks. The extracted data symbol is the one that corresponds to the codebook with minimum quantization error. In general, the decision boundaries for each data segment can be completely specified by the centroids of the codebooks [6].

One implementation of particular importance in (QIM) embedding is dither modulation [7]. The embedding process is parameterized by three sets of parameters: $\{\Delta_k\}_{k=1:L}$, $\{\underline{d}_1(k)\}_{k=1:L}$, and $\{\underline{d}_2(k)\}_{k=1:L}$, where Δ_k is the quantization step for the kth component, $\underline{d}_1$ and $\underline{d}_2$ are pseudorandom sequences that correspond to 0 and 1, respectively, and $|\underline{d}_1(k)|$, $|\underline{d}_2(k)| < \Delta_k/2$ for $k=1:L$. The host signal is segmented into segments of length L. One bit is embedded per segment. The kth component of the ith segment is modified according to [6]

$$\underline{y}_i(k) = q(\underline{x}_i(k) + \underline{d}_i(k)) - \underline{d}_i(k), \qquad k = 1, 2, \ldots, L \qquad (2.5)$$

where $q(\cdot)$ is a scalar quantization using quantization steps Δ_k and $\underline{d}_i \in \{\underline{d}_1, \underline{d}_2\}$. As discussed in Reference 6, the decision boundaries are determined by the values of $\{\Delta_k\}$. In general, the boundaries are symmetric cells around the reconstruction points. The quantization cells and the reconstruction points of any quantizer are shifted versions of the quantization cells and the reconstruction points of the other quantizer. The decoding is done by the following steps:

1. Add $\underline{d}_1$ and $\underline{d}_2$ to the modified segments.
2. Quantize the resulting segments using scalar quantization of each component in the segment with quantization steps $\{\Delta_k\}_{k=1:L}$.
3. Measure the overall quantization error of each segment in both cases.
4. The bit that corresponds to the smaller quantization error (at each segment) is decided.

For the above scheme, the embedding process can be undone if $\{\Delta_k, \underline{d}_1(k), \underline{d}_2(k)\}_{k=1:L}$ are estimated correctly. In section "Attack on Quantization-Based Schemes," we provide an attack that unveils these parameters and removes the watermark with minimum distortion.

Note that, in Reference 6, 2 $\underline{d}_2(k)$ is expressed in terms of $\underline{d}_1(k)$ and Δ_k to maximize the robustness. In this case,

$$\underline{d}_2(k) = \underline{d}_1(k) + \Delta_k/2 \qquad \text{if } \underline{d}_1(k) < 0$$
$$= \underline{d}_1(k) - \Delta_k/2 \qquad \text{if } \underline{d}_1(k) \geq 0$$

This further reduces the number of unknowns and, hence, reduces the estimation complexity.

Quantized Projection Watermarking. This scheme is based on projecting the signal (or some features derived from it) onto an orthogonal set of vectors. The projection value is then quantized using scalar quantization and the quantization index is forced to be odd or even to embed 1 or 0, respectively [8,9]. The embedding relation for modifying each vector v of the host signal is [8]

$$\tilde{v} = v - Pv + B_i \cdot \Delta_i \cdot Q_i\left(\frac{B_i^H v}{\Delta_i}\right) \tag{2.6}$$

where Δ_i is the quantization step of the projection value onto the ith base vector B_i (the ith column of the orthogonal matrix), P is the projection matrix to the subspace of B_i (i.e., $P = B_i B_i^H$), and Q_i is the quantization to the nearest even integer and odd integers (according to the corresponding data bit). Different orthogonal sets can be used in Equation 2.6. For example, in Reference 8, the columns of the Hadamard matrix are used as the orthogonal set.

Note that if a single vector is used in Equation 2.6 for embedding data (i.e., one bit per block) rather than the whole orthogonal set, then this is equivalent to the *hidden QIM* scheme [6], where the QIM occurs in the domain of the auxiliary vector B_i.

The decoding process is straightforward. Each vector v is projected onto the base vector B_i, and the projection value is rounded with respect to the quantization step Δ_i. If the result is even, then the corresponding bit is '0'; and if it is odd, the corresponding bit is '1'. Note that if the vector length is fixed, then the transformation between different orthogonal sets is linear. The decision boundary in this case is parameterized by the set $\{\underline{B}_i, \Delta_i\}$.

Comments

In this section, we analyzed the structure of the decision boundary of common watermark detectors. They share the common feature that the decision boundary at the detector (between the two hypotheses of the presence and absence of the watermark) is parameterized by a finite set of parameters. These parameters change according to the underlying test statistics. However, all of them can be estimated when the detector is publicly available, as will be discussed in the next section.

THE GENERIC ATTACK

Introduction

The decision boundaries of common watermarking schemes, which were discussed in the previous section, can be estimated using, for example, least square techniques if a sufficient number of points on the boundary is available. The estimation problem may be nonlinear in some cases, but in theory, it can still be applied and efficient techniques can be proposed to optimize the estimation. This is easy when the attacker has unlimited access to the detector device even as a black box.

In this case, the attacker can make *slight* changes to the watermarked signal until reaching a point at which the detector is not able to detect the watermark. This point can always be reached because a constant signal cannot contain a watermark. Therefore, by repeatedly replacing the samples of the watermarked signal by a constant value, the detector will respond negatively at some point. At this point, the attacker can go back and forth around the boundary until identifying a point on it with the required precision. Generating a large number of these points is sufficient for estimating the decision boundary for the cases discussed in the previous section.

Once the boundary is specified, any watermarked signal can be projected to the nearest point on the boundary to remove the watermark with the *smallest distortion*. For a correlation-based detector, the estimation of the decision boundary is equivalent to estimating the watermark itself. Hence, the projection is equivalent to successively subtracting components of the watermark from the watermarked signal until the detector responds negatively. The attack idea is illustrated in Figure 2.1.

The boundary estimation for both correlator and asymmetric detectors is a linear estimation problem in terms of the unknown parameters, which are $\{w[n]\}_{n=1:L}$ for the correlator detector and $\{a_{n,m}\}_{m,n=1:L}$ for the asymmetric detector. In both cases, the problem can be solved using least square techniques. However, for large-sized data, this may be expensive for an average attacker. For example, for an image of size 512×512, each data vector for the correlator detector is of size $512^2 = 262,144$, and at least 512^2 independent vectors are needed for the least square problem to be well conditioned. The direct least square will require inversion of a matrix of size $512^2 \times 512^2$, which may be expensive. Even if recursive least square (RLS) is employed, it will require manipulation of a matrix of size $512^2 \times 512^2$ at each iteration step, which may be also impractical for the average attacker. However, the workhorse for adaptive filtering, namely the least mean square (LMS)

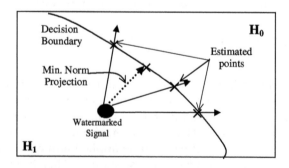

Figure 2.1. The generalized attack.

algorithm, works extremely well in this case and gives satisfactory results. In the next subsection, we give an effective implementation of the generalized attack using the simple LMS algorithm for the class of correlator detectors.

For quantization-based embedding, the attack is simpler. Simple statistical analysis is sufficient to estimate the unknown parameters without the need for recursion. The attack on quantization-based schemes is introduced in section "Attack on Quantization-Based Schemes."

Attack on Linear Detectors

The problem of estimating the decision boundary for the correlation detector fits the system model of classical adaptive filtering, which is shown in Figure 2.2. In this model, the system tries to track the reference signal $d(t)$ by filtering the input $\underline{r}(t)$ by the adaptive filter $\underline{w}(t)$. The optimal solution for this problem for stationary input is the *Weiner* filter, which is impractical to implement if the input statistics are not known *a priori*. The LMS algorithm [10] approximates Weiner filtering and the basic steps of the algorithm are:

1. Error calculation: $e(t) = d(t) - \underline{r}^*(t) \cdot w(t)$
2. Adaptation: $\underline{w}(t+1) = \underline{w}(t) + \mu \cdot \underline{r}(t) \cdot e^*(t)$

For algorithm stability, the adaptation step μ should be less than $2/(\Sigma_i \lambda_i)$, where $\{\lambda_i\}_{i=1:L}$ are the eigenvalues of the data covariance matrix. A conservative value of μ that is directly derived from the data and guarantees stability is $\mu = 2/(L \cdot P)$, where P is the signal power.

First, we will describe the generalized attack if the attacker has knowledge of the correlation value in Equation 2.2 for every input. Later, this assumption will be relaxed to study the more practical case.

For this problem, $\underline{r}(t)$ are the different samples of the watermarked signal after modification, $d(t)$ are the corresponding correlation values (output of the detector), and $\underline{w}(t)$ is the estimated watermark at time t. It is important to have the input vectors as uncorrelated as possible. If we have a single watermarked signal, the different samples that are derived

Figure 2.2. Adaptive filtering topology.

from it and are reasonably uncorrelated can be obtained by changing a random number of the signal values in a random order. For images, this is done by reordering the image blocks (or pixels) in a random fashion and replacing the first K blocks (where K is a random integer) by the image mean. If the watermark is binary, then the estimated coefficients should be approximated to binary values by taking the sign of each component. If the watermark is embedded in some transform coefficients, then the watermark values are not approximated. In Figure 2.3, we give an example of the convergence of the binary watermark components for the mandrill image of size 128×128. It represents the evolving of the matching between the estimated watermark and the actual watermark with the number of iterations. It should be noted that the shown convergence curve is obtained using a single watermarked signal. If more than one signal is employed in estimating the watermark, better convergence is obtained (see Figure 2.5).

After estimating the decision boundary, the watermark can be removed by successively subtracting the estimated watermark from the watermarked signal until the detector responds negatively. If all the watermark components are subtracted without reaching the boundary, then they are subtracted again. This is typical if the strength of the embedded watermark is greater than unity. In Figure 2.4, an example of the projection is given for the watermarked *Pepper* image when the threshold is half-way between the maximum correlation (of the correct random sequence) and the second maximum correlation (of all other random sequences). We show the ideal case when the watermark is known exactly and the cases when only 90% and 80% of the watermark is recovered correctly. From Figure 2.4, it is noticed that the difference is very small among the three cases. However, with large errors in estimating the watermark (e.g., if the matching is less than 70%), the projection

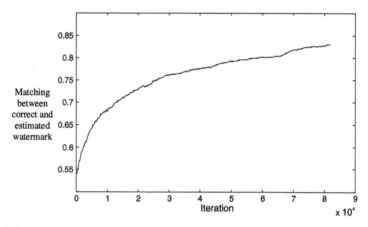

Figure 2.3. Convergence example of the LMS realization.

a. Watermarked image

b. After nearest projection
(watermark known)

c. After nearest project on
(90% recovered)

d. After nearest projection
(80% recovered)

Figure 2.4.   Example of watermark removal with minimum distortion.

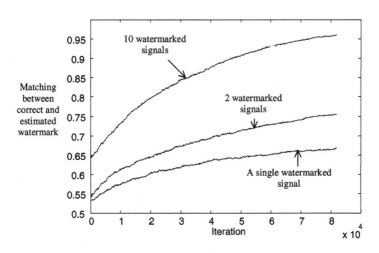

Figure 2.5.   LMS convergence when only the detector decisions are observed.

71

becomes noticeable because subtracting the erroneous components boosts the correlation in Equation 2.2 and it needs more iterations to be canceled.

Now we consider the practical case when the attacker does not have access to the internal correlation values but can only observe the detector decisions. In this case, the only points that can be determined accurately are the ones close to the boundary at which the detector changes its decision. As mentioned earlier, these points can be estimated by successively replacing the signal samples by a constant value until reaching a point at which the detector responds negatively. Starting from this point, small variations in the signal will cause the detector to go back and forth around the boundary until reaching a point on the boundary with the required precision.

The main problem in this case is the high correlation between the different modified samples of the same watermarked signal in the neighborhood of the decision boundary. This slows down the convergence significantly. However, convergence can be accelerated by employing multiple watermarked signals, and this is not a problem for public detectors. In Figure 2.5, we give a convergence example when one, two, and ten watermarked signals (all are images of size 128×128) are used for estimating the decision boundary.

The correlation threshold γ may be unknown to the attacker as well. However, if she uses any positive estimate of it, this will do the job because it will result in a scaled version of the watermark. The progressive projection described earlier will take care of the scaling factor.

A third possible scenario at the detector is when the detector decision is associated with a confidence measure about its correctness. This confidence measure is usually a monotonic function of the difference between the correlation value and the threshold. In principle, the attacker can exploit this extra information to accelerate the attack. Denote the confidence measure by η. In general, we have

$$\eta = f(l(\underline{R}) - \gamma)$$

where $l(\underline{R})$ is the correlation value and γ is the detection threshold. Assume, without loss of generality, that η is negative when the watermark is not detected; that is, it is a confidence measure of negative detection as well. We consider the worst-case scenario when the attacker does not know the formula of the confidence measure. In this case, the attacker can view η as an estimate of the correlation value and proceed as if the correlation value is available. However, it was found experimentally that the threshold γ must be estimated along with the watermark to accelerate the convergence. Hence, the LMS iteration of the attack is modified as follows:

1. Calculate the confidence measure $\eta(t)$ of the image instance
2. Error calculation: $e(t) = \eta(t) - [\underline{r}^*(t) \cdot \underline{w}(t) - \gamma(t)]$
3. Adaptation: $[\underline{w}(t+1), \gamma(t+1)] = [\underline{w}(t), \gamma(t)] + \mu \cdot e^*(t) \cdot [\underline{r}(t), -1]$

Note that we do not need to find points exactly on the decision boundary because the confidence measure can be computed for any image, not only the instances on the decision boundary. This significantly accelerates the algorithm.

The above attack works well when the confidence measure is *linear* with the correlation. A nonlinear confidence measure does not fit the linear model of the LMS and results in substantial reduction in the algorithm speed. In Figure 2.6, we show the algorithm convergence when ten watermarked images are used. The nonlinear function in the figure is quadratic in the difference $l(\underline{R}) - \gamma$. By comparing Figures 2.5 and 2.6, we note that the algorithm is accelerated only with the linear confidence measure. For the nonlinear confidence measure, it is better to ignore the confidence measure and run the attack with points only on the decision boundary, as discussed earlier.

If the watermark is embedded in the transform coefficients, the watermark will not be, in general, binary in the signal domain. In this case, the actual estimated values of the watermark components are used rather than their signs. However, if the attacker knows which transform

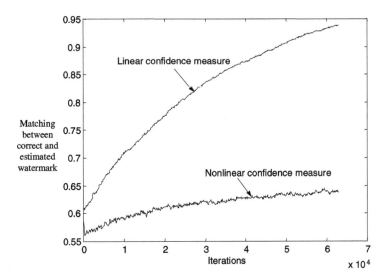

Figure 2.6. **Convergence of the LMS attack when a confidence measure is available.**

is used, then the above algorithm can be applied to the transformed signal rather than the signal.

Although we have used images to illustrate the attack, the algorithm discussed in this section works as well with audio and video watermarking. If the watermark is embedded in blocks, there is no need to get the blocks' boundaries, as we assume that the watermark exists at each individual sample of the watermarked signal.

Attack on Quantization-Based Schemes

The basic idea of the attack on quantization-based schemes is to estimate the entries of the different codebooks and use them to remove the watermark with *minimum* distortion. It turns out that, from the attacker viewpoint, both quantization-based schemes are similar and do not need special consideration, as will be discussed in the following subsections.

Attack on QIM Scheme. The objective of the attack is to estimate Δ_k, $\underline{d}_1(k)$, and $\underline{d}_2(k)$ for $k = 1, 2, \ldots, L$, and then use the estimated parameters to remove the watermark with minimum distortion.

First, we assume that the segment length L is known. Later, we will discuss how to estimate it. At the decoder, we have the modified segments in the form of Equation 2.5. If the correct quantization step Δ_k is used, then the quantization error for the kth component will be either $\underline{d}_1(k)$ or $\underline{d}_2(k)$. Hence, the histogram of the quantization error is concentrated around the correct value of $\underline{d}_1(k)$ and $\underline{d}_2(k)$. Based on this remark, the attack can be performed as follows:

1. Define a search range $[0, \Delta_{M(k)}]$ for the quantization step Δ_k. This range is determined by the maximum allowable distortion $\Delta_{M(k)}$ of each component.

2. Within this range, search is done for the best quantization step by performing the following steps for each candidate value of Δ_k:

    a. Each quantization step candidate is used to quantize the kth component of each segment. The quantization error is calculated. Positive quantization errors are accumulated together and negative quantization errors are accumulated together.

    b. For each quantization step candidate, the standard deviations of the positive and negative quantization errors are calculated.

    c. The best quantization step is the one that minimizes the sum of the standard deviations of the positive and negative quantization errors. A typical plot of the sum of the standard deviation for different values of Δ is shown in Figure 2.7.

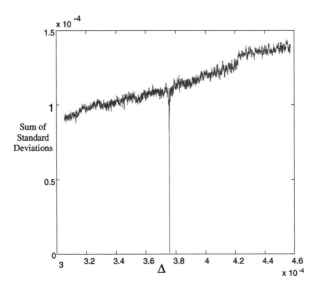

Figure 2.7. Example of Δ search.

3. After estimating Δ_k, $\underline{d}_1(k)$ and $\underline{d}_2(k)$ are simply the means of the positive and negative quantization errors, respectively. Note that the signs of $\underline{d}_1(k)$ and $\underline{d}_2(k)$ are chosen such that the different components of $\underline{d}_1$ or $\underline{d}_2$ within each segment are consistent.

The estimation of L follows directly from the analysis of the quantization error. Note that for any quantization step Δ (even if it is incorrect), the quantization error pattern of similar components at different segments is quite similar. This is basically because the reconstruction points of these segments are discrete. Recall that the kth component of each segment is modified according to Equation 2.5. Assume that the quantization function with step Δ is $G(\cdot)$. The quantization error of the kth component after using Δ is

$$\underline{e}_i(k) = G(q(\underline{x}_i(k) + \underline{d}_i(k)) - \underline{d}_i(k)) - q(\underline{x}_i(k) + \underline{d}_i(k)) + \underline{d}_i(k) \qquad (2.7)$$

Let $z_k = G(q(\underline{x}_i(k) + \underline{d}_i(k)) - \underline{d}_i(k)) - q(\underline{x}_i(k) + \underline{d}_i(k))$. If $\underline{d}_i(k)$, $\Delta \ll \underline{x}_i(k)$, then z_k is approximately distributed as a uniform random variable (i.e., $z_k \sim U[-\Delta/2, \Delta/2]$). Hence, the autocorrelation function (ACF) of the quantization error at lags equal to a multiple of L will be approximately

$$\text{ACF}_{e(k)} (nL) \approx (1/2) \sum_k (\underline{d}_1(k) + \underline{d}_2(k)) \qquad (2.8)$$

and the autocorrelation is almost zero elsewhere. This is illustrated in Figure 2.8 where we plot the ACF of the quantization error of part of an audio signal when $\underline{d}_1$ has random amplitude and $|\underline{d}_1(k) - \underline{d}_2(k)| = \Delta_k/2$.

Figure 2.8. Autocorrelation of the quantization error with incorrect Δ and $L = 1000$ (d_1 is arbitrary and $|d_1(k) - d_2(k)| = \Delta_k/2$).

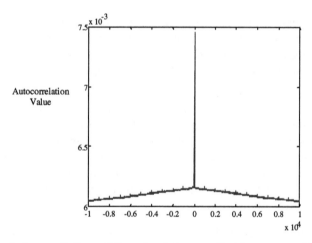

Figure 2.9. Autocorrelation of the *absolute* quantization error with incorrect Δ and $L = 1000$ ($d_1(k)$, $d_2(k) = \pm \Delta_k/4$).

However, if $\underline{d}_1(k)$, $\underline{d}_2(k) = \pm \Delta_k/4$, then the peaks at lags nL are much weaker. This can be treated by computing the ACF of the *absolute* quantization error rather than the quantization error itself. This is illustrated in Figure 2.9, where the peaks at multiple of nL are clear although weaker than the case with a dither vector with arbitrary amplitude.

Note that the procedure for estimating the key parameters of QIM embedding is not recursive. Hence, it is simpler than that of the correlator detector.

The removal of the watermark with minimum distortion after estimating the unknown parameters is straightforward. Note that $\underline{d}_1(k)$, $\underline{d}_2(k) \in [-\Delta_k/4, \Delta_k/4]$. For the specific implementation in Reference 6, we have $|\underline{d}_1(k) - \underline{d}_2(k)| = \Delta_k/2$. The idea of the attack is to increase the quantization error for the correct dither vector (which corresponds to decreasing the quantization error for the incorrect dither vector). Let the kth component of the modified segment be y_k. The modified value after the attack is

$$z_k = y_k \pm \delta_k, \qquad k = 1, 2, \ldots, L \qquad (2.9)$$

where δ_k is a positive quantity slightly larger than $\Delta_k/4$. Note that adding or subtracting δ_k is equally good, as it makes the quantization error of the incorrect dither vector smaller.

Rather than modifying the whole segment, it is sufficient to modify some components such that the quantization error of the incorrect dither vector is less than the quantization error of the correct dither vector. This can be achieved if a little more than half of the components of each segment is modified according to Equation 2.9. Moreover, not all of the segments are modified. The segments are modified progressively until the detector responds negatively.

In Figure 2.10, we give an example of the attack. In Figure 2.10, dither modulation is used to modify the 8×8 DCT coefficients of the image. The quantization step of each coefficient is proportional to the corresponding JPEG quantization step. The PSNR of the watermarked image is 40.7 dB. The attack as described above is applied with each component perturbed by an amount δ_k, whose amplitude is slightly larger than $\Delta_k/4$. If we assume that the detector fails when half of the extracted bits are incorrect, then only half of the blocks need to be modified. The

a. Watermarked image   b. After removing watermark (PSNR = 44 dB)

Figure 2.10. **Example of attack on the QIM scheme.**

resulting image is shown in Figure 2.10 and it has PSNR of 44 dB (compared to the watermarked image). In this attack, the watermark can be completely removed or it can be partially damaged to the degree that the detector cannot observe it.

Attack on the Quantized Projection Scheme. The projection values of a signal on a set of orthogonal vectors are equivalent to changing the basis for representing each vector from the standard set (which is the columns of an identity matrix) to the new orthogonal set. If the projection values are quantized according to Equation 2.6, then the reconstruction points will be discrete and uniformly spaced. Discrete reconstruction points of the projection values result in discrete reconstruction points in the signal domain. However, the quantization step in the signal domain is variable. It changes from one block to another according to the embedded data, as will be discussed.

Consider a projection matrix B. A vector of the projection values (of the ith block) $\underline{y}_i$ is related to the signal samples $\underline{x}_i$ by $\underline{y}_i = B \cdot \underline{x}_i$. Equivalently, we have $\underline{x}_i = B^T \underline{y}_i$. If the original quantization step vector is $\underline{q} = [\Delta_1 \cdots \Delta_L]$, then the discrete projection values will have the general form

$$\underline{y}_i = D_i \cdot \underline{q} \tag{2.10}$$

where D_i is a diagonal matrix with the quantization indices (that correspond to the embedded data) on its diagonal. In this case the reconstructed signal is $\underline{x}_i = B^T \cdot D_i \cdot \underline{q}$. If we assume that $\underline{x}_i$ is quantized by another quantization vector $\underline{q}' = [\Delta'_1 \cdots \Delta'_L]$, then we have $\underline{x}_i' = D_i' \cdot \underline{q}'$; that is,

$$D_i' \cdot \underline{q}' = B^T \cdot D_i \cdot \underline{q} \tag{2.11}$$

Now the objective of the attack is to find $\underline{q}'$ and remove the watermark with the minimum distortion. The problem is that $\underline{q}'$ is data dependent, as noted from Equation 2.11. It has to be estimated within each block and this is difficult in general. However, if $\underline{q}'$ is averaged over all blocks, the average quantization vector $\underline{q}'_{av}$ will be a good approximation, as will be discussed. Note that all the entries of $\underline{q}$ are positive. However, the entries of $\underline{q}'$, in general, may have negative signs. Estimating the signs of the quantization steps in the signal domain is necessary to be able to change the quantization values correctly in the transform coefficients.

The estimation of the block length is the same as described in the previous subsection because of the similarity in the distribution of the quantization noise at the corresponding samples of each block. This is illustrated in Figure 2.11, where we plot the ACF of the quantization error in the signal domain while the data is embedded by quantizing

Figure 2.11. **ACF with quantized projection embedding.**

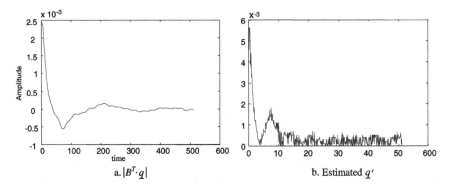

Figure 2.12. **Optimum and estimated values of the average q'.**

the DCT coefficients of blocks of size $L = 512$. The peaks at multiples of L are clear. This is analogous to Figure 2.8 for the QIM scheme.

The estimation of the average quantization step is the same as estimating Δ in the previous subsection. It is interesting to note that the relative amplitude of the average quantization step is quite similar to $B^T \cdot q$, as illustrated in Figure 2.12, where we plot the average quantization step in the time domain and $B^T \cdot q$. In this example, the data is embedded in the first 40 DCT coefficients (with $L = 512$).

The estimation of the signs of q' is done by analyzing the signs of pairs of its entries. Note that we are interested in the *relative* signs of the coefficients rather than their absolute values. If the signs are estimated in reverse order (i.e., positive instead of negative, and the reverse), it will have the same effect of moving the quantization values in the transform domain to the adjacent slot. The idea of the estimation is to study the

79

type of superposition between pairs of $\underline{q'}$ components. If the superposition is constructive, then the signs of the pair elements are the same and vice versa. First, consider the case with one embedded bit per segment (i.e., the data is projected onto one direction) and the projection value is quantized. The estimation of the signs proceeds as follows:

1. Select one coefficient in the signal domain and assume that its sign is positive.
2. Change the value of this coefficient by a sufficient amount δ such that the detector changes its decision.
3. Return the sample to its original value and then perturb it by $\delta/2$.
4. Perturb each other entry by $\delta/2$ (one at a time). If the perturbation results in changing the detector decision to its original value, then the sign of the corresponding entry is negative; otherwise, it is positive.

The extension to multibit embedding is straightforward. The above procedure is applied for each embedded bit in the segment and the majority rule is applied to decide the sign of each component. In Figure 2.13, we give an example of the sign algorithm for the scheme in Figure 2.12.

After estimating the quantization step in the signal domain, the watermark is removed by perturbing each segment in the signal domain by $\pm q'_{av}/\alpha$. In Figure 2.14, we show typical results of the percentage damage of the watermark (i.e., the fraction of bits that are decoded incorrectly) vs. the SNR of the output signal (after the attack). In this simulation, the SNR of the watermarked signal is 31.5 dB. Note that modifying the segments significantly results in moving to slots that match

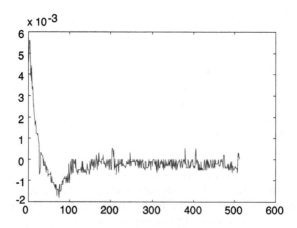

Figure 2.13.   Estimated q' after sign correction.

Figure 2.14.   Fraction of damaged watermark vs. the output SNR.

the original slot. This results in decreasing the error rate, as noted in Figure 2.14.

Note that if multiple codebooks are used for data embedding (as described in Reference 6), with the entries of the codebooks replacing the original data segments, then the estimation is much simpler. In this case, each codebook can be constructed by just observing the segments of watermarked data and the detector decisions. Once all codebooks are estimated, the embedded data can be simply modified by moving each segment to another codebook.

Comments on Attacks on Quantized-Based Schemes. The proposed attack on quantization-based schemes is simpler than the LMS attack for linear detectors because it does not iterate. We assumed that the data is embedded regularly in blocks of fixed size L. This is the typical scheme proposed in the original works that employ quantization for embedding (e.g., References 6 and 9). However, if the block boundaries are varying, then the attacker may use multiple watermarked items and perform the same statistical analysis on the different items. In this case, a unique quantization step is assumed for each sample and it is evaluated from the different watermarked items rather than blocks.

Discussion

The problem discussed in this subsection and the previous one motivated the search for decision boundaries that cannot be parameterized. For such boundaries, even if the attacker can change individual watermarked signals to remove the watermark, the modification will be *random* and the minimum distortion modification cannot be attained as earlier. The only choice for the attacker is to try to approximate the boundary numerically. This will require extra cost and the projection will be extremely difficult.

SECURE DETECTOR STRUCTURE

Introduction

In this section, we describe the structure of the decoder with nonparametric decision boundary. The new decision boundary is generated by changing the original decision boundary to a fractal curve (or any other nonparametric curve). Clearly, the resulting decoder is suboptimal. However, we will show that the degradation in performance is slight.

In the next subsection, we give an overview of the suggested decoder structure. Then we give a brief review of fractals generation and we provide a practical implementation procedure for the proposed decoder. Next, we show that the performance of the proposed detector is similar to the original detector. Finally, we establish the robustness of the proposed detector against the attack proposed in the previous section.

Algorithm

Rather than formulating the test statistic in a functional form, it will be described by a nonparameterized function. We select fractal curves to represent the new decision boundary. The fractal curves are selected because they are relatively simple to generate and store at the decoder. Random perturbation of the original decision boundary can also be used. However, in this case, the whole boundary needs to be stored at the decoder rather than the generation procedure in the fractal case.

Instead of the test statistic of Equations 2.2 and 2.4, we employ a fractal test statistic whose argument is R and has the general form

$$f(\underline{R}) > \text{threshold} \tag{2.12}$$

where $f(\cdot)$ is a fractal function. The basic steps of the proposed algorithms are:

1. Start with a given watermarking algorithm and a given test statistic $f(x)$ (e.g., a correlation sum 2.2). The decision is positive if $f(x) > \gamma$.
2. Fractalize the boundary using a fractal generation technique, which will be discussed in the next subsection.
3. Use the same decision inequality but with a new test statistic using the new fractal boundary.
4. (Optional at the encoder) Modify the watermarked signal if necessary to ensure that the *minimum distance* between the watermarked signal and the decision boundary is preserved.

Fractal Generation

This class of curves [11] has been studied for representing self-similar structures. Very complicated curves can be constructed using simple repeated structures. The generation of these curves is done by repetitively replacing each straight line by the generator shape. Hence, complicated shapes can be completely constructed by the initiator (Figure 2.15a) and the generator (Figure 2.15b). Different combinations of the generator and the initiator can be employed to generate different curves. This family of curves can be used to represent statistically self-similar random processes (e.g., the Brownian random walk [12, chap. 11]).

The family has the feature that it cannot be described using a finite set of parameters if the initiator and the generator are not known. Hence, they are good candidates for our particular purpose. Also, a Brownian motion process or a random walk can be used as well, but in this case, the whole curve should be stored at the detector.

Modifying the Decision Boundary

The most important step in the algorithm is modifying the decision boundary to have the desired fractal shape. In Figure 2.16, we give an example with a decision boundary of the correlator in R^2. The original boundary is a line, and the modified decision boundary is as shown in Figure 2.16.

There is a trade-off in designing the decision boundary. The maximum difference between the old decision and the modified one should be

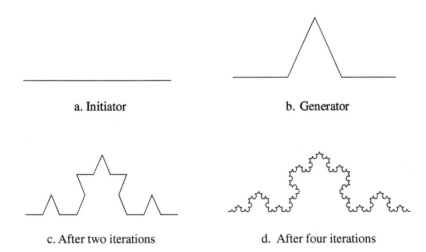

a. Initiator   b. Generator

c. After two iterations   d. After four iterations

Figure 2.15.   Fraction example.

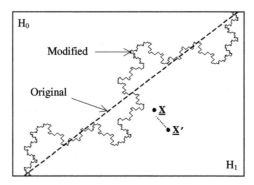

Figure 2.16. Example of modifying the decision boundary.

large enough so that the new boundary cannot be approximated by the old one. On the other hand, it should not be very large in order to avoid performance degradation.

After modifying the decision boundary, the watermarked signal X may need some modification to sustain the same shortest distance from X to the decision boundary. This is done by measuring the shortest distance between X and the new boundary and moving X along the direction of the shortest distance in the opposite direction (from X to X'). However, this modification is not critical for the performance, especially if the variance of the test statistic is small (which is usually the case) or if the distance between X and the original boundary is large compared to the maximum oscillation of the fractal curve.

Instead of evaluating the log-likelihood function of Equations 2.2 and 2.4, the fractal curve is evaluated for the received signal and is compared with the same threshold (as in Equation 2.10) to detect the existence of the watermark.

Practical Implementation

Instead of applying multidimensional fractalization, a simplified practical implementation that achieves the same purpose is discussed in this subsection. If the Gaussian assumption is adopted, then the test statistic in Equation 2.2 is optimal according to the Neyman–Pearson theorem [3, chap. 3]. Instead of this test statistic, two test statistics are used for the even and odd indexed random subsequences $r[2k]$ and $r[2k + 1]$ (or any two randomly selected subsequences), respectively:

$$T_1(\underline{R}) = (2/L) \cdot \sum_k r[2k] \cdot w[2k], \qquad T_2(\underline{R}) = (2/L) \cdot \sum_k r[2k + 1] \cdot w[2k + 1]$$

$$\underline{T} = (T_1 \, T_2) \tag{2.13}$$

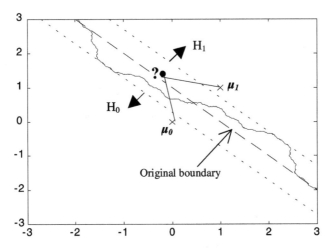

Figure 2.17. Detector operation.

Under H_0, $E(\underline{T}) = (0,0)$ and under H_1, $E(\underline{T}) = (1,1)$ if the watermark strength is assumed to be unity. In both cases, $\text{cov}(\underline{T}) = (2\sigma^2/L)I$, where σ^2 is the average of the variances of the signal coefficients. The Gaussian assumption of both T_1 and T_2 is reasonable if L is large by invoking the central limit theorem. Moreover, if the original samples are mutually independent, then T_1 and T_2 are also independent. The decision boundary in this case is a line (with slope -1 for the given means). If this line is fractalized, as discussed in the previous subsection, then the corresponding decision boundary in the multidimensional space will be also nonparametric.

The detection process is straightforward in principle but nontrivial. The vector $\underline{T}$ is classified to either hypothesis if it falls in its partition. However, due to the fractal nature of the boundary, this classification is not trivial. First, an unambiguous region is defined as shown in Figure 2.17 (i.e., outside the maximum oscillation of the fractal curve, which are the regions outside of the dotted lines). For points in the ambiguous area, we extend two lines between the point and means of both hypotheses. If one of the lines does not intersect with the boundary curve, then it is classified to the corresponding hypothesis. It should be emphasized that the boundary curve is stored at the detector and it should be kept secret.

Algorithm Performance

The technique proposed in the previous subsection is quite general. It can be applied to any watermarking scheme without changing the embedding algorithm. The algorithm performance is, in general, similar to

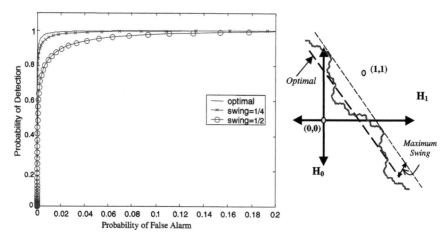

Figure 2.18.   ROC of the proposed algorithm.

the performance of the underlying watermarking algorithm with its optimal detector. However, for some watermarked items, we may need to increase the watermark strength, as illustrated in Figure 2.16.

Note that, in practice, the variance of the two statistics is small, so that the performances under the old and the new decision boundaries are essentially the same. For example, for an image of size 512×512 and 8 bits/pixel, if we assume a uniform distribution of the pixel values, then the variance of both statistics will equal to 0.042 according to Equation 2.3. Hence, the joint pdf of the two statistics is very concentrated around the means of both hypotheses. Consequently, the degradation in performance after introducing the new boundary is slight.

The receiver operating characteristic (ROC) of the proposed algorithm is close to the ROC of the optimal detector, and it depends on the maximum *oscillation* of the fractal boundary around the original one. In Figure 2.18, we illustrate the performance of the detector discussed in the previous subsection, when the mean is $(0, 0)$ under H_0 and is $(1, 1)$ under H_1, and the variance for both hypotheses is 0.1. As noticed from Figure 2.18, the performance of the system is close to the optimal performance, especially for a small curve oscillation. The degradation for a large perturbation is minor. This minor degradation can be even reduced by slightly increasing the strength of the embedded watermark.

Attacker Choices

In the discussion in section "The Generic Attack," the estimation of the watermark is equivalent to the estimation of the decision boundary for the correlator detector. After introducing the new algorithm, the two

86

estimations are decoupled. The attacker has to *simultaneously* estimate the watermark and the nonparametric boundary. This makes the estimation process prohibitively complex.

The practical choice for the attacker is to assume that the fractal oscillation is so small that the new boundary can be approximated by a hyperplane and proceed as before. We tested the attack described in section "Attack on Linear Detectors" with the same encoder that is used in generating Figure 2.5 but using the new decision boundary. The points on the decision boundary were estimated in exactly the same way as before. We used the same ten watermarked signals as the ones used in Figure 2.5. We used a fractal curve with a maximum swing of 0.25. The learning curve of the attack is *flat* around 67%, as shown in Figure 2.19. Comparing with Figure 2.5, it is clear that the attack is ineffective with the new algorithm. No information about the watermark is obtained. This even makes the estimation of the decision boundary more difficult.

To conclude the chapter, we compare the performance of the LMS attack when the correlator and fractal detectors are used. The comparison is in terms of the mean square error (MSE) between the watermarked image and the image after the attack. In Figure 2.20, we plot the MSE of the modified image vs. the number of iterations of the LMS attack. The same encoder parameters are used for both algorithms and the same number of images (ten images) is used for estimating the watermark. Note that the MSE for the fractal detector is higher because the new boundary is such that the *average* distance between the boundary and the centroid corresponding to H_1 increases. Note also that

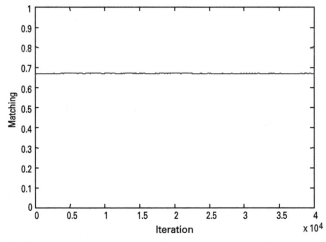

Figure 2.19. LMS convergence for a fractal boundary with ten watermarked images.

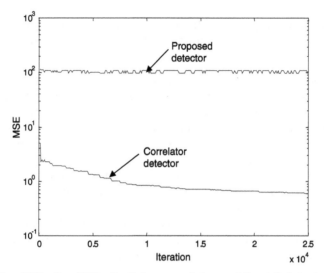

Figure 2.20. MSE after LMS attack for correlator and fractal detectors.

the MSE of the fractal detector is almost constant, as expected from the learning curve in Figure 2.19.

DISCUSSION

In this work, we analyzed the security of watermarking detection when the detector is publicly available. We described a generalized attack for estimating the decision boundary and gave different implementations of it. Next, we proposed a new class of watermark detectors based on a nonparametric decision boundary. This detector is more secure than traditional detectors, especially when it is publicly available. The performance of the new algorithm is similar to the traditional ones because of the small variance of the test statistics.

The proposed detector can work with any watermarking scheme without changing the embedder structure. However, with some watermarking procedures, the strength of the watermark may need to be increased slightly to compensate for the new boundary.

REFERENCES

1. Furon, T. and Duhamel, P., Robustness of Asymmetric Watermarking Technique, in *Proceedings of IEEE International Conference on Image Processing*, 2000, Vol. 3, pp. 21–24.
2. Furon, T., Venturini, I., and Duhamel, P., A Unified Approach of Asymmetric Watermarking Schemes, in *Proceedings of SPIE Conference on Security and Watermarking Multimedia Contents*, 2001, pp. 269–279.

3. Kay, S., *Fundamentals of Statistical Signal Processing: Detection Theory*, Prentice-Hall, Englewood Cliffs, NJ, 1998.

4. Kolmogorov, A. and Fomin, S., *Introductory Real Analysis*, Dover, New York, 1970, chap. 4.

5. Mansour, M. and Tewfik, A. Secure Detection of Public Watermarks with Fractal Decision Boundaries, in *Proceedings of XI European Signal Processing Conference, EUSIPCO-2002*, 2002.

6. Chen, B. and Wornell, G., Quantization Index Modulation, a class of provably good methods for digital watermarking and information embedding, *IEEE Trans. Inform. Theory*, 47(4), 1423–1443, 2001.

7. Chen, B. and Wornell, G., Dither Modulation: A New Approach to Digital Watermarking and Information Embedding, in *Proceedings of SPIE Conference on Security and Watermarking Multimedia Contents*, 1999, pp. 342–353.

8. Lan, T., Mansour, M., and Tewfik, A., Robust high capacity data embedding, *Proc. ICIP*, 2000.

9. Swanson, M., Zhu, B., and Tewfik, A., Data hiding for video-in-video, *Proc. ICIP*, 1996.

10. Haykin, S., *Adaptive Filter Theory*, Prentice-Hall, Englewood Cliffs, NJ, 1995.

11. Mandelbrot, B., *The Fractal Geometry of Nature*, W.H. Freeman, San Francisco, 1983.

12. Papoulis, A., *Probability, Random Variables, and Stochastic Processes, 3rd ed.*, McGraw-Hill, New York, 1991.

13. Abramowitz, M. and Stegun, A., *Handbook of Mathematical Functions*, Dover, New York, 1972.

14. Cox, I. and Linnartz, J., Public Watermarks and Resistance to Tampering, in *Proceedings of IEEE International Conference in Image Processing, ICIP*, 1997, Vol. 3, pp. 3–6.

15. Hernandez, J.R., Amado, M., and Perez-Gonzalez, F., DCT-domain watermarking techniques for still images: detector performance analysis and a new structure, *IEEE Trans. on Image Process.*, 9(1), 55–68, 2000.

16. Kalker, T., Linnartz, J., and Dijk, M., Watermark Estimation through Detector Analysis, in *Proceedings of IEEE International Conference on Image Processing, ICIP*, 1998, Vol. 1, pp. 425–429.

17. Linnartz, J. and Dijk, M., Analysis of the Sensitivity Attack against Electronic Watermarks in Images, in *Proceedings of 2nd International Workshop on Information Hiding*, 1998, pp. 258–272.

18. Mansour, M. and Tewfik, A., Techniques for Data Embedding in Image Using Wavelet Extrema, in *Proceedings of SPIE on Security and Watermarking of Multimedia Contents*, 2001, pp. 329–335.

19. Press. W. et al., *Numerical Recipes in C*, Cambridge University Press, Cambridge, 1992.

3
Fundamentals of Multimedia Encryption Techniques

Borko Furht, Daniel Socek, and
Ahmet M. Eskicioglu

INTRODUCTION

The recent advances in the technology, especially in the computer industry and communications, allowed a potentially enormous market for distributing digital multimedia content through the Internet. However, the proliferation of digital documents, multimedia processing tools, and the worldwide availability of Internet access have created an ideal medium for copyright fraud and uncontrollable distribution of multimedia content [1]. A major challenge now is the protection of the intellectual property of multimedia content in multimedia networks.

To deal with the technical challenges, two major multimedia security technologies are being developed:

1. Multimedia encryption technology to provide end-to-end security when distributing digital content over a variety of distribution systems

2. Multimedia watermarking technology as a tool to achieve copyright protection, ownership trace, and authentication

In this chapter, we present the current research efforts in multimedia encryption.

OVERVIEW OF MODERN CRYPTOGRAPHY

The three most important objectives of cryptography with respect to multimedia information security include (1) confidentiality, (2) data integrity, and (3) authentication [2].

Confidentiality refers to the protection of information from unauthorized access. An undesired communicating party, called an adversary, must not be able to access the communication material. *Data integrity* ensures that information has not been manipulated in an unauthorized way. Finally, *authentication* methods are studied in two groups: *entity* authentication and *message* authentication. Message authentication provides assurance of the identity of the sender of a message. This type of authentication also includes evidence of data integrity because if the data is modified during transmission, the sender cannot be the originator of the message. Entity authentication ensures the receiver of a message of both the identity of the sender and his active participation.

Modern cryptographic techniques provide solutions for these three objectives. In general, there are two types of cryptosystems: (1) symmetric (private) key cryptosystems and (2) asymmetric (public) key cryptosystems.

Symmetric Key Cryptosystems

All classical cryptosystems (i.e., cryptosystems developed before the 1970s) are examples of symmetric key cryptosystems. In addition, most modern cryptosystems are symmetric. Some of the most popular examples of modern symmetric key cryptosystems include AES (Advanced Encryption Standard), DES (Data Encryption Standard), IDEA, FEAL, RC5, and many others. The AES algorithm will be discussed further in section "Advanced Encryption Standard."

All symmetric key cryptosystems have a common property: they rely on a shared secret between communicating parties. This secret is used both as an encryption key and as a decryption key (thus the keyword "symmetric" in the name). This type of cryptography ensures only confidentiality and fails to provide the other objectives of cryptography.

Even more important, the disadvantage of symmetric key cryptography is that it cannot handle large communication networks. If a node in a communication network of n nodes needs to communicate confidentially with all other nodes in the network, it needs $n-1$ shared secrets. For a large value of n, this is highly impractical and inconvenient. On the other hand, an advantage over public key cryptosystems is that symmetric cryptosystems require much smaller key sizes for the same level of security. Hence, computations are much faster and memory requirements are smaller.

Public Key Cryptosystems

In public key cryptosystems, there are two keys: a public key, which is publicly known, and the private key, which is kept secret by the owner. The system is called "asymmetric" because different keys are used for encryption and decryption — the public key and the private key. If data is encrypted with a public key, it can only be decrypted using the corresponding private key, and vice versa. Today, all public key cryptosystems rely on computationally intractable problems. For example, the cryptosystem RSA relies on the difficulty of factoring large integers, whereas the El-Gamal cryptosystem relies on the discrete logarithm problem (DLP), which is the problem of finding a logarithm of a group element with a generator base in a finite Abelian group.

Public key cryptosystems do not need to have a shared secret between communicating parties. This solves the problem of the large confidential communication network introduced earlier. In addition, public key cryptography opened the door for ways of implementing technologies to ensure all goals of cryptography. By combining public key cryptography, public key certification, and secure hash functions, there are protocols that enable digital signatures, authentication, and data integrity.

Due to the increase in processor speed and even more to smart modern cryptanalysis, the key size for public key cryptography grew very large. This created a disadvantage in comparison to symmetric key cryptosystems: public key cryptography is significantly slower and requires a large memory capacity and large computational power. As an example, a 128-bit key used with the DES cryptosystem has approximately the same level of security as the 1024-bit key used with the RSA pubic key cryptosystem [3].

To solve these problems, researchers introduced different approaches. In order to decrease the key size so that public key cryptography can be used in smaller computational environments (such as smartcards or handheld wireless devices), Neil Koblitz introduced the idea of using a more exotic group in the public key underlying algebraic structure: the elliptic curve group. Elliptic curve cryptography (much of whose implementation is credited to CertiCom) enables smaller key sizes of public key cryptosystems that rely on DLP. The elliptic-curve-group algebra is much more complex, so the related cryptanalysis is much harder, resulting in smaller key requirements. Another solution came from public key cryptosystems that initially used more complex computational problems, such as the lattice reduction problem. The relatively new cryptosystem NTRU, based on the algebra of a ring of truncated polynomials, relies on the lattice reduction problem and it is the only public key cryptosystem that has the speed, memory, and computational complexity comparable to symmetric key cryptosystems. However, the security aspects of NTRU have yet to be investigated [4,5]. The most common implementation solution is to combine symmetric key cryptosystems with public key cryptography; namely, to overcome the problems related to applying the symmetric key encryption only, the plaintext is encrypted using a fast symmetric key scheme, and only the secret key used for symmetric encryption is encrypted with a slow public key scheme such as RSA. In this way, all goals of cryptography can be achieved with much better performance.

Cryptanalysis

Cryptanalysis is the art of deciphering an encrypted message, in whole or in part, when the decryption key is not known. Depending on the amount of known information and the amount of control over the system by the adversary (cryptanalyst), there are several basic types of cryptanalytic attack:

Ciphertext-only attack. The adversary only has access to one or more encrypted messages. The most important goal of a proposed cryptosystem is to withstand this type of attack.

Brute force attack. This is a type of ciphertext-only attack. It is based on exhaustive key search; and for well-designed cryptosystems, it should be computationally infeasible. By today's standards, 128-bit keys are considered secure against the brute force attack.

Known-plaintext attack. In this type of attack, an adversary has some knowledge about the plaintext corresponding to the given ciphertext. This may help determine the key or a part of the key.

Chosen-plaintext attack. Essentially, an adversary can feed the chosen plaintext into the black box that contains the encryption algorithm and the encryption key. The black box produces the corresponding ciphertext, and the adversary can use the accumulated knowledge about the plaintext–ciphertext pairs to obtain the secret key or at least a part of it.

Chosen-ciphertext attack. Here, an adversary can feed the chosen cipher-text into the black box that contains the decryption algorithm and the decryption key. The black box produces the corresponding plaintext, and the adversary tries to obtain the secret key or a part of the key by analyzing the accumulated ciphertext–plaintext pairs.

Advanced Encryption Standard (AES)

The AES algorithm is essentially a Rijndael [6] symmetric key crypto-system that processes 128-bit data blocks using cipher keys with lengths of either 128, 192, or 256 bits. Rijndael is more scalable and can handle different key sizes and data blocksizes; however, they are not included in the standard. Table 3.1 lists the basic AES parameters.

The AES algorithm's internal operations are performed on a two-dimensional array of bytes called the *State*. The State consists of four rows of bytes, each containing Nb bytes, where Nb is the blocksize divided by 32 (because the size of a word is 32 bits), which is, in the case of AES, equal to 4. At the beginning of the encryption or decryption procedure, the input array *in* is copied to the State array *s* according to the following rule: $s[r, c] = in[r+4c]$, where $0 \leq r < 4$ and $0 \leq c < Nb$. Similarly, at the end of each procedure, the State is copied to the output array *out* as follows: $out[r+4c] = s[r, c]$, where $0 \leq r < 4$ and $0 \leq c < Nb$. Clearly, in this notation, r stands for row and c for column.

AES Encryption. At the beginning of the AES encryption procedure, the input is copied to the State array using the above-described conventions. After an initial Round Key addition (see "AES Key Schedule"), the State array is transformed by implementing a round function 10, 12, or 14 times (depending on the key length), with the final round differing slightly from the first $Nr-1$ rounds. The final State is then copied to the output as described above. Figure 3.1 shows the pseudocode for AES encryption.

Table 3.1. The Basic AES Parameters

	Key Length (Nk words)	Blocksize (Nb words)	Number of Rounds (Nr)
AES-128	4	4	10
AES-192	6	4	12
AES-256	8	4	14

```
AesEncrypt (byte in[4*Nb], byte out [4*Nb], word w[Nb*(Nr+1)])
begin
        byte state[4,Nb]
        state = in
        AddRoundKey(state, w[0, Nb-1])

        for round = 1 step 1 to Nr-1
            SubBytes(state)
            ShiftRows(state)
            MixColumns(state)
            AddRoundKey(state, w[round*Nb, (round+1)*Nb-1])
        end for

        SubBytes(state)
        ShiftRows(state)
        AddRoundKey(state, w[Nr*Nb,(Nr+1)*Nb-1])

        out = state
end
```

Figure 3.1. Pseudocode for the AES encryption algorithm.

Table 3.2. AES Encryption S-box: Substitution Values for the Byte xy (in hexadecimal representation)

x							y									
	0	**1**	**2**	**3**	**4**	**5**	**6**	**7**	**8**	**9**	**a**	**b**	**c**	**d**	**e**	**f**
0	63	7c	77	7b	f2	6b	6f	c5	30	01	67	2b	fe	d7	ab	76
1	ca	82	c9	7d	fa	59	47	f0	ad	d4	a2	af	9c	a4	72	c0
2	b7	fd	93	26	36	3f	f7	cc	34	a5	e5	f1	71	d8	31	15
3	04	c7	23	c3	18	96	05	9a	07	12	80	e2	eb	27	b2	75
4	09	83	2c	1a	1b	6e	5a	a0	52	3b	d6	b3	29	e3	2f	84
5	53	d1	00	ed	20	fc	b1	5b	6a	cb	be	39	4a	4c	58	cf
6	d0	ef	aa	fb	43	4d	33	85	45	f9	02	7f	50	3c	9f	a8
7	51	a3	40	8f	92	9d	38	f5	bc	b6	da	21	10	ff	f3	d2
8	cd	0c	13	ec	5f	97	44	17	c4	a7	7e	3d	64	5d	19	73
9	60	81	4f	dc	22	2a	90	88	46	ee	b8	14	de	5e	0b	db
a	e0	32	3a	0a	49	06	24	5c	c2	d3	ac	62	91	95	e4	79
b	e7	c8	37	6d	8d	d5	4e	a9	6c	56	f4	ea	65	7a	ae	08
c	ba	78	25	2e	1c	a6	b4	c6	e8	dd	74	1f	4b	bd	8b	8a
d	70	3e	b5	66	48	03	f6	0e	61	35	57	b9	86	c1	1d	9e
e	e1	f8	98	11	69	d9	8e	94	9b	1e	87	e9	ce	55	28	df
f	8c	a1	89	0d	bf	e6	42	68	41	99	2d	0f	b0	54	bb	16

The SubBytes() transformation is essentially an S-box type of transform, which is a nonlinear byte substitution that operates independently
on each byte of the State. The simplest representation of this S-box
function is the lookup table. The lookup table associated with
SubBytes() is shown in Table 3.2.

In the `ShiftRows()` transformation, the bytes in the last three rows of the State are cyclically shifted over different numbers of bytes, whereas the first row is not shifted. The `ShiftRows()` transformation is defined as follows: $s'[r, c] = s[r, (c + shift(r, Nb)) \bmod Nb]$ for $0 \leq r < 4$ and $0 \leq c < Nb$, where the shift value $shift(r, Nb)$ is defined in as follows: $shift(1, 4) = 1$, $shift(2, 4) = 2$, and $shift(3, 4) = 3$.

The `MixColumns()` transformation operates on the State column by column. The columns are considered as polynomials over the Galois Field $GF(2^8)$ and multiplied modulo $x^4 + 1$ with a fixed polynomial $a(x) = \{03\}x^3 + \{01\}x^2 + \{01\}x + \{02\}$. Here, the notation $\{h_1 h_2\}$ denotes a byte in the hexadecimal format. This can be accomplished by applying the following four equations to the State columns:

1. $s'[0, c] = (\{02\} \bullet s[0, c]) \otimes (\{03\} \bullet s[1, c]) \otimes s[2, c] \otimes s[3, c]$
2. $s'[1, c] = s[0, c] \otimes (\{02\} \bullet s[1, c]) \otimes (\{03\} \bullet s[2, c]) \otimes s[3, c]$
3. $s'[2, c] = s[0, c] \otimes s[1, c] \otimes (\{02\} \bullet s[2, c]) \otimes (\{03\} \bullet s[3, c])$
4. $s'[3, c] = (\{03\} \bullet s[0, c]) \otimes s[1, c] \otimes s[2, c] \otimes (\{02\} \bullet s[3, c])$

Here, the $\bullet$ operation denotes multiplication in $GF(2^8)$ modul of the polynomial $x^4 + 1$, whereas the $\otimes$ denotes the usual bitwise XOR operation.

Finally, in the `AddRoundKey()` transformation, a Round Key is added to the State by a simple bitwise XOR operation. Each Round Key consists of Nb words from the key schedule (to be described in the AES Key Schedule section), each of which is each added into the columns of the State.

AES Key Schedule. In the AES algorithm, the initial input symmetric key is expanded to create a key schedule for each round. This procedure, given in Figure 3.2, generates a total of $Nb(Nr + 1)$ words that are used in

```
KeyExpansion (byte key[4*Nk], word w[Nb*(Nr+1)], Nk)
begin
        word temp

        i = 0
        while (i < Nk)
                w[i] = word(key[4*i], key[4*i+1], key[4*i+2], key[4*i+3])
                i = i+1
        end while
        i = Nk
        while (i < Nb * (Nr+1))
                temp = w[i-1]
                if (i mod Nk = 0)
                        temp = SubWord(RotWord(temp)) xor Rcon[i/Nk]
                else if (NK > 6 and i mod NK = 4)
                        temp = SubWord(temp)
                end if

                w[i] = w[i -NK] xor temp
                i = i+1
        end while
end
```

Figure 3.2. Pseudocode of the key schedule stage of the AES algorithm.

the `AddRoundKey()` procedure. In this algorithm, `SubWord()` is a function that takes a 4-byte input word and applies the S-box to each of the 4 bytes to produce an output word. The function `RotWord()` takes a word $[a_0, a_1, a_2, a_3]$ as input, performs a cyclic permutation, and returns the word $[a_1, a_2, a_3, a_0]$. The round constant word array, Rcon[i], contains the values given by $[x^{i-1}, \{00\}, \{00\}, \{00\}]$, with x^{i-1} being powers of x (x is denoted as $\{02\}$) in the field GF(2^8).

AES Decryption. AES decryption, the inverse of AES encryption, also consists of four stages in each round that are simply the inverses of the transformations described earlier. Each AES decryption round performs the following four transformations: `InvShiftRows()`, `InvSubBytes()`, `InvMixColumns()`, and `AddRoundKey()`. The pseudocode for the AES decryption process is given in Figure 3.3

The `InvShiftRows()` is the inverse of the `ShiftRows()` transformation, which is defined as follows: $s[r, c] = s'[r, (c + shift(r, Nb)) \bmod Nb]$ for $0 \le r < 4$ and $0 \le c < Nb$. Similarly, `InvSubBytes()` is the inverse of the byte substitution transformation, in which the inverse S-box is applied to each byte of the State. The inverse S-box used in the `InvSubBytes()` transformation is presented in Table 3.3.

The `InvMixColumns()` is the inverse of the `MixColumns()` transformation. The transformation `InvMixColumns()` operates on the State column by column, treating each column as a polynomial over the field GF(2^8) modulo $x^4 + 1$ with a fixed polynomial $a^{-1}(x)$, given by $a^{-1}(x) = \{0b\}x^3 + \{0d\}x^2 + \{09\}x + \{0e\}$. This can be accomplished by applying the following four equations to the State columns:

1. $s'[0, c] = (\{0e\} \bullet s[0, c]) \otimes (\{0b\} \bullet s[1, c]) \otimes (\{0d\} \bullet s[2, c]) \otimes (\{09\} \bullet s[3, c])$

```
AesDecrypt (byte in[4*Nb], byte out [4*Nb], word w[Nb*(Nr+1)])
begin
        byte state[4,Nb]
        state = in
        AddRoundKey(state, w[Nr*Nb, (Nr+1) *Nb-1])

        for round = Nr-1 step -1 downto 1
            InvShiftRows(state)
            InvSubBytes(state)
            AddRoundKey(state, w[round*Nb, (round+1)*Nb-1])
            InvMixColumns (state)
        end for

        InvShiftRows(state)
        InvSubBytes(state)
        AddRoundKey(state, w[0, Nb-1])

        out = state
end
```

Figure 3.3. Pseudocode of AES decryption algorithm.

Table 3.3. **AES Decryption S-box: Substitution Values for the Byte** *xy* **(in hexadecimal representation)**

x	0	1	2	3	4	5	6	*y* 7	8	9	a	b	c	d	e	f
0	52	09	6a	d5	30	36	a5	38	bf	40	a3	9e	81	f3	d7	fb
1	7c	e3	39	82	9b	2f	ff	87	34	8e	43	44	c4	de	e9	cb
2	54	7b	94	32	a6	c2	23	3d	ee	4c	95	0b	42	fa	c3	4e
3	08	2e	a1	66	28	d9	24	b2	76	5b	a2	49	6d	8b	d1	25
4	72	f8	f6	64	86	68	98	16	d4	a4	5c	cc	5d	65	b6	92
5	6c	70	48	50	fd	ed	b9	da	5e	15	46	57	a7	8d	9d	84
6	90	d8	ab	00	8c	bc	d3	0a	f7	e4	58	05	b8	b3	45	06
7	d0	2c	1e	8f	ca	3f	0f	02	c1	af	bd	03	01	13	8a	6b
8	3a	91	11	41	4f	67	dc	ea	97	f2	cf	ce	f0	b4	e6	73
9	96	ac	74	22	e7	ad	35	85	e2	f9	37	e8	1c	75	df	6e
a	47	f1	1a	71	1d	29	c5	89	6f	b7	62	0e	aa	18	be	1b
b	fc	56	3e	4b	c6	d2	79	20	9a	db	c0	fe	78	cd	5a	f4
c	1f	dd	a8	33	88	07	c7	31	b1	12	10	59	27	80	ec	5f
d	60	51	7f	a9	19	b5	4a	0d	2d	e5	7a	9f	93	c9	9c	ef
e	a0	e0	3b	4d	ae	2a	f5	b0	c8	eb	bb	3c	83	53	99	61
f	17	2b	04	7e	ba	77	d6	26	e1	69	14	63	55	21	0c	7d

2. $s'[1, c] = (\{09\} \bullet s[0, c]) \otimes (\{0e\} \bullet s[1, c]) \otimes (\{0b\} \bullet s[2, c]) \otimes (\{0d\} \bullet s[3, c])$

3. $s'[2, c] = (\{0d\} \bullet s[0, c]) \otimes (\{09\} \bullet s[1, c]) \otimes (\{0e\} \bullet s[2, c]) \otimes (\{0b\} \bullet s[3, c])$

4. $s'[3, c] = (\{0b\} \bullet s[0, c]) \otimes (\{0d\} \bullet s[1, c]) \otimes (\{09\} \bullet s[2, c]) \otimes (\{0e\} \bullet s[3, c])$

Finally, the `AddRoundKey()` is identical to the one from the AES encryption procedure because this transformation is its own inverse.

Today, the security level of AES is substantial because there are no known effective attacks discovered thus far. For more information about AES, see Reference 6.

INTRODUCTION TO MULTIMEDIA SECURITY

Multimedia security in general is provided by a method or a set of methods used to protect multimedia content. These methods are heavily based on cryptography and they enable either communication security or security against piracy (Digital Rights Management [DRM] and watermarking), or both. Communication security of digital images and textual digital media can be accomplished by means of standard symmetric key cryptography. Such media can be treated as a binary sequence and the complete data can be encrypted using a cryptosystem such as AES or DES [7]. In general, when the multimedia data is static (not a real-time streaming), we can treat it as regular binary data and use conventional encryption techniques. Encrypting the entire multimedia stream using standard encryption methods is often referred to as the *naive approach*.

However, due to a variety of constraints (such as near-real-time speed, etc.), communication security for streaming audio and video media is harder to accomplish. Communication encryption of video and audio multimedia content is not simply the application of established encryption algorithms, such as DES or AES, to its binary sequence. It involves careful analysis to determine and identify the optimal encryption method when dealing with audio and video data. Current research is focused on modifying and optimizing the existing cryptosystems for real-time audio and video. It is also oriented toward exploiting the format-specific properties of many standard video and audio formats in order to achieve the desired speed and enable real-time streaming. This is referred to as *selective encryption*.

For textual data, most applications of still images, and some low-quality audio and video streaming multimedia, we can still apply real-time packet encryption by means of SRTP (Secure Real-time Transport Protocol) [8], which is based on AES and encrypts the entire multimedia bit stream. This is essentially an application of the naive approach.

Deciding upon what level of security is needed is harder than it looks. To identify an optimal security level, we must carefully compare the cost of the multimedia information to be protected and the cost of the protection itself. If the multimedia to be protected is not very valuable in the first place, it is sufficient to choose a relatively light level of encryption. On the other hand, if the multimedia content is highly valuable or represents government or military secrets, the cryptographic security level must be the highest possible.

For many real-world applications such as pay-per-view, the content data rate is typically very high, but the monetary value of the content may not be high at all. Thus, very expensive attacks are not attractive to adversaries, and light encryption (often called *degradation*) may be sufficient for distributing MPEG video. For these applications, DRM is of much more interest. In contrast, applications such as videoconferencing or videophone (or even the Internet phone) may require a much higher level of confidentiality. If the videoconference is discussing important industrial, governmental, or military secrets, then the cryptographic strength must be substantial. Maintaining such a high level of security and still keeping the real-time and limited-bandwidth constraints is not easy to accomplish.

Comprehensive survey studies of multimedia encryption techniques are given in References 9 through 11. In Reference 10, Liu and Eskicioglu present a comprehensive classification that summarizes most of the presented algorithms. An updated version of that classification is shown in Table 3.4.

VIDEO ENCRYPTION TECHNIQUES

In this section, we discuss different research directions that were taken in the area of video communication encryption. As discussed earlier, a naive approach can be used to encrypt multimedia content. The whole multimedia stream is encrypted using a symmetric key cryptosystem. However, even the fastest modern symmetric schemes, such as DES or AES, are computationally very expensive for many real-time video and audio data.

Video Scrambling

Scrambling is a popular method of applying fast, yet very insecure distortion of the video signal. In general, scrambling was the product of an immediate industrial need by cable companies for a fast solution to make the free viewing of paid cable channels more difficult than doing nothing to the video signal.

Even though there is no distinct definition of scrambling, it refers to the simplest possible encryption attempts such as simple substitution or simple transposition ciphers whose security in the modern world is the lowest possible. Early work on signal scrambling was based on using an analog device to permute the signal in the time domain or distort the signal in the frequency domain by applying filter banks or frequency converters [29]. However, these schemes seriously lack security and they are extremely easy to crack using modern computers. As far as the attacker is concerned, these methods represent a temporary inconvenience in getting the original video or audio signal.

In many instances, this is still a solution that serves cable companies around the world quite effectively because most people lack the knowledge and engineering skills to crack the scrambled video signal, but the modified cable boxes that can unscramble all scrambled material are quite easy to manufacture. However, scrambling is out of the question for applications that require a more serious level of security.

Selective Video Encryption

In order to meet real-time constraints for audio and video multimedia playback, *selective encryption* techniques have been proposed. The basic idea of selective encryption is to encrypt only a portion of the

Table 3.4. Classification of Selective Encryption Schemes

Type of Data	Domain	Proposal	Encryption Algorithm	What is Encrypted?
Image	Frequency domain	Cheng and Li, 2000 [12]	No algorithm is specified	Pixel- and set-related significance information in the two highest pyramid levels of SPIHT
		Van Droogenbroeck and Benedett, 2002 [13]	DES, Triple DES, and IDEA	Bits that indicate the sign and magnitude of the nonzero DCT coefficients
		Pommer and Uhl, 2003 [14]	AES	Subband decomposition structure
	Spatial domain	Cheng and Li, 2000 [12]	No algorithm specified	Quadtree structure
		Droogenbroeck and Benedett, 2002 [13]	XOR	Least significant bitplanes
		Podesser, Schmidt, and Uhl, 2002 [15]	AES	Most significant bitplanes
Video	Frequency domain	Meyer and Gadegast, 1995 [16]	DES, RSA	Headers, parts of I-blocks, all I-blocks, I-frames of the MPEG stream
		Spanos and Maples, 1995 [17,18]	DES	I-frames, sequence headers, and ISO end code of the MPEG stream
		Tang, 1996 [19]	Permutation, DES	DCT coefficients
		Qiao, and Nahrstedt, 1997 [20]	XOR, permutation, IDEA	Every other bit of the MPEG bit stream
		Shi and Bhargava, 1998 [21]	XOR	Sign bit of DCT coefficients

Category	Reference	Algorithm	Description
	Shi et al., 1999 [22]	IDEA	Sign bit of motion vectors
	Alattar et al., 1999 [23]	DES	Every nth I-macroblock, headers of all the predicted macroblocks, header of every nth predicted macroblock
	Shin et al., 1999 [24]	Permutation, RC4	Sign bits of DC coefficients of I pictures; random permutation of the DCT coefficients
	Cheng and Li, 2000 [12]	No algorithm specified	Pixel- and set-related significance information in the two highest pyramid levels of SPIHT in the residual error
	Wen et al., 2002 [25]	DES, AES	The information-carrying fields, either fixed length code (FLC) codewords or variable length code (VLC) codewords
	Zeng and Lei, 2002 [26]	Permutation, XOR	Selective bit scrambling, block shuffling, block rotation of the transform coefficients (wavelet and JPEG), and JPEG motion vectors
	Wu and Mao, 2002 [27]	Any modern cipher, random shuffling on bitplanes in MPEG-4 FGS	Bit stream after entropy coding, quantized values before run-length coding (RLC) or RLC symbols, intra-bit-plane shuffling in MPEG-4 FGS
Spatial domain	Cheng and Li, 2000 [12]	No algorithm specified	Quadtree structure of motion vectors and quadtree structure of residual errors
Entropy codec	Wu and Kuo, 2000 [28]; Wu and Kuo, 2001 [29]	Multiple Huffman tables, multiple state indices in the QM coder	Encryption of data by multiple Huffman coding tables and multiple state indices in the QM coder
Compressed domain / Speech	Wu and Kuo, 2000 [28]	DES, AES	Most significant bits of the LSP codebook indices, the lag of pitch predictor, the pitch gain vectors, the fixed codebook gains, and the VAD mode flag coefficients of the G.723.1 speech codec

(Continued)

Table 3.4. Continued

Type of Data	Domain	Proposal	Encryption Algorithm	What is Encrypted?
		Servetti and De Martin, 2002 [30]	Not specified	1st stage vector of LSP quantizer, 2nd stage lower vector of LSP quantizer, pitch delay 1st subframe, pitch delay 2nd subframe, gain codebook (stage 1) 1st subframe, gain codebook (stage 2) 1st subframe, gain codebook (stage 1) 2nd subframe, gain codebook (stage 2) 2nd subframe
Audio	Compressed domain	Servetti et al., 2003 [31]	Not specified	File header (that contains the original *table_select*, and *big_value* values) at the beginning of the audio track; a subset of region1 bits and a subset of region2 bits
		Thorwirth et al., 2000 [32]	Not specified	Audio quality layers associated with the compressed audio data

Source: Adapted from Liu, X. and Eskicioglu, A.M., *IASTED International Conference on Communication, International and Information Technology (CIIT 2003),* 2003. With permission.

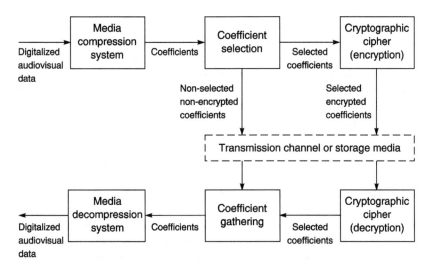

Figure 3.4. A common selective encryption scheme.

compressed bit stream. A common approach in selective encryption is to integrate compression with encryption, as shown in Figure 3.4.

For example, we can select only the most important coefficients from either the final or intermediate steps of a compression process and encrypt those coefficients. Less important coefficients are left unencrypted. Still, some schemes prefer to lightly encrypt even the less important coefficients. By "light" encryption we mean applying a simple encryption scheme whose speed is high and whose security level is low (there is always a trade-off between the speed and security). In this manner, we define *variable encryption* as an approach that applies different encryption schemes with different security strengths. Selective encryption can be treated as a special case of variable encryption [11].

SECMPEG by Meyer and Gadegast, 1995. In 1995, Meyer and Gadegast introduced the selective encryption method called *Secure MPEG (SECMPEG)*, designed for the MPEG-1 video standard [16]. SECMPEG contains four levels of security. At the first level, SECMPEG encrypts the headers from the sequence layer to the slice layer, and the motion vectors and DCT blocks are unencrypted. At the second level, the most relevant parts of the I-blocks are additionally encrypted (upper left corner of the block). At the third level, SECMPEG encrypts all I-frames and all I-blocks. Finally, at the fourth level, SECMPEG encrypts the whole MPEG-1 sequence (the naive approach). The authors chose the DES symmetric key cryptosystem, which was the natural choice, given that this cryptosystem had been around since 1976 and was the official symmetric encryption algorithm standardized by NIST and adopted by the U.S. Government. Because DES is a symmetric key cryptosystem, it could only be used to achieve confidentiality. Meyer and Gadegast targeted solving the problem of data integrity as well. For that reason, the Cyclic Redundancy Check (CRC) was incorporated as a low-level solution to integrity. The real data integrity mechanisms that included public key cryptography and cryptographically good hash functions such as MD4, MD5, or SHA were left for further research.

The selective encryption in SECMPEG (levels 1, 2, and 3) has some weaknesses [33,34]. It is shown that even though a single P- or B-frame carries almost no information without the corresponding I-frame, a series of P- or B-frames can tell much if their base I-frames are correlated. The experiments by Agi and Gong showed that encrypting I-frames only might leave visible I-blocks in other frames [33]. The same authors then proposed a few trade-off improvements: increasing the frequency of the I-frames or encrypting all P- and B-frames. These improvements decrease speed and further disrupt the compression ratio. Because SECMPEG introduces changes to the MPEG-1 format, a special encoder and decoder are needed to handle SECMPEG streams.

Nevertheless, the SECMPEG paper [16] and implementation by Meyer and Gadegast was one of the first important research initiatives for selective encryption of multimedia streams. These authors were among the first to realize the benefits of encrypting only selected bits in a video bit stream. Their experiments confirmed that the visual disruption was substantial only by encrypting the DC coefficients and the first three to eight AC coefficients in the 8×8 JPEG block of the MPEG-1 I-frames.

Aegis by Maples and Spanos, 1995. Another important research achievement on selective encryption of a MPEG video stream appeared in 1995 by Maples and Spanos [17,18], and it introduced the secure MPEG video mechanism called *Aegis*. Aegis was initially designed for MPEG-1 and MPEG-2 video standards. It encrypts I-frames of all MPEG groups of frames in an MPEG video stream, and B- and P-frames are left unencrypted. In addition, Aegis also encrypts the MPEG video sequence header, which contains all of the decoding initialization parameters that include the picture width, height, frame rate, bitrate, buffer size, and so forth. Finally, this method also encrypts the ISO end code (i.e., the last 32 bits of the stream). As a result, the bit stream's MPEG identity is further concealed. The Aegis behind-the-scenes encryption engine chosen by Maples and Spanos was DES. In a way, Aegis is very similar to level 3 of SECMPEG by Meyer and Gadegast, and the security weaknesses that are applicable to SECMPEG are carried over to Aegis.

As discussed earlier, Agi and Gong criticized encrypting only I-frames by Aegis and SECMPEG, in view of the fact that their experiments showed

106

that it was possible to discern some aspects from the scene from the decoded P-and B-frames [33], For example, they were able to conclude that the talking head was present at the scene. Alattar and Al-Regib presented a similar argument regarding the security of SECMPEG in Reference 35. It is important to notice that this type of security is not particularly good for applications where security is one of the top priorities (such as important military or business teleconferencing), but it might be sufficient for the quality degradation of the entertainment videos, such as the pay TV broadcast.

Aegis is also considered one of the pioneering research accomplishments in the area of selective video encryption. The experimental results for selective encryption published by Maples and Spanos in References 17 and 18 confirmed the enormous gain in speed over the naive approach.

Zigzag Permutation Algorithm by Tang, 1996. Tang's *zigzag permutation algorithm* [19] is based on embedding the encryption into the MPEG compression process. The JPEG images and the I-frames of MPEG video undergo a zigzag reordering of the 8×8 blocks. The zigzag pattern forms a sequence of 64 entries that are ready to enter the entropy-encoding stage. The main idea of this approach is to use a random permutation list to map the individual 8×8 blocks to a 1×64 vector. The algorithm consists of three stages:

- *Stage 1:* A list of 64 permutations is generated.
- *Stage 2:* Splitting procedure on an 8×8 block is performed as follows: We denote the DC coefficient by an eight-digit binary number with digits $b_7b_6b_5b_4b_3b_2b_1b_0$. This binary sequence is then split into two equal halves: $b_7b_6b_5b_4$ and $b_3b_2b_1b_0$. Finally, we place the number $b_7b_6b_5b_4$ into the DC coefficient and then assign the number $b_3b_2b_1b_0$ to AC_{63} (the last AC coefficient), which is the least important value in the block. This will result in no visible degradation of the quality.
- *Stage 3:* The random permutation is applied to the split block.

However, the zigzag permutation algorithm is not particularly secure [34,36]. Qiao and Nahrstedt introduced two types of attack on zigzag permutation: a known-plaintext attack and a ciphertext-only attack. A known-plaintext attack is particularly applicable to the videos with known clips such as blank screens, the movie rating screens, the MGM roaring lion, and so forth. If these known frames are used as a comparison, the adversary can easily generate the secret permutation list.

Because Tang realized the significant vulnerability to known-plaintext attack, he introduced an improvement of the zigzag permutation technique using the binary coin-flipping sequence method together with two different permutation lists. Two different permutation lists are generated, and for each 8×8 block, a coin is randomly flipped. The outcome event determines which list to apply (i.e., if the head is flipped we apply one list and if the tail is flipped we apply the other list). As shown in References 34 and 36, this addition turns out to be useless. If we know some of the original frames in advance (known plaintext), then, by simple comparison, both permutation lists can be found. Because of certain statistical properties of the blocks (upper left corner gathering of the AC coefficients within a block), we can easily determine which list of permutations to use.

In addition, Qiao and Nahrstedt showed that Tang's splitting method is just a subset of SECMPEG with a second level; thus, its security is not good. Finally, Qiao and Nahrstedt showed that Tang's zigzag permutation algorithm is susceptible to the ciphertext-only attack. The attack relies on the statistical properties of the discrete cosine transform (DCT) coefficients, for which most nonzero terms are gathered in the top left corner of the I-block. Statistical analysis shows the following observation [34]: the DC coefficient always has the highest frequency value, the frequencies of AC_1 and AC_2 coefficients are among the top six, and frequencies of AC_3 and AC_4 are among the top ten. Applying these observations, one can reconstruct the original video to relatively good accuracy using only five DCT coefficients. Therefore, the zigzag permutation cipher seriously lacks the desired level of security.

Video Encryption Algorithm by Qiao and Nahrstedt, 1997. The *Video Encryption Algorithm* (VEA) by Qiao and Nahrstedt [20] is constructed with the goal of exploiting the statistical properties of the MPEG video standard. The algorithm consists of the following four steps:

- *Step 1:* Let the $2n$-byte sequence, denoted by $a_1a_2\ldots a_{2n}$, represent the chunk of an I-frame
- *Step 2:* Create two lists, one with odd indexed bytes $a_1a_3\ldots a_{2n-1}$, and the other with even indexed bytes $a_2a_4\ldots a_{2n}$
- *Step 3:* XOR the two lists into an n-byte sequence denoted by $c_1c_2\ldots c_n$
- *Step 4:* Apply the chosen symmetric cryptosystem E (e.g., DES or AES) with the secret key $KeyE$ on either the odd list or even list and, thus, create the ciphertext sequence $c_1c_2\ldots c_n\, E_{KeyE}(a_1a_3\ldots a_{2n-1})$ or $c_1c_2\ldots c_n E_{KeyE}(a_2a_4\ldots a_{2n})$, respectively.[1]

---

[1] The authors' choice was to encrypt the even sequence, creating the ciphertext $c_1c_2\ldots c_n E_{KeyE}(a_2a_4\ldots a_{2n})$.

Clearly, the decryption mechanism at the other end of the communication channel consists of two easy steps: apply the symmetric cryptosystem E with the appropriate key to the second half of the ciphertext to obtain the first half of the original sequence, and XOR this result with the first half of the ciphertext to obtain the other half of the original sequence.

Even though the security of the system is based on the security of the chosen underlying cryptosystem, if an adversary obtains either the even or odd list, the system is completely broken. Thus, the authors suggest an even more secure approach. Instead of dividing the list into even and odd lists, the random $2n$-bit key, called *KeyM*, is generated and used to split the $2n$-byte chunk of MPEG stream into two lists. The method of partitioning the $2n$-byte MPEG sequence into two subsequences is as follows: if the ith bit in *KeyM* is 1, then the ith byte of the MPEG sequence goes into the first subsequence, and, similarly, if the ith bit in *KeyM* is 0, then the ith byte of the MPEG sequence goes into the second subsequence. It is required that *KeyM* be a binary sequence with exactly n ones and n zeros, in order to ensure that the two lists are of equal length. The suggested value for n is 64 or 128. By applying this approach, the attacker will have a very hard time ordering the resulting sequence of bytes in the case that the encrypted subsequence is somehow cracked, assuming that the binary sequence *KeyM* remained secret. This means that *KeyM* must be securely transmitted to the receiver before the decryption can take place.

Another consideration is that a possible pattern repetition in the $2n$ stream chunk represents a significant security hole in the method proposed be Qiao and Nahrstedt. According to the statistical analysis of MPEG stream sequences, it was observed that the nonrepeating patterns have a lifetime over only one 1/16 chunk [20]. Therefore, to obtain the nonrepeating pattern with a length of 1/2 frame, which consists of eight such chunks, it is sufficient to shuffle only these eight chunks. However, each of these chunks must be shuffled using different keys, which are here denoted by Key_1, Key_2,..., Key_8. The authors suggest using the permutations of degree 32 (even though degree 24 was shown to be sufficient), so that each Key_i is stored as a random permutation of degree 32. Hence, the length of a Key_i is 20 bytes, resulting in the total length of 160 bytes for Key_1, Key_2, ..., Key_8. Once the keys are generated, the Key_1 permutation is applied to the first 32 bytes of the even list, the Key_2 permutation is applied to the next 32 bytes, and so on, repeating this process after the eighth key. This procedure will ensure nonrepetition in the MPEG stream, thus significantly decreasing the vulnerability of the system to the repetitive pattern attacks. Furthermore, the increase in the bit-stream size caused by including these extra keys is at a negligible level.

Finally, Qiao and Nahrstedt proposed the use of one more additional key, denoted by *KeyF*. The experiments have shown that the pattern of selecting the even list and the odd list should be changed for every frame in order to ensure the anticipated security level [20]. For this reason, a 64-bit key *KeyF* is randomly generated for every single frame in the MPEG sequence. However, this key is subject to the constraint that every four consecutive bits represent a unique number from 0 to 15 (i.e., so that any *KeyF* represents a permutation of degree 16). To get the new keys for each frame, we permute *KeyM* and the Key_i's repeatedly using the permutation defined by *KeyF* assigned to that frame.

In order to securely transmit these additional keys (*KeyM*, Key_i's and *KeyF*'s), they must be encrypted using the encryption function E with *KeyE*. As a final point, the secret key *KeyE* has to be securely transmitted to the decoder's side (the receiver), possibly using public key cryptography or using a separate secure channel. Alternatively, the separate secure channel can be used for the transmission of keys

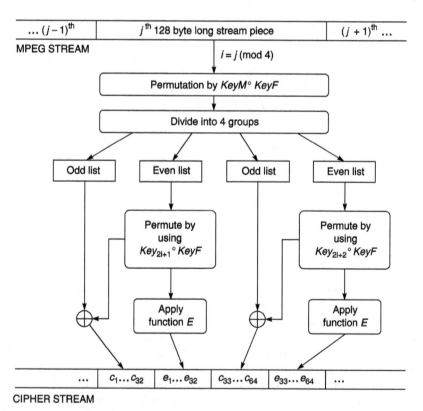

Figure 3.5. **Selective video encryption algorithm by Qiao and Nahrstedt. (From Qiao, L. and Nahrstedt, K.,** *Proceedings of the 1st International Conference on Imaging Science, Systems and Technology (CISST '97),* **1997. With permission.)**

KeyM and the *Key$_i$*'s. The diagram of the proposed algorithm is shown in Figure 3.5.

The experiments that were originally performed in 1997 were mainly using DES and IDEA cryptosystems; however, the newer choice for the underlying cryptosystem *E* would probably be the recently standardized AES cryptosystem (Rijndael). The security of the method proposed by Qiao and Nahrstedt is very close to the security of the encryption scheme *E* that is internally used. The speed of this algorithm is roughly half the speed of the naive algorithm, but that is arguably still a large amount of computation for high-quality, real-time video applications that have high bit rates [29].

Video Encryption Algorithms by Shi, Wang, and Bhargava, 1998 and 1999. In Reference 37, Shi, Wang, and Bhargava classified their previous work into four different video encryption algorithms: *Algorithm I*, *Algorithm II* (VEA), *Algorithm III* (MVEA), and *Algorithm IV* (RVEA). The original work was published by the same authors years earlier [21,22]. The basic idea of these algorithms is to apply selective encryption on selective coefficients in the JPEG/MPEG schemes, as illustrated in Figure 3.6.

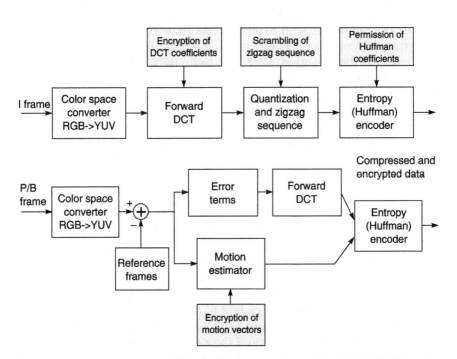

Figure 3.6.   Selective encryption of selective coefficients in MPEG/JPEG coding schemes: DCT and its zigzag sequence, coefficients in the Huffman table, and motion vectors.

Algorithm I. The first algorithm, denoted simply by Algorithm I, uses the permutation of Huffman codewords in the I-frames. This method incorporates encryption and compression in one step. The secret part of the algorithm is a permutation π, which is used to permute the standard JPEG/MPEG Huffman codeword list. In order to save the compression ratio, the permutation π must be such that it only permutes the codewords with the same number of bits. In addition, the distance between the original and the permuted codeword list must be greater than the encryption quality parameter β, which is chosen by the user.

The security of Algorithm I is not particularly good. In Reference 38, it is shown that Algorithm I is highly vulnerable to both known-plaintext attack and ciphertext-only attack. If some of the video frames are known in advance (such as standard introductory jingles and similar), one can reconstruct the secret permutation π by comparing the original and encrypted frames. Vulnerability to this type of attack was also discussed in Reference 37. However, Algorithm I is also subject to ciphertext-only attack. The low-frequency error attack can be applied on ciphertext produced by Algorithm I [38]. Basically, because permutation π has a special form (i.e., it only shuffles codewords with the same length), most of the security comes from shuffling the 16-bit codewords in the AC coefficient entropy table. However, because there is a very limited number of codewords with length of less than 16 bits, it is very easy to reconstruct all of the DC coefficients and most frequent AC coefficients (as these will be encoded with less than 16-bit codewords). In other words, the only hard part would be to figure out how the permutation π shuffles the 16-bit codewords. However, these appear to be extremely rare, and the reconstructed video may be of almost the same quality as the original. Furthermore, the rare pixels that do contain 16-bit codewords can easily be interpolated to get rid of the noise effect and to create the reconstruction image that, at least to the human visual system, appears as flawless as the original.

Algorithm II (VEA). Algorithm II (VEA) uses the following selective encryption observation: it is sufficient to encrypt only the sign bits of the DCT coefficients in an MPEG video. Algorithm II simply XORs the sign bits of the DCT coefficients with a secret m-bit binary key $k = k_1 k_2 \ldots k_m$. The effect of this scheme is that the encryption function randomly changes the sign bits of the DCT coefficients, depending on the corresponding bit value of k. Let us denote the sign bits of the DCT coefficients in an MPEG stream that belong to the same GOP (Group of Pictures) by $s_1 s_2 \ldots s_n$. Then, a bit s_i will not be changed if the value of the key bit $k_{i \pmod m}$ is 0, and it will be flipped if the value of the key bit $k_{i \pmod m}$ is 1. The next GOP would simply reuse the secret key, which serves for resynchronization purposes. The ability to resynchronize the video stream is important in the case of unreliable networks, transmission errors, and VCR-like functionality such as fast forwarding or rewinding.

The security of Algorithm II depends on the length of the key. The authors encourage the use of a long binary key; however, too long a key may be infeasible and impractical. On the other hand, if the key is short, the system can be easily broken. If the key is as long as the video stream and it is unique and used only once, it would correspond to the Vernam cipher (also referred to as the one-time pad), which is known to be absolutely secure. However, this is highly impractical for mass applications such as VOD (Video-on-Demand). On the other hand, if the key is too short, the whole method simply becomes the Vigenére-like cipher, a well-studied classical cipher for which there are many attacks developed (e.g., the Kasiski analysis) [38]. In addition, Vigenére is highly sustainable to the known-plaintext attack (one can literally read off the secret key). The authors of Reference 17 suggest the use of a pseudorandom generator that generates a stream of pseudorandom bits to be the key k of arbitrary length. The trouble with this approach is the security, randomness, and speed of this P-RNG (pseudo-random number generator). The additional issues include the synchronization of the P-RNG and the secure transmission of the seed (the secret key) for the P-RNG.

Algorithm III (MVEA). Algorithm III (MVEA) is an improvement to Algorithm II (VEA). It includes the following addition: the sign bits of differential values of motion vectors in P- and B-frames can also be randomly changed. This type of improvement makes the video playback more random and more nonviewable. When the sign bits of differential values of motion vectors are changed, the directions of motion vectors change as well. In addition, the magnitudes of motion vectors change, making the whole video very chaotic. The authors found that the encryption of sign bits of motion vectors makes the encryption of sign bits of DCT coefficients in B- and P-frames unnecessary.

Furthermore, the original Algorithm III (MVEA) was designed to encrypt only the sign bits of DC coefficients in the I-frames of the MPEG video sequence, leaving the AC coefficients unencrypted. This significantly reduces the computational overhead but it opens up new security risks; namely, because the DC coefficient and the sum of all AC coefficients within the block are related, an adversary may use the unencrypted AC coefficients to derive the unknown (encrypted) DC coefficients [22,37]. For that reason, the authors recommend encrypting all DCT coefficients in the I-frames for applications that need a higher level of security.

Just like Algorithm II (VEA), Algorithm III (MVEA) relies on the secret m-bit key k. Also, the resynchronization is done at the beginning of a GOP.

Unfortunately, the fundamental security issues and problems that are applicable to VEA are also applicable to MVEA.

Algorithm IV (RVEA).   Finally, Algorithm IV (RVEA) is a significantly more secure approach than the previous three algorithms. This approach is considered robust under both ciphertext-only and known-plaintext. The difference between the RVEA and MVEA/VEA algorithms is that RVEA uses conventional symmetric key cryptography to encrypt the sign bits of DCT coefficients and the sign bits of motion vectors. The conventional cryptosystems are mathematically well understood and thoroughly tested by experts in the field, which definitely adds to the security aspect of RVEA. The selective approach significantly speeds up the process of conventional encryption by only encrypting certain sign bits in the MPEG stream. The experiments show that the encryption quality is quite good considering the amount of information changed.

In Algorithm IV (RVEA), the sign bits of DCT coefficients and motion vectors are simply extracted from the MPEG video sequence; encrypted using a fast, conventional cryptosystem such as AES; and then restored back to their original position in the encrypted form. The effect of this is similar to VEA/MVEA, for which the sign bits are either flipped or left unchanged. The authors limited the number of bits for encryption to at most 64 for each MPEG stream macroblock, for the purposes of reducing and bounding the computation time. Next, we describe exactly how these sign bits are selected for encryption.

Each MPEG video slice consists of one or more *macroblocks*. The macroblock corresponds to a 16×16 pixel square, which is composed of four 8×8 pixel luminance blocks denoted by Y_1, Y_2, Y_3, and Y_4, and two 8×8 chrominance blocks Cb and Cr. Each of these six 8×8 blocks can be expressed as a sequence $ba_1a_2...a_n$, where n is at most 64 since b is the code for DC coefficient and a_i is the code for a nonzero AC coefficient. Then, for each such 8×8 block, we can define the sequence $\beta\alpha_1\alpha_2...\alpha_n$, which corresponds to the sign bits of the matching DCT coefficients b, a_1, $a_2, ...$, and a_n. Figure 3.7 shows the order of selection of the sign bits for each macroblock. The obvious reason for this selection order is that the DC and higher-order AC coefficients are carrying much more information than the low-order AC coefficients.

In conclusion, RVEA only encrypts the fraction (typically about 10%) of the whole MPEG video using conventional secure cryptographic schemes such as DES, IDEA, AES, and so forth. Therefore, Algorithm IV (RVEA) is a much better method than the previous three algorithms in terms of security. Furthermore, it saves up to 90% of the computation time compared to the naive approach.

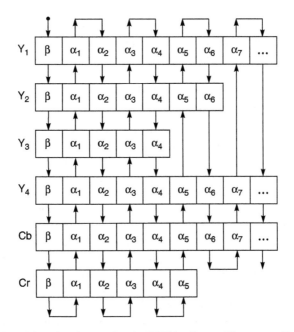

Figure 3.7. **The bit selection order in RVEA. (From Bhargava, B., Shi, C., and Wang, Y., http://raidlab.cs.purdue.edu/papers/mm.ps).**

Video Encryption Methods by Alattar, Al-Regib, and Al-Semari, 1999. In 1999, Alattar, Al-Regib, and Al-Semari presented three methods for selective video encryption based on DES cryptosystem [23]. These methods, called simply *Method I*, *Method II*, and *Method III*, were computationally improved versions of the previous work from two of the co-authors [35], which is referred to as *Method 0*.

The first algorithm (Method 0), proposed by Alattar and Al-Regib in Reference 35, essentially encrypts all macroblocks from I-frames and the headers of all prediction macroblocks using the DES cryptosystem. This method performs relatively poorly because encryption is carried out on 40 to 79% of the MPEG video stream [11].

In Method I, the data of every nth macroblock from the I-frame of MPEG video stream is encrypted using the DES cryptosystem, and the information from all of the other I-frame macroblocks is left unencrypted. The value of n was not specified and it can be chosen depending on the application needs. If the value of n is 2, then the encryption is performed on approximately one half of all I-frame macroblocks, but the security level is higher. On the other hand, if the value of n is higher, the computational savings are greater, yet the security level is lower. An important observation is that even though a certain number of I-macroblocks are left unencrypted, they are not expected to reveal any information about the encrypted ones [23]. However, this method does not hide the motion information and the authors suggest an improved algorithm, which will be discussed next.

To improve the security of Method I, Alattar, Al-Regib, and Al-Semari suggested Method II, which additionally encrypts the headers of all predicted macroblocks using DES. Because DES is a block cipher that operates on 64-bit blocks, a 64-bit segment starting from the header of a predicted macroblock is processed in the beginning. This segment may include exactly the whole header (which is the rare case when the header size is equal to 64 bits), a part of the header (when header size is larger than 64 bits), or the whole header along with the part of the macroblock data (when the header size is smaller than 64 bits). In the case when the encrypted segment contains part of the header, an adversary would have serious problems with synchronization, which adds to the security regarding motion vectors [23]. The security is further increased if the encrypted segment also contains a part of the macroblock data. The computation performed using Method II is clearly faster than that of Method 0, but slower than that of Method I.

Finally, Alattar, Al-Regib, and Al-Semari proposed Method III to reduce the amount of computation of Method II; namely, instead of encrypting all predicted macroblocks, the encryption in Method III is performed on every nth predicted macroblock, along with encrypting every nth I-macroblock.

Partial Encryption Algorithms for Videos by Cheng and Li, 2000. The partial encryption schemes for still images introduced by Cheng and Li are also extended to video [12]. The approaches proposed by Cheng and Li are not suitable for JPEG image compression and, thus, also not suitable for the MPEG video compression standard. Instead, the partial encryption algorithms are designed for video compression methods, which use either quadtree compression or wavelet compression based on zerotrees for video sequence intraframes, motion compensation, and residual error coding. For example, the proposed approach is applicable to video that is based on the Set Partitioning in Hierarchical Trees (SPIHT) image compression algorithm, which is an implementation of zerotree wavelet compression.

Cheng and Li's partial encryption algorithms are designed to disguise the intraframes (I-frames), the motion vectors, and the residual error code of the given video sequences. In both quadtree-compression- and wavelet-compression-based videos, all I-frames are encrypted using the previously discussed methods for partial encryption of still images by Cheng and Li [12].

In addition, it is also important to encrypt the motion vectors. If the motion vector information is unencrypted, the adversary may be able to use an image frame to obtain approximations to the successive frames. Almost all motion estimation algorithms divide the frame into blocks and try to predict their movement (the position in the next frame) by constructing the estimated motion vector for each block. The blocks that belong to the same large object often have identical motion vectors and it is efficient to encode these vectors together. The authors employ video encryption algorithms that use a quadtree for merging these blocks [12]. Then, quadtree partial encryption is used to encrypt the motion vectors.

Finally, for security purposes, it is important to encrypt the residual error as well. Unencrypted residual error may reveal the outline of a moving object. The residual error is often treated as an image frame and then compressed using some standard image compression algorithm. Again, we restrict ourselves to video compression algorithms that use either a quadtree- or wavelet-based image compression algorithm to compress the residual error frames. Thus, partial encryption schemes for both quadtree and wavelet compression can be applied to the residual error encryption.

MHT-Encryption Scheme and MSI-Coder by Wu and Kuo, 2000 and 2001. In their recent work [28,29], Wu and Kuo proposed two selective encryption algorithms for MPEG video sequences: the *MHT-encryption scheme* (where MHT stands for Multiple Huffman Tables) and the *MSI-coder* (where MSI stands for Multiple State Indices).

The MHT-encryption scheme is based on changing the standard Huffman table to a different one based on a secret key. Shi, Wang, and Bhargava's Algorithm I, which was discussed earlier, proposed a similar idea. The basic procedure for generating the entropy code based on different Huffman trees (the "encryption") is summarized in the following three steps:

1. Generate 2^k different Huffman tables, numbered from 0 to $2^k - 1$.
2. Generate a random vector $P = (p_1, p_2, \ldots, p_n)$, where each p_i is a k-bit integer ranging from 0 to $2^k - 1$.
3. For the ith symbol in the Huffman entropy encoding stage, use the Huffman table indexed by $p_{(i-1(\mathrm{mod}\ n))+1}$ to encode it.

As the compression ratio should not be affected, it is important to select optimal Huffman tables that perform similarly to the standard one. This, of course, creates an additional constraint that may be a security risk [38]. The authors propose creating a number of so-called training multimedia elements (images or audio data) that can be used to represent the majority of the multimedia data in the world, so that the associated Huffman code that can be easily generated is optimal for general use. The authors' experimental results show a relatively small increase in the size of output images on average, which means that in this approach, the compression performance will be satisfactory, even though the symbols are chosen from multiple Huffman tables.

Another method for obtaining optimal Huffman trees is proposed in Reference 28 and 29; namely, only four base optimal Huffman trees are generated, and the other optimal tables are produced by what is referred to as a *Huffman tree mutation process*. The label pairs are permuted using the secret permutation, as illustrated by the example in Figure 3.8. Clearly, there is no change in the optimality. In addition, the authors propose two slight security enhancements for the MHT-encryption scheme to increase the resistance against known-plaintext and chosen-plaintext attacks (see Reference 29).

The second method (MSI-coder) is designed for video codecs that use QM coding instead of Huffman coding. The QM coder is an adaptive coder based on low-cost probability estimation. It dynamically adjusts the statistical model to a received binary sequence symbols, whose probability is updated at a low computational cost via table lookup. In the standard QM coder, there is a total of 113 possible values for the state index, whose initial value is 0, indicating the equal probabilities of 0's and 1's. Because there are only 113 possibilities to initialize the state index, initializing it to a different "secret" value is pretty useless. Therefore, the MSI-coder uses four indices, which are initially set to different secret values and used alternatively in a secret order. The MSI-coder consists of the following four steps:

1. Generate a random key $K = \{(s_0, s_1, s_2, s_3), (p_0, p_1, \ldots, p_{n-1}), (o_0, o_1, \ldots, o_{n-1})\}$, where each s_i is a 4-bit integer, whereas each p_i and o_i is a 2-bit integer.

Figure 3.8. The Huffman tree mutation process. (From Wu, C.-P. and Kuo, C.-C.J., in *SPIE International Symposia on Information Technologies 2000*, pp. 285–295; Wu, C.-P. and Kuo, C.-C.J., in *Proceedings of SPIE Security and Watermarking of Media Content III*, 2001, Vol. 4314.)

2. Initialize four state indices (I_0, I_1, I_2, I_3) to (s_0, s_1, s_2, s_3).

3. To encode the ith bit from the input, we use the index $Ip_{i \pmod n}$ to determine the probability estimation value Q_e.

4. If the state update is required after encoding the ith bit from the input, all state indices are updated except for $Io_{i \pmod n}$.

The not-so-obvious step 4 is included to ensure that the state indices will become different even if they become the same at some point. By experiments, Wu and Kuo showed that the MSI-encoded data is increased in size by only 0.82 to 4.16% when compared to the data encoded with the original QM coder. Like the previous scheme, the MSI-coder can similarly be slightly enhanced against the known-plaintext and chosen-plaintext attacks [29].

Format-Compliant Configurable Encryption by Wen et al., 2002. This approach, introduced in Reference 25, is a generalization of the ideas of selective encryption into a format-compliant method. It stresses the importance of maintaining compliance to a standard (such as MPEG-4 codec). In this model, the data is divided into information-carrying and not-information-carrying portions. We only need to encrypt the information-carrying fields. These fields are either fixed-length code (FLC) codewords or variable-length code (VLC) codewords. To achieve format compliance, we extract the bits that are chosen to be encrypted, concatenate them, and then encrypt with a secure scheme such as DES. Finally, we put the encrypted bits back to their original positions. For FLC coded fields, this operation most likely creates a compliant bit stream. If it does not, we apply the same approach for VLC coded fields. For VLC coded fields, encrypting concatenated codewords may not result in another valid codeword. In order to still maintain compliance, we assign a fixed-length index to each codeword in the VLC codeword list, encrypt the index concatenation, and map it back to the codewords. This, however, introduces the overhead, but the percentage of overhead is content dependent. In their proposal, Wen et al. stress the importance of preserving the format of standard multimedia codecs when including the additional filters such as encryption and decryption.

Selective Scrambling Algorithm by Zeng and Lei, 2002. Zeng and Lei proposed the frequency domain scrambling algorithm that groups the transform coefficients into blocks or segments that undergo some or all of the following three operations: (1) selective bit scrambling, (2) block shuffling, and (3) block rotation [27].

Most of the video/image compression algorithms are based on either the wavelet transform or the DCT. Therefore, the selective scrambling algorithm proposed by Zeng and Lei was designed for two types of compression: wavelet transform based and 8×8 DCT based.

In the case of wavelet-transform-based codecs, selective bit scrambling is performed on the sign bits because they are not highly compressible. Other kinds of bits are refinement bits and significance bits. Significance bits are the worst candidates for selective scrambling because they have the lowest entropy and, therefore, they are highly compressible. On the other hand, refinement bits are somewhere in the middle as far as compressibility is concerned and, thus, they can be scrambled too, but the degradation level is not as high as in sign bit scrambling. In the block shuffling procedure, each subband is divided into a number of blocks of equal size, but for different subbands, the blocksize can vary. These blocks can be shuffled using the table that is generated by some secret key. Visual effects of this procedure are dramatic, whereas the output data increases by only about 5% [26]. Finally, the set of blocks can further be rotated by a cyclic shift controlled by the secret key.

For 8×8 DCT-based algorithms, each I-frame is divided into segments, each containing several macroblocks. Within each segment, the DCT coefficients with the same frequency location are shuffled. In addition, the sign bits of each coefficient can be encrypted. They are flipped "randomly" according to some secret key. The authors suggest that scrambling the P- and B-frames, as well as the motion vectors, is a good idea for security purposes, because they give some information about the original I-frames. If that is computationally expensive, at least the I-blocks in P- and B-frames should be scrambled.

IMAGE ENCRYPTION TECHNIQUES

When dealing with still images, security is often achieved using the naive approach to completely encrypt the entire image. However, there are a number of applications for which naive-based encryption and decryption represent a major bottleneck in communication and processing. For example, a limited bandwidth and processing power in small mobile devices calls for a different approach. Additionally, different image encryption techniques are used as a basis for selective video encryption. In this section, we introduce a few newly proposed techniques for image encryption, based on encrypting only certain parts of the image in order to reduce the amount of computation. This is referred to as *selective image encryption*. A similar idea was already explored in the previous section.

Partial Encryption Algorithms by Cheng and Li, 2000

In Reference 12, Cheng and Li proposed partial encryption methods that are suitable for images compressed with two specific classes of compression algorithms: quadtree-compression algorithms and wavelet-compression algorithms based on zerotrees. The encryption/decryption function is not specified, but, in general, the user can select the conventional cryptosystems such as IDEA, AES, and so forth.

The quadtree image compression produces the quadtree structure and the parameters describing each block in the tree. For simplicity of argument, it is assumed that the only parameter that describes each block is the average intensity. The intensity for each block does not provide enough information about the original image, but the quadtree decomposition allows the reconstruction of outlines of objects in the original frame [12]. Therefore, the quadtree encryption method proposed by Cheng and Li encrypts only the quadtree structure, and the block intensities, located at leaf nodes of a quadtree, are left unencrypted. The quadtree partial encryption can be applied to both lossless and lossy image compression. Another consideration is the ordering of the leaf nodes for the transmission. Figure 3.9 illustrates the different leaf orderings to be discussed. The four branches of each tree node in Figure 3.9 correspond to NE (northeast), SW (southwest), SE (southeast), and NE (northeast) quadrants, in that order; the black leaf node has value 0 and the white leaf node has value 1. Vulnerability to certain cryptanalytical attacks exists if the ordering of leaf nodes is done using Leaf Ordering I, where leaves are encoded via the inorder traversal of the quadtree. If we would apply Leaf Ordering I to the tree in Figure 3.9, the result would be binary sequence 0010011011110010. Therefore, the authors suggest using Leaf Ordering II, where leaves are encoded via the opposite of breadth-first traversal of the tree. This increases the security level [12]. For illustration, applying Leaf Ordering II to the quadtree from Figure 3.9 would result in the binary sequence 1111000001100101.

The wavelet-compression algorithm based on zerotrees generally transmits the structure of the zerotree, along with the significant coefficients. A typical example of this kind of compression algorithm is the SPIHT compression algorithm, which transmits the significance of the

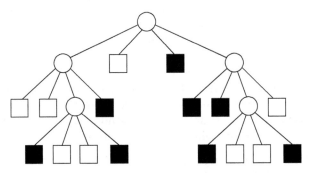

Figure 3.9. An example of a quadtree for a black-and-white (binary) image. (From Cheng, H. and Li, X., *IEEE Trans. Signal Process.,* **48(8), 2439–2457, 2000. With permission.)**

coefficient sets that correspond to the trees of coefficients. The SPIHT algorithm uses the significance of the coefficient sets to reconstruct the zerotree structure. In addition, the structure of the tree strongly affects the execution of the SPIHT algorithm. The SPIHT-encoded image contains different types of data such as the sign bits, the refinement bits, and the significance bits (significance of pixels and significance of sets). Even a small amount of incorrect information at the beginning of the encoded block containing the significance bits causes failure in the decoding process. Incorrect significance bits often cause the misinterpretation of future bits, unlike the incorrect sign bits or refinement bits, which do not. Therefore, Cheng and Li propose encrypting only the significance information of pixels and sets, as well as the initial threshold parameter n that determines which coefficients are significant [12]. Furthermore, the wavelet transform creates a hierarchy of coefficient bands called *pyramid decomposition*, and the number in the band label is referred to as the *pyramid level*. The authors restrict themselves to encrypting only those significant bits that are in the two highest pyramid levels, because all other pixels and sets are derived by decomposing the sets from the two highest pyramid levels. Information about the significant bits from the first two pyramid levels cannot be deduced just by observing the lower levels.

Selective Encryption Methods for Raster and JPEG Images by Droogenbroeck and Benedett, 2002

In 2002, Droogenbroeck and Benedett proposed selective encryption methods for uncompressed (raster) images and compressed (JPEG) images [13].

An uncompressed (raster) gray-level image defines eight bitplanes. The highest (most significant) bitplanes are highly correlated to the original gray-level image. On the other hand, the least significant bitplanes appear randomlike. Encrypting only the bitplanes that contain nearly uncorrelated values would decrease the vulnerability to the known-plaintext attacks [13]. The authors propose the encryption scheme that consists of XORing the selected bitplanes with a key that has the same number of bits as the bits that are to be encrypted. According to Droogenbroeck and Benedett, at least four to five least significant bitplanes should be encrypted to achieve satisfactory visual degradation of the image. It is important to note that partial degradation of the image is not sufficient for applications where high security is a must.

The second method is designed to selectively encrypt the JPEG compressed images. Huffman entropy encoding creates the symbols based on the run-length coding. In particular, zero coefficients are encoded into the symbols that contain the run of zeros and the magnitude categories for the nonzero coefficients that terminate the runs. These symbols are encoded with the 8-bit Huffman codewords, followed by the appended bits that specify the sign and magnitude of the nonzero coefficients. In the proposed method, only the appended bits that correspond to the selected AC coefficients are encrypted. The DC coefficients are left unencrypted because their values are highly predictable [13]. On the other hand, the codewords are left unencrypted for synchronization purposes.

Selective Bitplane Encryption Algorithm by Podesser, Schmidt, and Uhl, 2002

In Reference 15, Podesser, Schmidt, and Uhl proposed a selective encryption algorithm for the uncompressed (raster) images, which is in contrast with the first method by Droogenbroeck and Benedett [13]. In the raster image that consists of eight bitplanes, Schmidt and Uhl's algorithm encrypts only the most significant bitplanes. The proposed underlying cryptosystem for this method was AES. However, without loss of generality, any fast conventional cryptosystem can be chosen.

After performing the experiments, Podesser, Schmidt, and Uhl came to the same conclusion in Reference 15 as Droogenbroeck and Benedett did in Reference 13; that is, encrypting only the most significant bitplane (MSB) is not secure. Podesser, Schmidt, and Uhl argue that the MSB bitplane can be reconstructed with the aid of the unencrypted remaining bitplanes. Therefore, they suggest encrypting at least two or four bitplanes. Encrypting only two bitplanes is sufficient if severe alienation of the image data is acceptable, whereas encrypting four bitplanes provides higher security. It is up to the user to determine if the degradation method by encrypting only two bitplanes is sufficient for the given application or if the more secure approach of encrypting four bitplanes is needed.

AUDIO AND SPEECH ENCRYPTION TECHNIQUES

In many applications, the audio sequences need confidentiality during transmission. Sometimes, it is enough to apply the naive approach, but, in many instances, this is too computationally expensive (e.g., in small mobile devices). As far as security is concerned, perhaps the most important type of audio data is speech. Unlike in the case of music files and similar entertainment audio sequences, in many applications speech requires a substantial level of security. This section discusses the methods for speech protection, as well as the protection of general audio compressed sequences such as MP3.

Encryption of Compressed Speech

Traditional speech scrambling has a long history. As in the case of analog video signals, the early work was based on analog devices that simply permute speech segments in the time domain or distort the signal in the frequency domain by applying inverters and filter banks. These schemes are very insecure by today's computing standards [28]. Today's research is shifted toward securing the speech in digital form, by applying partial or selective encryption [28,30,31].

Selective Encryption Algorithm for G.723.1 Speech Codec by Wu and Kuo, 2000. One of the most popular digital speech codecs is the ITU recommendation G.723.1 compression standard. It has a very low bitrate and it is extremely suitable for voice communications over packet-switching-based networks. It is also a part of the ITU H.324 standard for videoconferencing/telephony over regular public telephone lines.

The compression is based on the analysis-by-synthesis method. The encoder incorporates the entire decoder unit, which synthesizes a segment of speech according to given input coefficients. The encoder then changes these coefficients until the difference between the original speech and the synthesized speech is within the acceptable range. The decoding is performed with three decoders: the LSP decoder, the pitch decoder, and the excitation decoder; the G.723.1 coefficients can be categorized depending on the decoder to which they are fed. In addition, this codec can work in either 6.3-Kbps or 5.3-Kbps mode.

In Reference 28, Wu and Kuo suggest applying selective encryption to the most significant bits of all important G.723.1 coefficients. They identified the following coefficients as the important ones: the LSP codebook indices, the lag of pitch predictor, the pitch gain vectors, the fixed codebook gains, and the VAD mode flag. The total number of selected bits for encryption is 37 in each frame, which is less than one fifth of the entire speech stream at the 6.3-Kbps rate and less than one fourth of the entire speech stream at the 5.3-Kbps rate.

Perception-Based Partial Encryption Algorithm by Servetti and De Martin, 2002. In 2002, Servetti and De Martin published a perception-based algorithm for partial encryption of telephone bandwidth speech [30]. The algorithm was implemented for the ITU-T G.729 codec for a rate of 8 Kbps.

Servetti and De Martin suggested two methods for partial telephony speech encryption. The goal of the method was to have low security but high bitrate (similar to the degradation schemes for videos and images). The purpose was to degrade the speech enough to prevent immediate eavesdropping. However, more substantial cryptanalysis could reveal the encrypted speech. The second algorithm encrypts more of the bit stream and its goal is to provide more security. Servetti and De Martin argue that even though it encrypts only about half of the bit stream, the algorithm's security level is comparable to that of the naive algorithm.

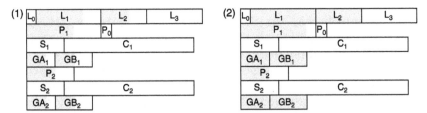

Figure 3.10. Partial encryption for G.729 speech codec (grayed bits are selected for encryption): (1) low-security algorithm and (2) high-security algorithm. (From Servetti, A. and De Martin, J.C., *IEEE Trans. Speech Audio Process.*, 10(8), 637–643, 2002. With permission.)

There is a total of 15 segments from the ITU-T G.729 codec output: L_0 (1 bit), L_1 (7 bits), L_2 (5 bits), L_3 (5 bits), P_1 (8 bits), P_0 (1 bit), S_1 (4 bits), C_1 (13 bits), GA_1 (3 bits), GB_1 (4 bits), P_2 (5 bits), S_2 (4 bits), C_2 (13 bits), GA_2 (3 bits), and GB_2 (4 bits). Rather than describing it in words, the selected bits for encryption in Servetti and De Martin's low- and high-security algorithms are shown in Figure 3.10. The experiments showed that by applying the high-security selective encryption algorithm, the speech is highly scrambled, it cannot be reconstructed from the known bits, and the total computational savings is more than 50%.

Encryption of Compressed Audio

There are numerous applications for which general audio data needs to be protected and the expensive naive approach might be infeasible. This demand created some research initiatives toward developing selective encryption approaches for compressed audio streams.

MP3 Security Methods by Thorwirth, Horvatic, Weis, and Zhao, 2000. Thorwirth et al. proposed a selective encryption algorithm for perceptual-audio-coding (PAC)-based compression standards, such as MPEG-I Layer-3 (MP3) [32]. In their proposal, the authors concentrated on analyzing encryption of MP3-encoded audio files.

In the late 1980s, researchers at Fraunhofer Institute developed the audio coding technique called MPEG-I Layer-3, or simply MP3. This codec achieved the stunning compression ratio of 1:10 to 1:12 while still maintaining the CD sound quality. It is a PAC that uses perceptual masking algorithms to discard the redundancy from the raw audio digital signal. All components of the raw audio signal that are inaudible to the human hearing system are identified as redundant data by the perceptual models. The compression in MP3 audio standard is based on the Huffman entropy code.

The hearable frequency spectrum is divided into segments called *audio quality layers*. The 20 Hz to 4 KHz range represents the lowest audio quality layer, whereas the CD quality range is 20 Hz to 22 KHz. The authors propose encrypting the audio quality layers associated with the compressed audio data, in order to enforce audio quality control by means of encryption. The algorithm identifies the frequency spectrum boundaries that are used to determine the audio quality layers. Each known layer is then grouped into blocks of equal size and a block cipher is applied. After the encryption stage, the encrypted data can be easily plugged back to the MP3 bit stream, thus preserving the format. Such encrypted MP3 sequences are decodable and playable by any valid MP3 player [32].

SUMMARY

In this chapter, many of the current important multimedia encryption techniques were presented and analyzed. In brief, the best way of protecting multimedia data is by means of the naive algorithm (i.e., by encrypting the entire multimedia bit sequence using a fast conventional cryptosystem). Yet, in many instances, this is not possible due to the expensive computational overhead introduced by the encryption and decryption stages. Much of the past and current research targets encrypting only a carefully selected part of the multimedia bit stream in order to reduce the computational load and yet keep the security level high. Many of the proposed schemes only achieved moderate to low security, which may find applications in which quality degradation is preferred over absolute security. However, only a few of the proposed methods promise to achieve substantial security, which is the number-one requirement in many multimedia applications. It is also worthwhile mentioning that many of the above-proposed audiovisual encryption techniques are flexible in terms of selecting the underlying cryptosystem, regardless of the choice made by the authors. In general, a well-studied, fast, and secure conventional cryptosystem should be chosen. Surely, AES is a good candidate, but there are numerous other successful modern cryptosystems with similar and, in some aspects, even better performances.

Further research should be directed toward developing substantially secure encryption schemes for high-bitrate and high-quality audiovisual data. Furthermore, the experts should investigate the security aspects of the newly proposed multimedia encryption techniques.

REFERENCES

1. *IEEE Transactions on Circuits and Systems for Video Technology* (Special issue on authentication, copyright protection, and information hiding), 13(8), 2003.
2. Eskicioglu, A.M., Protecting intellectual property in digital multimedia networks, *IEEE Computer*, 36(7), 39–45, 2003.

3. Van Oorschot, P.C., Menezes, A.J., and Vanstone, S.A., *Handbook of Applied Cryptography*, CRC Press, Boca Raton, FL, 1997.
4. Seidel, T., Socek, D., and Sramka, M., Parallel Symmetric Attack on NTRU using Non-Deterministic Lattice Reduction, *Designs, Codes and Cryptography*, Kluwer Academic Publishers, May 2004, Vol. 32, Iss. 1–3, pp. 369–379(11).
5. Howgrave-Graham, N., Nguyen, P., Pointcheval, D., Proos, J., Silverman, J.H., Singer, A., and Whyte, W., The Impact of Decryption Failures on the Security of NTRU Encryption, in *Proceedings of Crypto 2003*, Santa Barbara, CA, 2003.
6. Daemen, J. and Rijmen, V., AES Proposal: Rijndael, AES Algorithm Submission, September 3, 1999, available at http://www.nist.gov/CryptoToolkit.
7. Stinson, D.R., *Cryptography Theory and Practice*, CRC Press, Boca Raton, FL, 2002.
8. McGrew, D., Naslund, M., Norman, K., Blom, R., Carrara, E., and Oran, D., The Secure Real Time Transport Protocol (SRTP), RFC 3711, March 2004.
9. Furht, B. and Socek, D., Multimedia Security: Encryption Techniques, IEC Comprehensive Report on Information Security, International Engineering Consortium, Chicago, IL, 2003.
10. Liu, X. and Eskicioglu, A.M., Selective Encryption of Multimedia Content in Distribution Networks: Challenges and New Directions, presented at *IASTED International Conference on Communications, Internet and Information Technology (CIIT 2003)*, Scottsdale, AZ, 2003.
11. Lookabaugh, T., Sicker, D.C., Keaton, D.M., Guo, W.Y., and Vedula, I., Security Analysis of Selectively Encrypted MPEG-2 Streams, presented at *Multimedia Systems and Applications VI Conference*, Orlando, FL, 2003.
12. Cheng, H. and Li, X., Partial encryption of compressed images and video, *IEEE Trans. Signal Process.*, 48(8), 2439–2451, 2000.
13. Van Droogenbroeck, M. and Benedett, R., Techniques for a Selective Encryption of Uncompressed and Compressed Images, in *Proceedings of Advanced Concepts for Intelligent Vision Systems (ACIVS) 2002*, Ghent, 2002.
14. Pommer, A. and Uhl, A., Selective encryption of wavelet-packet encoded image data, *ACM Multimedia Syst. J.*, 9(3), pp. 279–287, 2003.
15. Podesser, M., Schmidt, H.-P., and Uhl, A., Selective Bitplane Encryption for Secure Transmission of Image Data in Mobile Environments, presented at *5th Nordic Signal Processing Symposium*, Hurtigruten, Norway, 2002.
16. Meyer, J. and Gadegast, F., Security Mechanisms for Multimedia Data with the Example MPEG-1 Video, Project Description of SECMPEG, Technical University of Berlin, 1995.
17. Maples, T.B. and Spanos, G.A., Performance Study of Selective Encryption Scheme for the Security of Networked Real-Time Video, in *Proceedings of the 4th International Conference on Computer and Communications*, Las Vegas, NV, 1995.
18. Spanos, G.A. and Maples, T.B., Security for Real-Time MPEG Compressed Video in Distributed Multimedia Applications, presented at *Conference on Computers and Communications*, 1996, pp. 72–78.
19. Tang, L., Methods for Encrypting and Decrypting MPEG Video Data Efficiently, in *Proceedings of the 4th ACM International Multimedia Conference*, Boston, 1996, pp. 219–230.
20. Qiao, L. and Nahrstedt, K., A New Algorithm for MPEG Video Encryption, in *Proceedings of the 1st International Conference on Imaging Science, Systems and Technology (CISST '97)*, 1997, pp. 21–29.
21. Shi, C. and Bhargava, B., A Fast MPEG Video Encryption Algorithm, in *Proceedings of the 6th International Multimedia Conference*, Bristol, U.K., 1998.
22. Shi, C., Wang, S.-Y., and Bhargava, B., MPEG Video Encryption in Real-Time Using Secret key Cryptography, in *1999 International Conference on Parallel and Distributed Processing Techniques and Applications (PDPTA'99)*, Las Vegas, NV, 1999.

23. Alattar, A.M., Al-Regib, G.I., and Al-Semari, S.A., Improved Selective Encryption Techniques for Secure Transmission of MPEG Video Bit-Streams, in *Proceedings of the 1999 International Conference on Image Processing (ICIP '99)*, Kobe, 1999, Vol. 4, pp. 256–260.

24. Shin, S.U., Sim, K.S., and Rhee, K.H., A Secrecy Scheme for MPEG Video Data Using the Joint of Compression and Encryption, *Lecture Notes in Computer Science*, Vol. 1729, Springer-Verlag, Berlin, 1999, pp. 191–201.

25. Wen, J., Severa, M., Zeng, W., Luttrell, M., and Jin, W., A format-compliant configurable encryption framework for access control of video, *IEEE Trans. Circuits Syst. Video Technol.*, 12(6), 545–557, 2002.

26. Zeng, W. and Lei, S., Efficient frequency domain selective scrambling of digital video, *IEEE Trans. Multimedia*, 5(1), 118–129, 2002.

27. Wu, M. and Mao, Y., Communication-Friendly Encryption of Multimedia, presented at *2002 International Workshop on Multimedia Signal Processing*, St. Thomas, 2002.

28. Wu, C.-P. and Kuo, C.-C.J., Fast Encryption Methods for Audiovisual Data Confidentiality, presented at *SPIE International Symposia on Information Technologies 2000*, Boston, MA, 2000, pp. 284–295.

29. Wu, C.-P. and Kuo, C.-C.J., Efficient Multimedia Encryption via Entropy Codec Design, in *Proceedings of SPIE Security and Watermarking of Multimedia Content III*, San Jose, CA, 2001,Vol. 4314.

30. Servetti, A. and De Martin, J.C., Perception based partial encryption of compressed speech, *IEEE Trans. Speech Audio Process.*, 10(8), 637–643, 2002.

31. Servetti, A., Testa, C., and De Martin, J.C., Frequency-Selective Partial Encryption of Compressed Audio, presented at *IEEE International Conference on Aucoustics, Speech and Signal Processing*, Hong-Kong, 2003.

32. Thorwirth, N.J., Horvatic, P., Weis, R., and Zhao, J., Security Methods for MP3 Music Delivery, presented at *Conference Record of the Thirty-Fourth Asilomar Conference on Signals, Systems and Computers*, 2000, Vol. 2, pp. 1831–1835.

33. Agi, I. and Gong, L., An Empirical Study of Secure MPEG Video Transmission, in *Proceedings of the Symposium on Network and Distributed Systems Security*, 1996.

34. Qiao, L. and Nahrstedt, K., Comparison of MPEG encryption algorithms, *Int. J. Computer Graphics*, 22(3), 1998.

35. Alattar, A. and Al-Regib, G., Evaluation of Selective Encryption Techniques for Secure Transmission of MPEG Video Bit-streams, in *Proceedings of the IEEE International Symposium on Circuits and Systems*, 1999, Vol. 4, pp. IV-340–IV-343.

36. Qiao, L., Nahrstedt, K., and Tam, I., Is MPEG Encryption by Using Random List Instead of Zigzag Order Secure?, in *IEEE International Symposium on Consumer Electronics*, 1997.

37. Bhargava, B., Shi, C., and Wang, Y., MEPG Video Encryption Algorithms, available at http://raidlab.cs.purdue.edu/papers/mm.ps, 2002.

38. Seidel, T., Socek, D., and Sramka, M., Cryptanalysis of Video Encryption Algorithms, in *Proceedings of the 3rd Central European Conference on Cryptology TATRACRYPT 2003*, Bratislava, Slovak Republic, 2003.

4

Chaos-Based Encryption for Digital Image and Video

Shujun Li, Guanrong Chen, and Xuan Zheng

INTRODUCTION

Many digital services, such as pay TV, confidential videoconferencing, and medical and military imaging systems, require reliable security in storage and transmission of digital images and videos. Because of the rapid progress of the Internet in the digital world today, the security of digital images and videos has become more and more important. In recent years, more and more consumer electronic services and devices, such as mobile phones and personal digital assistants (PDAs), have also started to provide additional functions of saving and exchanging multimedia messages. The prevalence of multimedia technology in our society has promoted digital images and videos to play a more significant role than the traditional dull texts, which demands a serious protection of users' privacy. To fulfill such security and privacy needs in various applications, encryption of images and videos is very important to frustrate malicious attacks from unauthorized parties.

From the early 1990s, many efforts have been made to investigate specific solutions to image and video encryption. Due to the tight relationship between chaos theory and cryptography, chaotic cryptography has also been extended to design image and video encryption schemes. This chapter focuses on different image and video encryption algorithms based on chaos and clarifies some experiences, lessons, and principles of using chaos to design such encryption schemes. To start, a comprehensive discussion on the state of the art of image and video encryption will first be given as background and motivation for the discussion of the chapter.

The organization of this chapter is as follows. In section "Image and Video Encryption: Preliminaries," some preliminaries on image and video encryption are given. Section "Image and Video Encryption: A Comprehensive Survey" is a comprehensive review of today's image and video encryption technology without using chaos theory. Chaos-based image and video encryption schemes are then surveyed in section "Chaos-Based Image and Video Encryption." Some experiences, lessons, and principles drawn from existing chaos-based image and video encryption algorithms are commented on and discussed in section "Experiences and Lessons." The final section concludes the chapter.

IMAGE AND VIDEO ENCRYPTION: PRELIMINARIES
A Brief Introduction to Modern Cryptography

To facilitate the following discussion, in this subsection, we give a brief introduction to the basic theory of modern cryptography [1].

An encryption system is also called a *cipher* or a *cryptosystem*. The message for encryption is called *plaintext*, and the encrypted message is called *ciphertext*. Denote the plaintext and the ciphertext by P and C, respectively. The encryption procedure of a cipher can be described as $C = E_{K_e}(P)$, where K_e is the encryption key and $E(\cdot)$ is the encryption function. Similarly, the decryption procedure is $P = D_{K_d}(C)$, where K_d is the decryption key and $D(\cdot)$ is the decryption function. Following Kerckhoffs' principle [1], the security of a cipher should only rely on the decryption key K_d, because adversaries can recover the plaintext from the observed ciphertext once they get K_d. See Figure 4.1 for a diagrammatic view of a cipher.

There are two kinds of cipher following the relationship of K_e and K_d. When $K_e = K_d$, the cipher is called a *private key cipher* or a *symmetric cipher*. For private key ciphers, the encryption–decryption key must be transmitted from the sender to the receiver via a separate secret channel. When $K_e \neq K_d$, the cipher is called a *public key* cipher or an *asymmetric*

Figure 4.1. Encryption and decryption of a cipher.

cipher. For *public key* ciphers, the encryption key K_e is published and the decryption key K_d is kept private, for which no additional secret channel is needed for key transfer.

According to the encryption structure, ciphers can be divided into two classes: *block ciphers* and *stream ciphers*. Block ciphers encrypt the plaintext block by block and each block is mapped into another block with the same size. Stream ciphers encrypt the plaintext with a pseudorandom sequence (called *keystream*) controlled by the encryption key.

A cryptographically secure cipher should be strong enough against all kinds of attack. For most ciphers, the following four attacks should be tested: (1) *ciphertext-only attack* — attackers can get the ciphertexts only; (2) *known-plaintext attack* — attackers can get some plaintexts and the corresponding ciphertexts; (3) *chosen-plaintext attack* — attackers can choose some plaintexts and get the corresponding ciphertexts; (4) *chosen-ciphertext attack* — attackers can choose some ciphertexts and get the corresponding plaintexts. It is known that many image and video encryption schemes are not secure enough against known- or chosen-plaintext attack, as shown in the following subsections.

The Need for Image and Video Encryption Schemes

The simplest way to encrypt an image or a video is perhaps to consider the two-dimensional (2-D) or 3-D stream as a 1-D data stream and then encrypt this 1-D stream with any available cipher [2–5]. Following References 6 to 8, such a simple idea of encryption is called *naive encryption*. Although naive encryption is sufficient to protect digital images and videos in some civil applications, the following issues have to be taken into consideration when advanced encryption algorithms are specially designed for sensitive digital images and videos, because their special features are very different from texts:

1. *Trade-off between bulky data and slow speed.* Digital images and videos are generally bulky data of large sizes, even if they

are efficiently compressed (see discussion below). Because the encryption speed of some traditional ciphers is not sufficiently fast, especially for software implementations, it is difficult to achieve fast and secure real-time encryption simultaneously for large-sized bulky data.

2. *Trade-off between encryption and compression.* If encryption is applied before compression, the randomness of ciphertexts will dramatically reduce the compression efficiency. Thus, one has to apply encryption after compression, but the special and various image and video structures make it difficult to embed an encryption algorithm into the integrated system. For example, some popular compression standards (such as MPEG-x) are antagonistic toward selective encryption [9]; that is, there exist notable trade-offs between the compression and the encryption [10].

3. *Dependence of encryption on compression.* The lossy compression technique is widely used for images and videos to dramatically reduce the size of the data for encryption, and it is natural to expect that the design and implementation of fast encryption schemes will be easier. However, it was pointed out [11] that the encryption cannot benefit much from such a data reduction, because generally the time consumed by the compressor is much longer than that by the encryption algorithm. This implies that the encryption efficiency depends heavily on the involved compression algorithm.

4. *Incapability of compression to reduce data size.* In general, lossy compression of images and videos is not acceptable in some applications due to legal considerations. Medical imaging systems are well-known examples, for which the diagnostic images and videos of all patients are required to be stored in lossless forms. In this case, the only choice is to use lossless compression or to leave the images and videos uncompressed, which emphasizes, once again, the trade-off between bulky data and slow encryption speed.

5. *Intractable high redundancy.* There exists high (short distance and long distance) redundancy in uncompressed images and videos, which may make block ciphers running in the ECB (electronic code book) mode fail to conceal all visible information in some plain-images and plain-videos. As a result, block cipher running in the CBC (cipher block chaining) mode (or other modes [1]) or stream ciphers should be used to encrypt uncompressed images and videos with high redundancy.

   • If an image contains an area with a fixed color, which means large redundancy, the edge of this area will be approximately

(a)

(b)

Figure 4.2. An uncompressed plain image (a) containing many areas with fixed gray levels and its corresponding cipher image (b) encrypted by 128-bit Advanced Encrytion Standard (AES) running in the ECB mode.

preserved after encryption. This is because those consecutive identical pixels lead to the same repeated patterns when a block cipher is used in the ECB mode. See Figure 4.2 for a real example of this phenomenon.

- Interestingly, a recent work [12] reported that encrypted BMP images (uncompressed) are less random than encrypted JPEG images (compressed), which implies that the high redundancy cannot be removed efficiently after encryption.

6. *Loss of the avalanche property.* Apparently, a direct use of traditional ciphers in image and video encryption cannot provide the avalanche property at the level of the image and video frame. For example, for two images with only 1-bit difference at the

133

position (i,j), all cipher-pixels except for the ones at (i,j) will be identical in the ECB mode, and all cipher-pixels before (i,j) will be identical in the CBC mode. To maintain the avalanche property, special algorithms should be developed.

7. *New concepts of security and usability.* The diverse multimedia services need different security levels and usability requirements, some of which should be defined and evaluated with human vision capabilities. A typical example is the so-called perceptual encryption, with which only partial visible information is encrypted and the cipher-image and cipher-video gives a rough view of the high-quality services.

Some Special Features of Image and Video Encryption Schemes

In image and video encryption systems, some features are required to support special functions of diverse multimedia services in different environments. These features are generally realized with a combination of compression and encryption and impose some limits on the design of the image and video encryption algorithms.

- *Format compliance* (also called *transcodability* [13], *transparency*, or *syntax-awareness* [14]). This feature means that the encrypted image and video are still decodable at the receiver end without knowledge about the decryption key. For online stream multimedia services, especially those running in wireless environments, the transparency property is desirable to eliminate the problems caused by loss or uncorrected data. The transparency property is also useful for the ease of concatenating other postprocessing devices (such as digital watermarking) to the whole compression or encryption system errors [14,15]. To achieve transparency, the encryption procedure should not destroy the syntax structure of the encrypted file or stream; that is, the descriptive information of the file or stream should be left unencrypted.

- *Scalability.* Scalability means multilevel security for different applications with flexible parameter settings [16–25]. The embedded multilayer structure (i.e., the fine granularity scalability [FGS]) of JPEG2000 images [26] and MPEG-2/4 videos [27] makes scalable encryption easy and natural. The basic idea in realizing scalability is to encrypt partial layers and partial data in selected layers. Scalability can be considered a control mechanism for the visual quality of the encrypted image and video.

- *Perceptibility.* Perceptibility means partial encryption of visible information of the plain-image or plain-video, which is useful for pay-after-trial services of digital multimedia, such as pay TV and video-on-demand (VoD) services [13]. It is a generalization of scalable (multilayered) encryption and does not depend on the embedded multilayered structure of the encrypted image and video. Two typical perceptual encryption schemes for JPEG images and MP3 music were proposed in References 28 and 29, respectively. The selective image encryption schemes proposed in References 30 to 35 and video scrambling schemes in References 36 and 37 are also examples of perceptibility, although this term was not explicitly used.

- *Error tolerability.* The concept of *error-tolerating* (or *error-resilient*) encryption was investigated in References 22 and 38 and also mentioned in References 14 and 15. It is undesirable if an encrypted stream cannot be decoded when some bit errors are introduced, which frequently occurs in multimedia applications, particularly in wireless environments (error-correction mechanism may fail in some situations). However, the avalanche property of good ciphers means high sensitivity to errors, which may lead decryption to fail in some cases. To solve this problem, the idea of selective encryption was used in Reference 22 to a provide better error-tolerating property; in Reference 38, the possibility of designing an *error-preserving* encryption algorithm was studied.

Generally speaking, there exist tight relationships among the above-discussed features: (1) transparency and the idea of *selective encryption* (see section "Selective Encryption" for more details) are requirements of scalability and perceptibility, and (2) multilevel security is achieved by providing perceptibility in some scalable encryption schemes.

IMAGE AND VIDEO ENCRYPTION: A COMPREHENSIVE SURVEY

Generally speaking, there are two basic ways to encrypt a digital image: in the spatial domain or in the transform domain. Because digital videos are generally compressed in the DCT (discrete cosine transform) domain, almost all video encryption algorithms work in the DCT domain. Due to the recent prevalence of the wavelet compression technique and the adoption of the wavelet transform in the JPEG2000 standard [26], in recent years image and video encryption algorithms working in the wavelet domain have also attracted some attention [35,39–43]. In addition, some novel image and video compression algorithms have also been proposed to realize joint compression–encryption schemes.

Although many efforts have been devoted to better solutions for image and video encryption, the current security analyses of many schemes are not sufficient, especially for the security against known-plaintext and chosen-plaintext attacks. What is worse, many selective encryption schemes are, indeed, insecure against ciphertext-only attack, due to the visible information leaking from unencrypted data.

In this section, we provide a comprehensive survey of image and video encryption schemes without using chaos theory, as a background for chaos-based encryption schemes. Before that, a widely used idea in the image and video encryption community, called selective (or partial) encryption, was introduced in order to facilitate the security evaluations of selective image and video encryption schemes to be carried out later.

Selective Encryption

Since the 1990s, selective encryption has been widely suggested and adopted as a basic idea for the encryption of digital images and videos, aiming to achieve a better trade-off between the encryption load and the security level. In Reference 22, it was pointed out that selective encryption is also useful for realizing the error-tolerating property in wireless video transmission. The MPEG-4 IPMP (Intellectual Property Management and Protection) extensions standard also supported selective encryption [44]. In addition, as mentioned earlier, scalability and perceptibility are generally realized via selective encryption.

Some reviews of selective encryption methods and their performances can be found in References 9 and 45 to 47, among which Reference 47 gave a partial list of some representative selective encryption methods and Reference 9 analyzed the potential insecurity of different selective syntactic elements in the MPEG-2 video stream against possible attacks. Although it seems that selective encryption is a good idea for the design of high-efficiency image and video encryption schemes, some essential defects of selective encryption have been pointed out, showing its incapability to provide a satisfactory balance between security and usability. For selective encryption methods of MPEG videos, for instance, the following defects have been clarified [9–11,14,47–50]:

1. Although the energy of a compressed image concentrates on lower DCT coefficients, the visible information does not concentrate on partial coefficients, but scatters over all DCT coefficients. Actually, only one DCT coefficient is enough to recover some visible information of the concerned plain-frame, as shown in Figure 2d of Reference 10 and Figure 5.2 of Reference 51 on some experimental images. By setting all encrypted DCT coefficients to fixed values, it is possible for an attacker to recover a rough view of the plain-frame. A more detailed discussion of this defect can be found in Section IV of Reference 14, where this defect is used to realize the so-called *error-concealment attack* (also called *perceptual attack* [9]).

2. The scattering effect of visible information also exists in different bits of DCT coefficients, which makes it insecure to partially

encrypt significant bits of DCT coefficients. In Figure 3 of Reference 10, it was shown that neither encrypting the sign bits nor encrypting multiple significant bits is secure enough against ciphertext-only attack utilizing the unencrypted bits.

3. Only encrypting I-frames of a video cannot provide sufficient security against ciphertext-only attack. The unencrypted I-blocks and motion vectors in B- and P-frames can be still used to uncover partial visible information of the original videos.

4. Because all I-frames occupy about 30 to 60% or even more of an MPEG video [8,25], the reduction of computation load of encrypting I-frames only is not significant. If all I-macroblocks in B- and P-frames are also encrypted, the encryption load will be close to that of full encryption. In Reference 11, it was further pointed out that selective encryption of compressed images and videos cannot significantly save the overall processing time, because the compression procedure generally consumes more time than the encryption of the compressed images and videos.

5. If selective encryption is exerted before the entropy-coding stage, compression performance will decrease; whereas if selective encryption is exerted after the entropy-coding stage, format compliance may be lost. If the entropy-coding algorithm is kept secret, the secret entropy codec is generally insecure against plaintext attack, because the sizes of the Huffman tables are too small from a cryptographical point of view.

Apparently, the first two defects of selective encryption of MPEG videos are due to the orthogonality of DCT. Because all transforms used in image and video compression algorithms have the orthogonal property, the two defects exist for all transform-based image and video compression algorithms. The first two defects on uncompressed images were also pointed out in Reference 50, and the second defect was used in Reference 33 to achieve perceptual encryption with controllable quality of cipher-images.

In Reference 9, a comparison of the performances of selectively encrypting different syntactic elements of MPEG-2 was given, and three kinds of relationships between the compressor and the selective encryption system were clarified: cooperative, neutral, and antagonistic. Although it was thought in Reference 9 that the relationship between the MPEG compressor and most selective MPEG encryption schemes is neutral, the aforementioned defects of selective MPEG encryption imply that the MPEG compressor plays an antagonistic role with respect to selective encryption.

In summary, considering the security defects of selective image and video encryption, it is difficult to simply use the idea of selective encryption alone to achieve a high security level. From a conservative point of view, the meaningful use of selective encryption is to realize perceptual encryption (i.e., to degrade the visible quality of the encrypted plain-image and plain-video), rather than to provide cryptographically strong security. It has been argued that selective encryption can work well with model-based compression algorithms, such as context-based arithmetic coding [53] and model-based speech coding [10], but further studies are still needed to confirm the security level of selective encryption in such compression models.

Joint Image and Video Encryption Schemes

Due to the similarity between MPEG videos and JPEG images, most MPEG encryption methods can be used to encrypt JPEG images directly [33,54,55]. On the other hand, some encryption techniques proposed for images can also be extended to encrypt videos with similar structures. Therefore, the distinction between image encryption and video encryption is not prominent. In this subsection, we discuss those schemes lying on their boundary: the joint image and video encryption schemes.

- Almost all *DCT-based encryption schemes* can be used to encrypt both JPEG images and MPEG videos, although most DCT-based encryption schemes were originally proposed for MPEG videos, with a few for JPEG images [33,55]. Video encryption schemes for MPEG will be further discussed in section "Video Encryption Schemes."

- Because entropy coding is widely used in image and video compression algorithms, the idea of *making entropy codec secret* can work for both image and video encryptions.

  In References 56 and 57, the secretly permuted Huffman table is used to encrypt the input image or video stream. This scheme is not secure enough against known-plaintext or chosen-plaintext attacks and its key space is too small.

  In Reference 10, multiple Huffman tables (MHTs) are employed and a random index is used as the secret key to select a Huffman table for each codeword. This scheme cannot resist the chosen-plaintext attack. Later, two methods were proposed to enhance its security: secretly inserting pseudorandom bits [58] and changing the random index frequently [58,59].

  In Reference 60, another encryption scheme based on secret Huffman tables was proposed. Random flipping of the last bit of each codeword was introduced to further adaptively change the Huffman table.

In References 14 and 15, the Huffman tables are left untouched and the secret entropy codec is achieved as follows. Map each plain-codeword to an index representing its position in the Huffman table, encrypt the index, and then remap the encrypted index back to generate the cipher-codeword.

- All *wavelet-based* image *encryption schemes* can be extended to encrypt videos based on wavelet compression algorithms, such as motion JPEG2000 [26]. Wavelet-based image encryption schemes will be surveyed in the next subsection.

In References 61 and 62, it was suggested to use the following three operations for encryption of wavelet-compressed videos: selective bit scrambling, block shuffling, and block rotation. It appears that this scheme cannot resist the chosen-plaintext attack.

In References 51, 63, and 64, the use of selective encryption in SPIHT-encoded images was studied, in which SPIHT coding is cooperative with the selective encryption.

- In References 51 and 63 to 65, the use of selective encryption in *quadtree decomposition* of digital images was discussed in detail. It was pointed out that Leaf Ordering I (from top to bottom) is not sufficiently secure in the selective encryption framework. This scheme was also extended to selective video encryption.

- In Reference 53, a selective encryption scheme based on *context-based arithmetic coding* of DWT (discrete wavelet transform) coefficients was proposed. This scheme uses a traditional cipher to selectively encrypt partial leading bits of the compressed bit stream. Without knowledge of the leading bits, it is cryptographically difficult to decompress the bit stream due to the sensitivity of the decompression to the leading bits (i.e., to the modeling context). This scheme is a good example that exhibits the cooperative relationship between compression and selective encryption.

Image Encryption Schemes

- One of the simplest ideas to selectively encrypt images in the spatial domain is to *encrypt one or more bitplanes* [33,66,67]. Because the MSB (most significant bit) contains the most defining information on the image, it serves as the first bitplane for encryption. As a result, the selection order is generally from MSB to LSB (least significant bit) [66,67], but the order should be reversed for perceptual encryption schemes so as to reserve some visible information [33].

- In Reference 68, a *VQ-based image encryption* algorithm was proposed. In this scheme, the codebook is first extended, then transformed to another coordinate system, and, finally, permuted to make a shuffled codebook in a larger size. The parameters used in the above three processes are encrypted with a traditional cipher. It was claimed [68] that this scheme can resist all kinds of known attack, and the encryption load is very light.

- In Reference 39, *secret permutations* were suggested to shuffle the *DWT coefficients* in each subband of wavelet compressed images. An enhanced version of this scheme suggested encrypting the lowest subband with a traditional cipher. In Reference 69, some permutation methods of DWT coefficients were compared, and a novel method was proposed to realize a stronger confusion of shuffled coefficients. Because of the scattering effect of visible information in all DWT coefficients (see Figures 1 and 3 of Reference 39), such permutations alone are not secure enough against the ciphertext-only attack, if not all subbands are permuted. Also, the secret permutations can be reconstructed under known-plaintext and chosen-plaintext attacks.

- In References 32 and 35, several perceptual encryption schemes were proposed by *selectively encrypting partial DWT coefficients*. The bit-shift encryption function used in Reference 35 is not secure enough against known-plaintext and chosen-plaintext attacks. In References 67 and 76, the use of selective encryption in JPEG2000 image encryption was discussed. It was pointed out that at least 20% of encrypted data is needed to provide sufficient security.

- In Reference 43, *encryption of sign bits of partial DWT coefficients* was suggested. This scheme is not secure due to the aforementioned second defect of selective encryption.

- In Reference 71, the idea of *encrypting wavelet filters* was proposed to develop a new encryption system. Later, in References 40, 41, and 72, this algorithm was studied with wavelet packet decomposition and it was shown that such an encryption scheme is not secure enough against the ciphertext-only attack based on a heuristic cryptanalytic method.

- In References 41, 42, 73, and 74, the possibility of *encrypting the quadtree decomposition structure* was studied for images compressed with *wavelet packet algorithms*. Uniform scalar quantization of wavelet coefficients was found insecure against the ciphertext-only attack, and the zerotree coder was suggested to provide higher security.

- *Encryption schemes based on fractal compression* were proposed in References 30 and 31. Selected parameters are encrypted to achieve perceptibility.

- In Reference 75, an image encryption scheme was proposed based on the so-called *base-switching lossless compression algorithm*. The base-switching compression is a simple lossless algorithm, which compresses each 3×3 block of the image into a 3-tuple data (m, b) and an integer with nine b-base bits. The base b of each block is encrypted with a secret polynomial function to generate the cipher-image. Apparently, this scheme cannot resist known-plaintext and chosen-plaintext attacks, because using a polynomial function is not sufficiently secure from a cryptographical point of view.

Video Encryption Schemes
MPEG Encryption Schemes

- The most frequently used idea of MPEG encryption is to *encrypt selective frames, macroblocks, DCT coefficients*, and *motion vectors*. The following is a list of selective data for encryption in different schemes (from light to heavy encryptions):

  All header information (and partial blocks) [76]

  Selective AC coefficients of Y/V blocks in all I-frames [77]

  Selective leading DCT coefficients of each block [78]

  Selective DCT coefficients of each block and motion vectors[61,62]

  All or selective motion vectors [36]

  All I-frames[34,79] and the header of the MPEG video sequence [48,80]

  All I- and P-frames [79], or all I-frames and I-macroblocks in B- and P-frames [76]

  All or selective I-macroblocks and the headers of all predicted macroblocks [81]

Note that almost all selective MPEG encryption schemes have the defects mentioned in section "Selective Encryption" and the encryption of the headers will cause the loss of format compliance.

- Another frequently used idea is to *secretly permute* all *or selective macroblocks, blocks, DCT coefficients*, and *motion vectors*.

  In Reference 54, DCT coefficients are secretly permuted within each block, and the DC coefficient is split into two halves and the 63rd AC coefficient is set to be the higher half of the DC coefficient.

  In References 61 and 62, the following three operations are combined to encrypt images: secret permutations of DCT coefficients, selective encryption of DCT coefficients, and motion vector scrambling. In this scheme, several blocks compose a segment, and DCT coefficients in different blocks at the same frequency are secretly permuted.

In Reference 82, the secret permutations of DCT coefficients and the encryption of sign bits of DC coefficients are combined to realize a selective encryption scheme.

In References 14 and 83, different basic units are secretly permuted: macroblocks, 8×8 blocks, and run-level codewords. The secret permutation tables are pseudorandomly generated from some encrypted local-content-specific bits.

The first three of the above schemes are all insecure against ciphertext-only attack [6,7,49,84,85] and known-plaintext and chosen-plaintext attacks [6,7,49,84]. Another disadvantage of the secret permutation of DCT coefficients is the expansion of the video size [61,62].

- In References 57 and 86 to 88, three encryption schemes were proposed that *encrypt selective sign bits of DCT coefficients and motion vectors*, which are respectively called VEA (video encryption algorithm) [87], MVEA (modified VEA) [86], and RVEA (real-time VEA) [88]. Note that the encryption of sign bits was also involved in other designs [14,82].

  VEA is a simple cipher XORing all sign bits with a repeated m-bit key. It is too simple to resist ciphertext-only attack and known-plaintext and chosen-plaintext attacks.

  MVEA is a simple modification of VEA, in which only sign bits of DC coefficients in I-frames and sign bits of motion vectors in B- and P-frames are XORed with the secret key. In fact, MVEA is weaker than VEA [57, appendix].

  RVEA is a combined version of VEA and MVEA, where the XOR operations are replaced by a traditional cipher. For each macroblock, at most 64 sign bits are encrypted with the order from low frequency to high frequency (see Figure 5 of Reference 57). Although RVEA is the strongest VEA cipher, the attempt of using unencrypted AC coefficients to reconstruct some visible information is still possible.

Generic Video Encryption Schemes.

- In References 6,7, and 52, another VEA was proposed to encrypt video stream. Divide each 128-byte piece of the plain-video into two 64-byte lists: an Odd List and an Even List, and the Even List is XORed by the Odd List and then encrypted. This VEA can reduce the encryption load by 50%. An extended VEA with a lower encryption cost was proposed in Reference 22 to support the error-tolerability property.

- In Reference 89, a simple video encryption scheme was proposed that applies a *secret linear transformation* on each pixel value. All pixels in the same macroblock are encrypted with the same secret parameters set. In Reference 37, a similar encryption scheme was proposed. Both schemes are insecure against known-plaintext and chosen-plaintext attacks.

- In Reference 90, *combining a fast (stream) cipher and a secure (block) cipher* was suggested to achieve overall fast encryption of digital videos. The encryption procedure can be described as follows. Assume that C and M, respectively, mean the ciphertext and the plaintext, and that **SE** and **FE**, respectively, mean the secure cipher and the fast cipher,

$$C = \{\mathbf{SE}(K, M_{ik+1}), \mathbf{FE}(K_{i+1}, M_{ik+2}M_{ik+2} \cdots M_{(i+1)k})\}_{i=0}^{t}$$

where $K_{i+1} = \mathbf{SE}(K, \mathbf{SE}(K, M_{ik+1}))$. Two ciphers with high encryption speeds were designed. Because partial plaintexts are selected to be encrypted by a more secure cipher but others are selected to be encrypted by a faster cipher, such a mechanism can be regarded as a generalized version of selective encryption.

CHAOS-BASED IMAGE AND VIDEO ENCRYPTION

Due to the tight relationship between chaos and cryptography, in the past two decades it was widely investigated how to use chaotic maps to construct cryptosystems. For a comprehensive survey of digital chaos ciphers, see Chapter 2 of Reference 91. Basically, there are two typical ways to use chaos in image and video encryption schemes: (1) use chaos as a source to generate pseudorandom bits with desired statistical properties to realize secret encryption operations and (2) use 2-D chaotic maps (or fractallike curves) to realize secret permutations of digital images and frames. The first way has been widely used to design chaotic stream ciphers, whereas the second has been specially employed by chaos-based image encryption schemes.

Image Encryption Schemes Based on 2-D Chaotic Maps

The idea of using 2-D chaotic maps to design permutation-based image encryption schemes was initially proposed in References 92 to 95 and later systematized in References 96 to 98. Assuming that the size of the plain-image is $M \times N$, the encryption procedure can be described as follows (see Figure 4.3):

- Define a discretized and invertible 2-D chaotic map on an $M \times N$ lattice, where the discretized parameters serve as the secret key.

Figure 4.3. **A general framework of image encryption systems based on 2-D chaotic permutations (substitution part is run in CBC mode to resist chosen-plaintext attack).**

- Iterate the discretized 2-D chaotic maps on the plain-image to permute all pixels.
- Use a substitution algorithm (cipher) so as to modify the values of all pixels to flatten the histogram of the image (i.e., to enable the confusion property).
- Repeat the permutation and the substitution for k rounds to generate the cipher-image.

To resist the chosen-plaintext attack, the substitution part should be used in context-sensitive modes (generally in CBC mode). This provides the needed diffusion property for the cipher-image with respect to small changes in the plain-image. The most favorable 2-D chaotic map for discretization is the Baker map whose continuous form is defined as follows:

$$B(x, y) = \begin{cases} (2x, y/2), & 0 \leq x < 1/2 \\ (2x - 1, y/2 + 1/2), & 1/2 \leq x < 1 \end{cases}$$

It is also possible to use the Cat map and the Standard map as discussed in References 97 and 98, but it was found that these two maps are not as good as the Baker map.

In Reference 99, it was pointed out that there exist some weak keys in Fridrich's image encryption scheme [96–98]. This problem is caused by the short recurrent-period effect of the discretized Baker map: for some keys, the recurrent period of the chaotic permutation is only 4. Although this issue was discussed from a statistical point of view in Section 5 of Reference 98 and Section 4.2 of Reference 97, the existence of such a short period was not noticed. To overcome this defect, in Reference 100, a modified Fridrich's image encryption scheme was proposed. An extra permutation (shifting pixels in each row) is introduced to avoid a short recurrent period of the discretized chaotic permutation. The existence of weak keys signifies the importance of the dynamical properties of the discretized chaotic permutations. However, until now, only limited results on a subset of all chaotic possible permutations have been reported [101]; therefore, further theoretical research is needed to clarify this issue and its negative effect on the security of image encryption schemes.

Recently, 2-D discretized chaotic maps were generalized to 3-D counterparts: the 3-D Baker map in References 102 to 104 and the 3-D Cat map in Reference 105. Based on the proposed 3-D discretized chaotic maps, after rearranging the 2-D plain-image into a 3-D lattice (over which the 3-D chaotic map is iterated), the plain-image can be encrypted in a procedure similar to Fridrich's original scheme. Another difference between the two schemes and Fridrich's scheme is that a chaotic pseudorandom number generator (PRNG) based on the 1-D Logistic map is used to realize the substitution algorithm.

In References 106 and 107, a different discretized rule for the Baker map was proposed and a generalized version of the original Scharinger–Fridrich image encryption schemes [92–98] was developed. For a $2^l \times 2^l$ image, the new discretized Baker map was controlled by a 2^{2l-1}-size sequence $\{b_k^{(1)}, \ldots, b_k^{(2^{2l-1})}\}$, which determines 2^{2l-1} rotation directions of local pixels. Let the encryption key be of 2^{2l-1} addresses $\{a_0^{(1)}, \ldots, a_0^{(2^{2l-1})}\}$. The encryption procedure is realized by running the following two combined operations n times:

1. Use selected bits from the pixel values indexed by the 2^{2l-1} addresses to generate $\{b_k^{(1)}, \ldots, b_k^{(2^{2l-1})}\}$, so as to control the secret permutations.

2. Use selected bits from the Y coordinates of the permuted pixels in the last round to substitute the pixel values in the current round.

The above two operations are similar to those used in the original Scharinger–Fridrich schemes. This generalized encryption scheme has two special features: (1) the decryption key is different from the encryption key and (2) the decryption key depends on both the encryption key and the plain-image. In fact, the decryption key is a permutation of the addresses contained in the encryption key. A defect of this scheme is that its key size is too long.

Image Encryption Schemes Based on Fractallike Curves

The permutations defined by discretized 2-D chaotic maps can also be generated from a large group of fractallike curves, such as the Peano–Hilbert curves [108]. Due to the tight relationship between chaos and fractals, permutation encryption schemes based on fractallike curves can be designed, and are further discussed in this subsection.

This basic idea of using fractallike curves to generate noiselike images can be retrospected to early work in image-understanding on noiselike coding of associate memories [109]. In such noiselike associative memories, associative keys are used to store and retrieve data, and the keys can be generated in a manner similar to image encryption. For example, in Reference 108, the Peano–Hilbert curve is used to permute all pixels and a pseudorandom mechanism is used to substitute the gray values. In Reference 110, the idea of using chaos to generate keys for noiselike coding memories was also suggested.

In Reference 111, a simple video scrambling scheme was proposed, which encrypts images or uncompressed video frames by scanning all pixels with a secret space-filling curve (SFC). Although it is called a video scrambling method, it actually is an image scrambling algorithm. This scheme can be broken under ciphertext-only attack, as reported in Reference 112. In addition, it is insecure against known-plaintext and chosen-plaintext attacks because the secret permutation can be reconstructed easily with some pairs of plain-images and cipher-images.

Since the 1990s, a number of image and video encryption schemes based on SCAN, which is a fractal-based image processing language [113], have been proposed [114–121] and realized in hardware [122–124]. All SCAN-based image and video encryption schemes can be divided into two generations: the first generation uses secret permutations to encrypt plain-images and the second combines secret permutations and the substitution algorithm. It has been pointed out that the first generation is not secure enough against known-plaintext and chosen-plaintext attacks [51,64,125,126], and the second can enhance the security of the first generation. In all SCAN-based encryption schemes, the secret permutations are generated from 13 different SCAN patterns and 24 different partition patterns, where the SCAN words serve as the secret key. Figure 1 to Figure 3 of Reference 121 illustrate details about how these SCAN patterns are combined to generate a secret permutation (or a scan order) of the image. In the following, a brief introduction is given to all SCAN-based image and video encryption schemes.

- *The first generation* [114–119]:

  In References 114 to 116, SCAN language was used to design a SCAN transposition cipher (STC), which is then combined with a stream cipher to compose a product cipher. Following the analyses given in References 51, 64, and 215, STC is insecure against known-plaintext and chosen-plaintext attacks and its security is ensured by another stream cipher.

In Reference 117, the SCAN language is combined with quadtree decomposition to encrypt images, where the SCAN language is used to permute the order of four nodes in each level of the quadtree structure. This scheme was insecure due to many security weaknesses, which were discussed in detail in Reference 51.

In Reference 118, the SCAN language is slightly modified and then combined with the 2DRE (two-dimensional run-encoding) technique to encrypt binary images. It was pointed out that this cryptosystem cannot resist the known-plaintext attack [126].

In Reference 119, the SCAN language is used to compress the image into a shorter binary string, then rearrange the compressed string into multiple $2^n \times 2^n$ blocks, and, finally permute each $2^n \times 2^n$ block with two different SCAN patterns m times. Apparently, this scheme corresponds to a single STC, which is insecure against known-plaintext and chosen-plaintext attacks [51,64,126].

- *The second generation* [120,121]: The following substitution mechanism is exerted after permutation, so as to resist known-plaintext and chosen-plaintext attacks (just like those image encryption schemes based on 2-D chaotic maps):

$$C[j] = (B[j] + (C[j-1]+1) \cdot R[j]) \quad \text{mod } 256$$

where $R[j]$ is a pseudorandom integer between 0 and 255. Apparently, the substitution algorithm corresponds to a stream cipher with ciphertext feedback. The mixing of different SCAN patterns (two secret SCAN patterns and two public SCAN patterns — the sprial pattern $s0$ and the diagonal pattern $d0$) and the substitution part makes the new SCAN-based encryption scheme much more secure against known-plaintext and chosen-plaintext attacks.

Image Encryption Schemes Based on 1-D Chaotic Maps

All chaos-based cryptosystems using 1-D chaotic maps can be used to encrypt digital images. It is common to use images to show visible performances of the designed cryptosystems [127–130]. In this subsection, discussion is focused on the chaos-based encryption algorithms specially designed for digital images.

Yen et al.'s Image Encryption Schemes. Yen et al. [131–147] proposed a series of chaos-based image and video encryption schemes. In these proposed algorithms, the employed chaotic map is the Logistic map $f(x) = \mu x(1-x)$ realized in finite computing precision, and the secret key always includes the initial condition $x(0)$ and the control parameter μ (for some schemes, the secret key includes some additional parameters).

All of these encryption schemes follow a similar basic idea of using chaos to realize encryption:

- Run the Logistic map to generate a pseudorandom binary sequence $\{b(i)\}$ from the n-bit representation of each chaotic state $x(k) = 0.b(n \cdot k)b(n \cdot k + 1) \cdots b(n \cdot k + n - 1)$, where n may be less than the finite computing precision.

- Use the chaotic binary sequence $\{b(i)\}$ to pseudorandomly control permutations and value substitutions of all pixels.

Note that the generated sequence $\{b(i)\}$ is generally not balanced; that is, the number of 0's is different from that of 1's, because the variant density function of the Logistic map is not uniform [148]; that is, the Logistic map is not a good choice for encryption, so it is better to use other 1-D chaotic maps with uniform variant density. However, in the following, one can see that Yen et al.'s encryption schemes are not secure even when $\{b(i)\}$ satisfies the balance property.

- BRIE (*Bit Recirculation Image Encryption*) [137]. $\{b(i)\}$ is used to pseudorandomly control shift operations exerted on each pixel. This scheme has been cryptanalyzed in Reference 149. Due to the essential defects of rotation shift operations, the encryption performance of this scheme is rather poor when some specific secret keys are used. Also, it cannot resist known-plaintext and chosen-plaintext attacks, because a mask image that is equivalent to the secret key can be derived from a pair of plain-image and cipher-image.

- CKBA (*Chaotic Key-Based Algorithm*) [138]. $\{b(i)\}$ is used to pseudo-randomly XOR (or NXOR) each pixel with *key*1 or *key*2, where *key*1 and *key*2 are also included in the secret key. According to Reference 150, CKBA cannot resist known-plaintext and chosen-plaintext attacks. Only one pair of known-plain-image or chosen plain-image and cipher-image is enough to reconstruct *key*1 and *key*2 and then derive $\{b(i)\}$. From $\{b(i)\}$, $x(0)$ and an approximate value of μ can also be found.

- HCIE (*Hierarchical Chaotic Image Encryption*) [131,133,139]. In this scheme, an $M \times N$ plain-image is divided into $S_M \times S_N$ blocks for encryption, where $\sqrt{M} \leq S_M \leq M$ and $\sqrt{N} \leq S_N \leq N$. $\{b(i)\}$ is used to pseudorandomly control *no*-round $4(S_M + S_N) - 2$ shift operations with four different directions to permute all blocks and all pixels in each block. The CIE (Chaotic Image Encryption) algorithm propo-sed in Reference 132 is a simplified version of HCIE. Because HCIE is a permutation-only image encryption scheme, it cannot resist the chosen-plaintext attack, and a mask image that is equivalent to the key can still be reconstructed from a small number of pairs of plain-images and cipher-images.

- MLIE (*Mirror-Like Image Encryption*) [134] and CMLIE (*Chaotic MLIE*) [141,142]. {$b(i)$} is used to pseudorandomly control four different mirrorlike swapping operations within the images. Because the two schemes are both permutation-only image encryption schemes, they cannot resist known-plaintext and chosen-plaintext attacks.

- CNNSE (*Chaotic Neural Network for Signal Encryption*) [135,140,143]. {$b(i)$} is used to control the weights of a neutral network, which is then used to encrypt each pixel bit by bit. The final function of the chaotic neutral network is very simple: $d_i'(n)=d_i(n) \oplus b(8 \times n + i)$, where $d_i(n)$ and $d_i'(n)$, respectively, represent the ith plain-bit of the nth plain-pixel and the ith cipher-bit of the nth cipher-pixel. Apparently, this scheme works like a stream cipher, and so CNNSE is vulnerable to known-plaintext and chosen-plaintext attacks: only one known-plaintext or chosen-plaintext is enough to reveal the sequence b and then to derive the secret key. It is the least secure image encryption scheme among all those proposed by Yen et al.

- TDCEA (*The 2-D Circulation Encryption Algorithm*) [144]. This scheme is an enhanced version of BRIE [136,137]. For a bit-matrix M composed of eight consecutive pixel values, {$b(i)$} is used to make bit-shift operations in four different directions. TDCEA has better capability against the known-plaintext attack than BRIE, but it is still not secure enough against the chosen-plaintext attack.

- DSEA (*Domino Signal Encryption Algorithm*) [145]. For the nth plain-byte $f(n)$, `true_key=initial_key` if $i \bmod L=0$, else `true_key=` $f'(n-1)$, where $f'(n)$ denotes the nth cipher-byte. {$b(n)$} is used to pseudorandomly select an encryption function from XOR and NXOR: if $b(n)=1$, then $g'(n)=g(n)$ XOR `true_key`, else $g'(n)=g(n)$ NXOR `true_key`. Because a NXOR $b=a$ XOR b, DSEA cannot resist known-plaintext and chosen-plaintext attacks.

- RSES (*Random Seed Encryption Subsystem*) [147] and RCES (*Random Control Encryption Subsystem*) [146]. RSES and RCES are actually the same encryption scheme, which is an enhanced version of CKBA [138]. The two masking keys, *key*1 and *key*2, used in CKBA become time-variant and are pseudorandomly controlled by {$b(i)$}. {$b(i)$} is also used to control swap operations exerted on neighboring pixels. Although this scheme is much more complex than CKBA, it is still insecure against known-plaintext and chosen-plaintext attacks [151].

Other Image Encryption Schemes on 1-D Chaotic Maps.

- In Reference 152, another permutation-only image encryption scheme was proposed for binary images. The 1-D chaotic map $x(k+1)=\sin(a/x(k))$ is used to pseudorandomly permutate all pixels. Apparently, it cannot resist known-plaintext and chosen-plaintext attacks, but it is generally difficult to derive the secret key by breaking the permutation matrix.

- In References 103 and 104, the Logistic map is used as a chaotic stream cipher (more than a chaotic PRNG) to mask the SPIHT-encoding bit stream of a wavelet-compressed image. To resist known-plaintext and chosen-plaintext attacks, three different masking operations are used and the selected operation at each position is dependent on previous cipher-bits.

A Related Topic: Chaos-Based Watermarking

Due to the similarity between image encryption and image watermarking, some ideas of chaos-based image encryption have also been used in the area of digital watermarking [153–157]. Generally speaking, there are two ways to use chaos in a watermarking system: directly generating watermark signals (pattern) from chaos and mixing (2-D) watermark patterns via chaos. The first way corresponds to chaotic PRNG, and the second corresponds to chaotic permutations of 2-D images (i.e., the secret permutation used in image encryption schemes based on 2-D chaotic maps). At present, almost all chaos-related techniques used in watermarking systems are borrowed from chaotic cryptography (especially chaos-based image encryption), but it can be expected that some new ideas in chaos-based digital watermarking will also benefit the image encryption community in the future.

Chaos-Based Video Encryption

- *SCAN-based encryption for losslessly compressed videos.* The new generation of SCAN-based image encryption schemes were also extended to encrypt videos [120,121,123,124]. The plain-video is compressed with a frame-difference-based light lossless compression algorithm and then encrypted with the new SCAN-based encryption algorithm.

- *Yen et al.'s encryption schemes for MPEG videos.* Some of Yen et al.'s image encryption schemes [134–136,138,140–143,145,146] were recommended for encrypting MPEG videos, thanks to their high encryption speed. The idea of selective encryption was also used in References 136 and 138: motion vectors are selected as data for encryption using BRIE or CKBA. However, the insecurity of Yen et al.'s encryption schemes makes their use in video encryption unacceptable.

- *Chiaraluce et al.'s chaos-based H.263+ encryption scheme.* In Reference 158, a chaotic video encryption scheme was proposed for encrypting the following selective data of an H.263+ encoded video: most sign bits of DC coefficients, the AC coefficients of I-macroblocks, sign bits of AC coefficients of P-macroblocks, and sign bits of motion vectors. The proposed scheme is a stream cipher based on three chaotic maps: the skew tent map, the skew sawtooth map, and the discretized Logistic map. The outputs of the first two chaotic maps are added and then the addition is scaled to be an integer between 0 and 255. Each scaled integer is used as the initial condition of the third map to generate a 64-size key stream to mask the plaintext with XOR operation. To further enhance the security against known-plaintext and chosen-plaintext attacks, it was suggested to change the key every 30 frames.

- *CVES (Chaotic Video Encryption Scheme)*. In Reference 159, a chaos-based encryption scheme called CVES using multiple chaotic systems was proposed. CVES is actually a fast chaotic cipher that encrypts bulky plaintext frame by frame. The basic idea is to combine a simple chaotic stream cipher and a simple chaotic block cipher to construct a fast and secure product cipher. In Chapter 9 of Reference 91, it was pointed out that the original CVES is not sufficiently secure against the chosen-plaintext attack, and an enhanced version of CVES was proposed by adding ciphertext feedback. Figure 4.4 gives a diagrammatic view of the enhanced CVES, where CCS and ECS(1) to ECS(2^n) are all piecewise linear chaotic maps, and m-LFSR$_1$ and m-LFSR$_2$ are the perturbing PRNG of CCS and ECS, respectively. The encryption procedure of CVES can

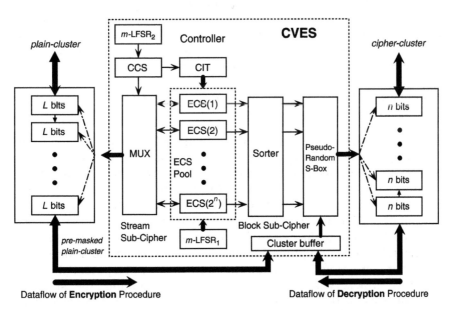

Figure 4.4. The enhanced CVES proposed in Chapter 9 of Reference 91.

be described as follows. Each plain-block is first XORed by a chaotic signal pseudorandomly selected from chaotic orbits of the 2^n ECSs (Encryption Chaotic Systems) and then substituted by a pseudorandom S-box generated from all chaotic orbits of the 2^n ECSs. Initial tests have shown that the encryption speed of CVES is competitive with most traditional ciphers and is only a little slower than the AES reference code.

EXPERIENCES AND LESSONS

From the above survey on chaos-based image and video encryption schemes, one can learn about some experiences and also lessons on how to design fast and secure image and video encryption schemes with or without using chaos. Although some experiences and lessons are merely common rules in modern cryptography, for some reason they have not been widely accepted by the image and video encryption community. In this section, we summarize these learned experiences and lessons in the following list of remarks.

Remark 1. *Permutation-only image/video encryption schemes are generally insecure against known-plaintext and chosen-plaintext attacks.*

Under known-plaintext and chosen-plaintext attacks, a mask image that is equivalent to the secret key can be obtained to decrypt cipher-images encrypted with the same key. In addition, permutation-only image ciphers cannot change plain-histograms, which contain some useful information about the plain-images; for example, cartoon pictures and real photos have different histograms, and photos of human faces usually have narrower histograms than photos of natural scenes.

Remark 2. *Secret permutation is NOT a prerequisite of secure image and video encryption schemes.*

This is because the substitution part running in CBC mode is sufficient for achieving confusion and diffusion properties and for ensuring security against the chosen-ciphertext attack. In fact, comparing Figure 8 and Figure 13 of Reference 98, one can see that the substitution algorithm can make the cipher-image look "chaotic" much faster than a chaotic permutation. This implies the incapability of chaotic permutations. It is believed that the main reason for using secret chaotic permutation in image and video encryption schemes is that secret permutation may be useful for increasing the computational complexity of a potential chosen-plaintext attack. With the use of secret permutation, the statistical cryptanalysis of the concerned encryption scheme will become much more complicated or impractical.

Remark 3. *Ciphertext feedback is very useful for enhancing the security against known-plaintext and chosen-plaintext attacks.*

Most image encryption schemes based on 2-D chaotic maps, the new generation of SCAN-based image encryption schemes, and the enhanced CVES all utilize the ciphertext feedback mechanism to resist the chosen-plaintext attack.

Remark 4. *Combining ciphertext feedback and a (secret) permutation can achieve the diffusion (i.e., avalanche) property at the level of image and video frame.*

Although secret permutations are commonly used together with ciphertext feedback to provide the diffusion property, the permutation can actually be publicized. Apparently, using a public permutation only means that the secret key of the secret permutation is publicized so that the security relies on other parts of the whole cryptosystem.

Remark 5. *Combining a simple stream cipher and a simple block cipher running in the CBC mode can yield a secure and fast encryption scheme, where the stream cipher is used to create the confusion property, the block cipher is used to realize the diffusion property, and ciphertext feedback in the CBC mode is used to resist the chosen-plaintext attack.*

The modified CVES proposed in Chapter 9 of Reference 91 is a one-round version of such a simple but fast encryption scheme. In CVES, the avalanche property is sacrificed in order to increase the encryption speed. The loss of the avalanche feature may not influence the security of the schemes, however.

Remark 6. *The diffusion methods used in most chaos-based encryption schemes are too slow due to the multiple time-consuming iterations of chaotic permutations.*

In fact, only two rounds are enough to achieve diffusion: encrypt the data in CBC mode from top to bottom and then encrypt the partially encrypted data again in the CBC mode from bottom to top.

Remark 7. *Selective encryption may provide enough security if the unencrypted data depends on the encrypt data.*

An example of such selective encryption schemes is the one proposed in Reference 53, which is based on the context-sensitive compression algorithm. More studies are needed to clarify the relationship between the selective encryption and the model-based compression algorithms.

Remark 8. *Although selective encryption is generally insecure from a cryptographical point of view, it can be generalized to provide a more general way of designing fast and secure video encryption* *schemes: use a slow (but stronger) cipher to encrypt selective data and use a fast (but weaker) cipher to encrypt the rest of the data.*

Two video ciphers were constructed in Reference 90 to show the potential of this idea. For the case that the compression algorithm is antagonistic to simple selective encryption, this generalized version of selective encryption will be very useful as a replacement for the simple one.

CONCLUSIONS

Image and video encryption plays a more and more important role in today's multimedia world. Although many encryption schemes have been proposed to provide security for digital images and videos, some of them are too weak to resist various attacks designed by cryptanalysts. Basically, many efforts have been devoted to study the security issue, but for multimedia, the security is still not strong from a serious crypto-graphic point of view. To design truly secure image and video encryption schemes, classical cryptology must be employed.

As an emerging tool for the design of digital ciphers, chaos theory has been widely investigated, especially to develop image and video encryption algorithms. The simplicity of many discrete chaotic maps and the well-established chaos theory make it possible to approach practically good solutions to image and video encryption. The success and failure of chaos-based encryption schemes have led to some valuable experiences and lessons, which can be used as the fundamentals of future research on the chaos-based multimedia encryption technology. At this point, chaos theory for image and video encryption appears to be promising but not yet mature. More efforts are needed for its further development toward a marketable future.

ACKNOWLEDGMENTS

The authors would like to thank Dr. Gonzalo Álvarez at Instituto de Física Aplicada of Consejo Superior de Investigaciones Científicas (Spain), Dr. Ennio Gambi at Universitá di Ancona (Italy), and Mr. Chengqing Li at Zhejiang University (China) for their valuable comments on the manuscript of this chapter.

REFERENCES

1. Schneier, B., *Applied Cryptography: Protocols, Algorithms, and Souce Code in C*, 2nd ed., John Wiley & Sons, New York, 1996.
2. Dang, P.P. and Chau, P.M., Image encryption for secure Internet multimedia applications, *IEEE Trans. Consumer Eletron.*, 46(3), 395–403, 2000.
3. Dang, P.P. and Chau, P.M., Implementation IDEA algorithm for image encryption, in *Mathematics and Applications of Data/Image Coding, Compression, and Encryption III, Proc. SPIE*, Vol. 4122, Mark S. Schmalz, Ed., 2000, pp. 1–9.

4. Dang, P.P. and Chau, P.M., Hardware/software implementation 3-way algorithm for image encryption, in *Security and Watermarking of Multimedia Contents II, Proc. SPIE,* Vol. 3971, Ping W. Wong and Edward J. Delp III, Eds., 2000, pp. 274–283.
5. McCanne, S. and Van Jacobson. vic: a flexible framework for packet video, in *Proceedings of 3rd ACM International Conference on Multimedia,* 1995, pp. 511–522.
6. Qiao, L., Multimedia Security and Copyright Protection, Ph.D. thesis, University of Illinois at Urbana–Champaign, Urbana, IL, 1998.
7. Qiao, L. and Nahrsted, K., Comparison of MPEG encryption algorithms, *Computers Graphics,* 22(4), 437–448, 1998.
8. Agi, I. and Gong, L., An empirical study of secure MPEG video transmission, in *Proceedings of ISOC Symposium on Network and Distributed Systems Security (SNDSS'96),* 1996, pp. 137–144.
9. Lookabaugh, T.D., Sicker, D.C., Keaton, D.M., Guo, W.Y., and Vedula, I., Security analysis of selectively encrypted MPEG-2 streams, in *Multimedia Systems and Applications VI, Proc. SPIE,* Vol. 5241, Andrew G. Tescher, Bhaskaran B. Vasudev, V. Michael Bove Jr., and Ajay Divakaran, Eds., 2003, pp. 10–21.
10. Wu, C.P. and Kuo, C.-C.-J., Fast encryption methods for audiovisual data confidentiality, in *Multimedia Systems and Applications III, SPIE,* Vol. 4209, 2001, pp. 284–285.
11. Pommer, A. and Uhl, A., Application scenarios for selective encryption of visual data, in *Proceedings of Multimedia and Security Workshop of 10th ACM International Conference on Multimedia,* 2002, pp. 71–74.
12. Ziedan, I.E., Fouad, M.M., and Salem, D.H., Application of data encryption standard to bitmap and JPEG images, in *Proceedings of 12th National Radio Science Conference (NRSC'2003),* 2003, pp. C16/1–C16/8.
13. Macq, P.M., and Quisquater, J.J., Cryptology for digital TV broadcasting, *Proc. IEEE,* 83(6), 944–957, 1995.
14. Wen, J., Severa, M., Zeng, W., Luttrell, M.H., and Jin, W., A format-compliant configurable encryption framework for access control of video, *IEEE Trans. Circuits Syst. Video Technol.,* 12(6), 545–557, 2002.
15. Wen, J., Severa, M., Zeng, W., Luttrell, M.H., and Jin, W., A format-compliant configurable encryption framework for access control of multimedia, in *Proceedings of IEEE 4th Workshop on Multimedia Signal Processing (MMSP'2001),* 2001, pp. 435–440.
16. Wee, S.J. and Apostolopoulos, J., Secure scablable streaming and secure transcoding with JPEG2000, in *Proceedings of IEEE International Conference on Image Processing (ICIP'2003),* Vol. I, 2003, pp. 205–208.
17. Yu, H.H. and Yu, X., Progressive and scalable encryption for multimedia content access control, in *Proceedings of IEEE International Conference on Communications (ICC'2003),* Vol. 1, 2003, pp. 547–551.
18. Yuan, C., Zhu, B.B., Wang,Y., Li, S. and Zhong, Y., Efficient and fully scalable encryption for MPEG-4 FGS, in *Proceedings of IEEE International Symposium on Circuits and Systems (ISCAS'2003),* Vol. II, 2003, pp. 620–623.
19. Eskicioglu, A.M. and Delp, E.J., An integrated approach to encrypting scabable video, in *Proceedings of IEEE International Conference on Multimedia and Expo (ICME'2002),* 2002, pp. 573–576.
20. Wee, S.J. and Apostolopoulos, J.G., Secure scablable streaming enabling transcoding without decryption, in *Proceedings of IEEE International Conference on Image Processing (ICIP'2001),* Vol. 1, 2001, pp. 437–440.
21. Wee, S.J. and Apostolopoulos, J.G., Secure scablable video streaming for wireless networks, in *Proceedings of IEEE International Conference on Acoustics, Speech, and Signal Processing (ICASSP'2001),* Vol. 4, 2001, pp. 2049–2052.
22. Tosun, A.S. and Feng, W., Lightweight security mechanisms for wireless video transmission, in *Proceedings of IEEE International Conference on Information Technology: Coding and Computing,* 2001, pp. 157–161.

23. Tosun, A.S. and Feng, W., Efficient multi-layer coding and encryption of MPEG video streams, in *Proceedings of IEEE International Conference on Multimedia and Expo (ICME'2000)*, 2000, pp. 119–122.

24. Kunkelmann, T. and Horn, U., Partial video encryption based on scalable coding, in *Proceedings of 5th International Workshop on Systems, Signals and Image Processing (IWSSIP'98)*, 1998.

25. Dittmann, J. and Steinmetz, A., Enabling technology for the trading of MPEG-encoded video, in *Information Security and Privacy: Second Australasian Conference (ACISP'97) Proceedings*, *Lecture Notes in Computer Science*, Vijay Varadharajan, Josef Pieprzyk, and Yi Mu, Eds., Vol. 1270, Springer-Verlag, New York, 1997, pp. 314–324.

26. Taubman, D.S. and Marcellin, M.W., JPEG2000: standard for interactive imaging, *Proc. IEEE*, 90(8), 1336–1357, 2002.

27. Li, W., Overview of fine granularity scalability in MPEG-4 video standard, *IEEE Trans. Circuits Syst. Video Technol.*, 11(3), 301–317, 2001.

28. Torrubia, A. and Mora, F., Perceptual cryptography of JPEG compressed images on the JFIF bit-stream domain, in *Digest of Technical Papers of IEEE International Conference on Consumer Electronics (ICCE'2003)*, 2003, pp. 58–59.

29. Torrubia, A. and Mora, F., Perceptual cryptography on MPEG layer III bit-streams, *IEEE Trans. Consum. Eletron.*, 48(4), 1046–1050, 2002.

30. Roche, P., Dugelay, J.-L., and Molva, R., Multi-resolution access control algorithm based on fractal coding, in *Proceedings of IEEE International Conference on Image Processing (ICIP'96)*, Vol. 3, 1996, pp. 235–238.

31. El-Khamy, S.E. and Abdou, H.E.M., A novel secure image coding scheme using fractal transformation, in *Proceedings of 15th (Egypt) National Radio Science Conference (NRSC'98)*, 1998, pp. C23/1–C23/9.

32. Grosbois, R., Gerbelot, P., and Ebrahimi, T., Authentication and access control in the JPEG 2000 compressed domain, in *Applications of Digital Image Processing XXIV, Proc. SPIE*, Vol. 4472, Andrew G. Tescher, Ed., 2001, pp. 95–104.

33. Van Droogenbroeck, M. and Benedett, R., Techniques for a selective encryption of uncompressed and compressed images, in *Proceedings of Advanced Concepts for Intelligent Vision Systems (ACIVS'2002)*, 2002, pp. 90–97.

34. Simitopoulos, D., Zissis, N., Georgiadis, P., Emmanouilidis, V. and Strintzis, M.G., Encryption and watermarking for the secure distribution of copyrighted MPEG video on DVD, *Multimedia Syst.*, 2003, 9(3), 217–227.

35. Kiya, H., Imaizumi, D., and Watanabe, O., Partial-scrambling of images encoded using JPEG2000 without generating marker codes, in *Proceedings of IEEE International Conference on Image Processing (ICIP'2003)*, Vol. III, 2003, pp. 205–208.

36. Bodo, Y., Laurent, N., and Dugelay, J.-L., A scrambling method based on disturbance of motion vector, in *Proceddings of 10th ACM International Conference on Multimedia*, 2002, pp. 89–90.

37. Pazarci, M. and Dipçin, V., A MPEG2-transparent scrambling technique, *IEEE Trans. Consumer Eletron.*, 48(2), 345–355, 2002.

38. Tosun, A.S. and Feng, W., On error preserving encryption algorithms for wireless video transmission,in *Proceedings of 9th ACM International Conference on Multimedia*, 2001, pp. 302–308.

39. Uehara, T., Safavi-Naini, R., and Ogunbona, P., Securing wavelet compression with random permutations, in *Proceedings of IEEE Pacific-Rim Conference on Multimedia (IEEE-PCM'2000)*, 2000, pp. 332–335.

40. Pommer, A. and Uhl, A., Wavelet packet methods for multimedia compression and encryption, in *Proceedings of IEEE Pacific Rim Conference on Communications, Computers and Signal Processing (PACRIM'2001)*, Vol. 1, 2001, pp. 1–4.

41. Pommer, A., Selective Encryption of Wavelet-Compressed Visual Data, Ph.D. thesis, University of Salzburg, Austria, 2003.

42. Pommer, A. and Uhl, A., Selective encryption of wavelet-packet encoded image data: efficiency and security, *Multimedia Syst.*, 9(3), 279–287, 2003.

43. Seo, Y.-H., Kim, D.-W., Yoo, J.-S., Dey, S., and Agrawal, A., Wavelet domain image encryption by subband selection and data bit selection, in *Proceedings of World Wireless Congress (WCC'03/3GWireless'2003)*, 2003.

44. ISO, MPEG4 IPMP (Intellectual Property Management and Protection) Final Proposed Draft Amendment (FPDAM), ISO/IEC 14496-1:2001/AMD3, ISO/IEC JTC 1/SC 29/WG11 N4701, 2002.

45. Kunkelmann, T., Reinema, R., Steinmetz, R., and Blecher, T., Evaluation of different video encryption methods for a secure multimedia conferencing gateway, in *From Multimedia Services to Network Services: 4th International COST 237 Workshop Proceedings, Lecture Notes in Computer Science*, Vol. 1356, André V. Dantine and Christophe Diot, Eds., Springer-Verlag, Berlin, 1997, pp. 75–89.

46. Kunkelmann, T. and Horn, U., Video encryption based on data partitioning and scalable coding—a comparison, in *Interactive Distributed Multimedia Systems and Telecommunication Services: 5th International Workshop (IDMS'98) Proceedings, Lecture Notes in Computer Science*, Vol. 1483, Thomas Plagemann and Vera Goebel, Eds., Springer-Verlag, Berlin, 1998, pp. 95–106.

47. Liu, X. and Eskicioglu, A.M., Selective Encryption of Multimedia Content in Distribution Networks: Challenges and New Directions, in *Proceedings of IASTED International Conference on Communications, Internet and Information Technology (CIIT'2003)*, 2003.

48. Spanos, G.A. and Maples, T.B., Security for Real-Time MPEG Compressed Video in Distributed Multimedia Applications, in *Proceedings of IEEE 15th Annual International Phoenix Conference on Computers and Communications*, 1996, pp. 72–78.

49. Dolske, J.H., Secure MPEG video: techniques and pitfalls, available online at http://www.dolske.net/old/gradwork/cis788r08/, 1997.

50. Skrepth, C.J. and Uhl, A., Selective Encryption of Visual Data, in *Proceedings of IFIP TC6/TC11 6th Joint Working Conference on Communications and Multimedia Security (CMS'2002)*, 2002, pp. 213–226.

51. Cheng, H.C.H., Partial Encryption for Image and Video Communication, Master's thesis, University of Alberta, Edmonton, Alberta, Canada, 1998.

52. Qiao, L. and Nahrstedt, K., A New Algorithm for MPEG Video Encryption, in *Proceedings of 1st International Conference on Imaging Science, Systems, and Technology (CISST'97)*, 1997, pp. 21–29.

53. Wu, X. and Moo, P.W., Joint Image/Video Compression and Encryption via High-Order Conditional Entropy Coding of Wavelet Coefficients, in *Proceeding of IEEE Conference on Multimedia Computing and Systems (CMS'99)*, 1999, pp. 908–912.

54. Tang, L. Methods for Encrypting and Decrypting MPEG Video Data Efficiently, in *Proceedings of 4th ACM Internationa of Conference on Multimedia*, 1996, pp. 219–230.

55. Kailasanathan, C., Safavi-Naini, R., and Ogunbona, P., Compression Performance of JPEG Encryption Scheme, in *Proceedings of 14th International Conference on Digital Signal Processing (DSP'2002)*, Vol. 2, 2002, pp. 1329–1332.

56. Shi, C. and Bhargava, B., Light-weight MPEG Video Encryption Algorithm, in *Proceedings of International Conference on Multimedia (Multimedia'98, Shaping the Future)*, 1998, pp. 55–61.

57. Bhargava, B., Shi, C., and Wang, S.-Y., MPEG video encryption algorithm, *Multimedia Tools Applic.*, 24(1), 57–79, 2004.

58. Wu, C.-P. and Kuo, C.-C.J., Efficient multimedia encryption via entropy codec design, in *Security and Watermarking of Multimedia Contents III, Proc. SPIE*, Vol. 4314, Sethuraman Panchanathan, V. Michael Bove, Jr., and Subramania, I. Sudharsanan, Eds., 2001, pp. 128–138.

59. Xie, D. and Kuo, C.-C.J., An enhanced MHT encryption scheme for chosen plaintext attack, in *Internet Multimedia Management Systems IV, Proc. SPIE*, Vol. 5242, John R. Smith, Sethuraman Panchanathan and Tong Zhang, Eds., 2003, pp. 175–183.
60. Kankanhalli, M.S. and Guan, T.T., Compressed-domain scrambler/descrambler for digital video, *IEEE Trans. Consumer Eletron.*, 48(2), 356–365, 2002.
61. Zeng, W. and Lei, S., Efficient Frequency Domain Video Scrambling for Content Access Control, in *Proceedings of 7th ACM International Conference on Multimedia*, 1999, pp. 285–294.
62. Zeng, W. and Lei, S., Efficient frequency domain selective scrambling of digital video, *IEEE Trans. Multimedia*, 5(1), 118–129, 2003.
63. Li, X., Knipe, J., and Cheng, H., Image compression and encryption using tree structures, *Pattern Recogn. Lett.*, 18(8), 2439–2451, 1997.
64. Cheng, H. and Li, X., Partial encryption of compressed images and videos, *IEEE Trans. Signal Process.* 48(8), 2439–2451, 2000.
65. Cheng, H. and Li, X., On the Application of Image Decomposition to Image Compression and Encryption, in *Communications and Multimedia Security II: Proceedings IFIP TC6/TC11 International Conference (CMS'96)*, 1996, pp. 116–127.
66. Podesser, M., Schmidt, H.-P., and Uhl, A., Selective Bitplane Encryption for Secure Transmission of Image Data in Mobile Environments, in *Proceedings of 5th IEEE Nordic Signal Processing Symposium (NORSIG'2002)*, 2002.
67. Norcen, R., Podesser, M., Pommer, A., Schmidt, H.-P., and Uhl, A., Confidential storage and transmission of medical image data, *Computers in Biol. Med.*, 33(3), 277–292, 2003.
68. Chang, C.-C., Hwang, M.-S., and Chen, T.-S., A new encryption algorithm for image cryptosystems, *J. Syst. Software*, 58(2), 83–91, 2001.
69. Lian, S. and Wang, Z., Comparison of Several Wavelet Coefficients Confusion Methods Applied in Multimedia Encryption, in *Proceedings of International Conference on Computer Networks and Mobile Computing (ICCNMC'2003)*, 2003, pp. 372–376.
70. Norcen, R. and Uhl, A., Selective Encryption of the JPEG2000 Bitstream, in *Proceedings IFIP TC6/TC11 7th Joint Working Conference on Communications and Multimedia Security (CMS'2003), Lecture Notes in Computer Science*, Vol. 2828, Antonio Lioy and Daniele Mazzocchi, Eds., Springer-Verlag, Berlin, 2003, pp. 194–204.
71. Vorwerk, L., Engel, T., and Meinel, C., A Proposal for a Combination of Compression and Encryption, in *Visual Communications and Image Processing 2000, Proc. SPIE*, Vol. 4067, King N. Ngan, Thomas Sikora and Ming-Ting Sun, Eds., 2000, pp. 694–702.
72. Pommer, A. and Uhl, A., Multimedia Soft Encryption using NSMRA Wavelet Packet Methods: Parallel Attacks, in *Proceedings of International Workshop on Parallel Numerics (Par-Num'2000)*, 2000, pp. 179–190.
73. Pommer, A. and Uhl, A., Selective Encryption of Wavelet Packet Subband Structures for Obscured Transmission of Visual Data, in *Proceedings of 3rd IEEE Benelux Signal Processing Symposium (SPS'2002)*, 2002, pp. 25–28.
74. Pommer, A. and Uhl, A., Selective Encryption of Wavelet Packet Subband Structures for Secure Transmission of Visual Data, in *Proceedings of Multimedia and Security Workshop of 10th ACM International Conference on Multimedia*, 2002, pp. 67–70.
75. Chuang T.-J. and Lin, J.-C., New approach to image encryption, *J. Electron. Imaging*, 7(2), 350–356, 1998.
76. Meyer, J. and Gadegast, F., *Security Mechanisms for Multimedia-Data with the Example MPEG-1 Video*. Berlin, 1995; available online at http://www.gadegast.de/frank/doc/secmeng.pdf.
77. Taesombut, N., Huang, R., and Rangan, V.P., A Secure Multimedia System in Emerging Wireless Home Networks, in *Communications and Multimedia Security (CMS'2003), Lecture Notes in Computer Science*, Vol. 2828, Antonio Lioy and Daniele Mazzocchi, Eds., 2003, pp. 76–88.

78. Kunkelmann, T. and Reinema, R., A Scalable Security Architecture for Multimedia Communication Standards, in *Proceedings of IEEE International Conference on Multimedia Computing and Systems (ICMCS'97)*, 1997, pp. 660–661.

79. Li, Y., Chen, Z., Tan, S.-M., and Campbell, R.H., Security Enhanced MPEG player, in *Proceedings of International Workshop on Multimedia Software Development (MMSD'96)*, 1996, pp. 169–175.

80. Spanos, G.A. and Maples, T.B., Performance Study of a Selective Encryption Scheme for the Security of Networked, Real-Time Video, in *Proceedings of 4th International Conference on Computer Communications and Networks (IC3N'95)*, 1995, pp. 2–10.

81. Alattar, A.M. and Al-Regib, G.I., Evaluation of Selective Encryption Techniques for Secure Transmission of MPEG Video Bit-Streams, in *Proceedings of IEEE International Symposium on Circuits and Systems (ISCAS'99)*, Vol. IV, 1999, pp. 340–343.

82. Shin, S.U., Sim, K.S., and Rhee, K.H., A Secrecy Scheme for MPEG Video Data using the Joint of Compression and Encryption, in *Information Security: Second International Workshop (ISW'99) Proceedings, Lecture Notes in Computer Science*, Vol. 1729, Masahiro Mambo and Yuliang Zheng, Eds., Springer-Verlag, Berlin, 1999, pp. 191–201.

83. Zeng, W., Wen, J., and Severa, M., Fast Self-Synchronous Content Scrambling by Spatially Shuffling Codewords of Compressed Bitstream, in *Proceedings of IEEE International Conference on Image Processing (ICIP'2002)*, Vol. III, 2002, pp. 169–172.

84. Qiao. L. and Nahrstedt, K., Is MPEG Encryption by using Random List instead of ZigZag Order Secure?, in *Proceedings of IEEE International Symposium on Consumer Electronics (ISCE'97)*, 1997, pp. 332–335.

85. Uehara, T. and Safavi-Naini, R., Chosen DCT Coefficients Attack on MPEG Encryption Schemes, in *Proceedings of IEEE Pacific-Rim Conference on Multimedia (IEEE-PCM'2000)*, 2000, pp. 316–319.

86. Shi, C. and Bhargava, B., An Efficient MPEG Video Encryption Algorithm, in *Proceedings of IEEE Symposium on Reliable Distributed Systems*, 1998, pp. 381–386.

87. Shi, C. and Bhargava, B., A Fast MPEG Video Encryption Algorithm, in *Proceedings of 6th ACM International Conference on Multimedia*, 1998, pp. 81–88.

88. Shi, C., Wang, S.-Y., and Bhargava, B., MPEG Video Encryption in Real-Time using Secret Key Cryptography, in *Proceedings of International Conference on Parallel and Distributed Processing Techniques and Applications (PDPTA'99)*, 1999, pp. 191–201.

89. Pazarci, M. and Dipçin, V., A MPEG-transparent scrambling technique, *IEEE Trans. Consumer Eletron.*, 48(2), 2002, 345–355.

90. Bao, F., Deng, R., Feng, P., Guo, Y., and Wu, H., Secure and Private Distribution of Online Video and Some Related Cryptographic Issues, in *Information Security and Privacy: The 6th Australasian Conference (ACISP 2001) Proceedings, Lecture Notes in Computer Science*, Vol. 2119, Vijay Varadharajan and Yi Mu, Eds., 2001, pp. 190–205.

91. Li, S., Analyses and New Designs of Digital Chaotic Ciphers, Ph.D. thesis, School of Electronics & Information Engineering, Xi'an Jiaotong University, Xi'an, China, 2003; available http://www.hooklee.com/pub.html (in both Chinese and English).

92. Pichler, F. and Scharinger, J., Finite Dimensional Generalized Baker Dynamical Systems for Cryptographic Applications, in *Proceedings of 5th International Workshop on Computer Aided Systems Theory (EuroCAST'95), Lecture Notes in Computer Science*, Vol. 1030, Franz Pichler, Robert Moreno-Díaz and Rudolf F. Albrecht, Eds., 1996, pp. 465–476.

93. Scharinger, J., Fast Encryption of Image Data using Chaotic Kolmogorov Flows, in *Storage and Retrieval for Image and Video Databases V, Proc. SPIE*, Vol. 3022, Ishwar K. Sethi and Ramesh C. Jain, Eds., 1997, pp. 278–289

94. Scharinger, J., Secure and Fast Encryption using Chaotic Kolmogorov Flows, in *Proceedings of IEEE Information Theory Workshop (ITW'98)*, 1998, pp. 124–125.

95. Scharinger, J., Fast encryption of image data using chaotic Kolmogorov flows, *J. Electronic Imaging*, 7(2), 318–325, 1998.

96. Fridrich, J., Image Encryption based on Chaotic Maps, in *Proceedings of IEEE International Conference on Sysytems, Man and Cybernetics (ICSMC'97)*, Vol. 2, 1997, pp. 1105–1110.

97. Fridrich, J., Secure Image Ciphering Based on Chaos, Technical Report RL-TR-97-155, the Information Directorate (former Rome Laboratory) of the Air Force Research Laboratory, New York, 1997.

98. Fridrich, J., Symmetric ciphers based on two-dimensional chaotic maps, *Int. J. Bifurcat. Chaos*, 8(6), 1259–1284, 1998.

99. Salleh, M., Ibrahim, S., and Isinn, I.F., Ciphering Key of Chaos Image Encryption, in *Proceedings of International Conference on Artificial Intelligence in Engineering and Technology (ICAIET'2002)*, 2002, pp. 58–62.

100. Salleh, M., Ibrahim, S., and Isinn, I.F., Enhanced Chaotic Image Encryption Algorithm based on Baker's Map, in *Proceedings of IEEE Int. Symposium on Circuits and Systems (ISCAS'2003)*, Vol. II, 2003, pp. 508–511.

101. Qi, D., Zou, J., and Han X., A new class of scrambling transformation and its application in the image information covering, *Sci. in China E (Engl. Ed.)*, 43(3), 304–312, 2000.

102. Mao, Y., Chen, G., and Lian, S., A novel fast image encryption scheme based on 3D chaotic Baker maps, *Int. J. Bifurcat. Chaos*, in press.

103. Mao, Y. and Chen, G., Chaos-based image encryption, in *Handbook of Computational Geometry for Pattern Recognition, Computer Vision, Neural Computing and Robotics*, Bayco-Corrochano, E., Ed., Springer-Verlag, Heidelberg, 2004.

104. Mao, Y., Research on Chaos-based Image Encryption and Watermarking Technology, Ph.D. thesis, Nanjing University of Science & Technology, Nanjing, China, 2003 (in Chinese).

105. Mao, Y., Chen, G., and Chui, C.K., A symmetric image encryption scheme based on 3D chaotic Cat maps, *Chaos, Solitons Fractals*, 21(1), 749–761, 2004.

106. Miyamoto, M., Tanaka, K., and Sugimura, T., Truncated Baker transformation and its extension to image encryption, in *Mathematics of Data/Image Coding, Compression, and Encryption II, Proc. SPIE*, Vol. 3814, Mark S. Schmalz, Ed., 1999, pp. 13–25.

107. Yano, K. and Tanaka, K., Image encryption scheme based on a truncated Baker transformation, *IEICE Trans. Fundamentals*, E85-A(9), 2025–2035, 2002.

108. Zunino, R., Fractal circuit layout for spatial decorrelation of images, *Electron. Lett.*, 34(20), 1929–1930, 1998.

109. Bottini, S., An algebraic model of an associative noise-like coding memory, *Biol. Cybern.*, 36(4), 221–228, 1980.

110. Parodi, G., Ridella, S., and Zunino, R., Using chaos to generate keys for associative noise-like coding memories, *Neural Networks*, 6(4), 559–572, 1993.

111. Matias, Y. and Shamir, A., A video scrambing technique based on space filling curve (extended abstract), in *Advances in Cryptology–Crypto'87, Lecture Notes in Computer Science*, Vol. 293, Carl Pomerance, Ed., Springer-Verlag, Berlin, 1987, pp. 398–417.

112. Bertilsson, M., Brickell, E.F., and Ingemarson, I., Cryptanalysis of video encryption based on space-filling curves, in *Advances in Cryptology–EuroCrypt'88, Lecture Notes in Computer Science*, Vol. 434, Jean-Jacques Quisquater and Joos Vandewalle, Eds., Springer-Verlag, Berlin, 1989, pp. 403–411.

113. Bourbakis, N.G. and Alexopoulos, C., A fractal-based image processing language: formal modeling, *Pattern Recogn.*, 32(2), 317–338, 1999.

114. Bourbakis, N.G. and Alexopoulos, C., Picture data encryption using SCAN patterns, *Pattern Recogn.*, 25(6), 567–581, 1992.

115. Alexopoulos, C., Bourbakis, N.G., and Ioannou, N., Image encryption method using a class of fratcals, *J. Electron. Imaging*, 4(3), 251–259, 1995.

116. Bourbakis, N.G., Image Data Compression-Encryption using G-SCAN Pattern, in *Proceedings of IEEE International Conference on Systems, Man and Cybernetics*, Vol. 2, 1997, pp. 1117–1120.

117. Chang, H.K.-C. and Liu, J.-L., A linear quadtree compression scheme for image encryption, *Signal Process.: Image Commun.*, 10(4), 279–290, 1997.

118. Chung, K.-L. and Chang, L.-C., Large encryption binary images with higher security, *Pattern Recogn. Lett.*, 19(5–6), 461–468, 1998.

119. Maniccam, S.S. and Bourbakis, N.G., SCAN based Lossless Image Compression and Encryption, in *Proceedings of IEEE International Conference on Information Intelligence and Systems (ICIIS'99)*, pp. 490–499, 1999.

120. Bourbakis, N.G. and Dollas, A., SCAN-based compression–encryption-hiding for video on demand, *IEEE Multimedia*, 10(3), 79–87, 2003.

121. Maniccam, S.S. and Bourbakis, N.G., Image and video encryption using SCAN pattern, *Pattern Recogn.*, 37(4), 725–737, 2004, http://www.sciencedirect.com, 2003.

122. Bourbakis, N.G., Brause, R., and Alexopoulos, C., SCAN image compression/ encryption hardware system, in *Digital Video Compression: Algorithms and Technologies 1995, Proc. SPIE*, Vol. 2419, Arturo A. Rodriguez, Robert J. Safranek and Edward J. Delp III, Eds., 1995, pp. 419–428.

123. Dollas, A., Kachris, C., and Bourbakis, N.G., Performance Analysis of Fixed, Reconfigurable, and Custom Architectures for the SCAN Image and Video Encryption Algorithm, in *Proceedings of 11th Annual IEEE Symposium on Field-Programmable Custom Computing Machines (FCCM'2003)*, 2003, pp. 19–28.

124. Kachris, C., Bourbakis, N.G., and Dollas, A., A reconfigurable logic-based processor for the SCAN image and video encryption algorithm, *Int. J. Parallel Program.*, 31(6), 489–506, 2003.

125. Jan, J.-K. and Tseng, Y.-M., On the security of image encryption method, *Inf. Process. Lett.*, 60(5), 261–265, 1996.

126. Chang, C.-C., and Yu, T.-X., Cryptanalysis of an encryption scheme for binary images, *Pattern Recogn. Lett.*, 23(14), 1847–1852, 2002.

127. Roskin, K.M. and Casper, J.B., From Chaos to Cryptography, http://xcrypt.theory. org/paper, 1999.

128. Murali, K., Yu, H., Varadan, V., and Leung, H., Secure communication using a chaos based signal encryption scheme, *IEEE Trans. Consumer Eletron.*, 47(4), 709–714, 2001.

129. Peng, J., Liao, X., and Wu, Z., Digital Image Secure Communication using Chebyshev Map Sequences, in *Proceedings of IEEE International Conference on Communications, Circuits and Systems and West Sino Expositions (ICCCS'2002)*, 2002, pp. 492–496.

130. Murali, K., Leung, H., Preethi, K.S., and Mohamed, I.R., Spread spectrum image encoding and decoding using ergodic chaos, *IEEE Trans. Consuming Eletron.*, 49(1), 59–63, 2003.

131. Yen, J.-C. and Guo, J.-I., A New Hierarchical Chaotic Image Encryption Algorithm and Its Hardware Architecture, in *Proceedings of 9th (Taiwan) VLSI Design/CAD Symposium*, 1998.

132. Yen, J.-C. and Guo, J.-I., A New Chaotic Image Encryption Algorithm, in *Proceedings (Taiwan) National Symposium on Telecommunications*, 1998, pp. 358–362.

133. Guo, J.-I., Yen, J.-C., and Jen-Chieh Yeh., The Design and Realization of a New Hierarchical Chaotic Image Encryption Algorithm, in *Proceedings of International Symposium on Communications (ISCOM'99)*, 1999, pp. 210–214.

134. Guo, J.-I. and Yen, J.-C. A New Mirror-like Image Encryption Algorithm and Its VLSI Architecture, in *Proceedings of 10th (Taiwan) VLSI Design/CAD Symposium*, 1999, pp. 327–330.

135. Yen, J.-C. and Guo, J.-I., A Chaotic Neural Network for Signal Encryption/Decryption and Its VLSI Architecture, in *Proceedings of 10th (Taiwan) VLSI Design/CAD Symposium*, 1999, pp. 319–322.

136. Yen, J.-C. and Guo, J.-I., A New MPEG/Encryption System and Its VLSI Architecture, in *Proceedings of international Symposium on Communications (ISCOM'99)*, 1999, pp. 215–219.

137. Yen, J.-C. and Guo, J.-I., A New Image Encryption Algorithm and Its VLSI Architecture, in *Proceedings of IEEE Workshop on Signal Processing Systems (SiPS'99)*, 1999, pp. 430–437.

138. Yen, J.-C. and Guo, J.-I., A New Chaotic Key-Based Design for Image Encryption and Decryption, in *Proceedings of IEEE Int. Symposium on Circuits and Systems 2000*, Vol. 4, 2000, pp. 49–52.

139. Yen, J.-C. and Guo, J.-I., Efficient hierarchical chaotic image encryption algorithm and its VLSI realisation, *IEEE Proc. Vis. Image Signal Process.*, 147(2), 167–175, 2000.

140. Su, S., Lin, A., and Yen, J.-C., Design and Realization of a New Chaotic Neural Encryption/Decryption Network, in *Proceedings of IEEE Asia–Pacific Conference on Circuits and Systems (APCCAS'2000)*, 2000, pp. 335–338.

141. Yen, J.-C. and Guo, J.-I., A new chaotic mirror-like image encryption algorithm and its VLSI architechture, *Pattern Recogn. Image Anal. (Adv. Math. Theory Applic.)*, 10(2), 236–247, 2000.

142. Guo, J.-I., Yen, J.-C., and Lin, J.-I., The FPGA Realization of a New Image Encryption/Decryption Design, in *Proceedings of 12th (Taiwan) VLSI Design/CAD Symposium*, 2001.

143. Yen, J.-C. and Guo, J.-I.,The design and realization of a chaotic neural signal security system, *Pattern Recogn. and Image Anal. (Adv. in Math. Theory, Applic)*, 12(1), 70–79, 2002.

144. Yen, J.-C. and Guo, J.-I., Design of a New Signal Security System, in *Proceedings of IEEE International Symposium on Circuits and Systems (ISCAS'2002)*, Vol. IV, 2002, pp. 121–124.

145. Yen, J.-C. and Guo, J.-I., The design and realization of a new domino signal security system, *J. Chin. Inst. Electr. Engi. (Trans. Chin. Inst. Engi. E)*, 10(1), 69–76, 2003.

146. Chen, H.-C., and Yen, J.-C., A new cryptography system and its VLSI realization, *J. Systems Architechture*, 49(7–9), 355–367, 2003.

147. Chen, H.-C., Yen, J.-C., and Guo, J.-I., Design of a New Cryptography System, in *Advances in Multimedia Information Processing — PCM 2002: Third IEEE Pacific Rim Conference on Multimedia Proceedings, Lecture Notes in Computer Science*, Vol. 2532, Yung-Chang Chen, Long-Wen Chang, and Chiou-Ting, Hsu, Eds., Springer-Verlag, Berlin, 2002, pp. 1041–1048.

148. Lasota, A. and Mackey, M.C., *Chaos, Fractals, and Noise: Stochastic Aspects of Dynamics*, 2nd ed., Springer-Verlag, New York, 1997.

149. Li, S. and Zheng, X., On the Security of an Image Encryption Method, in *Proceedings of IEEE International Conference on Image Processing (ICIP'2002)*, Vol. 2, 2002, pp. 925–928.

150. Li, S. and Zheng, X., Cryptanalysis of a Chaotic Image Encryption Method, in *Proceedings of IEEE International Symposium on Circuits and Systems (ISCAS'2002)*, Vol. II, 2002, pp. 708–711.

151. Li, S., Li, C., Chen, G., and Mou, X., Cryptanalysis of the RCES/RSES image encryption scheme, submitted to *IEEE Trans. Image Processing*, 2004.

152. Belkhouche, F. and Qidwai, U., Binary Image Encoding using 1D Chaotic Maps, in *Proceedings of Annual Conference of IEEE Region 5*, 2003, pp. 39–43.

153. Voyatzis, G. and Pitas, I., Digital image watermarking using mixing systems, *Computers Graphics*, 22(4), 405–416, 1998.

154. Scharinger, J., Secure Digital Watermark Generation based on Chaotic Kolmogorov Flows, in *Security and Watermarking of Multimedia Contents II, Proc. SPIE*, Vol. 3971, Ping W. Wong and Edward J. Delp III, Eds., 2000, pp. 306–313.
155. Nikolaidis, N., Tsekeridou, S., Nikolaidis, A., Tefas, A., Solachidis, V., and Pitas, I., Applications of Chaotic Signal Processing Techniques to Multimedia Watermarking, in *Proceedings of IEEE workshop on Nonlinear Dynamics in Electronic Systems*, 2000, pp. 1–7.
156. Lou, D.-C., Yin, T.-L., and Chang, M.-C., An efficient steganographic approach, *Computer Syst. Sci. Eng.*, 17(4/5), 263–273, 2002.
157. Tefas, A., Nikolaidis, A., Nikolaidis, N., Solachidis, V., Tsekeridou, S., and Pitas, I., Performance analysis of correlation-based watermarking schemes employing Markov chaotic sequences, *IEEE Trans. Signal Process.*, 51(7), 1979–1994, 2003.
158. Chiaraluce, F., Ciccarelli, L., Gambi, E., Pierleoni, P., and Reginelli, M., A new chaotic algorithm for video encryption, *IEEE Trans. Consumer Eletron.*, 48(4), 838–844, 2002.
159. Li, S., Zheng, X., Mou, X., and Cai, Y., Chaotic Encryption Scheme for Real-Time Digital Video, in *Real-Time Imaging VI, Proc. SPIE*, Vol. 4666, Nasser Kehtarnavaz, Ed., 2002, pp. 149–160.

5

Key Management and Protection for IP Multimedia

Rolf Blom, Elisabetta Carrara, Fredrik Lindholm, Karl Norrman, and Mats Näslund

INTRODUCTION

IP multimedia services have, as the name indicates, the Internet Protocol (IP) suite as a common communication platform. However, the open Internet has achieved a poor reputation with respect to security and, today, security problems end up in media headlines and users have become much more security-aware. Thus, strong security of multimedia applications will be an absolute requirement for their general and widespread adoption. This chapter describes a general framework for how to secure multimedia services.

The popularity of multimedia applications is not only a growing market for the fixed-access Internet users, but it is also an increasing and promising market in the emerging third generation (3G) of mobile communications. This calls for more adaptive multimedia applications, which can work both in a more constrained environment (such as cellular or modem access) and broadband networks. Environments with a mixture of different network types are usually referred to as heterogeneous networks.

The main topic of interest in this chapter is restricted to the protection of streaming media (e.g., audio and video sessions) in heterogeneous environments. Protection of downloadable content and session establishment is also handled, but only to give the needed context. The focus is on a few specific IP multimedia applications and their security, the key management protocol Multimedia Internet KEYing (MIKEY) [1], and the media security protocol Secure Real-time Transport Protocol (SRTP) [2]. Both of these protocols have been developed by the Internet Engineering Task Force (IETF).

A basic overview of the main threats for IP multimedia applications is provided, together with a brief summary of common countermeasures. It is often critical to provide security from a service acceptance point of view, but it may also have major impact on service performance. There are, in particular, some constrained environments where security solutions may encounter problems (e.g., in the emerging heterogeneous networks as documented later). SRTP and MIKEY together can implement an efficient security solution for IP multimedia applications in heterogeneous environments. Basic scenarios and a walk-through of typical multimedia session instances are described to show how the two security protocols are used.

Some parts of the chapter assume that the reader is somewhat familiar with cryptography, and we refer to Reference 3 for extended background on this area.

Threats and Countermeasures

There are several security threats that can undermine the deployment of multimedia applications. Some of the more urgent threats to prevent are the following:

Unauthorized access to services

Unauthorized access to sensitive data (violation of confidentiality)

Message manipulation

Rogue or replayed messages

Disturbance or misuse of network services (often leading to reduced availability)

Common security countermeasures against such threats are the following:

User authentication, which can be used to mitigate unauthorized access to services and which is commonly achieved using digital signatures

Confidentiality protection, which can be achieved by encrypting data

Integrity protection, which can be achieved by applying a so-called Message Authentication Code (MAC) on the message or by applying a digital signature

Replay protection, which is usually achieved by keeping track of previously received messages in combination with integrity protection of the messages

Assertion of data origin authentication is an important security function in certain group-communication scenarios. Integrity protection alone does not always guarantee that the message actually comes from a given source. It does so in peer-to-peer communication, where integrity protection is also a form of data origin authentication (though repudiable [i.e., the sender can deny the transmission of the message]), as only the two peers know the secret key. However, in a group scenario, where the key is shared among the members, integrity protection can only guarantee that the message comes (unmodified) from a member of the group. A malicious member could alter the message sent from another member or could send the message impersonating another member and would not be discovered. Data origin authentication is commonly provided by use of certificates and digital signatures. This also guarantees nonrepudiation, a security function that, however, is seldom implemented for media or signaling traffic, as it is computationally expensive.

Finally, the threat of misusing content in the form of duplicating it, copying it, and so forth may be an important aspect in applications requiring Digital Rights Management (DRM), but it is largely out of the scope of this chapter. However, it should be noted that a security protocol, coupled with proper key management, can serve as a central ingredient in providing DRM.

Basic Mechanisms

The security of data in transmission is implemented by a *security protocol*. A security protocol provides rules and formatting of the packet so that security functions such as encryption and integrity protection can be applied to the transmitted message.

There exist a few different mechanisms to secure general IP communication. The IP Security Protocol (IPsec) [4] is a well-known security protocol for protecting IP traffic, operating at the network layer. Virtual private networks (VPNs) based on IPsec are a common way to secure traffic, especially network-to-network traffic. The International Telecommunication Union (ITU) H.323 [5] forms a set of protocols for voice, video, and data conferencing over packet-based networks and also defines its security solution in the H.235 specification [6]. H.235 uses an application security protocol for protecting the media traffic. A later version of H.235 (version 3) [7] adopts, as well, the IETF protocol SRTP.

The parameters needed by the security protocols, such as keys and which cryptographic algorithms to use, are exchanged via a *key management protocol* executed prior to the data transmission, typically at session setup time.

The Transport Layer Security (TLS) protocol [8] is functioning both as a key management protocol and as a security protocol mostly for applications using the Transport Control Protocol (TCP) and may, for example, be used to secure signaling protocols like H.323 and the Session Initiation Protocol (SIP) [9]. Internet Key Exchange (IKE) [10] is the key management protocol used for exchanging parameters for IPsec. H.323 exchanges the security parameters for securing the media session within the signaling protocol (already protected by TLS or IPsec). IETF has developed a few key management protocols for multicast and groups; among them is MIKEY, which is also adopted in the new version of H.235.

In this chapter, the main focus is on IP multimedia applications based on IETF-based protocols, such as SIP for signaling and the Real-Time Transport Protocol (RTP) [11], together with the Real-Time Transport Control Protocol (RTCP) [11] for the media transport. Figure 5.1 gives an overview of the protocols and their placement in the stack in relation to other protocols. As already discussed, security may be applied on different levels, either at the network layer by applying IPsec or higher

Figure 5.1. Overview of the IP multimedia protocols and their relationships to other protocols.

up in the stack by, for example, using SRTP to protect the RTP traffic and TLS to protect the signaling traffic.

Security in Heterogeneous Networks

The design of protocols suitable for heterogeneous environments forces the designers to consider worst-case scenarios, in terms of bandwidth limitation, bit errors, round-trip delays, and so forth. Hence, the heterogeneous environments pose constraints, both on the multimedia applications as such and on the security solutions. In other words, when a communication path consists of several links with very different characteristics, it is the most restrictive link (with respect to bandwidth, bit-error rate, etc.) that dictates the requirements when end-to-end protection is desired. Indeed, true end-to-end protection is the only method that will guarantee security in this case, as one usually cannot be sure that all "hops" along the path are sufficiently secured. Although it is, in general, possible to apply security at lower layers (e.g., secure VPNs based on IPsec), applying security at the application layer allows one to better tune the security protocols to a given scenario and application.

A first concern when designing protocols for heterogeneous environments is that the addition of security should not affect the service in any drastic way (e.g., in terms of convenience and resource consumption). In cellular networks, spectrum efficiency is clearly a major factor for the though-break of any service. To a great extent, this has been the motivation for the work in (robust) header compression for IP protocols, particularly important for applications with short packets such as Voice-over-IP-over-Wireless. Encryption may obstruct header compression when applied before it, as it introduces randomness, hence effectively causing a major increase in bandwidth cost. Other common properties to strive for when designing a security protocol are low bandwidth overhead, low number of extra round-trips, and low computational cost.

SCENARIOS

There are many different types of multimedia applications, all with different characteristics and requirements. The targeted environments, with all the assumptions that can be made of the underlying network and end devices, also affect these applications. When considering security, it may not always be possible to use one single solution for all types of multimedia applications; instead, the scenario and environment may force different types of solution. As an example, an application may use TLS to secure downloadable content. However, the application would not be able to reuse the TLS session to also secure the streaming session that uses RTP over UDP (instead, it could use SRTP to secure the RTP session).

This section gives an overview of the scenarios considered in this chapter and also specific security requirements that these scenarios may put on a security solution. For all these scenarios, it is assumed that the network environment is of a heterogeneous nature.

Conversational Multimedia Scenario

In a conversational multimedia scenario, two (or more) users interact with each other in real-time, usually using, for example, a Voice/Video-over-IP application between the involved parties. To be able to send the media between the involved parties, the users must first locate and contact each other using some type of session establishment protocol (see section "Session Establishment"). The session establishment protocols are specially designed to handle the media sessions between the parties, which include operations such as creating new media sessions, tearing down media sessions, and negotiating codecs and other media-specific parameters. As will be shown in section "Protecting the IP Multimedia Sessions," session establishment can also play an important role in media security establishment.

In the example scenario of Figure 5.2, Alice uses SIP to establish a call to Bob (see also section "Session Establishment" for more discussion about SIP). This is done by first contacting Alice's SIP proxy, which, in turn, locates Bob's SIP proxy. As Bob's SIP proxy knows the whereabouts of Bob, it can, in turn, contact Bob. When Bob answers and accepts the incoming call, this is also signaled with SIP (along the same path). In general, SIP signaling is sent in hop-by-hop fashion with the SIP proxies as intermediate nodes.

Figure 5.2. Example of the establishment of a two-party SIP call.

The media traffic is, in contrast to the signaling traffic, sent directly between the end nodes. The reason why this can be done is simply because when session establishment has been executed, the parties will have the direct contact information of the others.

In an unprotected environment, Mallory (the malicious attacker) can launch many different types of attack. The unprotected session establishment is vulnerable to attacks such as media session redirection or hijacking (i.e., directing the media streams to a destination other than the intended one), fake calls, and different types of denial-of-service attack (e.g., by tearing down established media sessions). The unprotected media itself is vulnerable to attacks such as eavesdropping and message manipulation.

Small-Size Group Scenario

In a two-party conference, it is sometimes desired to have the possibility of inviting further participants into the call in an ad hoc manner. The most straightforward approach is, as in the example of Figure 5.3, to have one of the current participants invite the new member and also handle the media flows between the new and existing members. This scenario has its limitations, as it will put high resource demands (both on the processing power and the available bandwidth) on the members as the number of members in the group increases. From a security point of view, this approach will not need much extra security functionality compared to the normal conversational multimedia scenario. However,

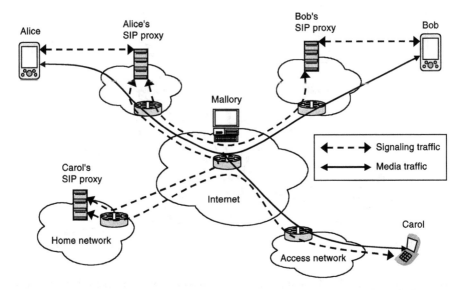

Figure 5.3. Example of a two-party SIP call with the invitation of a third party.

171

the member controlling the group will need to have one security relationship with each participant to protect the direct communication with the other group members. An additional requirement may be that of backward (forward) security: a party that joins (leaves) the group must not have access to previous (future) communication. This is a key management issue.

One way to circumvent the scalability problem is to use a multicast conference. In that case, the media traffic will be sent on the multicast channel to all available members, and only the signaling traffic will need to be sent on a peer-to-peer basis between the member handling the group and all other members. However, it should be noted that multicast groups are usually prearranged and are not generally set up on an ad hoc basis. From a security perspective, a multicast conference will imply demands, both on the security protocol for the media (e.g., it must be possible to use for multicast delivery) and on the key management protocol (i.e., it must be possible to deliver a group key that can be used by all members).

In the scenario of Figure 5.4, a centralized group controller is used, commonly referred to as a multipoint control unit (MCU). The MCU is the contact point for all members in the group. A benefit of this approach is, of course, that the media mixing is done on a dedicated server and that the conference is not dependent on the equipment and availability of one member only.

Figure 5.4. Example of a multiparty SIP conference with a centralized control unit.

Securing the media traffic and signaling will not be much different from the conversational multimedia scenario, as individual security relationships between the MCU and the members are needed. However, this scenario assumes that the members can trust the MCU to act fairly and not leak information (so any server could not function as a secure MCU).

One issue that has not been treated so far for these scenarios is authorization for the groups (i.e., who is allowed to join the group and what are they privileged to do). In a peer-to-peer environment, it is common practice to base the authorization on preshared keys, certificates, and so forth. In a group, this can sometimes be more complicated, as, for example, two communicating parties may have different authorization policies. One simple approach for handling group authorization is to allow the group controller to be the only one handling these policies (assuming the existence of a group controller). In the case where no group controller exists or the controller delegates the possibility of inviting new members to other controllers or members, the group authorization policies are negotiated and distributed when the group is set up.

Streaming Scenario

Figure 5.5 shows a streaming scenario where one sender distributes media to multiple receivers (using a normal client/server model). The media distribution can be done either by using unicast distribution (e.g., by a video-on-demand application) or by using multicast distribution (e.g., Web TV broadcast application). Signaling is often done on

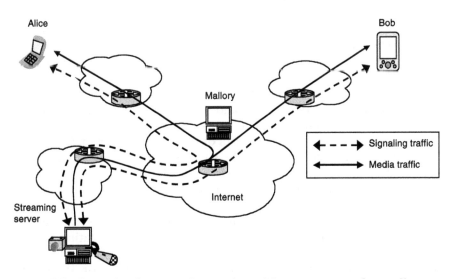

Figure 5.5 Example of a streaming session with one server and two clients.

173

an individual basis between the client and the server. From a security perspective, this scenario is quite similar to the multicast group scenario (without a centralized controller).

SESSION ESTABLISHMENT

The scenarios described above show the use of signaling protocols for the setup of the communication. Two major standard signaling protocols are the ITU H.323 and the IETF SIP. They are both intended for setup, control, and tear-down of sessions, although their designs are based on very different network models. The IETF RTSP [12] is another example of signaling protocol, aimed at client-to-server streaming communication. These signaling protocols often carry a protocol describing the session parameters, such as codecs and ports. One such protocol is the Session Description Protocol (SDP) [13]. There are then cases where the session is just announced (e.g., for multicast communications), where announcement protocols like SAP [14] are used.

The threats against signaling protocols are clearly many, as they control the entire session; it is, therefore, particularly important to provide them with protection. The security applicable to signaling protocols is strongly dependent on the protocol architecture and is defined in the correspondent standards. H.323 (with its security solution, H.235) and SIP make use of hop-by-hop IPsec or TLS, and SIP defines the use of the Secure Multipurpose Internet Mail Extensions (SMIME) protocol [15] for end-to-end protection. The Real-Time Streaming Protocol (RTSP) currently uses HTTP security, whereas SAP has no real security solution defined.

A trust model identifies the relation between different actors in a system. The trust model is very dependent on the setting in which the application is used. However, some generalization can be made. Figure 5.6 depicts the trust model for a general SIP call. As shown, there may be a need to have one trust relationship with and between all the proxies to secure the signaling traffic and another trust relationship to secure the media traffic on an end-to-end basis. The reason for this is that the proxies need to be able to read parts of the signaling messages in order to route the message correctly (in some situations, the proxies may also need to modify parts of the message). Thus, to "feel secure," one needs to trust each pair of proxies to sufficiently protect the signaling between them against "third parties" and also that they do not try to read or manipulate the signaling in a malicious way. However, as the media traffic is sent directly between the two communicating parties, the proxies will not need to access the media traffic, which, therefore, can be sent protected end-to-end. Sometimes, mixers or translators

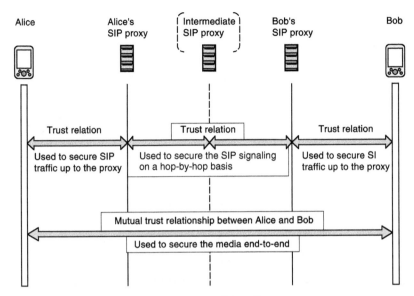

Figure 5.6. A typical trust model for an SIP call.

are needed to harmonize the media communications; in this case, the middlebox typically operates as security endpoints as it needs to have full access to the media.

MULTIMEDIA INTERNET KEYING

Any security protocol providing security functions such as confidentiality and integrity protection requires that the sender and receivers have established a so-called Security Association (SA), which describes how to enable and use the security protocol in a trusted manner. The SA is generally represented by a shared set of data and security parameters (e.g., the cryptographic key used and the encryption/ authentication algorithm used). Typically, these parameters are agreed upon with the aid of a key management protocol. The term "key management protocol" is a slightly misleading but commonly used term for protocols that establish security associations between two or more entities. This section describes the key management protocol Multimedia Internet KEYing (MIKEY).

Overview

A multimedia application in general includes more than one media session that needs protection; for example, a conversational multimedia application can be expected to have two audio streams (one in each

Figure 5.7. The tasks and main objects of MIKEY.

direction) and two video streams (also one in each direction) between the involved parties. To protect these media sessions, a security protocol needs to be applied for each separate session (e.g., SRTP in the case of RTP traffic; see also section "The Secure Real-Time Transport Protocol"). It would be inconvenient to separately set up a security association for each protected media session, as that would increase both computational cost and the required number of message exchanges between the parties. MIKEY allows setting up security associations for multiple protected media sessions in one run of the protocol. In MIKEY, a protected media session is generally referred to as a crypto session (CS). A collection of CSs is called a crypto session bundle (CSB) (e.g., corresponding to a multimedia session).

The main target of MIKEY (see Figure 5.7) is to establish an SA and a corresponding set of traffic encryption keys (TEKs) for each CS. This is accomplished by first running the key transport and exchange mechanism, which establishes the SA and so-called TEK generation keys (TGKs) at all entities involved in the communication. When the TGK is in place, individual TEKs for each CS can be derived from these TGKs using a predetermined key derivation function.

The SA includes parameters required to protect the traffic for the security protocol such as algorithms used and key lifetimes. What parameters actually go into the SA is dependent on the security protocol used. Note that different media streams within the same multimedia session could for example use completely different protection algorithms or different key sizes.

176

Key Establishment Methods

Because the scope of MIKEY includes thin devices as well as computationally stronger ones, the main goal is to provide strong security but inducing as small a computational load as possible. Furthermore, the number of round-trips is a crucial factor for wireless networks, in particular for cellular networks, where the round-trip times can be quite long. To address both the most extreme scenario and the more general one, MIKEY provides three different key establishment methods. These methods are a transport method based on preshared symmetric keys, an asymmetric-key-based transport method, and a Diffie–Hellman (DH)-based key agreement method.

The messages used by MIKEY to establish a CSB are constructed by several building blocks, called payloads. For instance, each message does first include a header payload, which includes information on the crypto session identifier. After the header, additional payloads are added containing information such as timestamp, encrypted TGKs, and signature. This subsection will not go into depth on the payload and encoding of the messages, but will concentrate on the cryptographic characteristic of the different key establishment methods.

Preshared Key Method. The preshared key method is based on the assumption that the involved parties have established a trust relationship by agreeing on a preshared key. The agreement of the preshared key is outside the scope for the protocol but can, for example, be done by using another cryptographic protocol or by physical distribution of the key (e.g., using smartcards or CDs), other types of out-of-band signaling, or a previous run of MIKEY. The preshared key, K, is used to derive one encryption key, K_E, and one authentication key, K_A, in a cryptographically independent manner (see section "Deriving Keys"). These keys are later used to protect the MIKEY message.

The protocol is executed, as shown in Figure 5.8, by the Initiator creating a message P including the CSB identifier (ID_{CSB}) to which the

Figure 5.8. Message sequence chart for the preshared key method.

message corresponds, a timestamp (T), optionally its own identity (ID_I), a random number (R), and the TGKs protected using the encryption key K_E (E_{KE} [TGKs]). The message is then sent together with other required information (M), such as the security protocol parameters, to the Responder. The entire communication is integrity protected using a MAC, which is keyed using the authentication key, K_A.

The Responder verifies the MAC and, if correctly verified, processes the MIKEY message. (This order, verify-then-process, improves resistance to denial-of-service attacks.) The Responder can then extract the TGKs and other necessary information to create the SA out of the MIKEY message. If requested by the Initiator, the Responder creates a verification message, including a MAC, which is sent back to the Initiator as proof that the Responder correctly received the keys and parameters.

This method uses no computationally demanding operations and can be performed in less than or equal to one round-trip. Furthermore, the messages are short, because only symmetric key cryptography is involved, reducing the delay over delay-sensitive links. Hence, it is highly suitable for thin devices connected over cellular networks. A drawback is, of course, the fact that a preshared key must be in place, but there are several scenarios where this is likely to be the case, such as the streaming scenario described earlier.

Public-Key Method. The public-key method, outlined in Figure 5.9, is very similar to the preshared-key method, with the main difference being that there is no longer any dependency on prior establishment of a shared key. The Initiator, instead, uses public keys and a so-called envelope approach; that is, the Initiator chooses a (pseudo-)randomly generated symmetric envelope key K_{ENV}, which is used to derive the keys K_E and K_A. The encryption key, K_E, is used as in the preshared-key

Figure 5.9. Message sequence chart for the public-key method.

case, to encrypt the TGKs, and the authentication key is similarly used to compute a MAC over the encrypted TGKs (compare this with the preshared-key case, where the MAC is computed over the entire message). The main difference from the preshared case is that the envelope key K_{ENV} is encrypted using the Responder's public key Pk_R, which results in the public-key envelope $E_{Pk_R}(K_{ENV})$.

In other words, using the public key of the Responder, the Initiator can securely send a key (K_{ENV}), which then can serve the same purpose as the preshared key did in the previous case. It might seem simpler to protect the TGK directly using the public key Pk_R. The rationale for the two-layer approach, introducing the intermediate envelope key, is that no matter how much "TGK material" is transported, one single public-key operation suffices to protect all the TGK material. Put differently, it is a trade of possible multiple public-key operations for symmetric-key operations, a significant saving.

When the Initiator sends the message to the Responder, the message is also signed using the Initiator's signing key (Pr_I). The Responder can authenticate the Initiator by verifying the signature. As for the preshared-key method, the Responder can obtain all TGKs and other necessary information to create the SAs from the received message. If requested by the Initiator, the Responder creates a verification message, equivalent to the one created in the preshared-key method, which is then sent back to the Initiator.

The public-key-based method includes both an asymmetric key encryption and a signing, in addition to the symmetric key operations required to encrypt the TGKs. The Responder has to verify the signature and possibly also the corresponding certificate/certificate chain, the latter to verify the authenticity of the Responder's public key. This makes this method far heavier computationalwise, compared to the preshared-key method. In a typical case (using RSA), the public-key operations of decryption and signature generation imply modular arithmetic (exponentiation) on very large numbers. This is the price that is paid for the greater flexibility of not having the need of preshared keys in place prior to running MIKEY. Note, however, that once the envelope key is in place, this key can be used as a preshared key for future sessions.

Diffie–Hellman Method. The Multimedia Internet KEYing protocol also includes a DH method [3], which, in contrast to the other two methods, is not based on key transport. Instead, the DH method requires that both parts participate in the creation of the TGK. The method relies on a "cryptographically suitable" finite cyclic group, G, generated by an element, g, in this group, and where g^x denotes g multiplied by itself x times (e.g., $g^3 = g \cdot g \cdot g$).

Figure 5.10. **Message sequence chart for the Diffie–Hellman method.**

The DH method is depicted in Figure 5.10. The Initiator starts with creating a message P including the CSB identifier (ID_{CSB}), a timestamp (T), a random number (R), optionally its own identifier (ID_I) or certificate ($Cert_I$), and its public DH value (g^x). The DH value is computed using the generator g of a chosen DH group and a (pseudo-)randomly chosen and secret value x. The message is then signed by the Initiator and sent to the Responder.

The Responder authenticates the Initiator by verifying the signature in the received message. If correctly verified, the Responder creates a response message similar to the Initiator's message, but also including its own public DH value (g^y).

The Initiator authenticates the Responder by verifying the signature included with the response message. Once each party has both g^x and g^y, they can independently compute the TGK as g^{xy}. Note that anyone listening in on the communication channel will be able to retrieve both g^x and g^y, but under the assumption on the hardness of the DH problem, this information is not sufficient to efficiently compute g^{xy}.

The DH method is clearly limited compared to the transport methods, in the sense that it can only be used in peer-to-peer communications (it is not possible to establish group keys) and that it can only provide one single TGK. Furthermore, it is usually even more computation-intensive than the public-key-based method because it (compared to, for example, RSA public-key methods) requires one additional modular exponentiation. Also, note that the second message may introduce extra delay compared to the other methods, as the message is not optional to send and, most importantly, it is larger and more demanding to generate than for the other methods.

Deriving Keys

Many times, it is desired to have the possibility to derive one or more keys from a "Master key." This is usually to avoid the need for an "avalanche" of keys to be created and communicated for different media sessions and purposes. However, to avoid decreasing the security of the system, such a derivation cannot be done using any method, but must be done in a way so that one derived key cannot be used to obtain another derived key, nor the Master key. The first property is usually referred to as an "independence" property and the latter one is usually referred to as "forward secrecy."

Multimedia Internet KEYing utilizes a key derivation function in two different contexts. In the first context, it is used to derive independent TEKs for multiple protection protocols from one single TGK (without compromising the security); that is, the TGK acts as a Master key for a number of TEKs. In the second context, it is used to compute the encryption key (K_E) and the authentication key (K_A), which are used to protect the messages sent during the key establishment phase in the preshared-key and public-key methods. These keys are the result of applying the key derivation function to either the preshared key (preshared method) or to the envelope key (public-key method). In the DH method of the protocol, the derivation function is used with the DH key, g^{xy}, to directly derive TEKs.

One of the common ways to fulfill the basic security requirements for the key derivation functions is to use a so-called pseudorandom function (PRF). Intuitively, this is a keyed function, $f(k, x)$, such that even after observing a large number of input–output pairs, $(x, f(k, x))$, an adversary gains no significant advantage in predicting the output corresponding to a new input, x' (nor does he learn k). This means that even if the adversary learns one key generated by the PRF, other keys generated are still secure, and these are precisely the desired properties we described earlier.

The PRF in MIKEY is quite similar to the one used in TLS. The differences lie in how the input key data is split and the MAC used. The outline of the PRF is depicted in Figure 5.11. The PRF takes a key (inkey) of specified length and a specific label (a "string") as inputs and then returns a derived key of specified length. The PRF splits the inkey into blocks of 256 bits, and each block is fed into the so-called P-function together with the label. All outputs from each of the computations are then combined using bitwise Exclusive-OR (XOR), denoted $\otimes$ in Figure 5.11, which results in the final key (outkey).

The P-function takes a so-called P-inkey and a seed as input and produces a bit string of required length. The P-function is built upon the HMAC function [16], where at a first layer, HMAC is computed using a so-called Output Feedback Mode with the seed as initial input value and the P-key as key. Each output of the HMAC in the first layer is then concatenated (denoted $\oplus$ in Figure 5.11) with the seed and fed into

Figure 5.11. Overview of the PRF used in MIKEY.

another "masking" layer of HMACs, which produces the final bit string of the P-function.

THE SECURE REAL-TIME TRANSPORT PROTOCOL

The Secure Real-Time Transport Protocol (SRTP) [2] is an application layer security protocol designed by the IETF community for RTP. SRTP secures RTP as well as the control protocol for RTP (RTCP). This section goes through the building blocks of SRTP and its applications.

The SRTP is not the only mechanism that can be used to secure RTP. For example, IPsec may be used as the network security protocol. However, as mentioned, applying security at the application level allows tuning of the security protocol to the needs of the application within a particular scenario (e.g., to reduce bandwidth consumption).

Protocol Overview

The SRTP is a profile of the Audio-Video Profile (AVP) of RTP (called Secure AVP [SAVP]), as it defines extensions to RTP and RTCP specifically to secure the applications. SRTP is built as a framework, following general practice to allow for future extensions of the protocol. This makes it possible to add new, possibly even more efficient algorithms in the future, and it ensures that it is possible to replace the current cryptographic algorithms if they reveal weaknesses in the future.

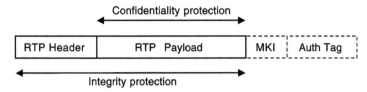

Figure 5.12. Overview of the SRTP packet.

The security parameters needed by SRTP are collected in the so-called cryptographic context. Parameters in the cryptographic context are, for example, the indication of the cryptographic algorithms used and the Master key. Some of the parameters are fixed during the session; others are updated per packets (e.g., replay protection information).

Protecting RTP. One of the main objectives of SRTP is to provide confidentiality, integrity, and replay protection for the RTP media stream. This is done by using a per-packet protection method, which is outlined in Figure 5.12. The confidentiality mechanism covers the original RTP payload, whereas integrity protection covers both the RTP payload and the RTP header.

An authentication tag is added after the RTP packet when integrity protection is desired. The authentication tag is created by computing a MAC over the RTP packet. The length of the authentication tag is variable and may, for example, be 32 or 80 bits (depending on the level of security needed vs. the desired bandwidth usage).

As an additional feature, a so-called Master Key Identifier (MKI) may be added to point to the current Master key used for confidentiality and integrity protection. The length of the MKI is dependent on the number of expected active Master keys but it would normally be on the order of 1 to 2 bytes. The MKI provides a simple way for the receiver to retrieve the correct key to process a received packet — in particular, in scenarios where the security policy is such that the sender changes the key frequently. In other, more simple configurations, such as with one stream per key and low-rate rekeying, the MKI can be omitted. Readers familiar with protocols such as IPsec can think of the MKI as a Security Parameter Index (SPI), with the difference that the MKI only identifies the key, not the other parameters.

Each SRTP packet is associated with an Index number. This Index number is used for the encryption algorithm and key synchronization and in conjunction with integrity protection to obtain replay protection. The Index number is a 48-bit number, where the lower 16 bits are the RTP sequence number (sent in the RTP packet header) and the remaining high-order 32 bits are a "rollover counter" (ROC), internal to SRTP. The

Figure 5.13.   Overview of the SRTCP packet.

ROC always starts at zero and is therefore only communicated explicitly when a receiver joins an ongoing session. The ROC is updated locally by observing wrap-arounds in the RTP sequence number space.

Protecting RTCP. The SRTP also provides confidentiality, integrity, and replay protection of the RTCP traffic (see Figure 5.13). Although optional for RTP, integrity protection is mandatory for RTCP. This is because RTCP is a control protocol, and, as such, it can inflict actions like termination of the session. The integrity of certain RTCP messages is therefore critical.

The definition of the Secure RTCP (SRTCP) packet is different from SRTP because the RTCP header does not carry a sequence number, which otherwise could have been reused. Therefore, SRTCP adds a 31-bit field at the end of the RTCP packet to synchronize the security processing, called the SRTCP Index. One extra bit preceding the SRTCP Index is the E-bit, a flag indicating if the packet is encrypted or not. This indication is required, as RTP allows the split of a compound RTCP packet into two lower-layer packets, of which one is encrypted and one is sent in the clear to facilitate network monitoring. Similar to SRTP packet construction, an MKI may be appended; the authentication tag is, as mentioned, always appended.

Efficiency. Because SRTP targets heterogeneous environments, one major design principle is bandwidth efficiency, which motivates several of the design choices. Limited message expansion is achieved by reusing existing fields for synchronization and by optionally adding variable-length fields, whose length can be policed according to the use case.

The encryption algorithms currently defined in SRTP are used in a way so that no additional field is needed (unless the MKI is used), nor is there any expansion of the payload due to padding. However, this may not hold with other encryption algorithms, possible to add in the future, for example, block ciphers, which require padding and explicit synchronization fields.

To allow further improvement in bandwidth savings, SRTP does not obstruct header compression of the RTP packet; that is, it is possible to apply header compression of the whole IP/UDP/RTP header while using SRTP. In order not to obstruct header compression, SRTP does not encrypt the headers; however, the RTP header may be integrity protected by SRTP (without conflicting with header compression). At the same time, this means that information such as payload type is not kept confidential, which, however, seems a reasonable compromise in most cases.

Note that the bandwidth factor is less critical with RTCP; therefore, adding some bytes and an authentication tag per packet is affordable. In fact, RTCP packets may be quite long and are sent less frequently than RTP packets, and RTP has rules for the bandwidth allocation to RTCP in a given session. Keeping in mind how many bytes SRTP adds to the RTCP packet allows for maintaining the same bandwidth sharing ratio (SRTCP packets are simply transmitted with slightly longer packet intervals).

Key Usage

Several cryptographic keys are needed by SRTP for different purposes. To make the key handling more manageable both for SRTP and the key management protocol, only one key (a so-called Master key) is required, from which SRTP can dynamically derive all other keys needed for the current session ("key splitting" procedure).

The SRTP may require as many as six session keys per instance of the protocol, according to which security functions are provided (a triplet for securing RTP and the equivalent but distinct triplet for RTCP):

A session encryption key to encrypt the data

A so-called session salt key, when required by the underlying encryption transform

A session authentication key to integrity protect the data

Similar to the MIKEY key derivation function (see section "Deriving Keys"), SRTP derives session keys using a PRF with the Master key and a specific Label as input. The selected unique value of the Label guarantees the uniqueness and independence of each generated session key. The PRF is different from the one in MIKEY and is currently implemented as the Advanced Encryption Standard (AES) [17] in counter mode, as that is also the default encryption algorithm (see section "SRTP Transforms") and thus reduces code size. Although it might seem desirable to reuse code also between MIKEY and SRTP, MIKEY needs to have a slightly more flexible PRF to cater to more general use. Conversely, using the MIKEY PRF in SRTP would be a general overkill, because SRTP could be running together with another key management protocol. Still, note that many of the transforms in MIKEY and SRTP are indeed the same (e.g., AES and HMAC).

SRTP Processing

The SRTP works logically as a so-called "bump in the stack" implementation; at the sender side, it intercepts the RTP packet, forms the SRTP packet from it, and forwards it to the lower layers of the stack for transmission. Conversely, at the receiver side, SRTP intercepts the packet, performs the needed security processing, and (if successful) forwards the RTP packet to the upper layer of the stack.

When an SRTP packet is to be transmitted or received, at first the cryptographic context under which the packet is secured has to be retrieved by looking at the triplet SSRC (which is a field in the RTP packet header to identify the source), destination IP address, and destination transport port number (from the UDP packet header); that is, the sender and receiver maintain a database of cryptographic contexts, indexed by this triplet.

On the sender side (see Figure 5.14), the correct session keys are derived from the Master key in the cryptographic context, by running the pseudorandom function with appropriate input. The packet then may be encrypted and an authentication tag may be added for integrity protection. Possibly an MKI field is also appended, to point to the correct Master key.

Figure 5.14. A simplified state chart for SRTP sender processing.

On the receiver side, after the cryptographic context retrieval (possibly using the MKI to identify the Master key), the correct session keys are derived from the Master key. The receiver first checks if the packet has been replayed, by comparing the Index of the packet that has just arrived against the replay list, and accepting it if not seen earlier. Replay protection is achieved by implicitly authenticating the RTP sequence number; hence, replay protection can only be securely implemented when integrity protection is provided. Then, the integrity of the packet is verified (when integrity protection is provided). If and only if the replay and integrity checks are successful, then the payload is finally decrypted (when confidentiality is enabled), replay information is updated, and the packet is passed to the upper layer application.

SRTP Transforms

An important aspect is the choice of the cryptographic algorithms, also called transforms. SRTP defines some default transforms to promote interoperability. Efficient algorithms are chosen to maintain low computational cost and a small footprint in code size, to accommodate the heterogeneous scenarios. As mentioned, transform reuse is also important.

The algorithm defined for integrity protection is HMAC, based on the Secure Hash Algorithm (SHA-1) [18], a common and rather efficient transform. Coverage of the HMAC is the RTP header and RTP payload, together with the local rollover counter. The HMAC is keyed using the session authentication key. The output is an authentication tag of variable length that is appended to the SRTP packet.

There are currently two different ciphers defined in SRTP. Both are stream ciphers, a class of ciphers that is tolerant to bit errors, which may occur in wireless environments. They also conserve payload size without adding any padding. Both ciphers operate on each packet independently: encryption/decryption of one packet does not depend on preceding packets, to allow for possible packet loss and re-ordering of packets. The two stream ciphers are based on the AES block cipher operating in special modes.

The inputs to the stream ciphers are the session encryption key and some synchronization data, called the Initialization Vector (IV). The output of the stream cipher is a keystream that is then XORed bit by bit with the message to encrypt. This generates the ciphertext (encrypted data) that is sent in the SRTP payload.

The SRTP default encryption transform is AES in counter mode, with the IV derived as a function of the SRTP Index, the SSRC field carried in the RTP header (to allow key sharing between streams), and a Salt key (i.e., a random value agreed upon by the key management and needed by stream ciphers to defeat certain attacks).

An optional cipher is defined: AES in f8 mode. AES in f8 mode operates similar to AES in counter mode. The IV is a function of the SRTP Index, Salt key, and SSRC, as with AES in counter mode, but also of other fields from the RTP packet header. This provides an implicit authentication of those fields when "real" integrity protection is not provided (modifications of those fields would result in erroneous decryption).

There are, in general, two security aspects that need to be considered when applying a stream cipher in SRTP. First, rekeying must be triggered as soon as one of the streams protected by a given key reaches 2^{48} SRTP packets or 2^{31} SRTCP packets (whichever occurs first). This is because stream ciphers can, if not used correctly, generate a so-called two-time pad: the same output keystream is used more than once to encrypt different content. In this case, an attacker could get information by applying bitwise XOR between the two ciphertexts, which will result in the XOR of the two plaintexts. Note that even at very high packet rates, the above-mentioned limits possess no practical problems, as they correspond to quite a long session time period. Furthermore, some parameter of cryptographic significance should be made unique per stream and packet. One easy way is to use different Master keys per each stream. Two-time pads could also happen by key management mistakes. To avoid two-time pads, automatic key management is needed, as manual key management can more easily lead to mistakes.

SRTP and Key Management

The SRTP is a security protocol independent of any specific key management protocol. This means that any general key management protocol can be used to negotiate the parameters needed for SRTP to work. This desire for modularity is also one of the reasons why SRTP only needs one Master key (which is then internally split into the necessary session keys).

Rekeying. Rekeying, which means changing the Master key during an ongoing session, is done by retrieving a new Master key by the key management protocol. Rekeying during the session lifetime may be triggered for different reasons. For example, in group-communication scenarios, a member leaving the group may trigger such an event to ensure that the leaving member cannot listen into future group communications (forward security). Similarly, the group policy may require rekeying when a new member joins a group (backward security).

There are other practical reasons why rekeying may be needed. For the currently defined transforms in SRTP, rekeying has to be triggered after at most 2^{48} RTP (or 2^{31} RTCP) packets have been secured. Finally, rekeying may simply be performed for security reasons, such as an unfortunate compromise of the Master key, or simply a conservative security policy that wants to strongly limit the amount of ciphertext under the same Master key. In the end, it is always a matter of policy of the key management protocol when the rekeying is actually triggered.

When a rekey event occurs, it is important that all of the parties involved in the secure communication know when to change the Master key. In SRTP, two different methods can be used. The most straightforward one, suitable in any scenario, is to add the MKI field to each packet, as a pointer to the correct Master key. A new MKI value in an SRTP packet indicates that the sender has switched the Master key and which key he used. The mapping between each MKI value and Master key is done, for example, by the key management protocol.

The alternative method for supporting rekeying is by SRTP Indices, called the <From, To> pair, indicating the range of packets (48-bit Indices) where the key is active. The new Master key is changed after the packet corresponding to the Index To. The advantage of this method is that no field is added to the packet. Such a method, however, is smoothly applicable only to simple cases — in particular when each Master key is used for a single stream. As a matter of fact, with multiple streams there is no defined way to indicate when to change the Master key simultaneously on all the streams. Indeed, also in the case of a single stream, the switching of the key on SRTCP is done as soon as the key is changed on the correspondent RTP stream, already quite an approximation.

Key Refresh. The key derivation provides an additional feature: key refresh. After the mandatory Master key "splitting" into session keys, it is possible to periodically further run the key derivation function, generating fresh session keys (independent from previous session keys). This is clearly different from rekeying, as the latter requires running the key management protocol (often an expensive operation). Use of fresh session keys prevents producing large amounts of ciphertext with a single fixed session key, from which an attacker potentially could take advantage.

Furthermore, a compromised session key discloses only the data protected by that key, as other session keys derived from the same Master key are not compromised, due to the use of the pseudorandom function (although compromising a Master key is catastrophic for all of the sessions under it). Therefore, the key refresh is a welcome security enhancement that can be implemented by already-existing code (the key derivation function) and does not require running the key management protocol.

PROTECTING THE IP MULTIMEDIA SESSIONS

Multimedia Internet KEYing and SRTP are two components that can be used to create an overall secure multimedia solution. When used together, they provide an end-to-end security solution of the media sessions. In a practical setting, instead of running it separately, MIKEY is generally transported within the session establishment protocol. This is done to reduce the number of round-trips and the overall delay.

Figure 5.15 describes how MIKEY can be used together with SIP to establish a secure call. The MIKEY message as such is carried within the SDP part of the SIP message. The SIP INVITE and the answer to this (the 200 OK message) carry the two-message MIKEY exchange [19]. Because MIKEY provides its own security in an end-to-end fashion, it is independent of the security of the underlying transport protocol. SRTP is used to efficiently protect the RTP sessions within the multimedia session, and its security parameters (cryptographic context) are therefore exchanged by MIKEY. The MIKEY crypto session is typically formed by an RTP stream and the corresponding RTCP stream. In particular, MIKEY distributes the SRTP Master key as the MIKEY traffic encryption key (TEK). It can be noted that the approach of Figure 5.15 is in line

Figure 5.15. SIP signaling, using MIKEY to set up media security.

190

Figure 5.16. **RTSP signaling, using MIKEY to set up media security.**

with the scenario of section "Conversational Multimedia Scenarios" and can easily be extended to work in scenarios such as the group scenarios of section "Small-Size Group Scenario."

An alternative to MIKEY is to transport the security parameters needed for the security protocol instantiation directly within SDP, completely relying on the security offered by it [20] (i.e., if SIP/SDP is only protected in a hop-by-hop fashion between the SIP proxies, then with this approach it is not possible to offer end-to-end security for the media as the keys will be exposed in each proxy). Hence, the security of this approach is conditioned by the trust model of SIP itself.

Figure 5.16 shows similarly how MIKEY can be integrated within RTSP. The streaming server sends the first MIKEY message within the answer to the RTSP DESCRIBE message. The client completes the MIKEY exchange using the RTSP SETUP message. When the exchange has completed successfully, both client and server will have the security parameters and keys needed to set up the SRTP session in a correct way. It can be noted that the approach of Figure 5.16 is in line with the scenario previously described.

In general, the use of MIKEY with SRTP creates a security solution that can be integrated with many different session establishment protocols and in a multitude of different scenarios. As noted, MIKEY and SRTP can be used together for efficient end-to-end protection of media traffic. The overall delay introduced by adding security is a crucial aspect to consider — in particular in the setup phase when the user is waiting for the communication to begin. The integration of MIKEY in the session establishment protocol, together with its ability to set up the security for multiple security associations in one run, are some of the important factors that keep the additional delay for the security setup low.

REFERENCES

1. Arkko, J. et al., MIKEY: Multimedia Internet KEYing, RFC 3830, Internet Engineering Task Force, 2004.
2. Baugher, M. et al., The Secure Real-time Transport Protocol, RFC 3711, Internet Engineering Task Force, 2004.
3. Menezes, A.J., van Oorschot, P.C., and Vanstone, S.A., *Handbook of Applied Cryptography*, CRC Press, Boca Raton, FL, 1997.
4. Kent, S. and Atkinson, R., Security Architecture for the Internet Protocol, RFC 2401, Internet Engineering Task Force, 1998.
5. Packet-Based Multimedia Communications Systems, ITU-T H.323, Telecommunication Standardization Sector of ITU, 2003.
6. Security and Encryption for H-Series (H.323 and other H.245-Based) Multimedia Terminals, ITU-T H.235, Telecommunication Standardization Sector of ITU, 2003.
7. Usage of the MIKEY Key Management Protocol for the Secure Real Time Transport Protocol (SRTP) within H.235, Draft ITU-T Recommendation H.235, Annex G, Telecommunication Standardization Sector of ITU, 2003.
8. Dierks, T. and Allen, C., The TLS Protocol, Version 1.0, RFC 2246, Internet Engineering Task Force, 1999.
9. Rosenberg, J. et al., SIP: Session Initiation Protocol, RFC 3261, Internet Engineering Task Force, 2002.
10. Harkins, D. and Carrel, D., The Internet Key Exchange (IKE), RFC 2409, Internet Engineering Task Force, 1998.
11. Schulzrinne, H. et al., RTP: A Transport Protocol for Real-Time Applications, RFC 3550, Internet Engineering Task Force, 2003.
12. Schulzrinne, H., Rao, A., and Lanphier, R., Real Time Streaming Protocol (RTSP), RFC 2326, Internet Engineering Task Force, 1998.
13. Handley, M. and Jacobson, V., SDP: Session Description Protocol, RFC 2327, Internet Engineering Task Force, 1998.
14. Handley, M., Perkins, C., Whelan, E., Session Announcement Protocol, RFC 2974, Internet Engineering Task Force, 2000.
15. Ramsdell, B., S/MIME Version 3 Message Specification, RFC 2633, Internet Engineering Task Force, 1999.
16. Krawczyk, H., Bellare, M., and Canetti, R., HMAC: Keyed-Hashing for Message Authentication, RFC 2104, Internet Engineering Task Force, 1997.
17. NIST, Advanced Encryption Standard (AES), Federal Information Processing Standard Publications (FIPS PUBS) 197, 2001.
18. NIST, Secure Hash Standard, Federal Information Processing Standard Publications (FIPS PUBS) 180–1, 1995.
19. Arkko, J. et al., Key Management Extensions for Session Description Protocol (SDP) and Real Time Streaming Protocol (RTSP), Internet Engineering Task Force, 2003.
20. Andreasen, F., Baugher, M., and Wing, D., Session Description Protocol Security Descriptions for Media Streams, Internet Engineering Task Force, 2003.

6

Streaming Media Encryption

Heather Yu

Imagine being able to use your home PC as a control center from which you can direct audio or video content (music, movies, and so on) from the Internet or your hard drive to play on your stereo or TV. Further imagine sitting on your couch with friends and family viewing your latest vacation pictures on your TV — a slide show streamed directly from your PC. Digital content, broadband access, and wired and wireless home networks are ushering in a new digital media age that will make such things possible.

—M. Jeronimo and J. Weast,
UPnP Design by Example, Intel Press, U.S., 2003

Advances in multimedia computing, compression, and communication are providing us with growing business opportunities and demands for multimedia services. For many multimedia services, security is an important component to restrict unauthorized content access and distribution. Today, high-quality audio and video are a reality on the Web. Digital audio and video streaming services are increasingly available to average consumers. Considering the facts that (1) a typical consumer-use personal computer (PC) has enough CPU power to decode a compressed video to a full screen in real-time, (2) the number of broadband (Digital Subscriber Line [DSL] and cable modem) Internet users is in the millions, and (3) the audio and video quality at low and medium resolutions over such broadband (> 400 kbps) connections is good enough to find a wide acceptance among consumers, streaming media application is becoming a serious challenger of broadcast and recorded audio and video applications. Consequently, various content providers face serious new challenges protecting the rights of their digital contents, which is an important part in building up a successful streaming media business model. In this chapter, we discuss an important aspect of streaming media content protection: streaming media encryption to ensure confidentiality and assist content access control.

STREAMING MEDIA, AN EXCITING APPLICATION ON THE INTERNET

What Is Streaming Media?

Streaming media [1] (more precisely, streaming digital media) refers to digital media being transmitted through a network, from a server to a client, in a streaming or continuous fashion. The streamed data is transmitted by a server application and received and displayed in real-time by client applications. These applications can start displaying video or playing back audio as soon as enough data has been received. In a packet-switch network, the server breaks the media into packets that are routed and delivered over the network. At the receiving end, a series of timestamped packets, called stream, is reassembled by the client and the media is played as it comes in. From the end user's perspective, streaming differs from conventional file download in that the client plays the media as it arrives, rather than waiting for the entire media to be downloaded before it can be played. In fact, a client may never actually download a streaming media; it may simply reassemble the media's packets, buffer, play, and then discard them. To an end user, the media stream should come in continuously without interruption. This is, indeed, one of the most important goals for which a media streaming system is designed.

In this chapter, we discuss digital media transmission through a packet-switch network, such as the Internet only. For simplicity, we use the term *streaming media* (or SM) instead of streaming digital media throughout this chapter, unless otherwise specified.

What Types of Media Can Be Streamed?

Conceptually, all types of digital media should be able to be streamed. For example, text, image, audio, video, software, and three-dimensional (3-D) data stream all can be streamed. In this chapter, though, we focus on time-varying media types, such as audio and video.

Streaming Media System

A sample generic streaming media system is illustrated in Figure 6.1, which represents the model for both on-demand and live streaming media services. In on-demand mode, a precoded medium is archived on a storage system and served to the client on demand, whereas in live streaming, the media stream is coded, packetized, and streamed to the client in real-time.

194

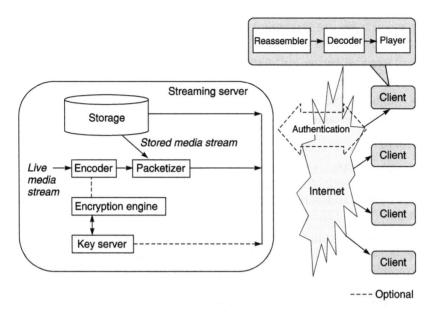

Figure 6.1. **General architecture of a streaming media system.**

Notice that the Internet is a best-effort network that is heterogeneous in nature. Packet loss and reordering caused by a constantly changing bandwidth and congestion condition may result in an undesirable playback experience at the client due to packet loss. Rate adaptation and error control schemes, along with a suitable protocol, are thus used to offer better user streaming media experiences [1].

A generic streaming media service may include the following basic components:

- Streaming media request
- Coding (compression)
- Packetization
- Packets transmission
- Rate adaptation
- Error control
- Reassembling
- Decoding (decompression)
- Client device playback

When security is required, the system should comprise additional components such as authentication, encryption, and key management. A good secure streaming media system should secure the end-to-end system at the server, during transmission, and within the client player.

A generic secure streaming media service requires some or all of the following additional elements:

- User and server authentication
- Media encryption
- Rights management
- Key distribution

Protocol

To transport streaming media over the Internet, an appropriate protocol aiming at delivery of delay-sensitive media streams is needed. Protocols for real-time and streaming media, such as the Real-time Transport Protocol (RTP) [2], are thus created.

The RTP is a standard protocol for the end-to-end network transport of real-time data, including audio and video. It can be used for both types of streaming media: media-on-demand and live media. RTP consists of a data part and a control part. The latter is called RTCP. In RTP, timing information and a sequence number contained in the RTP header are used to cope with packet loss and reordering. This allows the receivers to reconstruct the timing produced, so that chunks of streaming media are continuously played out. This timing reconstruction is performed separately for each source of RTP packets in the streaming media. The sequence number can also be used by the receiver to estimate how many packets are being lost. Furthermore, reception reports using RTCP are used to check how well the current streaming media is being received and may be used to control adaptive encodings.

Now let us look at how streaming media encryption can be done in various scenarios.

STREAMING MEDIA ENCRYPTION

Challenges of Streaming Media Encryption

Due to the large size of multimedia data streams, the time constraint for continuous playback of streaming media, and the potential cost overhead for decryption at the client device, streaming media encryption imposes challenges in many applications.

Real-Time Constraint. To transfer huge amounts of time-critical data (e.g., video), it is essential that all security features be implemented with minimal delay and jitter. Otherwise, it may easily amount to non-negligible loss of bandwidth. Thus, new encryption implementations that are fast to execute are needed.

To resolve the real-time constraint, selective encryption was proposed [3–8]; that is, only some parts of the entire bit stream are encrypted while the rest are left in the clear. For instance, only I-frames or I-frames plus

196

the I-blocks in P- and B-frames of an MPEG video are encrypted. Another algorithm is to encrypt only the sign bits and leave the rest in the clear.

As we introduced earlier, at the protocol level, RTP uses timing information and sequence number to ensure correct continuous playback of the media stream at the client.

Potential Cost Increase. The traditional online encryption model was designed to serve small amounts of data, such as credit card information (CCI), typically exchanged in a secure transactional manner. However, audio and video files are often multiple megabytes or more, larger than those data files like CCI by many orders of magnitude. Obviously, the larger the file, the more data needs to be encrypted online, the more processing power is required, and, hence, the higher the cost. A traditional small data stream based online encryption model does not address the computation intensity problem caused by large datasets. Because content is being viewed while streaming, the client player must be able to perform reassembling, decoding, decryption, error control, and reencryption if specified by usage. Computational overhead and additional hardware requirements at the client device are entailed. This processor-intensive routine can significantly deter the end-user experience if the computational overhead caused by the decryption and reencryption processes is more than the client device can handle. Yet, for average consumer streaming media applications, low decryption and reencryption cost overhead is critical for a successful business model. The essence of complexity trades security makes it harder to design a secure streaming media system with minimum additional client device cost. These imply the need for new ways to handle video and audio encryption.

To lower the cost, selective and lightweight encryption schemes have both been proposed. For instance, RTP allows partial packet encryption using a default algorithm — Data Encryption Standard (DES) — which is very fast. Details on RTP encryption are discussed in section "Encryption in RTP."

Potential Bitrate Increase. When a bit stream is scrambled, the original format of the bit stream may be compromised if care is not taken. This is especially serious for compressed multimedia data streams. If scrambling destroys certain inherent structure, compression efficiency can be compromised. With a fixed channel bandwidth, user experience could noticeably worsen due to quality reduction or playback delay at the client machine caused to bitrate increase. Let us look at a simple example. Assume we encrypt only the I-frames of MPEG video using intrablock discrete cosine transform (DCT) coefficient shuffling; that is, we shuffle the DCT coefficients within each DCT block. Assume a low-bitrate video transmission over a wireless network. As a result of shuffling, some clustered zero coefficients may be shuffled apart, which results in a considerable bitrate increase.

To guarantee full compatibility with any decoder, the bit stream should only be altered (encrypted) in ways that do not compromise compliance with the original format. This principle is referred to as *format compliance* [8]. Furthermore, careful design of the RTP packetization may avoid bitrate increase.

The Rate Variation Challenge. Consider the following consumer application scenario. A streaming video server streams video to clients with various playback devices, such as DTV, desktop PC, personal digital assistant (PDA), and cellular phone. To ensure access control to premium content, the server stores an encrypted copy on the server. Upon receiving access requests, the server needs to send the encrypted medium stream, at the rate suitable for the network channel condition and receiver device capability, to the client (see Figure 6.2). To meet the scalability requirement for plaintext audio and video streaming, simulcast as well as multiple description coding (MDC), scalable and fine-grained scalable (FGS) [9,10] compression algorithms were proposed to provide scalable access of multimedia with interoperability between different services and flexible support to receivers with different device capabilities. With simulcast, multiple bit streams of multiple bitrates for the same content are generated. Unlike simulcast, scalable coding and MDC-based schemes do not require the server to compute and save N copies of the source medium data stream. With MDC, multiple

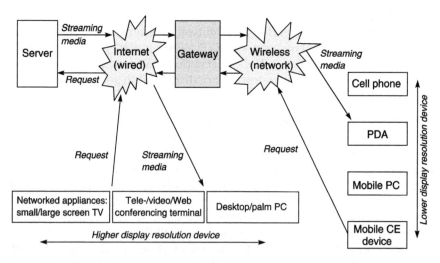

Figure 6.2. **Streaming media over heterogeneous networks to various devices: a general layout.**

descriptions of the content are generated and sent over different channels to the receiver. If all descriptions are received, the decoder can reconstruct the source medium data stream using all of them to achieve minimum distortion. If only some of the descriptions are received, the decoder can still reconstruct the source medium data stream, but with a higher level of distortion. The reconstruction quality is proportional to the number of descriptions received. The more descriptions the decoder can receive, the less distortion it achieves. However, if the decoder receives a partial description or it cannot receive all bits of the description correctly in time, that description may be rendered useless. With scalable coding, a bit stream is partially decodable at a given bitrate. With FGS coding, it is partially decodable at any bitrate within a bitrate range to reconstruct the medium signal with the optimized quality at that bitrate. In most applications, FGS is more efficient compared with simulcast [9], and it is one of the most efficient schemes with continuous scalability.

The format-compliant requirement indicates that encryption has to be compliant with the scalable coding schemes to provide adequate quality of service. For example, if a streaming medium compressed using scalable coding needs to be protected and nonscalable cryptography algorithms are used, the advantages of scalable coding may be lost. Previously proposed selective encryption algorithms can often be easily modified to offer two-level scalability. However, they are not specifically designed to be compatible with MDC or FGS coding. If a medium compressed using FGS coding needs to be protected and previous non-FGS-compatible cryptography algorithms are used, the advantages of FGS coding are lost. Also, observe that if an uncompressed medium is encrypted with non-FGS-compatible schemes and transmitted through a dynamic channel to various unknown receivers, reconstruction with optimized quality will be difficult to achieve.

Scalable cryptography schemes can also offer means for multilevel access control of multimedia content. A traditional security system commonly offers two states: access authorization and access denial. With scalable encryption algorithms, a single encrypted bit stream can suggest multiple levels of access authorization — for example, access denial, general preview access authorization that allows a preview of sample or part of the movie in low resolution on mobile handheld devices, high-quality preview access authorization that grants access to club members and a sneak preview of the content in high resolution, and full content with quality adapted to device capability.

In section "Scalable Streaming Media Encryption," we argue, in detail, how scalable encryption can be achieved. Several algorithms in the literature are addressed.

Further, recall that RTP uses reception report to control adaptive encoding. This is helpful in rate adaptation because of network congestion to provide optimal Quality of Service (QoS). For instance, in an audio conferencing application, each conference participant sends audio data in small chunks of, say, 20-msec duration. Each chunk of audio data is preceded by an RTP header; the RTP header and data are, in turn, contained in a User Datagram Protocol (UDP) packet. The RTP header indicates what type of audio encoding (such as Pulse Code Modulation (PCM), Adaptive Differential PCM (ADPCM) or Linear Predictive coding (LPC)) is contained in each packet so that senders can change the encoding during a conference, for example, to accommodate a new participant that is connected through a low-bandwidth link or react to indications of network congestion.

The Dynamic Network Challenge. In another scenario, a song is being streamed to a client through the Internet. As we already know, the Internet, like other packet-switch networks, may lose and reorder packets and delay them by variable amounts of time. These hinder the correct reception, decoding, playback of some portions of the audio and may affect the playback quality significantly. If privacy/confidentiality is desired, the data stream and the control packets (in RTP) encryption and streaming pose challenges. If the server encrypts each and every bit of the audio using a long block cipher and sends it to the receiver where it will be decrypted at the same rate as encrypted, it requires correct reception of each and every bit of the encrypted message to avoid subsequent plaintext being improperly decrypted or rendered useless. To do that, three or more assumptions are made: the channel capacity is known, the receiver can receive all the bits correctly in time for decryption, and the receiver is capable of reconstructing the media in time for streaming media playback. However, due to the dynamic characteristics of the Internet and the error-prone property of some networks, those assumptions are challenging. From a consumer's perspective, it is desirable that the changing network condition will not result in streaming interruption but only quality adaptation to the changing network conditions. That is, encryption should preserve the loss-resilient capability of the streaming media system.

At the end of section "Scalable Streaming Media Encryption," how to design a loss-resilient encryption scheme with the scalability of a streaming media system preserved is addressed and a sample algorithm is given.

The Transcoding Challenge. In a heterogeneous environment, where streaming media is transmitted through time-varying communication channels, transcoders are often used at intermediate network nodes to perform transcoding operations on compressed bit streams to provide proper QoS for different clients. If a transcoder requires decryption and reencryption of the encrypted streaming media for transcoding operations, an additional security threat at the intermediate network node is imposed. This further complicates the problem and signifies the need for a new set of cryptography implementations that are suitable for video and audio streaming applications.

Transcoding safe streaming media encryption has been reported in the literature. We discuss one such algorithm in section "Scalable Streaming Media Encryption" as well.

Other Challenges. Video cassette recorder (VCR)-like function, end-to-end system security, interoperability, upgradeability, and renewability are some other challenges of streaming media encryption.

User requirements for VCR-like function, such as fast forwarding or rewinding, make the problem even more complex. With traditional encryption methods, the entire file must be processed through the encryption cycle from the beginning to move to other locations within the file. The result can be a slow, linear process that diminishes the consumer experience.

An end-to-end content protection system ensures safe delivery and playback of encrypted streaming media in the entire process. It reduces the risk of a security breach and, hence, encourages the adaptation of new streaming media applications by various content providers.

The availability of interoperability, upgradability, and renewability in a streaming media system potentially reduces both manufacturing and customer costs in the long run. It is therefore desirable. RTP specifies a default encryption algorithm for maximum interoperability. In the meantime, it allows the use or upgrade of other encryption algorithms. In addition, it makes use of profiles for additional payload encryption, which allows encrypting only the data while leaving the headers in the clear for applications where that is desired.

A Brief Summary of Streaming Media Encryption System Requirements

There are a number of reasonable requirements that are necessary to maintain a user-friendly, yet secure, end-user experience. A secure streaming media system:

- Should be secure but low cost in implementation to appeal to more content creators and providers to present their media online via streaming means
- Should not reduce the playback quality of the streaming media (i.e., should not impact continuous playback, loss-resilient capability, and scalability of the system)

- Should sustain current and new heterogeneous environment to attract more applications and more customers
- Should be extendable from PCs to mobile devices and still remain secure, for flexible new business models
- Should be easily renewable
- Should be able to preserve entertainment-like experience; users should be able to fast forward or rewind content without any degradation in the viewing or playback experience

The rest of the chapter is dedicated to a discussion of how to design streaming media schemes, on both system and algorithm levels, to meet the requirements. First, we look at RTP encryption in the next subsection. Then, a sample streaming media encryption system that is RTP compliant is discussed. Several example algorithms with scalability and further with loss-resilient scalability to meet the secure streaming media transmission requirements are addressed.

Encryption in RTP

Today, RTP is often used through the Internet, which cannot be considered secure. To ensure the confidentiality of the media content, encryption has to be used. To support on-demand and live streaming media services, a streaming media system needs to support preencryption and live-encryption, respectively. Further, the system must be capable of delivering the decryption key to the authorized clients securely.

In RTP, when encryption is desired, all of the octets that will be encapsulated for transmission in a single lower-layer packet are encrypted as a unit. The presence of encryption and the use of the correct key are confirmed by the receiver through header or payload validity checks. The default encryption algorithm in RTP is specified to be the DES algorithm in cipher block chaining (CBC) mode. We discuss CBC in section "Scalable Streaming Media Encryption." Strong encryption algorithms, such as Triple-DES, can be used in place of the default algorithm for better security. In addition, profiles may define additional payload types for encrypted encodings. A framework for encryption of RTP and RTCP streams is provided in SRTP, the Secure Real-time Transport Protocol [11]. SRTP is a profile of RTP that defines a set of default cryptographic transforms. It allows new transforms to be introduced in the future. With appropriate key management, SRTP is secure for unicast and multicast RTP applications.

In RTP, a mixer is used to perform remixing of RTP streams, including encrypted streams. They are able to decrypt and reencrypt streams. Translators are another type of application-level device in RTP. They perform payload format conversions, tunnel the packets through firewalls, and add or remove encryption to enable the coexistence of the different networking technologies. Because in many applications not all information should be confidential, the use of a mixer and translator can help optimize network usage. As RTP is often used for transferring huge amounts of time-critical data (e.g., video), it is essential that all security features be implemented with minimal delay and jitter. It should be evident that with huge transmission rates, even a small timing overhead easily amounts to a huge loss of bandwidth [12]. RTP, implemented on an application basis, provides the flexibility to allow splitting of packets into encrypted and unencrypted parts.

Interested readers are directed to IETF's Real-time Transport Protocol [2] and the Secure Real-time Transport Protocol Internet draft [11] documents for more details about the protocols.

A Sample Streaming Media Encryption System

Encryptionite [12] by SecureMedia uses the Indexed Encryption technique for secure streaming media distribution. Based on the Diffie–Hellman cryptographic algorithm, it is fast (to provide good continuity at playback and low-cost overhead at client device) and can accommodate lost, garbled, or out-of-order packets. It works as follows.

Both the server and the client contain the same set of unique packet keys. The packet keys are contained in a virtual key chain called the *shared index*. The first step in the initialization process occurs when the client generates a private encryption key based on a true random number generation process that uses the client's mouse movement patterns. In the next step, a one-way function is applied to the client's private key to derive the public key. Unique key sets are generated for each client session, ensuring that software keys are not compromised by remote hackers. The client's public key is passed to the server, where it is used to create a synchronization token. The synchronization token determines which key in the index of keys will be used to begin the media encryption process. After the synchronization token is securely passed back to the client, the client index is synchronized with the server index. The client and the server are now ready to transmit secure packets of data. Each media packet is then encrypted based on the key indexing system. Using the unique packet ID associated with every packet, the encryption index will select a strong symmetric key that is derived from a mathematical relationship between the "home base," a randomly selected key determines where in the universe of Encryptonite keys the encryption process should begin, and the packet ID (see Figure 6.3). The encryption index is claimed to be secure because the "home base" is determined from a true random process on the client's system and is securely transmitted to the server. Only the client and the server know

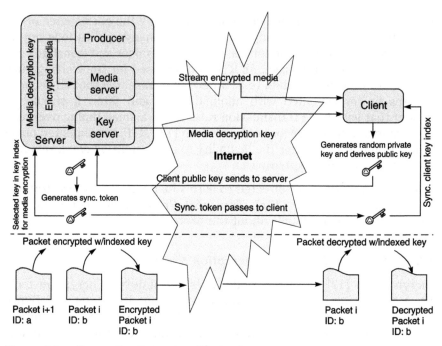

Figure 6.3.   Encryptionite system illustration.

which key is the starting key. Packet IDs by themselves cannot determine the "home base" because they contain no information that points to the starting key.

Figure 6.3 illustrates both the initialization and the media transmission processes of Encryptionite. Since the packets do not contain any keys, they can be streamed at higher rates (lower bit-rate increase) compared to those systems that place the decryption key inside the packets. In addition, in Encryptionite, packets do not need to be received in any particular order (partially loss resilient) because packet encryption is not based on a packet's relationship to other packets.

When the client receives an encrypted packet, the packet ID is used to determine which key should be used to decrypt the packet. All keys located within the encryption index are unique, random, and not mathematically related. Each packet in a stream has its own unique encryption key. In the rare case that one packet is decrypted by a hacker, that person would only have access to a single packet. Hacking additional packets would be a time-consuming and difficult process. The likelihood of a successful hack is further complicated by extra-strong encryption keys from 612 bits to over 2200 bits (application-adequate security level).

204

The system process is as follows:

1. Client and server key indexes are synchronized (see Figure 6.3).
2. Each packet of data is encrypted by keys that are determined based on a relationship between the starting key and the packet ID.
3. Each encrypted packet is sent to the client without key information.
4. The client receives the encrypted packet and decrypts it using the appropriate key as determined by the relationship between the packet ID and the starting key.
5. The packet of media is ready to be displayed.

Scalable Streaming Media Encryption

In section "Challenges of Streaming Media Encryption," we discussed the demand for scalable streaming media encryption schemes to cope with the heterogeneous environment, which can provide scalability to various multimedia content, different network topologies, changing bandwidth, and diverse device capabilities. In the subsequent sections we discuss several scalable encryption schemes that are suitable for streaming media applications, starting with the basic algorithms for stream message encryption.

Digital Data Stream Encryption. Block cipher and stream cipher are two basic encryption algorithms. Block ciphers operate on data with a fixed transformation on large blocks of plaintext data; stream ciphers operate with a time-varying transformation on individual plaintext digits [13].

Stream ciphers (SCs), which convert plaintext to ciphertext one bit at a time [14], offer means to decrypt an earlier portion of the ciphertext without the availability of the later portion. So does cipher block chaining (CBC) [14]. Therefore, the most intuitive way to provide scalable distribution of uncompressed and some types of compressed media using a single encrypted bit stream is to prioritize data, bit-by-bit or block-by-block, and encrypt the bit stream using SCs or CBC.

Cipher Block Chaining. In the CBC mode, the plaintext bit stream is first partitioned into blocks of plaintext bit streams. The ciphertext of a current block is a function of the current plaintext block and the previous ciphertext block. In other words, the ciphertext of a current block is a function of all the previous blocks of plaintext bit streams. For instance, the current plaintext block bit stream P^i may be XORed with the previous ciphertext block bit stream C^{i-1} before it is encrypted. Figure 6.4 illustrates the idea. Noticeably, the feedback in CBC causes error propagation; that is, a single error in the ciphertext bit stream will result in incorrect decryption of all the subsequent ciphertext blocks.

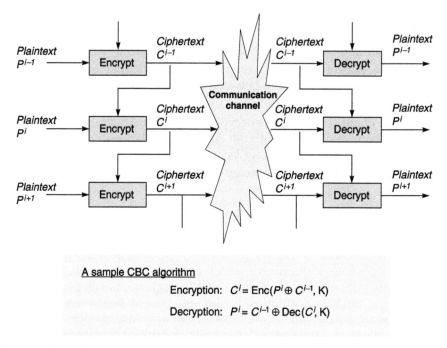

Encryption: $C^i = \text{Enc}(P^i \oplus C^{i-1}, K)$

Decryption: $P^i = C^{i-1} \oplus \text{Dec}(C^i, K)$

Figure 6.4. **Cipher block chaining.**

Stream Cipher. Stream cipher is to encrypt the plaintext one bit at a time. Figure 6.5a illustrates a basic SC architecture. Assume $P = P_1, P_2, \ldots, P_M$ is the plaintext bit stream, $C = C_1, C_2, \ldots, C_M$ is the ciphertext bit stream, and a key stream generator outputs a stream of key bits $K = K_1, K_2, \ldots, K_M$; a simple SC example is given in Figure 6.5b. The ciphertext bit stream C_i is produced by XORing the plaintext bit stream P_i and the key stream K_i bit by bit: $C_i = P_i \oplus K_i$, $i \in [1, M]$. If the medium stream is encrypted Most Significant Bit (MSB) first and Least Significant Bit (LSB) last, it can be truncated $(C_1, C_2, \ldots, C_M, \ M < N)$, transmitted, and reconstructed $(P_i = C_i \oplus K_i = (P_i \oplus K_i) \oplus K_i = P_i \oplus (K_i \oplus K_i) = P_i \oplus \ 0, \ i \in [1, M])$ at corresponding scale with corresponding quality. For an 8-bit gray-scale image, a maximum of eight scales can be achieved using the above simple algorithm. To provide finer-grained scalability, one can take advantage of various transformations, such as DCT and wavelet transformation, and a fine-tuned algorithm that can prioritize the DCT and wavelet coefficients to provide optimized quality at any given bitrate.

Clearly, in an SC system, the system security very much depends on the key stream, which is often generated using a key stream generator. The closer the key stream is to random, the harder it is to break it.

In a synchronous SC, the encryption and the decryption key streams are identical but independent of the plaintext data stream. When there is

Figure 6.5. Stream cipher.

any error, even if it is just one bit, in either the ciphertext bit stream or the key stream, a corresponding error will occur in the deciphered plaintext bit stream without error propagation. However, when there is a ciphertext bit loss, the subsequent ciphertext bit stream will decrypt incorrectly.

In a self-synchronizing SC, the key stream is a function of a fixed number of previous ciphertext bits; that is, the output ciphertext at encryption is fed back to the encryption engine to encrypt a subsequent bit.

Note that it is important to choose an SC (e.g., choose the use of synchronization mode, feedback or forward mode, and the key length) based on the security requirement and time constraint of each application.

Next, let us look at how CBC and SC can be used to facilitate secure transcoding for encrypted streaming media through a sample scheme.

A Scalable Streaming Media Encryption Scheme that Enables Transcoding without Decryption. Wee and Apostolopoulos [15] proposed a scalable streaming media encryption scheme, SSS, to enable transcoding without decryption. It utilizes CBC or SC to achieve progressive decryption ability. First, the input video frame is segmented into regions. Then, each region is coded into scalable video data and header data. Next, the scalable video data is encrypted with CBC- or SC-based progressive encryption, which allows truncation of the scalable video data stream and quality adaptation in accordance. Finally, secure scalable packets are created by combining the unencrypted header data with the progressively encrypted scalable video data. The unencrypted header contains information, such as recommended truncation points or hints, for subsequent transcoding and decoding operations.

The SSS transcoders simply read the unencrypted header data at the beginning of each packet, then use that information to discard packets or truncate packets at the appropriate locations. The SSS decoders then decrypt and decode the received packets; the resolution and quality of the reconstructed video will depend on the transcoding operation.

A FGS Streaming Media Encryption Algorithm. In Reference 16, a scalable encryption scheme for MPEG-4 FGS [9] is proposed. It can be used for streaming media to provide suitable fine-grained scalability. The algorithm provides a lightweight encryption that preserves the full fine-grained scalability and the error resilience performance of MPEG-4 FGS after encryption. It applies different encryption schemes to the base layer and the enhancement layer. The base layer is encrypted in either a selective or a full-encryption mode. Different encryption algorithms can be selected based on the application requirement. In Reference 16, the Chain and Sum encryption algorithm is chosen because it is fast with the least compression overhead. In the selective encryption mode, the DC values of a known number of bits, the sign bits of DCT coefficients, and the motion vector sign bits, as well as the motion vector residues, are extracted from each base Video Object Plane (VOP) to form an encryption unit that they call the encryption cell. After encryption, the corresponding bits in the ciphertext are played back to write over the original bits. In the full-encryption mode, the entropy-coded video data, except the VOP header, form an encryption cell for each base VOP. The VOP start code serves as the separator header for each encryption cell.

A lightweight selective encryption is applied to the enhancement layer to make the encryption transparent to intermediate processing stages. In this way, FGS fine-granularity scalability is fully preserved in an encrypted FGS stream. A content-based key K_c of a VOP is first generated. K_c combined with the video encryption key K_v and a fixed text key K_T is used as the input to a stream cipher to generate a random binary matrix of the same size as the VOP. The DCT sign bits, the motion vector sign bits, and the motion vector residues are encrypted by XORing the random bit at the same position in the random binary matrix. These ensure correct alignment of received packets with the random bits when packet loss presents. Because the proposed encryption is applied after entropy coding, negligible compression overhead is imposed. Because the enhancement layer is encrypted using an SC, error propagation is prevented. These ensure the same fine-granularity scalability and error resilience performance as an unencrypted FGS video stream. Because both the base-layer and the enhancement-layer encryption algorithms selected in Reference 16 are fast, no significant computational overhead is introduced. Hence, real-time continuous media streaming and playback at the client is enabled.

Achieving Loss-Resilient Scalability. The advantage of the above-discussed FGS SM encryption algorithm lies in its means to preserve the fine-grained scalability for MPEG-4 video stream transmission over heterogeneous networks, without departing from the streaming media encryption basic requirements. Introducing encryption service does not drop or reduce the scale of quality of service offered by FGS coding, which is optimally adapted to the network condition and device capability. The disadvantage it suffers from is that it is only partially loss resilient. If a base-layer packet is lost, no reconstruction is possible at the receiver end. Recall that Multiple Description Coding (MDC) [10] provides loss-resilient scalability by generating multiple descriptions of the content and transmitting over different channels to the receivers. If all descriptions are received, the decoder can reconstruct the source medium data stream using all of them to achieve minimum distortion. If only some of the descriptions are received, the decoder can still reconstruct the source medium data stream, but with a higher level of distortion. The reconstruction quality is proportional to the number of descriptions received. The more descriptions the decoder can receive, the less distortion it achieves. This implies the possibility of combining the MDC-based encryption algorithm with the FGS-based encryption algorithm for a hybrid encryption algorithm to achieve better loss resilience with application-suitable scalability [17]. Figure 6.6 demonstrates one possible configuration. For ease of presentation, a sample algorithm for a noncompressed medium data stream is presented:

Algorithm I:

- Generate M descriptions: $D_1, D_2, \ldots, D_M$.
- For $m = [1, M]$, decompose description D_m into base layer D_{bm} and enhancement layer D_{em}: $D_m = D_{bm} + D_{em}$.
- Partition $D_m = D_{bm} + D_{em}$ into $Q_m = Q_{bm} + Q_{em}$ units.
- Encrypt each unit of D_{bm}, $D^q_{bm} = \text{Enc}(K_{enc}, D^q_{bm})$ using any encryption algorithm with suitable security and computational complexity for the application. In the RTP default mode, DES in the CBC mode should be used. When SRTP is used, AES can be used.
- Encrypt each unit of D_{em}, $D^q_{em} = \text{Enc}(K_{enc}, D^q_{em})$ using the FGS SM encryption algorithm such as the one described in the previous section.
- Packetize each unit of the stream D^q_{bm} and D^q_{em}.

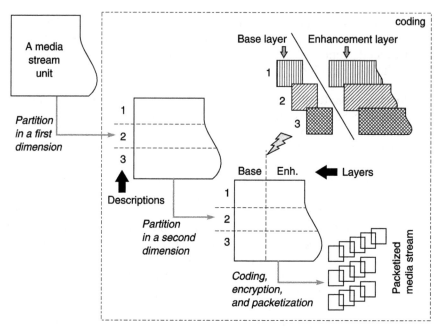

Figure 6.6.   A three-description, two-layer hybrid configuration.

At the decoder, assume descriptions D'_j, $D'_{j+1}, \ldots, D'_J$ $(J-j) < M$, $j > 0$, $J > 0$, $Q'_j \geq Q_{bm}$ are received, where Q'_j denotes the number of errorless packets, which include all base-layer packets of D'_j and $Q'_j - Q_{bm}$ enhancement-layer packets, received for description D'_j:

- Decrypt D'_{bj} using all the Q_{bm} packets of D'_j.
- Decrypt D'_{ej} using the $Q'_j - Q_{bm}$ packets of D'_j.
- For $m = [j, J]$, construct each description.
- Reconstruct the media stream using descriptions D_j, $D_{j+1}, \ldots, D_J$.

Assume a base-layer packet $D^{q'}{}_{bm}$, $j < m < J$, is lost during transmission; reconstruction is done using packets $D'_j, \ldots, D'_{m-1}$, $D'_{m+1}, \ldots, D'_J$. The reconstruction quality is proportional to the total number of descriptions $J - j - 1$ received.

Alternatively, a media stream can be partitioned into base layer and enhancement layer first. The base layer can be further partitioned into multiple descriptions. In this way, base-layer error-resilient capability is achieved through multiple description encoding and encryption whereas the enhancement-layer error-resilient capability may be achieved similar to that proposed in Reference 16.

Assume a base-layer packet D_m, $1 \leq m \leq M$, is lost during transmission and a base layer is reconstructed using packets D'_1, $D'_2, \ldots, D'_{m-1}$,

$D'_{m+1}, \ldots, D'_M$. Also assume that the media stream can be reconstructed using the received base- and enhancement-layer packets. Subsequently, quality adaptation to the channel condition and device capability with minimum distortion is achieved.

Notice that the MDC-based encryption algorithm by itself may be developed for a scalable streaming media encryption system. It will offer a certain level of loss-resilient scalability. However, if the decoder receives a partial description or it cannot receive all bits of the description correctly in time, that description may be rendered useless. The disadvantage is that many descriptions have to be generated to achieve fine-granularity scalability.

SUMMARY

The availability of streaming media services is providing us with an exciting new set of applications. The market for Internet audio and video streaming has been expanding quickly since the mid-1990s. Today, it is already a billion-dollar market and it continues to grow. Because the Internet is heterogeneous in nature with no QoS guarantee, especially for continuous media, it poses substantial challenges for streaming media applications and businesses. Meanwhile, traditional cryptography systems are not intended for large continuous media, such as video and audio, and are not designed for streaming media services in a heterogeneous environment with non-interrupted continuous playback, random access capability, and loss-resilient user experiences. These make the design of a secure streaming media system nontrivial. In this chapter, we presented an overview of streaming media encryption and addressed several critical issues for a successful system implementation. Sample system architecture and algorithms are given as references for readers.

The coverage of this chapter is by no means complete. Nevertheless, we hope it can provide application developers with the knowledge of existing and proposed solutions for streaming media encryption and can offer researchers some better understanding toward secure streaming media architecture, algorithms, the associated requirements, and remaining challenges for different secure streaming media applications.

Interested readers can also refer to the following literature for additional information about streaming media technologies, including streaming media encryption. In Reference18, an encryption algorithm for multiple access control of MPEG-4 FGS coded stream is proposed. SMIL, Synchronized Multimedia Integration Language, is the standard markup language for streaming multimedia presentations. It was approved by the World Wide Web Consortium in 1998. SMIL is the language used to lay out audio and video presentations like those found using RealPlayer G2 and, now, QuickTime 4.1. Examples of what SMIL can do are applications like interactive video, video-on-demand, online training, and any other conceivable opportunity where streaming-rich media could captivate a given audience. References 19 and 20 provide a good introduction to SMIL, and Reference 21 is the standard SMIL specification by W3C. In the meantime, information about Secure XML, which includes encryption, authentication, and key management for enabling the secure transmission of data across the World Wide Web, can be found in Reference 22. In addition, the Web sites listed in References 23 to 26 offer a comprehensive set of information on streaming media, which includes streaming media security and other technologies related to streaming media.

REFERENCES

1. Lu, J., Signal processing for Internet video streaming: a review, *Image and Video Communications and Processing, Proc. SPIE*, 2000.
2. Schulzrinne, H., Casner, S., Frederick, R., and Jacobson, V., RTP: A Transport Protocol for Real-Time Applications, IETF Internet Draft, RFC-1889, 1996.
3. Agi, I. and Gong, L., An Empirical Study of MPEG Video Transmissions, in *Proceedings of Internet Society Symposium on Network and Distributed System Security*, 1996.
4. Li Y., Chen, Z., Tan, S., and Campbell, R., Security Enhanced MPEG Player, in *Proceedings of IEEE First International Workshop on Multimedia Software Development*, 1996.
5. Qiao, L. and Nahrstedt, K., A New Algorithm for MPEG Video Encryption, in *Proceedings of the First International Conference on Imaging Science, Systems and Techonology*, 1997.
6. Wu, C.-P. and Kuo, C.-C.J., Fast Encryption Methods for Audiovisual Data Confidentiality, in *Proceedings of SPIE Voice, Video and Data Communications*, Boston, MA, November, 2000.
7. Servetti, A. and De Martin, J.C., Perception-Based Selective Encryption of G.729 Speech, in *Proceedings of IEEE International Conference on Acoustics, Speech, and Signal Processing 2002*, 2002.
8. Zeng, W., Format-Compliant Selective Scrambling for Multimedia Access Control, in *Proceedings of IEEE International Conference on Information Technologies: Coding and Computing 2002*, 2002.
9. Li, W., Overview of fine granularity scalability in MPEG-4 video standard, *IEEE Trans. Circuits Syst. Video Technol.* 11(3), 301–317, 2001.
10. Goyal, V.K., Multiple description coding: compression meets the network, *IEEE Signal Process. Mag.*, 18(5), 74–93, 2001.
11. Baugher, M., McGrew, D., Carrara, E., Naslund, M., and Norrman, K., The Secure Real-time Transport Protocol, IETF Internet Draft, 2003.
12. SecureMedia—Encryptonite product brief, http://www.stelzner.com/PDF/SecureMedia-PB.pdf, SecureMedia, 2000.
13. Hallivuori, V., Real-Time Transport Protocol (RTP) Security, Helsinki University of Technology, Telecommunications Software and Multimedia Laboratory, http://kotiweb.kotiportti.fi/vhallivu/files/rtp_security.pdf. 2000.
14. Schneier, B., *Applied Cryptography: Protocols, Algorithms, and Source Code in C*, 2nd ed., John Wiley & Sons, New York, 1996.
15. Wee, S.J. and Apostolopoulos, J.G., Secure Scalable Streaming Enabling Transcoding Without Decryption, in *Proceedings of IEEE International Conference on Image Processing*, 2001.

16. Yuan, B., Zhu, B., Wang, Y., Li, S., and Zhong, Y., Efficient and Fully Scalable Encryption for MPEG-4 FGS, *IEEE International Symposium on Circuits and Systems*, Bangkok, 2003.
17. Yu, H., On Scalable Encryption for Mobile Consumer Multimedia Applications, in *Proceedings of IEEE International Conference on Communications*, 2004.
18. Yuan, C., Zhu, B. B., Su, M., Wang, X., Li, S., and Zhong, Y., Scalable Access Control Enabling Rate Shaping without Decryption for MPEG-4 FGS Video, in *Proceedings of IEEE International Conference on Image Processing*, Barcelona, 2003.
19. SMILe with Rich Media, white paper by Confluent Technologies, http://www.smilsoftware.com/docs/SMILwithRichMedia.pdf.
20. Creat Rich Media and SMILe, white paper by Confluent Technologies, http://www.smilsoftware.com/docs/RichMediaandSMIL.pdf.
21. W3C Synchronized Multimedia Working Group, Synchronized Multimedia Integration Language (SMIL) 1.0 Specification, W3C REC-smil-19980615, W3C Recommendation, 1998.
22. Eastlake, D.E. and Niles, K., *Secure XML: The New Syntax for Signatures and Encryption*, Addison-Wesley, Reading, MA, 2002.
23. Streaming Media Land, http://streamingmedialand.com/technology_frameset.html.
24. Streaming Media Inc., http://www.streamingmedia.com/.
25. Streaming Media World, http://smw.internet.com/.
26. Streaming Magazine, http://www.streamingmagazine.com/.

7
Digital Media Fingerprinting:
Techniques and Trends

William Luh and Deepa Kundur

INTRODUCTION

The ease with which digital data can be exactly reproduced has made piracy, the illegal distribution of content, attractive to pirates. As illegal copies of digital data, such as video and audio, proliferate over the Internet, an emerging interest in protecting intellectual property and copyright material has surfaced. One such method of protecting copyright material is called *digital fingerprinting*. Although other means of digital data security exist, fingerprinting aims to deter pirates from distributing illegal copies, rather than actively preventing them from doing so. Fingerprinting is a method of embedding a unique, inconspicuous serial number (fingerprint) into every copy of digital data that would be legally sold. The buyer of a legal copy is discouraged from distributing illegal copies, as these illegal copies can always be traced back to the owner via the fingerprint. In this sense, fingerprinting is a *passive* form of security, meaning that it is effective after an attack has been applied, as opposed to *active* forms of security, such as encryption, which are effective from the point they are applied to when decryption takes place.

In fingerprinting a given dataset, all legal copies of the digital data are "similar," with the exception of the unique imperceptible fingerprints; that is, all copies of the digital data appear to be visually or audibly indifferent. A coalition of pirates can, therefore, exploit this weakness by comparing their digital data, looking for differences and then possibly

215

detecting as well as rendering the fingerprint unreadable. Such an attack is known as *collusion*. One goal of fingerprinting is to ensure that some part of the fingerprint is capable of surviving a collusion attack, so as to identify at least one of the pirates.

For multimedia, an additional extra level of protection is required. In general, multimedia can withstand some amount of (single) user-generated distortion, such that the modifications are imperceptible to the end user. A coalition of pirates might add noise to the multimedia in addition to their collusion attack. Hence, a fingerprinting scheme for multimedia should also be robust to some amount of user-generated distortion. Examples of user-generated distortions are additive white Gaussian noise, linear filtering such as blurring with Gaussian or Laplacian point spread functions, JPEG compression, geometric distortions such as cropping and resizing, and many other attacks found in References 1 and 2. Fingerprinting has the goal of traceability; hence, fingerprinting for multimedia should be robust to both collusion as well as user-generated distortions.

The scope of this chapter encapsulates symmetric fingerprinting as well as fingerprinting in a broadcast channel environment, which involves sending one encrypted copy of the multimedia to several end users, where symmetric fingerprinting at decryption takes place. A formal presentation of symmetric fingerprinting as well as fingerprinting in a broadcast channel environment is presented, and a survey of selected articles follows.

THE DIGITAL FINGERPRINTING PROBLEM

The problem of digital fingerprinting consists of many components that can be formulated separately. Figure 7.1 shows a breakdown of the overall problem into smaller problems, presented as the leaves of a tree diagram. The problem of designing a fingerprinting scheme consists of designing a fingerprinting code and a watermarking scheme used to embed the code into multimedia as discussed in the next subsections. Fingerprinting in a broadcast channel environment is described in a later section.

Fingerprinting Code

A fingerprinting code consists of a codebook and a tracing algorithm.

Definition 1: A *codebook* is a set $\Gamma = \{\gamma^1, \gamma^2, \ldots, \gamma^M\} \subseteq \Sigma^l :=$ $\{s_1 s_2 \cdots s_l | s_i \in \Sigma\}$, of M codewords of length l, over some finite alphabet Σ. Any subset $\Gamma' \subset \Gamma$ is also a valid codebook. Also, γ^i can be written as $\gamma^i = \gamma_1^i \gamma_2^i \cdots \gamma_l^i$.

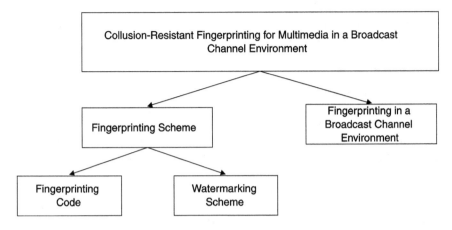

Figure 7.1. Components of the digital fingerprinting problem.

Definition 2: A *tracing algorithm A* is a function $\Sigma^l \mapsto 2^{\Sigma^l} \setminus \{\emptyset\}$, where 2^{Σ^l} is the power set of Σ^l.

In a fingerprinting scheme, each codeword from Γ is assigned to a different user. The goal of a malicious coalition of users is to combine their codewords, producing a new codeword η, such that η cannot be traced back to the coalition.

Definition 3: A *successful collusion attack* by a coalition of M users with codewords in Γ is a function Z such that $\eta = Z(\Gamma) \in \Sigma^l$ and $A(\eta) \notin 2^{\Gamma} \setminus \{\emptyset\}$.

While the adversaries of fingerprinting must design a successful attack function Z, the advocates of fingerprinting must design a codebook and a tracing algorithm to counter collusion attacks.

Definition 4: The triple (Γ, A, Θ) consisting of codebook Γ of cardinality M, tracing algorithm A, and a family of attack functions Θ is said to be *M-collusion resistant to* Θ with ε error if the following properties are satisfied: *Given* $\eta = Z(\Gamma')$ for $Z \in \Theta$ and $\Gamma' \subseteq \Gamma, \Pr[A(\eta) \in 2^{\Gamma'} \setminus \{\emptyset\}] > 1 - \varepsilon$.

Note: Definition 4 also resists framing of innocent users, as the tracing algorithm A will produce a subset of codewords from Γ', the codebook belonging to the colluders. A typical family of attack functions is the family of Marking Assumption attacks [3], which will be discussed in section "Fingerprinting under the Marking Assumption."

Once the fingerprinting code is designed, a means to imperceptibly embed it into multimedia is necessary. The technique of embedding codewords imperceptibly into multimedia is called *modulation and watermarking*, as defined in the next subsection.

Watermarking Scheme

A digital watermark is an imperceptible mark, such as a logo, that is embedded into multimedia. To quantify the meaning of imperceptibility, a metric $d(\cdot, \cdot) \geq 0$ is defined to measure the similarity between any two multimedia c and $\tilde{c}_i$. Let $T > 0$ be a threshold variable such that $d(c, \tilde{c}_i) \gg T$ implies c and $\tilde{c}_i$ are not visually similar and $d(c, \tilde{c}_i) < T$ implies they are visually similar. For example, $d(c, \tilde{c}_i)$ can represent the Euclidean distance, or mean square error (MSE), between c and $\tilde{c}_i$. The threshold T is a factor of the human visual system for images and video or a factor of the human audio system for audio.

A watermarking algorithm takes a host multimedia, a watermark, a key, and embeds the watermark into the host in an imperceptible manner.

Definition 5: A *watermarking algorithm* is a function $\omega : C \times W \times L \rightarrow C$, where C is a set of multimedia, W is a set of watermarks, and L is a set of keys. In addition, for any $c \in C$, $w \in W$, and $l \in L$, $\omega(c, w, l)$ is the watermarked multimedia, such that $d(\omega(c, w, l), c) < T$.

Watermarks are extracted from watermarked multimedia via an extraction function X.

Definition 6: A *blind watermark extraction function* X is a function $C \times L \mapsto W$, such that $X(\omega(c, w, l), l) = w$.

In addition to the imperceptibility requirements of a watermarking algorithm, $\omega(c, w, l)$ should also be robust to some attacks.

Definition 7: A *feasible attack* F on watermarked multimedia, given w, but not l, is a function $C \mapsto C$, such that $d(F(\omega(c, w, l)), c) < T$.

The attack defined in Definition 7 allows the attacker to have knowledge of the watermarking algorithm but not the key, which is known as Kerckhoff's Principle in cryptography [4]. In addition, the attack should have imperceptible effects on the watermarked multimedia. A blind watermarking scheme is said to be robust to a particular attack if the extraction function is able to extract the watermark after that particular attack.

218

Definition 8: A blind watermarking scheme that is strictly robust to a feasible attack F is a *triple* (ω, X, F), such that $X(F(\omega(c, w, l)), l) = w$. A blind watermarking scheme that is τ-robust to a feasible attack F is a *triple* (ω, X, F), such that $X(F(\omega(c, w, l)), l) = \tilde{w}$ and $d(\tilde{w}, w) < \tau$.

An example of a feasible attack is additive white Gaussian noise (AWGN). Here, F is AWGN with noise power σ^2, defined as

$$F(\omega(c, w, l), l) = \omega(c, w, l) + n \tag{7.1}$$

n is a noisy video whose frames are Gaussian random processes, with a constant power spectral density (PSD) at σ^2. The attack in Equation 7.1 is made feasible by controlling σ^2.

In order to integrate the fingerprinting code into a watermarking scheme, a modulation function is required to map the codewords into unique watermarks. A demodulation function is used to map watermarks back to codewords.

Definition 9: A modulation function $m : \Gamma \rightarrow W$ is a *bijection*, and its inverse function is the demodulation function $m^{-1} = B : W \rightarrow \Gamma$.

Definition 9 ties together the fingerprinting code and the watermarking scheme, thus completing the problem formulation of the fingerprinting scheme. The modulation and watermarking process, along with its inverse operations, are depicted in Figure 7.2. In the next subsection, we discuss possible attacks for which we must effectively design fingerprints.

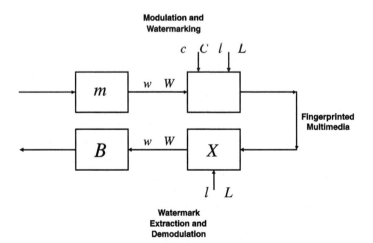

Figure 7.2. **Modulation and watermarking and inverse operations.**

Attacks

As discussed in the previous subsections, attacks on fingerprinted multimedia can be classified as either single-user attacks or collusion attacks directly on the multimedia.

Single-User Attacks. Feasible attacks on multimedia as defined in Definition 7 are now presented. These attacks involve one copy of the multimedia in question and can be categorized into *unintentional attacks* and *intentional attacks* [2]. Unintentional attacks are those that occur due to bandwidth constraints, such as lossy copying and transcoding (i.e., compression, change in frame rate, format conversion, conversion in display format). Intentional attacks are those user-generated attacks that aim to remove the watermark or fingerprint in the multimedia. Intentional attacks on video can be categorized into *single-frame attacks* and *statistical attacks* [2]. Single-frame attacks can be categorized into *signal processing attacks* (i.e., band-pass filtering, adaptive Wiener denoising [2], etc.) and *desynchronizing attacks* (i.e., affine transformations, scaling, cropping, etc.) [2]. Statistical attacks for video are sometimes also called collusion. However, there is only one copy of the video in question and the term arises from the fact that consecutive frames in the video are used together to remove the watermark or fingerprint. A simple statistical attack on video is to average a small set of consecutive frames in hopes that this will remove the watermark. A more sophisticated statistical attack is to first estimate the watermark in each individual frame and then average the estimated watermarks to obtain a final estimation, which is then subtracted from each frame.

Section "Multimedia Collision" presents collusion attacks directly on multimedia, by comparing several copies of the same video with different fingerprints embedded. The attacks involve combining matching frames from each copy as opposed to consecutive frames from one copy.

General Notation. Although we focus at times on video fingerprinting to elucidate concepts, much of our insight can be generalized to other types of digital media. Let c represent a plaintext video. The variable $\hat{c}$ is the encrypted version of c (denoted by the caret), and $\tilde{c}_i$ is a plaintext version of c (denoted by the tilde) with an imperceptible fingerprint for User i denoted by a subscript i. For example, the codeword $\gamma^i \in \Gamma$ is modulated and watermarked into c. Furthermore, the video can be broken down according to frame and pixel index, $c^j(x, y)$, where the superscript j denotes the frame number and (x, y) denotes the pixel index. In the next subsection, collusion applied directly on the video will be introduced, and $\underline{c}$ (using the underscore) is the notation used to denote a video obtained by collusion via a set of fingerprinted videos $\{\tilde{c}_i\}$. At times, a probabilistic approach is required, and the pixels in a video can

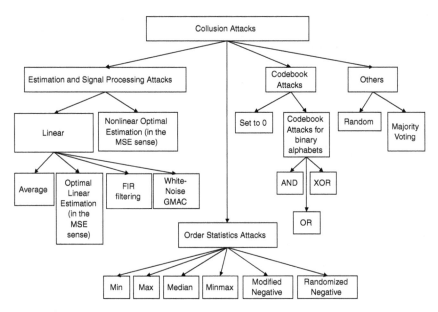

Figure 7.3. Collusion attacks.

be regarded as a random variable. A random variable is denoted by the uppercase version [i.e., $\tilde{C}_i^j(x, y)$]. Random variables are required when the probability density function is used; otherwise, a particular sample or outcome denoted by the usual lowercase is used.

Multimedia Collusion. Up to this point, collusion has only been addressed for codebooks as in Definition 3. This subsection will give examples of attacks that can be applied to the codebook and attacks that are applied directly to the multimedia. Figure 7.3 presents an example of some collusion attacks. It is assumed User 1 to User M collude without loss of generality, where $M \leq |\Gamma|$.

In general, attacks that are strictly applied to codebooks are not practically useful for multimedia fingerprinting because they do not effectively model collusion directly applied to media files; however, they are discussed because these attacks can serve as a basis for designing collusion-resistant codes, as in References 5 to 7. If Σ is binary, such as $\Sigma = \{0, 1\}$, any binary operator such as AND, OR, and XOR can be used as attacks. In the Set to 0 attack, $\eta = \eta_1 \eta_2 \cdots \eta_l$ is the codeword created by colluders, where $\eta_i = 0$ if $\gamma_i^j \neq \gamma_i^k$ for some $j \neq k$, otherwise $\eta_i = \gamma_i^j$ where $\gamma_i^1 = \gamma_i^2 = \cdots = \gamma_i^M$. This attack sets any differing bits (in the case of a binary alphabet) to 0 while preserving bits that are the same across all users. This attack can be modified so that differing bits are always set to one alphabet that appears in the colluders' codewords.

Majority Voting, which can also be a codebook attack, is defined in Equation 7.2 using the MODE operation from statistics, which chooses the most common value from a set:

$$\underline{c}^j(x, y) = \text{MODE}\left(\tilde{c}^j_1(x,y), \tilde{c}^j_2(x,y), \ldots, \tilde{c}^j_M(x,y)\right) \tag{7.2}$$

The Random attack selects pixels from the fingerprinted multimedia with equal probability. Equation 7.3 defines the Random attack using the UNIFORM-RANDOM operation, which selects the indices 1 to M with equal probability:

$$\underline{c}^j(x, y) = \tilde{c}^j_{\text{UNIFORM-RANDOM}(1, 2, \ldots, M)}(x, y) \tag{7.3}$$

From the Estimation and Signal Processing Attacks category, the Nonlinear Optimal Estimation (in the MSE sense), given frames in $\{\tilde{c}_i\}^M_{i=1}$, is

$$\underline{c}^j(x, y) = \text{E}\left[c^j(x,y) | \tilde{c}^j_1(x, y), \tilde{c}^j_2(x, y), \ldots, \tilde{c}^j_M(x, y)\right]$$
$$= h\left(\tilde{c}^j_1(x, y), \tilde{c}^j_2(x, y), \ldots, \tilde{c}^j_M(x, y)\right)$$

where $\underline{c}^j(x, y)$ is an estimate of the jth frame at the (x,y)th pixel of the respective frame and pixel in the video c with no fingerprint, and $h(\tilde{c}^j_1(x, y), \tilde{c}^j_2(x, y), \ldots, \tilde{c}^j_M(x, y))$ is given in

$$h\left(\tilde{c}^j_1(x, y), \tilde{c}^j_2(x, y), \ldots, \tilde{c}^j_M(x, y)\right)$$
$$= \int_{-\infty}^{+\infty} z \frac{f_{C^j(x,y), \tilde{C}^j_1(x,y), \tilde{C}^j_2(x,y), \ldots, \tilde{C}^j_M(x,y)}\left(z, \tilde{c}^j_1(x, y), \tilde{c}^j_2(x, y), \ldots, \tilde{c}^j_M(x, y)\right)}{f_{\tilde{C}^j_1(x,y), \tilde{C}^j_2(x,y), \ldots, \tilde{C}^j_M(x,y)}\left(\tilde{c}^j_1(x, y), \tilde{c}^j_2(x, y), \ldots, \tilde{c}^j_M(x, y)\right)} dz$$

$$(7.4)$$

$f_{C^j(x,y), \tilde{C}^j_1(x,y), \tilde{C}^j_2(x,y), \ldots, \tilde{C}^j_M(x,y)}$ is the joint probability density function (pdf) of the jth frame, (x,y)th pixel random variables of c, and $\{\tilde{c}_i\}^M_{i=1}$. $f_{\tilde{C}^j_1(x,y), \tilde{C}^j_2(x,y), \ldots, \tilde{C}^j_M(x,y)}$ is the joint of the jth frame, (x, y)th pixel random variables $\{\tilde{c}_i\}^M_{i=1}$. To be practical, Equation 7.4 requires that the pdfs be somehow estimated or known. Colluders must therefore resort to more practical techniques, such as those found in the Linear category. The simplest Linear attack averages the set of fingerprinted multimedia, as in

$$\underline{c}^j(x, y) = \frac{1}{M} \sum_{i=1}^{M} \tilde{c}^j_i(x, y) \tag{7.5}$$

As noted in Reference 5, Equation 7.5 is fair; all members of the coalition contribute equally; hence, no member is at a higher risk of being caught than his colleagues.

Another linear attack that is more optimal in the MSE sense than Equation 7.5 is given by

$$\underline{c}^j(x,y) = \sum_{i=1}^{M} \alpha_i \left(\tilde{c}_i^j(x,y) - E\left[\tilde{C}_i^j(x,y) \right] \right) + E[C^j(x,y)] \tag{7.6}$$

The weights α_i in Equation 7.6 are obtained by solving

$$E\left[\left(C^j(x,y) - E[C^j(x,y)] - \sum_{i=1}^{M} \alpha_i \left(\tilde{C}_i^j(x,y) - E\left[\tilde{C}_i^j(x,y) \right] \right) \right) \right.$$
$$\left. \left(\tilde{C}_k^j(x,y) - E\left[\tilde{C}_k^j(x,y) \right] \right) \right] = 0 \tag{7.7}$$

for $k = 1, 2, \ldots, M$.

Although Equation 7.7 may seem intimidating, it is a linear equation of M equations (for $k = 1, 2, \ldots, M$) and M unknowns (α_i, for $i = 1, 2, \ldots, M$). The expected values are more easily estimated than the pdfs in Equation 7.4. The Fourier infrared (FIR) filtering attack averages $\{\tilde{c}^j(x,y)\}_{j=1}^{M}$, then applies a FIR filter as in Equation 7.8.

$$\underline{c}^j = h(x,y) \otimes \frac{1}{M} \sum_{i=1}^{M} \tilde{c}_i^j(x,y) \tag{7.8}$$

$h(x,y)$ is an FIR two-dimensional (2-D) spatial filter and $\otimes$ is the 2-D convolution operator. The goal of Equation 7.8 is to further attenuate the fingerprint by filtering the average. Additive noise can be added to Equation 7.8, as in the Gaussian medium access channel (GMAC) [8].

The Order Statistic attacks found in Reference 9 consist of the min, max, median, minmax, modified negative, and randomized negative defined in Equations 7.9 to Equation 7.14, respectively:

$$\underline{c}^j(x,y) = \min\left(\tilde{c}_1^j(x,y), \tilde{c}_2^j(x,y), \ldots, \tilde{c}_M^j(x,y) \right) \tag{7.9}$$

$$\underline{c}^j(x,y) = \max\left(\tilde{c}_1^j(x,y), \tilde{c}_2^j(x,y), \ldots, \tilde{c}_M^j(x,y) \right) \tag{7.10}$$

$$\underline{c}^j(x,y) = \text{median}\left(\tilde{c}_1^j(x,y), \tilde{c}_2^j(x,y), \ldots, \tilde{c}_M^j(x,y) \right) \tag{7.11}$$

$$\underline{c}^j(x,y) = \frac{1}{2}\left(\min\left(\tilde{c}_i^j(x,y) \right) + \max\left(\tilde{c}_i^j(x,y) \right) \right) \tag{7.12}$$

$$\underline{c}^j(x,y) = \min\left(\tilde{c}_i^j(x,y) \right) + \max\left(\tilde{c}_i^j(x,y) \right) - \text{median}\left(\tilde{c}_i^j(x,y) \right) \tag{7.13}$$

$$\underline{c}^j(x,y) = \begin{cases} \min\left(\tilde{c}_i^j(x,y)\right) & \text{with probability } p \\ \max\left(\tilde{c}_i^j(x,y)\right) & \text{with probability } 1-p \end{cases} \tag{7.14}$$

The Digital Fingerprinting Problem

The above subsections formulated the problem piece by piece. The complete problem is stated in this subsection. The goal is to design a transmitter (Γ, m, ω) and a receiver (A, B, X). (Γ, A) is M-collusion resistant with ε error to common attack families such as the family of Marking Assumption attacks. In addition, the entire system should be robust to higher-level attacks on the multimedia, such as those in Figure 7.3. The triplet (ω, X, F) should be τ-robust to common feasible watermarking attacks, such as $F = \text{AWGN}$, for $\sigma^2 < \tau$.

PREVIOUS WORK ON FINGERPRINTING

The fingerprinting schemes discussed are known as symmetric fingerprinting. In symmetric fingerprinting, the buyer has no protection against a dishonest merchant whose intent is to frame the innocent buyer. This problem led to a solution known as asymmetric fingerprinting [10], allowing the buyer to avoid being framed by dishonest merchants. The major drawback in this scheme is the amount of personal information that the buyer needs to disclose to merchants. The solution to this problem is known as anonymous fingerprinting [11], where there is a third party devoted to collecting and keeping personal information private. These two fingerprinting schemes are protocol heavy, and some existing symmetric fingerprinting schemes can be modified to adopt these protocols, hence inheriting their frame-proof and privacy advantages, respectively. The reader is referred to the relevant references for further information. The focus of this chapter is on algorithmic solutions to digital fingerprinting.

Symmetric fingerprinting can also be classified by where in the content distribution chain the fingerprint is embedded. The majority of symmetric fingerprinting schemes embed the fingerprint at the end nodes (source and destination) and directly into the media content. Methods for embedding a fingerprint into multimedia can be found in the watermarking literature. However, some fingerprinting schemes, such as traitor tracing [12], do not embed the fingerprint in the actual content and may even make use of intermediate network components to mark the media. The following subsections will delve into specific instances of symmetric fingerprinting. We begin by discussing symmetric fingerprinting methods that make use of intermediate nodes. The advantage of these techniques is that they are more scalable (i.e., make use of less bandwidth) as the number of fingerprinted copies to be transmitted grows. However, to be effective, the intermediate nodes such as routers must be trustworthy and, hence, secure. We then discuss symmetric methods that assume that the fingerprint is embedded directly into the media and only requires participation from the end nodes. The reader should note that, for the most part, the techniques are described using the same or similar notation and variables as the original articles.

Symmetric Fingerprinting through Intermediaries

In watercasting by Brown et al. [13], watermarked data packets are selectively dropped to form a fingerprint and, hence, provide an audit trail associating a media clip to a particular user. An active network topology for multicast communications is assumed in which routers are used for the fingerprinting process. The *depth* of the associated multicast distribution tree is assumed to be known and is denoted d. Instead of transmitting n distinct watermarked copies of the media from the source for each of the n users, m (where $d << m < n$) copies are transmitted, providing an immediate bandwidth and complexity savings from the standard approach of embedding the fingerprint at the source and making multicast efficiency difficult to exploit.

The original host media is packetized at the source. For each packet, m slightly different fingerprinted copies, called a transmission group, are generated such that their perceptual media quality is equivalent at any receiver. Each of the packets in the transmission group is encrypted and simultaneously transmitted into the multicast network. When the transmission group reaches the first router, the router pseudorandomly selects one of the m distinct packets to drop and forwards the others. Similarly, as the remaining packets continue downstream along the multi-cast distribution tree, the other intermediate routers also selectively drop packets. At each "last-hop" router (which communicates directly with a receiver), only one packet is pseudorandomly forwarded. Brown et al. discussed that if the pseudorandom packet dropping selection is keyed with the position of the associated router, then the identity of the dropped packets within the overall media data stream serves as an effective *route marker*. This marker can be employed along with a secure *timestamp* associated with the data stream to identify the user to whom the media was transmitted.

The advantage of watercasting is its scalability with respect to band-width; multicast communications can be employed and little packet flooding is required. The challenges include making the system robust to unintentional packet dropping due to network congestion (setting $m \gg d$ can account for packet loss, but will trade off bandwidth), the vulnerability to router compromise that may interfere with the fingerprinting process, the overhead associated with adding packet selection and dropping functions into active routers, and high logging requirements because the state of the network during the entire session must be saved. Furthermore, to determine the user associated with a media clip, the entire session and communication transmission events must be resimulated in order to identify the exact route taken by the media stream.

Another approach, called *watermarking multicast video with a hierarchy of intermediaries (WHIM)* [14] by Judge and Ammar, is a scalable fingerprinting and encryption system that distributes the fingerprinting process to intermediate entities called *intermediaries*. The authors argue that watercasting provides security from the source to the last-hop router, which may result in an ambiguous identification of users if there is more than one receiver connected to a last-hop router. In contrast, WHIM provides additional protection between each last-hop intermediary and the associated receivers. Their system makes use of an overlay network in order to implement incremental embedding of the fingerprint over the intermediaries such that each receiver obtains a uniquely fingerprinted copy of the media.

The WHIM architecture has two components. The first part is the WHIM backbone, which is comprised of a set of secure servers that performs the function of incremental embedding of unique intermediary IDs to create an audit trail. Because of the hierarchical nature of the intermediaries, the overall fingerprint received by a user is unique and secure [14]. The second part is the WHIM Last Hop, which works between the last-hop (or "leaf") intermediaries and their associated receivers. This system fingerprints a unique ID for each user, such as the IP address, and ensures secure transmission.

Thus, overall, the WHIM system can be employed to trace a user's location in the overlay network while ensuring bandwidth efficiency because the traffic is multicast. The main disadvantage of the system is that each intermediary must perform a decryption, fingerprint generation and embedding, and reencryption, which introduces a high overhead, especially for applications involving video distribution. In addition to the computational load, the system is more vulnerable to attacks that compromise the intermediary nodes. Neither watercasting nor WHIM specifies the embedding methodology required for fingerprinting, but both state that it must be effective and robust.

In contrast, Wang et al. [15] focused on the application of tracing leaks of intelligence images. For this application, the authors argued that the lack of lossy compression on intelligence images, coupled with their controlled distribution to a limited number of users, reduces the robustness requirements of the embedding process. The embedding does not have to be robust to attacks such as JPEG nor does it have to be robust to collusion attacks involving hundreds or even tens of fingerprinted copies.

Their system is based on a controlled tree distribution structure for images in which the root node distributes the host image to a number of intermediate nodes that each fingerprint the received image and pass the result onto other intermediate nodes that, in turn, also embed a fingerprint. The fingerprinted images propagate down the tree, with additional fingerprints being embedded along the way up to the leaf nodes that represent the users of the data. The fingerprinted copies at the user nodes are kept and all other intermediate copies are destroyed in the process for added security.

At each distributing node, the fingerprints are securely generated by the receiving nodes, and the specific discrete wavelet transform used to embed the print and details of the insertion process is randomly selected by the distributing node. The embedding process occurs at a separate location of any node in the distribution tree, which then passes on the fingerprinted copy to the rightful receiver and destroys any copy. This gives the system an asymmetric quality for added protection because both the distributor and the receiver are needed to generate the fingerprinted image and neither party can frame the other. Although the properties of the approach are appropriate for intelligence image distribution, as discussed by the authors it is not suited for other media distribution applications such as video-on-demand due to robustness issues.

Symmetric Fingerprinting via Data Embedding

In contrast to the previous subsection, this subsection surveys fingerprinting that is performed at the end nodes by embedding the data directly into the media or decrypting certain parts of the encrypted media to render a fingerprinted copy.

Limitations. It is no surprise that with a sufficient number of colluders, any embedding-based fingerprinting scheme can be defeated. In fact, under the framework of Reference 16 using the Euclidean distance as a measure of fidelity, at most $O(\sqrt{n/\ln n})$ colluders are required to render the fingerprinting scheme useless. Here, n represents the size of the data (i.e., number of pixels in an image). However, these findings do not necessarily suggest that fingerprinting research exists in vein. For example, in Reference 6, subgroup-based constructions of anticollusion codes are used to group buyers suspected of likely colluding. For small groups, this implies that the colluders either have to recruit more colluders or purchase additional copies. Hence, the goal of fingerprinting is to make it more costly, but not necessarily impossible, for colluders.

Fingerprinting under the Marking Assumption. One of the very first articles analyzing the feasibility of collusion-secure codes was presented by Boneh and Shaw in Reference 3. A mark in digital data is a position that can take on a finite number of states, including an unreadable state. A collection of marks is defined to be a fingerprint. A mark is said to be detectable by a coalition of colluders if at least one mark differs in state from the other copies. The marking assumption states that only the detectable marks can be altered by colluders, whereas the undetectable marks cannot be altered.

Under the marking assumption, there are no totally collusion-resistant fingerprinting codes; that is, there exists a nonzero probability of missed detection, or probability of false alarm. However, this probability can be made arbitrarily small with the fingerprinting code (Γ, A) introduced here. For $|\Gamma| = n$, construct the $n \times (n-1)$ matrix

$$\begin{bmatrix} 1 & 1 & 1 & \cdots & 1 \\ 0 & 1 & 1 & \cdots & 1 \\ 0 & 0 & 1 & \cdots & 1 \\ 0 & 0 & 0 & \ddots & \vdots \\ \vdots & \vdots & \vdots & \ddots & 1 \\ 0 & 0 & 0 & \cdots & 0 \end{bmatrix}$$

and each column is replicated $d = 2n^2 \log(2n/\varepsilon)$ times. A random permutation of the columns of the matrix is then performed. The n rows of this resulting matrix make up Γ and are assigned to n different users. The code is able to resist collusion up to n users with a false-alarm probability of ε/n.

The detection process is rather involved. Let B_m be the set of bit positions in which the first m users see a 1 and the rest see a 0, and the cardinality of B_m is d. Let $R_s = B_{s-1} \cup B_s$ for $s \in \{2, 3, \ldots, n-1\}$. Let weight$(x)$ be the number of 1's in x, where x is a binary string. Let $x_{\hat{S}}$ be the bits in x at positions given by the numbers in the set S. The tracing algorithm A operates on a binary string x produced by colluders:

1. If weight $(x_{\hat{B}_1}) > 0$, then output "User 1 is guilty."
2. If weight $(x_{\hat{B}_{n-1}}) < d$, then output "User n is guilty."
3. For all $s = 2$ to $n - 1$, do:

   Let $k = $ weight $(x_{\hat{R}_s})$.

   If

   $$\text{weight}(x|_{B_{s-1}}) < \frac{k}{2} - \sqrt{\frac{k}{2} \log \frac{2n}{\varepsilon}}$$

   then output "User s is guilty."

Note that the unreadable marks are set to 0. Unreadable marks are those states that are neither 0 nor 1 after demodulation B.

The idea behind (Γ, A) is now explained. Suppose that User s is innocent. Then $\gamma^s_{|R_s} = 00 \cdots 0011 \cdots 11$. It is assumed that for large d, a random permutation of $\gamma^s_{|R_s}$ will result in the 1's being evenly distributed in both halves of $\gamma^s_{|R_s}$; that is, weight$\left(\gamma^s_{B_{s-1}}\right) \approx$ weight$\left(\gamma^s_{B_s}\right)$. In addition, it is assumed that the attack does not change this distribution. Therefore, if the 1's are not evenly distributed in $x_{\hat{R}_s}$, then s is guilty, which is essentially step 3 in A. The first two steps are easy to see. If User 1 is innocent, then marks in B_1 are undetectable and cannot be changed by the marking assumption to frame User 1. The same reasoning applies for User n.

A modulation and watermarking scheme is not described in this chapter. However, the following content distribution approach is abstractly presented. A plaintext object P of length L is partitioned into l pieces. Each piece is embedded with a 0 and a 1, creating a pair of new pieces for each of the original L pieces. Each of the new $2L$ pieces is encrypted with a separate private key, and the $2L$ encrypted pieces are distributed to users. Each user is given a set of private keys that can only decrypt one of the two pairs. Figure 7.4 depicts the process of partitioning, embedding, and encrypting. Recall that each key is, in fact, a fingerprint; and given that the fingerprints are properly designed, keyholders that collude to create another key can be traced.

Figure 7.4. Distribution of encrypted data — a broadcast channel approach. At the user end, each user is given a set of keys that will only decrypt the data embedded with a 0 or a 1. The keys are labeled so that the user end knows which ones to decrypt.

The codebook (Γ, A) is created from the binary alphabet $\Sigma = \{0, 1\}$, although the theory applies to q-ary alphabets. Other researchers have implementations for the q-ary alphabet as well as methods for embedding in multimedia, such as images [17]. The work of Reference 3 has also been extended to anonymous fingerprinting [18].

Projective Geometric Codes. In Reference 19, Dittmann et al. described a fingerprint as a collection of marking positions that are either marked with 1 or not marked, being equivalent to 0. The idea is to construct fingerprint codewords that intersect with other fingerprint codewords in unique ways. Assuming that the unique intersection point cannot be changed, as in the marking assumption, it will determine all of the colluders.

The concept of unique intersections has a nice geometric interpretation. For fingerprinting codes that can detect at most two colluders, the codewords that make up Γ can be represented by the edges on the triangle in Figure 7.5. Any two users have a unique intersection point — being a vertex of the triangle. Even if the users remove the detectable marks, the intersection will remain intact, revealing the identities of the two colluders. If the colluders do not remove all of the detectable marks (i.e., some leftover edge), then the leftover edge can be used to detect the colluders. Hence, it is in the best interest of colluders to remove detectable marks. A possible attack that can cripple this system is to remove leftover edges but leave the vertices intact. As will be seen later, when the geometric shapes live in higher dimensions and the colluders do not know where a vertex may be embedded, it is difficult to generate this attack.

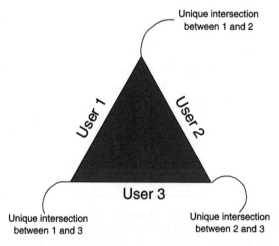

Figure 7.5. Geometric interpretation of two collusion-resistant codewords.

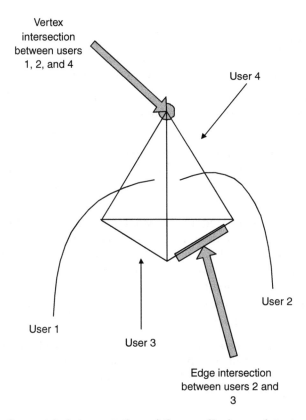

Figure 7.6. Geometric interpretation of three collusion-resistant codewords.

Figure 7.6 depicts a tetrahedron, where the sides represent the codewords that can detect at most three colluders. The four sides (planes) represent codewords for four users. When two users collude, they share a unique edge. When three users collude, they share a unique vertex.

For codewords that can detect at most four colluders, a geometric shape in four dimensions is used. In general, codewords that can detect at most n colluders require shapes in n dimensions, or $O(n)$ bases are required. The hyperplanes of the higher-dimension "hypertetrahedron" represent the codewords. These hyperplanes are derived from finite projective spaces PG(d, q), where d is the dimension that the hypertetrahedron lives in and $q+1$ is the number of points on a hyperplane, where q is a prime number. PG(d, q) is constructed from a vector space of dimension $d+1$ over the Galois field GF(q). The details of this construction can be found in References 20 and 21.

The tracing algorithm A detects the marked points that have not been removed, and it determines the largest projective subspace spanned by these points. In the theory of projective geometry, hyperplanes can be

231

described by a set of points that satisfy a linear equation. The coefficients of the linear equation are formed from any point in the subspace; hence, by choosing any point of the subspace and then solving the equation, a set of hyperplanes corresponding to fingerprints can be generated.

The modulation function m transforms the vectors of PG(d, q) to a binary string. The watermarking function W consists of the following steps:

1. The luminance channel of the image is split into 8×8 blocks, and a discrete cosine transform (DCT) is performed on each block.
2. The blocks are quantized with the quantization matrix given in Reference 19.
3. Each 8×8 quantized block will have one bit of the fingerprint binary string embedded into it. If the bit is a 1, a pattern is added to the block. If the bit is a 0, no pattern is added. Note that a different pattern is used for each block; however, all copies use the same block-pattern scheme.
4. The inverse operations of steps 2 and 1 are performed, resulting in a fingerprinted image.

The fingerprint is also embedded repeatedly, as redundancy adds an extra level of robustness. The demodulation function B requires the original unfingerprinted image. Basically, each 8×8 block is tested to see whether it is a 1 or 0.

Anticollusion Fingerprinting for Multimedia. The idea of using the unique intersection of codes to determine colluders is also used by Trappe et al. in References 5 and 6. Instead of taking a geometric approach, Γ is designed using the balanced incomplete block design (BIBD) from combinatorial design theory [22–24]. The drawback of BIBD codes is that they are only resilient to the AND operator, which is not always an effective model of collusion.

The work of References 5 and 6 also examines various modulation formats for fingerprint embedding, and it identifies coded modulation, a form of combining orthogonal basis signals, as suitable for fingerprinting. The anticollusion codes (ACCs) are then used as the weights for combining orthogonal basis signals as follows:

$$\vec{w}_j = m(b_{1j}b_{2j}\cdots b_{vj}) = \sum_{i=1}^{v} b_{ij}\vec{u}_i \qquad (7.15)$$

In Equation 7.15, $\vec{w}_j$ is the watermark created via modulation for user j, $\{\vec{u}_i\}_{i=1}^{v}$ is a set of v orthogonal basis signals, and $b_{1j}b_{2j}\cdots b_{vj}$ is an ACC for user j, where $b_{ij} \in \{\pm1\}$. ACCs have the property that the length $v = O(pn)$ and provides collusion resistance for up to n colluders. This is an improvement over the projective geometric codes requiring $O(n)$ bases. The watermark $\overrightarrow{w}_j$ is embedded into the multimedia using robust watermarking techniques such as in Reference 25.

The collusion attack is an equally weighted average of all copies. This attack is used because it is fair for all colluders [5]. Although this scheme is not the optimal estimate of the original host, all colluders have the same vulnerability of being caught. According to References 5 and 6, this attack has the effect of operating on the codewords using the AND operator. This assumption is usually only true for two colluders. However, by adjusting the threshold used in detection, the assumption can accommodate more colluders with a small probability of error (probability of false alarms and missed detections). Three detection processes are presented. The simplest detection scheme is known as hard detection, where the Z-statistic given in Equation 7.16 is compared to a fixed threshold

$$T(i) = \frac{\overrightarrow{y}^T \overrightarrow{u}_i}{\sqrt{\sigma^2 \left\| \overrightarrow{u}_i \right\|^2}} \qquad (7.16)$$

$\overrightarrow{y}$ is the received vector that has been attacked by collusion and AWGN with variance $\sigma^2 \cdot T(i)$ is compared to a threshold τ_e that is determined empirically from simulations. The output is

$$\begin{aligned} T(i) \geq \tau_e, \quad r_i = 1 \\ T(i) < \tau_e, \quad r_i = 0 \end{aligned} \qquad (7.17)$$

where $r = r_1 r_2 \cdots r_v$ is a bit string uniquely identifying the colluders and r should be the bit string resulting from the AND of the colluders' codewords. τ_e is chosen to minimize the probability of false alarms and the probability of missed detections, via simulation. The drawback of this scheme is that the empirically determined threshold τ_e is different for varying numbers of colluders; hence, simulations would be needed to select τ_e for more than two colluders.

In adaptive detection [7], the likelihood of $\overrightarrow{\Phi}$ is defined to be the conditional pdf

$$f\left(T(1), T(2), \ldots, T(v) | \overrightarrow{\Phi}\right) = N\left(\frac{\alpha_1}{K} B \overrightarrow{\Phi}, I_v\right)$$

where $\alpha_1 = \alpha \sqrt{\| \overrightarrow{u} \|^2 / \sigma_d^2}$ and K is the number of 1's in $\overrightarrow{\Phi}$. This is also the pdf of the Z-statistics under the alternate hypothesis that collusion has taken place. $\overrightarrow{\Phi}$ is a vector such that if $\Phi_j = 1$, then the jth user is guilty. The goal is to estimate $\overrightarrow{\Phi}$. The algorithm starts by assuming that all users are guilty; that is, $\vec{\Phi}_{est} = (1, 1, \ldots, 1)$. For each iteration, the number of 1's in $\vec{\Phi}_{est}$ is reduced by an element-wise multiplication with the jth row in the code matrix C, such that the $T(j)$'s are in nonascending order. The likelihood $\vec{\Phi}_{est}$ is compared to that of the previous iteration. If the likelihood is greater, then the iterations continue. If the likelihood is smaller, then the previous estimate is used. The advantage of adaptive detection over hard detection is that there is no need to empirically determine a fixed threshold. An improvement to the adaptive detection algorithm is to estimate $\vec{\Phi}_{est}$ at each stage using the likelihood function. This algorithm, termed sequential detection, reigns supreme over the two above-described algorithms in terms of lower probability of false alarm and lower probability of missed detection. However, the algorithm is more computationally intensive than the other two algorithms.

Fingerprinting in a Broadcast Channel Environment

In most fingerprinting schemes described in section "Symmetric Fingerprinting via Data Embedding," unique fingerprints are embedded into every copy of digital data before distribution to buyers. This is impractical for on-demand applications such as live-streaming video. The computational burden at the source, as well as the excessive bandwidth usage of embedding different fingerprints, and hence transmitting different copies of a video across a network, motivate a more clever design. Instead of embedding the fingerprint at the source, the fingerprints can be embedded at the user end during decryption of an encrypted video, thereby eliminating both of the above-mentioned problems. Such a scheme is referred to as fingerprinting in a broadcast channel environment.

There are other motivating factors behind fingerprinting at the decryption stage. The most significant are discussed in this subsection. First, tamper-proof hardware, such as pay-TV decoders, may not be needed, as the receiver is a private key decryptor. All receivers are identical, with the exception of a unique key assigned to each user. In many real-time, on-demand applications, where multimedia is being streamed to viewers, it is important to keep the computational cost of embedding fingerprints at a minimum. Even if the application in question is not real-time or on-demand, the time and cost of embedding fingerprints at the source may be too high to bear. For example, with users worldwide buying music online, several dedicated servers are required to embed fingerprints into the music before it is sent to the buyer. It would be easier to give the user a key and then have an executable file decrypt and embed the fingerprint at the user end.

A formal presentation is given next, outlining the criteria needed for fingerprinting in a broadcast channel environment. Some novel ideas for solving this problem are also provided.

234

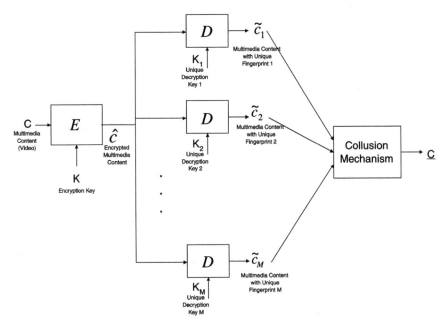

Figure 7.7. Problem formulation of fingerprinting in a broadcast channel environment.

Fingerprinting in a Broadcast Channel Environment Problem Formulation. We next consider how fingerprinting is integrated into a broadcast channel environment. Let c represent the multimedia to be distributed to buyers. In particular, c is a set of N frames, $c = \{c^1, c^2, \ldots, c^N\}$, that represent a perfectly compressed video. Let E represent an encryption function that maps from a set of videos C, and a set of keys K, to a set of encrypted versions of c, $\hat{C}$, such that any $\hat{c} \in \hat{C}$ cannot be understood by eavesdroppers without the appropriate key.

A particular $\hat{c}$ is sent to M receivers who have legally purchased the video content of c. Each receiver has unique keys, $K_1, K_2, \ldots, K_M$. A function D maps $\hat{C}$ and $\{K_1, K_2, \ldots, K_M\}$ to the set $\tilde{C}$, where $\tilde{c}_i \in \tilde{C}$ is a fingerprinted version of c, with a unique fingerprint for receiver i. This scheme is depicted in Figure 7.7. Referring to the notations introduced in Figure 7.7, the following requirements are necessary:

1. *Scrambled video signal: $d(c, \hat{c}) \gg T$.* The encrypted video $\hat{c}$ does not resemble the unencrypted video c, which means that eavesdroppers will be watching an unintelligible video.

2. *Unique fingerprinted videos: $\forall i \neq j, d(\tilde{c}_i, \tilde{c}_j) \neq 0$ and $d(c, \tilde{c}_i) < T$.* $\tilde{c}_i$ should also contain codewords that are collusion resistant (Definition 4), and the watermarking scheme should be robust to common feasible attacks found in the watermarking literature.

3. *Encryption security.* Without keys $K_1, K_2, \ldots, K_M$, an eavesdropper, or the function D, cannot derive a $\bar{c}$ given $\hat{c}$, such that $d(c, \bar{c}) < T$.

4. *Frame-proof.* It is impossible to create any set of keys $\{K_i\} \subset \{K_1, K_2, \ldots, K_M\}$, given another set of keys $\{K_j\} \subset \{K_1, K_2, \ldots, K_M\}$, where $\{K_i\} \cap \{K_j\} = \emptyset$.

The overall problem is tied together by noting that the function D performs decryption as well as modulation and watermarking (as in Figure 7.2) of the fingerprints. Collusion resistance of the keys is addressed by criteria 3 and 4, which state that only appropriate keys can be used to decrypt an encrypted video, and given a set of keys, it is impossible to create different keys that are appropriate.

A notation that encapsulates the process of modulation, watermarking, collusion, feasible attacks, extraction, and demodulation is now introduced. Suppose that $\tilde{c}_1, \tilde{c}_2, \ldots, \tilde{c}_M$ (in Figure 7.7) are fingerprinted with codewords from Γ. Then, define $x = B(X(F(\underline{c}), l))$, where $\underline{c}$ is the video after collusion, as in Figure 7.7, and x is the result of detecting a fingerprint from a signal that is the result of collusion and a feasible attack. Γ is called the underlying codebook of x and is denoted $\Gamma \longrightarrow x$. If Γ was not used, then the notation is $\Gamma \overset{\text{not}}{\longrightarrow} x$. This notation is useful, as it ties together the processes from the transmitter, through the attack channel, to the receiver.

The Chameleon Cipher. In Figure 7.4, the broadcasting scheme used approximately twice the bandwidth of the original plaintext data. The Chameleon cipher [26] allows the distributor to send one copy of the encrypted data to several end users, whereupon the encrypted data is decrypted and, at the same time, a fingerprint is embedded.

An example construct of the Chameleon cipher is now presented. Suppose that B is a key consisting of 2^{16} 64-bit words, and A is a key or seed for a pseudorandom number generator. The key A is applied to the pseudorandom number generator to select four words from B, which are then exclusive-ORed together, creating the keystream, which is then exclusive-ORed with a 64-bit plaintext, resulting in the ciphertext. When the ciphertext is decrypted, a key C is used, where C is almost the same as B, with the exception of some changed bits, called the marks. The marks can be placed in the least-significant-bit positions; hence, upon decryption, the result is similar to the original plaintext, with the exception that the least significant bits may be different. These differences are the fingerprints, and if enough marks are placed in C, the probability of any two users having a common marked bit will be high. The Chameleon cipher uses a random approach instead of a systematic codebook; however, the same idea can be applied using a systematic codebook.

The advantage of the Chameleon cipher is that bandwidth usage is efficient. The disadvantage is that because fingerprinting is performed at the user end, the user knows where the fingerprints are (i.e., the least significant bits) and, hence, the user can readily remove these fingerprints. Even if another key is employed to place these fingerprints in places other than the least significant bit, given knowledge of the key and algorithm, the user can still deduce where the fingerprints are.

Some ways around this are to either apply a black-box philosophy, where the joint fingerprinting and decryption mechanism has a component whose operations are unknown to the user, or the user is given a tamper-proof smartcard containing a key that must be authenticated; hence, the user cannot create a fraudulent key of her own. Furthermore, the key stored in the smartcard cannot be deduced by the user, unless expensive hardware is designed to read this smartcard. In the next section, such a scheme is proposed.

FRAMEWORK TOWARD A SOLUTION FOR FINGERPRINTING IN A BROADCAST CHANNEL ENVIRONMENT

This section presents some criteria and design methods for achieving a solution for fingerprinting in a broadcast channel environment.

Figures of Merit

Some traits that make a fingerprinting scheme strong are as follows:

1. *Code efficiency.* It is desirable that the fingerprinting codewords $\gamma^i \in \Gamma$ be short, while being resilient to a large coalition of pirates. That is, let $M = |\Gamma|$ and $l = \text{length}(\gamma^i)$; then it is desirable to make l/M as small as possible while satisfying the collusion-resistant criteria. Short codes are attractive because they can be embedded into the media several times, making them more robust.

2. *Encryption–decryption efficiency.* In Figure 7.7, $\hat{c}$ should be computed from c in polynomial time. In addition, the size of $\hat{c}$ should be close to that of c. In Figure 7.4, $\text{length}(\hat{c}) = 2 \times \text{length}(c)$. This is undesirable, as twice the bandwidth is required to transmit the encrypted video.

3. *Low probability of false alarms.* It should be difficult for pirates to generate digital data with fingerprints that frame innocent buyers; that is,

$$\Pr\left[A(x) \in 2^\Gamma \setminus \{\emptyset\} | \Gamma \xrightarrow{\text{not}} x\right] < \varepsilon \quad \text{for some small } \varepsilon$$

237

4. *High probability of detection.* After an attack, some portion of the fingerprint should survive to identify at least one pirate; that is,

$$\Pr\left[A(x) \in 2^{\Gamma} \backslash \{\emptyset\} | \Gamma \longrightarrow x\right] < 1 - \varepsilon \quad \text{for some small } \varepsilon$$

Smartcard Fingerprinting System

This subsection proposes a framework for fingerprinting in a broadcast channel environment that minimizes criterion 2 of subsection "Figures of Merit," such that $\text{length}(\hat{c}) = \text{length}(c)$.

Suppose (K, γ^i, l) is encrypted with a private key (in the context of Public Key Cryptography) at the distributor; then, (K, γ^i, l) and its encrypted version are stored on a tamper-proof smartcard, resulting in K_i, where K and K_i are as in Figure 7.7, $\gamma^i \in \Gamma$ is a codeword, and $l \in L$ is the watermarking key. The decryption function D first authenticates K_i using the distributor's public key, and then decrypts $\hat{c}$. The fingerprint is embedded using the watermarking key l. To increase security and make it more of a problem for pirates to break, (K, γ^i, l) can be changed, say, every 4 months, and the subscriber would receive a new smartcard at the time.

The use of smartcards decouples D from the unique keys, allowing manufacturers to mass-produce generic D's, and another plant may be responsible for creating the unique smartcards. This cuts costs, as production efficiency is increased. The smartcard fingerprinting system is depicted in Figure 7.8.

The security in this scheme requires tamper-proof hardware, as well as tamper-proof smartcards. The keys are stored in the smartcard and assumed to be unreadable by an average user. Attackers who are willing to spend more money can execute the following attacks. In the first expensive attack, the user builds a machine to read the keys on the smartcard. Once the keys and the watermarking algorithm are known, the

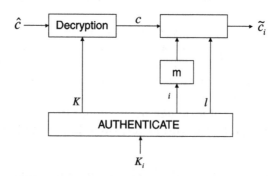

Figure 7.8. Smartcard fingerprinting system.

locations of the fingerprints can be located and removed. In the second expensive attack, the user builds D without the watermarking component, thus the resulting $\tilde{c}_i = c$ in Figure 7.8. The third expensive attack is to create fraudulent smartcards. A malicious user cannot easily create fraudulent smartcards unless the public key is retrieved from D and a machine for creating these smartcards is built. Once the public key is retrieved and a machine for creating these smartcards is built, the attacker can generate a key, say u_1, and use the public key to "decrypt" this user-generated key, creating u_2. Now, the user has a user-generated key, u_1, representing the encrypted version of (K, γ^i, l), and a "decrypted" user-generated key, u_2, representing the plaintext (K, γ^i, l). Of course, u_1 has to be generated, such that u_2 contains the actual K, as this is needed to decrypt $\hat{c}$. Additional computation time for searching for a u_1 that satisfies this is required. The attacker would also have to be able to read a genuine smartcard to retrieve K. Now, once u_1 and u_2 are generated, the machine for creating smartcards will create a smartcard containing these fraudulent keys. The authentication mechanism in D will apply the public key to the user-generated key, u_1; the result will match u_2 and the authentication test will pass with these fraudulent keys.

FINAL REMARKS

This chapter provides an introduction to the area of modern digital media fingerprinting. The digital fingerprinting problem is explicitly defined, common attacks are described, and three classes of digital fingerprinting techniques are identified. Several influential methods in the literature are summarized and analyzed. The chapter concludes with some novel insights into the use of chameleonlike ciphers for bandwidth-efficient, combined media decryption and fingerprinting.

From our discussion, it is clear that the design of a good digital fingerprinting method requires the consideration of advanced code development, signal processing, statistical and security analysis, and a little ingenuity or cleverness on the part of the designer. No proposed technique is absolutely robust to all possible attacks. In fact, we believe that given the constraints on the digital fingerprinting problem described here, it is impossible to develop such a method. However, as a passive form of security, digital fingerprinting needs only to be good enough to discourage the widespread propagation of such an attack; that is, overcoming the fingerprinting processes needs to be more expensive than the cost of the digital media content.

We focus, in this chapter, on digital fingerprinting for multimedia; in fact, the majority of literature in the area targets such applications. However, it is the belief of the authors that digital fingerprinting technology has potential for a broad number of other applications such as future sensor networks and computer forensics. Future work will focus on these emerging challenges.

REFERENCES

1. Cox, I.J., Kilian, J., Leighton, T.F., and Shamoon, T., Secure spread spectrum watermarking for multimedia, *IEEE Trans. Image Process.*, 6, 1673, 1997.
2. Deguillaume, F., Csurka, G., and Pun, T., Countermeasures for unintentional and intentional video watermarking attacks, in *IS&T/SPIE's 12th Annual Symposium, Electronic Imaging 2000: Security and Watermarking of Multimedia Content II*, 3971, Wong, P.W. and Delp, E.J., Eds., *SPIE Proceedings*, Vol. 3971, SPIE, 2000.
3. Boneh, D. and Shaw, J., Collusion-secure fingerprinting for digital data, *IEEE Trans. Inf. Theory*, 44, 1897, 1998.
4. Stinson, D.R., *Cryptography Theory and Practice*, CRC Press, Boca Raton, FL, 1995, p. 24.
5. Trappe, W., Wu, M., Wang, Z.J., and Liu, K.J.R., Anti-collusion fingerprinting for multimedia, *IEEE Trans. Signal Process.*, 51, 1069, 2003.
6. Trappe, W., Wu, M., and Liu, K.J.R., Collusion-Resistant Fingerprinting for Multimedia, presented at *IEEE International Conference on Acoustics, Speech, and Signal Processing (ICAPSS '02)*, Orlando, FL, 2002, Vol. 4, p. 3309.
7. Trappe, W., Wu, M., and Liu, K.J.R., Anti-collusion Fingerprinting for Multimedia. Technical Research Report, Institute for Systems Research, University of Maryland, Baltimore, 2002.
8. Su, J.K., Eggers, J.J., and Girod, B., Capacity of Digital Watermarks Subjected to an Optimal Collusion Attack, presented at *European Signal Processing Conference (EUSIPCO 2000)*, Tampere, Finland, 2000.
9. Zhao, H., Wu, M., Wang, Z.J., and Liu K.J.R., Nonlinear Collusion Attacks on Independent Fingerprints for Multimedia, in *Proceedings of IEEE International Conference on Acoustics, Speech, and Signal Processing (ICASSP '03)*, Hong Kong, 2003.
10. Pfitzmann, B. and Schunter, M., Asymmetric fingerprinting, in *Advances in Cryptology — EUROCRYPT '96, International Conference on the Theory and Application of Cryptographic Techniques*, Maurer, U.M., Ed., *Lecture Notes in Computer Science*, Vol. 1070, Springer-Verlag, Berlin, 1996, p. 84.
11. Pfitzmann, B. and Waidner, M., Anonymous Fingerprinting, in *Advances in Cryptology — EUROCRYPT '97, International Conference on the Theory and Application of Cryptographic Techniques*, Fumy, W., Ed., *Lecture Notes in Computer Science*, Vol. 1233, Springer-Verlag, Berlin, 1997, p. 88.
12. Chor B., Fiat, A., Naor, M., and Pinkas, B., Tracing traitors, *IEEE Trans. Inf. Theory*, 46, 893, 2000.
13. Brown, I., Perkins, C., and Crowcroft, J., Watercasting: Distributed Watermarking of Multicast Media, in *First International Workshop on Networked Group Communication '99*, Risa, L. and Fdida, S., Eds., *Lecture Notes in Computer Science*, Vol. 1736, Springer-Verlag, Berlin, 1999, p. 286.
14. Judge, P. and Ammar, M., WHIM: Watermarking multicast video with a hierarchy of intermediaries, *IEEE Commun. Mag.*, 39, 699, 2002.
15. Wang, Y., Doherty, J.F., and Van Dyck, R.E., A Watermarking Algorithm for Fingerprinting Intelligence Images, in *Proceedings of Conference on Information Sciences and Systems*, Baltimore, MD, 2001.
16. Ergun, F., Kilian, J., and Kumar, R., A Note on the Limits of Collusion-Resistant Watermarks, in *Advances in Cryptology — EUROCRYPT '99, International Conference on the Theory and Application of Cryptographic Techniques*, Stern, J., Ed., *Lecture Notes in Computer Science*, Vol. 1592, Springer-Verlag, Berlin, 1999, p. 140.

17. Safavi-Naini, R. and Wang, Y., Collusion Secure *q*-ary Fingerprinting for Perceptual Content, in *Security and Privacy in Digital Rights Management ACM CCS-8 Workshop DRM 2001*, Sander, T., Ed., *Lecture Notes in Computer Science*, Vol. 2320, Springer-Verlag, Berlin, 2002, p. 57.
18. Biehl, I. and Mayer, B., Cryptographic methods for collusion-secure fingerprinting of digital data, *Computers Electr. Eng.*, 28, 59, 2002.
19. Dittmann, J., Behr, A., Stabenau, M., Schmitt, P., Schwenk, J., and Ueberberg, J., Combining digital watermarks and collusion secure fingerprints for digital images, *SPIE J. Electron. Imaging*, 9, 456, 2000.
20. Beautelspacher, A. and Rosenbaum, U., *Projective Geometry*, Cambridge University Press, Cambridge, 1998.
21. Hirschfeld, J.W.P., *Projective Geometries over Finite Fields*, Oxford University Press, Oxford, 1998.
22. Dinitz, J.H. and Stinson, D.R., *Contemporary Design Theory: A Collection of Surveys*, John Wiley & Sons, New York, 1992.
23. Linder, C.C. and Rodger, C.A., *Design Theory*, CRC Press, Boca Raton, FL, 1997.
24. Colbourn, C.J. and Dinitz, J.H., *The CRC Handbook of Combinatorial Designs*, CRC Press, Boca Raton, FL, 1996.
25. Podilchuk, C. and Zeng, W., Image adaptive watermarking using visual models, *IEEE J. Selected Areas Commun.*, 16, 525, 1998.
26. Anderson, R. and Manifavas, C., Chameleon — A New Kind of Stream Cipher, in *Fast Software Encryption 4th International Workshop*, Biham, E., Ed., *Lecture Notes in Computer Science*, Vol. 1267, Springer-Verlag, 1997, p. 107.

8
Scalable Image and Video Authentication*

Dimitrios Skraparlis

INTRODUCTION

Because digital multimedia data is constantly increasing in quantity and availability, concerns are being expressed regarding the authenticity (by means of origin authentication) and integrity of multimedia data; the ease and efficiency of tampering with digital media has created a need for media authentication systems based on cryptographic techniques. In other words, the trustworthiness of digital media is in question.

Digital media are a key element to the consumer electronics industry. As technology penetrates more and more into everyday life, security has begun to emerge as a primary concern and media authentication technology will definitely play an important role in the success of present and future multimedia services. In any case, data origin and data integrity verification would enhance the quality of multimedia services.

Traditional authentication methods (cyclic redundancy checks [CRC], checks or cryptographic checksums, and digital signatures) are not fit for modern and future multimedia standards. Modern coding standards introduce scalability and tend to be more content oriented. Therefore, it would be necessary to devise image and video authentication methods

*© 2003 IEEE. Reprinted, with permission, from Skraparlis D., Design of an efficient authentication method for modern image and video, *IEEE Transactions on Consumer Electronics*, May 2003, pp. 417–426, Vol. 49, Issue 2.

that could offer scalability, regard the media content, be based on multimedia standards (and not be custom solutions, which are usually unsuccessful), and also be relatively simple to apply. So far, no authentication mechanism has been able to address all of these properties.

The main contributions of this chapter are the research for a technique to authenticate scalable media efficiently, the introduction of scalable content-based digital signatures, and a proposal of such a signature scheme based on stream signature techniques and a modern image and video coding scheme (JPEG2000 for image and MPEG-4 for video).

The applicability of such a scheme to real-world scenarios is further enhanced by the proposal of combining the scheme with special digital signature schemes, such as forward secure and group signatures. Application scenarios regard the security in modern multimedia standards or other applications such as reliable storage in unreliable entities. Examples are the transmission, distribution, or storage of digital photographic images and video on the Internet, press agencies, and similar organizations, reliable storage entities aiding in copyright and ownership disputes, and evidential camera and motion picture production and distribution.

The analysis of the authentication method begins in sections "Authentication System Considerations" and "Design of the Authentication Method" with an overview of the design considerations that will form a solid framework for the proposed technique. Prior art will then be reviewed in section "Prior Art," which will present fundamental techniques related to multimedia authentication. The complete proposed method will be presented in section "New Directions in Authentication Method Design." The analysis is finally complemented by the Appendix, which clarifies the concept of authentication and further justifies the design considerations. Throughout this chapter, emphasis will be given to the theory and general design rather than actual results of the implemented method, as actual implementation details will rely on the application and one of the author's intentions was to demonstrate a concise theoretical treatment of the subject.

AUTHENTICATION SYSTEM CONSIDERATIONS

In brief, a practical authentication system should provide the following:

Asymmetric security/source authentication. Asymmetric techniques based, for example, on public key cryptography provide data source and data integrity authentication. Symmetric techniques such as MACs (Message Authentication Codes) and symmetric encryption do not provide source authentication, because the same key is shared between two entities and impersonation is, therefore, possible.

Offline security. Offline security means that the creator does not need to be available for every authentication query. This is a fact in complex media distribution chains that contain one-way distribution links from the producer to the consumer (e.g., offline availability of compact disk [CD] and digital versatile disk [DVD] distributed works).

Open-system security. It is wise to address an open system such as the Internet for possible applications due to its popularity and constant growth. Furthermore, if the method achieves reasonable open-system security, then it could complement closed-systems security as a more secure mechanism.

Applied security. The term "applied security" implies that no custom cryptographic primitives and mechanisms are used (e.g., use public key cryptography infrastructures [PKIs]). PKI security comes from years of experience in security engineering. In any case, it is much easier and more economical to base an authentication mechanism on PKIs than establish a new custom authentication infrastructure that will probably fail to establish itself in the consumer electronics market.

For supplementary analysis on the authentication system design choices, please refer to the Appendix.

DESIGN OF THE AUTHENTICATION METHOD

In the following subsections, the design steps for an authentication method based on the considerations of the previous section will be presented.

How to Do Source and Integrity Authentication

A method to do source and integrity authentication for data that is transmitted through an insecure channel is by sending a cryptographically secure digest of the message (e.g., the output of a hash function) through a secure channel (Figure 8.1).

The channel could either be a secure physical line or a virtual channel provided by a cryptographic technique such as a digital signature. Verification is performed by comparing the authentic message digest with a calculated digest of the received message (Figure 8.2); if the two values are equal, then the message is authentic; that is, it comes from its reputed source. It should be noted that, as it will be clarified in the Appendix, the concept's source authentication and integrity authentication are inseparable.

There also exist methods to do source and integrity authentication using encryption, and they are briefly described in the Appendix.

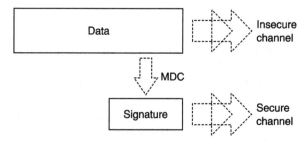

Figure 8.1. How to do source and integrity authentication without the need for feedback. MDC stands for message digest code (a hash function).

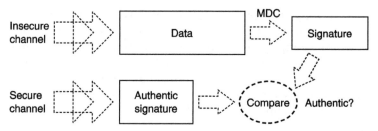

Figure 8.2. Source and integrity authentication verification with no need for feedback.

However, as encryption in a system is optional and encryption in general does not always provide authentication, such methods will not be discussed further in this chapter.

Application to Multimedia Data Formats

The method of the previous subsection, although essential, is not sufficient for still images and video data. Two problems exist. First, we should devise a way to incorporate the signature in the media file. Second, we should construct an authentic or secure channel for the signature's transmission.

For the first problem, possible solutions are watermarking and labeling. Watermarking is obtrusive, as it alters the original media. The method of watermarking is analyzed in more detail in section "Watermarking." Labeling (or captioning) is unobtrusive; that is, it does not alter the original media. Signature data accompanies the media file as an authentication label or tag (see section "Labeling (or Captioning)"). Labeling is the preferred technique in this chapter; please refer to section "Watermarking" for justification.

The second problem, the problem of the secure channel of Figure 8.1 and Figure 8.2, can be solved by mathematical methods that provide an authentic channel, such as MACs and digital signatures.

Principles and Requirements of Modern Coding Standards that the Designer of Modern Systems Should Consider

Modern coding standards were designed with new features in mind. Some of these features are progressive transmission or scalability and some features that relate to content-based encoding such as region-of-interest coding and random codestream access and processing. In this chapter, we will work mostly on the JPEG2000 standard [1]. Some introductory work on JPEG2000 is presented in References 2 to 6.

Scalability. Scalability enables users of different bandwidths or rights to all receive the same content in different qualities. It is also possible to transmit an image or video progressively, by progressive size enlargement or progressive quality enhancement (image is gradually rendered more accurate). Some applications of scalability are the following: multiquality network services, layered multicasting, and database browsing.

Content-Based Multimedia. The representation of visual information has a fundamental difference compared to other types of data: data is considered as a whole (i.e., every bit change is considered significant), whereas the representation of images provides information not directly linked to the binary representation of data. Every image holds information (meaning) that is associated with the human cognitive representations of the world. Modern coding standards such as JPEG2000 and MPEG-4 demonstrate a trend toward content encoding.

The contents of sections "Scalability" and "Content-Based Multimedia" constitute the new directions in research and these are presented in section "New Directions in Authentication Method Design."

Design of the Authentication Method Summary

To summarize, the design methodology for the authentication system is the following. For authentication via securely providing authentication information, the designer needs to:

- Provide an authentic channel (by the use of cryptography).
- Find a way to include labels in the data. Also make sure that it is efficient and that an unexpected termination in data transmission does not prove catastrophic for the authentication mechanism (such a desired property would also benefit multiscale data authentication). Image coding methods should therefore be investigated.
- Investigate the "content-based properties" of the label embedding method (i.e., how the position of authentication labels in the bit stream is related to the image content).

In addition, various design considerations in this chapter are as follows:

- Do not create a custom image coding method, but work on a standard.
- Make sure that the cryptographic part of the final method is efficient but as secure as desired for multimedia.

However, before tackling how to deal with the above, we will review prior art.

PRIOR ART

In the following subsections, we will review prior art in the form of either commercial applications or in the open literature. These will form an overview of prior art in the subject and present the shortcomings and inefficiencies of the methods, creating the need for more complete or advanced techniques. Moreover, some of the prior art techniques will form a base for the novel advances presented in section "New Directions in Authentication Method Design."

Traditional (General-Purpose and Multimedia) Authentication Systems

The general problem of data integrity authentication has traditionally been addressed by commercial picture authentication systems and image authentication cameras, which are based on common digital signature standards.

However, as digital signatures have proven to be rather inefficient for multimedia data, and hash and sign methods (section "Hash and Sign Method") are still deemed inefficient and inappropriate for streams and multicasting, other techniques based on stream signatures have been presented recently in the literature and are analyzed in the following subsection.

Efficient Data Authentication Techniques: Stream Signatures

Stream signatures aim to provide efficient source and data authentication for scalable data. For example, in modern image and video coding standards such as JPEG2000 and MPEG-4, some receivers opt for not receiving the multimedia data at the maximum rate (best quality). In that case, traditional authentication systems utterly fail, because verification is only possible when the media has been fully received.

Hash and Sign Method. The simplest but most inefficient stream signature is the hash and sign method (see Figure 8.3), which is used in commercial authentication systems. The bit stream is first divided into

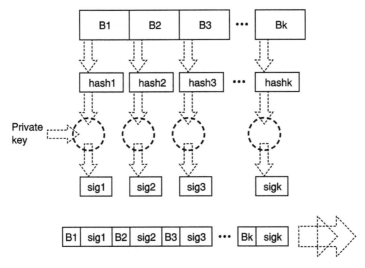

Figure 8.3. Hash and sign signature.

blocks of equal size and then the hash value of each block is signed by a digital signature algorithm (DSA). The signatures are then inserted between each block in the bit stream. The receiver calculates the signatures for each received block and compares them to the received signatures. If they match, the content is authenticated.

The performance cost of hash and sign is one digital signature calculation per block. That could be severely decreased without a significant compromise of security by introducing hash trees. The idea is to transfer the properties of a single digital signature to all of the blocks through hash trees or chain mechanisms.

Tree-Based Method. The tree-based method can be constructed in several ways, either the standard tree chaining method [7, 8, §13.4.1] or subinstances of the tree chaining method (e.g., star chaining method in the signed Java Applets technology).

As one can see in Figure 8.4, every node in the tree contains the hash of its children. During transmission, every packet p has overhead equal to the size of hash values that constitute the path in the tree that leads to the packet. For data comprising k packets, the number of hash values n_p that must precede each packet for successful authentication is either $\log_2(k)$, $\sum_{p=1}^{k} n_p = k \log_2(k)$, when packet-loss robustness is required, or $0 \leq n_p \leq \log_2(k)$, $\sum_{p=1}^{k} n_p = k$, when a minimum number of transmitted packets is required but by adding complexity to the receiver.

Offline or Recursive Method. The recursive stream authentication method of Reference 9 has less overhead than the tree methods,

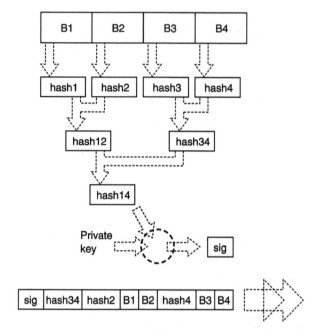

Figure 8.4. Example of a hash authentication tree method as a stream signature.

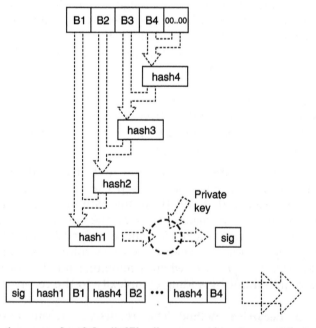

Figure 8.5. An example of the "offline" or recursive stream signature.

requiring less buffering at the receiver end. Looking at Figure 8.5, block processing is performed backward (from the end to the first block in the data). The recipient of the data verifies the digital signature sent at the start and then calculates and compares the hash for each block recursively, as shown in the Figure 8.5.

Other Methods. There has been research on stream signatures for streams that suffer from packet losses [10–13], but they will not be considered here. Other methods for embedding stream signatures into the file format do not offer offline security (as described in section "Authentication System Considerations"), as they are one-time signatures [10,14–16].

A stream signature cannot unfold its power unless we devise a way to embed the overhead packets in the data, as has been previously described in the design considerations of section "Design of the Authentication Method Summary." Stream signatures have been demonstrated to work in MPEG video streams [9] but have not previously been introduced in modern coding standards such as JPEG2000 and MPEG-4, although data embedding methods for these standards exist (section "Labeling (or Captioning)"). This fact led the author to the concept of multiscale image labeling, which will be analyzed in section "Scalability in an Authentication Technique: Multiscale Image Labeling."

Medium-Oriented Authentication Techniques

Watermarking. The basic idea behind watermarking technology is the slight import of information into the media, taking advantage of the imperfections of the human visual system. There also exist visible watermarking techniques; see Reference 17 as an example. An embedded watermark theoretically cannot be removed or modified without visible degradation of the medium. Watermarking is classified among information hiding methods. A bibliography for this subject is given in Reference 18.

Reasons for not choosing the technique of watermarking are the following:

- Watermarking techniques have not yet been convincing for their effectiveness. First-generation watermarking (and practically all of the commercial solutions) has proven exceptionally weak on simple attacks, a fact that renders their legal credit easily questionable. The watermarking techniques currently under research are not convincing for their reliability and the results are rather disappointing. The greatest problem, in general, is synchronization of the watermarking detector, which can easily be lost by very simple and also slight or imperceptible image transformations [19,20].

- An important characteristic of watermarking is that water-marking techniques do modify the data, although these modifications are supposed to be imperceptible to the consumer. Quality degradation and modification of the original artistic medium may dissatisfy the candidate recipients of this technology — artists and consumers. Also, certain applications may strictly not allow any modification of the data, as in the example of evidential images.
- The complexity and the computational power demand of state-of-the-art watermarking techniques are deemed to be unreasonable; this is a weak point when targeting consumer electronics' and portable devices' technology. Watermarking is probably better suited to the subject of intellectual property, rather than casual data integrity control.

It would also be possible for a security solution to utilize other methods of integrity authentication combined with watermarking. For an example of combining watermarking and labeling, see Reference 21 (refer to section "Labeling (or Captioning)" for a description of labeling).

Labeling (or Captioning). By using labeling, which is the insertion of authentication tags in the image or video data in a way that is transparent to a noncompliant decoder, offline source and integrity authentication is possible. Similar to traditional integrity schemes, the absence of the labels implies uncertainty of the image or video integrity. To support the credibility of the labeling method, several labeling schemes for state-of-the-art coding standards will be introduced in the following subsections.

Labeling in JPEG2000. There exist three possible methods to do labeling in the JPEG2000 coding standard:

- *Component extension.* In component extension, authentication tags are introduced as an extra component in the image, for certain progression orders that allow the multiplexing of the extra component with the other components in the image bit stream. It should be noted that this method is probably not compliant with the basic JPEG2000 standard.
- *After coding termination.* In Reference 22, a method that inserts data into a JPEG2000 codestream is presented. The method uses a detail of the JPEG2000 encoder: after each coding pass termination (between entropy coding and rate allocation), it is possible to insert data without affecting a normal JPEG2000-compliant decoder. More information on the encoder can be found in the standard [23, Annex C: §3.4, p. 90: Annex D, §4.1, p. 99] and in Reference 24. Behind the encoder lies the EBCOT algorithm [25].

- *Multiplexing (general method).* The JPEG2000 standard offers freedom in how to construct the bit stream. This fact allows the multiplexing of the authentication component with the basic image components (as in the component extension method) and additionally allows controlling its frequency of occurrence in the final bit stream with precision. This would, however, raise the complexity of an encoder. A similar technique is opting for using a more general file format, as follows in the next subsections.

Labeling in the jpm and jpx File Formats. The jpx format is described as an extension in JPEG2000–ISO/IEC FCD15444-2, Annex L: extended file format syntax. It allows the insertion of XML descriptors and MPEG-7 metadata. It also incorporates an Intellectual Property Rights (IPR) box and a Digital Signature box that uses certain hash and digital signature algorithms in order to protect any data part in the .jpx file.

The term "box" refers to a binary sequence that contains objects and has the general form |size|type|contents|. Unknown types of boxes are to be ignored by normal decoders (according to the standard's L.10 directive), so there is the possibility of creating custom boxes without losing compatibility. This, in fact, enables one to create more diverse labeling methods, such us the one presented in this chapter.

The jpm (ISO/IEC FCD15444-6) standard is about the transmission of images through the Internet and it also allows the use of XML and IPR boxes. In both of these formats, JPEG2000 codestreams in jpc and jp2 format can be inserted as boxes (named Media Data box and Contiguous Codestream box in the .jpm format).

The incorporation of labeling methods in the jpx and jpm standards is very simple and possibly more robust than using the JPEG2000 labeling methods described earlier.

Labeling in Motion-JPEG2000 and MPEG-4. The JPEG2000, Motion-JPEG2000, MPEG-4, and QuickTime standards have some common characteristics: they all share the same file format structure that comprises objects. Boxes in Motion-JPEG2000 are called atoms in QuickTime and MPEG-4, and they are formatted as |size|type|contents|. Furthermore, unknown objects are ignored, a directive that allows the definition of objects specifically designed for our authentication application. The reader is referred to References 26 and 27.

Content-Based Multimedia

Advanced data integrity techniques include content-based signatures. Content-based digital signatures are data integrity techniques applied to the data content, such as low-level image descriptors (edges [28] with the popular canny edge detector [29], textures, histograms [30],

DCT coefficients as feature codes [31], and wavelet coefficient heuristics [32]) or semantic nonautomatic descriptions (e.g., MPEG-7). A digital signature is applied not to the image bit stream, but to the image's content description, thereby authenticating the content of the image. Commercial automatic content-authentication systems typically claim to be highly robust. However, as cited by state-of-the-art research in computer vision, all automated content extraction methods are unreliable and perform satisfactorily only in custom and well-defined conditions. Therefore, human-assisted algorithms would ensure performance of content-based signatures.

Modern coding standards could provide the framework for higher-level human-assisted image descriptors. In modern coding standards, the creator can influence the coding of the image or video. This will be supported in more detail in section "The Example of JPEG2000." This idea is similar to the method of Perceptual Image Hashing with a noninversive compression technique presented in Reference 33. In addition, scalability is a new important trend in image and video coding standards, but commercial content-based authentication systems do not address scalability; so there is a need to optimize content-based signature methods with scalability robustness, a fact that can be tackled with modern scalable coding standards, leading to the term "scalable content-based digital signature" (section "The Example of JPEG2000").

NEW DIRECTIONS IN AUTHENTICATION METHOD DESIGN

Traditional (and commercial) media authentication systems are not designed for multiscale media and are, therefore, inappropriate for multicasting and other applications of scalability. Second, they are usually not content oriented or they did not consider this trend during their design.

Scalability in an Authentication Technique: Multiscale Image Labeling

To address scalability, each label should only be dependent on its corresponding layer (scale). A simple solution to the scalability of digital media is to insert a label containing a digital signature between each data part of the media, like the "hash and sign" method. However, this solution is inefficient. This can be solved by incorporating research on more advanced stream digital signatures (section "Efficient Data Authentication Techniques: Stream Signatures") that have the benefit that the cryptographic properties of a single digital signature can be spread over multiple data with low additional computational cost.

What Is the Relationship between Labeling and the Image Content?

State-of-the-art media coding techniques take steps toward encoding the media content.

The Example of JPEG2000. In JPEG2000, it is possible to ignore designing a content extraction algorithm, because the encoder indirectly provides a version of such an algorithm. More specifically, for JPEG2000:

- Signing the local maxima on the multiscale layers [34] is equivalent to authenticating the image edges [35]. Local maxima remain at high compression rates.

- The basic layer (LL) of the multiscale image is the most important layer and is encoded (and therefore authenticated) first.

- The image bit stream can be reallocated so that most of the image's information is transmitted first and the not-so-important details follow. Human intervention is therefore introduced in deciding which image context or information is important and which is not, a task that is yet impossible for the automatic content extraction tools. JPEG2000 includes ROI (region of interest) coding and, in general, provides the freedom to precisely choose the position of every encoded packet in the final bit stream, for every layer up to providing lossless coding for any image.

If one considers the scalability property of modern coding standards, then one may come up with the term "scalable content-based digital signatures," which provide content authentication of scalable versions of images and video.

Discussion of JPEG2000's Ability for Content-Oriented Encoding. One could object that JPEG2000 does not really encode the image content. In addition, content encoding implies that there exist subjective factors that influence image encoding. A good example is that content encoding could prove catastrophic to artistic image encoding; different people perceive the image in completely different ways that no automatic or human-assisted content description operation can ever predict.

In that case, we could say that the encoded image is not content oriented but, instead, that it is encoded hierarchically in a content-oriented way. This means that, on the one hand, the image is coded losslessly (no information is being left out), but, on the other hand, the encoded image's packet hierarchy is carefully chosen so that the most probably important image elements are encoded first.

To conclude, JPEG2000's design enables us to do integrity authentication of the scalable bit stream by using scalable labeling and at the same time establish a connection to the original image's content. This fact enables the characterization of the labeled encoded JPEG2000 image as a "self-contained content-based digital signature." This type of digital signature is very useful in reliable multimedia storage in insecure systems (section "Application Scenarios").

The Complete Authentication Method

The image authentication mechanism can take two forms. One is the self-contained autonomous content-based signature and the other is the authentication information targeted for embedding in specific code-streams. Examples of each type will be given as application scenarios in section "Application Scenarios." The implementation of the authentication method and related issues can be found in Reference 36.

Choosing Parameters and Primitives: Stream Signature, Labeling Technique, Digital Signature Technique. Some important factors for choosing cryptographic primitives are the proven security of the primitive (old, well-tested, and enhanced primitives like Rivest-Shamir-Adleman (RSA) may qualify for this), the primitive's throughput (it is important to work with fast algorithms), its availability internationally (possible imposed patents or restrictions are undesirable), and the implementation cost (hardware and software availability — depends on the design of the system). Another very important factor is key length, which should be chosen so that it could protect the data for a reasonable amount of time; in the case of multimedia, this should probably be at least a decade, although it is very difficult to foresee technological advances that will affect the security of the mechanism.

Based on the above, a brief selection procedure will result in the following choices:

- *Stream signature*. The efficiency of the authentication method clearly depends in the type of stream signature. The offline stream signature combined with secure hash algorithm (SHA-1) as a hash primitive and RSA of at least 1024 bits key length (and perhaps 2048 bits for more security) is very efficient compared to other constructions like "hash and sign," as has already been analyzed in section "Efficient Data Authentication Techniques: Stream Signatures."
- *Labeling method*. jpm, jpx for image and MPEG-4 and QuickTime and Motion-JPEG2000 for video are the most elegant file formats that allow the configuration of boxes as labels. However, a design should be oriented to a popular format, but this wide acceptance cannot be foreknown for modern standards at the time of writing.

An example of the complete authentication signature for the low-speed Internet is presented in Figure 8.6. In general, the length of the blocks that the stream signature operates on should actually be selected according to the application needs; the key factor would be the data rate, thus providing low overhead for the signature bits in each case.

Optimizing the Stream Signature Technique for Scalable Video. A modification to stream signatures that has existed since the creation of

| 3.194 | 50.352 | 63.292 | 159.953 |

Figure 8.6. These successive instances of the JPEG2000 image have 160-bit authentication tags embedded after each coding termination. Numbers show the file size in bytes after the insertion of each tag.

authentication trees [8, §15.2.1(iv)] is to apply the stream signature to streams where each individual packet could contain a substream. As an example, authentication trees could contain other authentication trees as leaves in the tree. This technique allows the designer of video (and, of course, image) authentication techniques to optimize for scalability:

- In video coding, there exists two-dimensional scalability: time scalability along with quality scalability. Instead of calculating one stream signature (which includes one digital signature) per time interval (e.g., per fixed number of frames), it is possible to expand the stream signature so that it includes blocks of substreams. For example, looking at Figure 8.7, B1 is frame 1, B2 is frame 2, and so on. Each frame's quality is addressable and time scalability

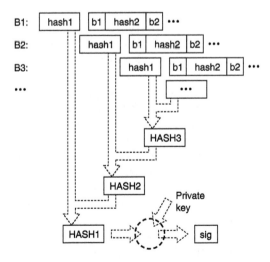

Figure 8.7. Optimized stream signature for scalable video.

257

is maintained, as each frame can be uniquely decoded and authenticated.

- The technique can be applied similarly to general object-based coding standards like jpx. The stream signature operates on groupings of objects (or boxes) so that a single digital signature operates to each group ("sig" operating in the figure's objects; Figure 8.7) while preserving scalability in each individual object (B1, B2,... in Figure 8.7).

Choice of Digital Signature Schemes for Adaptation to Real Models. Some unpopular digital signature schemes have been devised in the past that could greatly enhance an authentication method's applicability to real-world scenarios.

- *Group signatures.* Group signatures are a relevantly recent concept, introduced in Reference 37 in 1991. Group signatures can be used to conceal an organization's infrastructure (i.e., issue a single public key for the whole organization). Their description is as follows. A member of the group can sign anonymously on behalf of the group. In case of a dispute, the identity of the creator of the signature can be revealed only by a designated entity, the group manager. Nobody (even the group manager) can attribute a signature's origin to someone else or sign on behalf of another person in the group.

    Several group signature techniques have been presented in the literature, designed for small and for large groups. Some relevant publications are References 38 and 39. An application example of group signatures can be seen in Figure 8.9.

- *Forward-secure signatures.* The application of forward-secure signatures has the pleasant property that the validity of past signatures is maintained even if the present secret or private key is disclosed. Another property of forward-secure signatures is that it is not possible to forge signatures of past time intervals in cases of secret or private key disclosure. This property is very important, especially if we think that the problem of revealing secret or private keys exists in applications but no satisfactory solution has been given. For example, in Reference 40, the possible problem of a photographic camera being stolen or withheld, along with all the implications of this (key extraction by camera tampering and forging of later signatures), is discussed, however without suggesting any solution other than avoiding this situation.

    In general, it is desired and possible to construct forward-secure signatures based on, for example, RSA. Various techniques have been presented in the literature [41–44].

Application Scenarios

The application examples that follow are directly related to the general applications of scalability.

Image and Video Transmission on the Internet. Looking at Figure 8.8, a lossless image or video is gradually transmitted from the creator to another user up to a desired quality level, being authenticated at the same time. Please note that the public key could also be included in the final file, provided that a digital signature certificate is also included in the data. That is, of course, only if trust could be attributed to the entity responsible for keeping the certificates authentic.

Commercial Case: Secure Transmission and Distribution of Media. A commercial multimedia distribution scheme is presented and described in Figure 8.9. The scheme is complemented by utilizing group signatures. This scheme links the creator of the content to the distributor and then to all of the clients while preserving the uniqueness of the creator's signature, as no entity can forge a group signature. The scheme is straightforward, as there is no need to generate another version of the image or video for each customer. Bearing in mind that the original work is scalable, each customer can receive a quality-degraded part (according to bandwidth, requirements, subscription status, etc.) or even the lossless-complete version by simply cutting down the size or rate of the distributed media.

Reliable Storage of Multimedia Data in Unreliable Storage Entities. Thinking in a similar fashion as in Figure 8.9, the original creator of an image or video could store the work (with the embedded authentication signature) in a server (the distributor in the figure), which can later be accessed by another user or client. An important feature is that, due to the

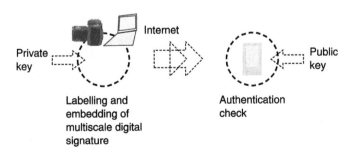

Figure 8.8. Simple case of image or video transmission on the Internet (identical to Figure 8.1 and Figure 8.2).

Creation of original work, labelling and embedding of multiscale digital signature

Creator

Private key

Possibly insecure channel

Work is checked for authenticity

Distributors group key

Distributors

Then distributed in different qualities (q1, q2, q3,..) according to end-user

Possibly insecure distribution channel

q1   q2   q3

Work is checked for authenticity

Distributors group key

Customers/clients

Figure 8.9. Image or video original content creation and commercial distribution. The distributor could be a press agency.

presence of a secure channel provided by the digital signature, the storage entity can be unreliable, as no attacker could tamper with the image without detection (based on a digital signature's high cryptographic strength). It is therefore possible to relax the requirements for a very secure server that is trusted to keep the integrity of the data stored. (In unreliable storage entities, it is possible that one could regenerate the signature for an original work and claim rights. This can be solved by the use of timestamping during the original work's creation.)

In addition, users can access the media files from the server at different qualities and speeds according to their bandwidth and access rights. This is a main feature of modern coding standards — scalability — so there is no need to store many files for every image or video. Furthermore, authentication for any user is straightforward, backed up by the public key mechanism.

The same concept could be used in human-assisted authentication queries: an image database that would hold a version of the content-oriented digital signatures (i.e., the original work with the embedded authentication signatures up to a certain bit-stream size) could be used by a human operator to authenticate the content of a downgraded image in question.

Credibility Problems of the Digital Photographic Image and Digital Video. The introduction of the technique suggested in this chapter in the hardware part of a complete solution could enhance the reliability of an image or video authentication system. This is, of course, not a new idea. Commercial authentication photographic cameras and image authentication systems already exist.

However, do such authentication systems have any credibility? The answer is not yet clear, as the suggestion of a hardware digital signature generation transfers the problem to a new domain — the reliability of security hardware — which has been questioned [45].

CONCLUSIONS AND FURTHER WORK

To recapitulate, an authentication method under various considerations has been presented. This method allows the source and integrity authentication of scalable images and scalable video sources in the form of the modern coding standards JPEG2000 and MPEG-4. The use of labeling has been exploited instead of modifications of the medium such as watermarking because of its efficiency and practicality. The above could all be summed up in a "scalable content-based digital signature" concept that has many practical applications.

Finally, it has been found that recent advances in cryptography present new potential dimensions to the manipulation of digital multimedia and could complement the application of the proposed method in real-world scenarios.

Further work on this subject could include investigations of techniques for packet-loss tolerance. A complete system would also involve the combination of all the special digital signature methods in a single primitive.

Another subject would be the investigation of the scalable authentication method in complete DRM systems, an area of current great interest.

ACKNOWLEDGMENT

The author would like to thank Associate Prof. Dimitrios Mitrakos of Aristotle University of Thessaloniki, Department of Electrical and Computer Engineering, for his encouragement and support during the early version of this work, as found in Reference 36.

APPENDIX: MULTIMEDIA SECURITY AND THE IMPORTANCE OF AUTHENTICATION

Two important concepts related to the security of digital media are:

- Source authentication (or data origin authentication)
- Integrity authentication (or message authentication)

These two concepts are bound under the term "authentication." Source authentication assures data origin (that data actually originated from its reputed source) and message authentication provides for message or media integrity. These two concepts are, by definition, inseparable: the tampering of data has the automatic effect that the tampered data originated from another source (the entity responsible for the modification), whereas claims about the integrity of data originating from an undefined source cannot be held [8, §9.6.1]. In the next subsections, we will clarify the concepts related to the security of digital media and establish a better understanding of security mechanisms and the importance of authentication in the overall design of a system.

Source and Integrity Authentication Should Not Be Confused with Entity Authentication

Source and message integrity authentication and entity authentication are different concepts: entity authentication (or identification) takes place during an online authentication protocol and its validity is confined to that transaction only.

Entity authentication can be found to be insufficient for large distribution systems, as the complexity of the system can vary and it would, therefore, be necessary to attribute trust to or set up authentication mechanisms for all of the entities that comprise the distribution system (starting from the creator of the content, all the way to all of the distributors and redistributors of multimedia content in the distribution chain).

Source and integrity (message) authentication and entity authentication contribute to classifying the authentication systems as either online or offline. However, they are not the absolute factors that classify the system as, for example, there exist both online and offline message authentication techniques. Online and offline methods have been briefly discussed in section "Authentication System Considerations."

Why Authentication and Not Encryption?

Although techniques that provide message authentication by utilizing encryption exist, it is a mistake to assume that encryption automatically does message authentication. See Reference 8 (§ 9.6.5) for details. Examples of methods that provide authentication by using encryption are the following:

- Embedding the hash value before encryption. Careful consideration should be given to the choice of cryptographic algorithms.
- Embedding a secret authenticator prior to encryption.

REFERENCES

1. ISO/IEC JTC 1/SC 29/WG 1, Coding of Still Pictures. JPEG 2000 Part I Final Committee Draft Version 1.0, ISO/IEC FCD15444-1: 2000 (V1.0, 16 March 2000).
2. Tutorial on JPEG2000 and Overview of the Technology, http://jj2000.epfl.ch/jj_tutorials/index.html.
3. Rabbani, M. and Santa-Cruz, D., The JPEG 2000 Still-Image Compression Standard, presented at *International Conference in Image Processing (ICIP)*, Thessaloniki, Greece, 2001.
4. Christopoulos, C., Skodras, A., and Ebrahimi, T., The JPEG2000 still image coding system: an overview, *IEEE Trans. Consumer Electron.*, 46(4), 1103–1127, 2000.
5. Special edition on JPEG 2000, Ebrahimi, T., Christopoulos, C., and Leed, D.T., Eds., *Signal Processing: Image Communication, Science Direct*, 17(1), January 2002.
6. Adams, M., The JPEG-2000 Still Image Compression Standard, ISO/IEC JTC 1/SC 29/WG 1 N 2412, December 2002.
7. Merkle, R., A certified digital signature, in *Advances in Cryptology, Crypto 89*, Brassard, G., Ed., *Lecture Notes in Computer Science*, Vol. 435, Springer-Verlag, New York, 1989, pp. 218–238.
8. Menezes, A., van Oorschot, P., and Vanstone, S., *Handbook of Applied Cryptography*. CRC Press, Boca Raton, FL, 1997.
9. Gennaro, N. and Rohatgi, P., How to Sign Digital Streams, presented at *Crypto 97*, 1997.
10. Perrig, A. et al., Efficient Authentication and Signing of Multicast Streams over Lossy Channels, presented at *IEEE Symposium on Security and Privacy 2000*, pp. 56–73.
11. Golle P. and Modadugu, N., Authenticating Streamed Data in the Presence of Random Packet Loss, presented at *ISOC Network and Distributed System Security Symposium*, 2001, pp. 13–22.
12. Wong, C. and Lam, S., Digital signatures for flows and multicasts, *IEEE/ACM Trans. on Networking*, 7(4), 502–513, 1999.
13. Miner, S. and Staddon, J., Graph-Based Authentication of Digital Streams, presented at *IEEE Symposium on Security and Privacy*, 2001.
14. Anderson, R. et al., A new family of authentication protocols, *ACM Operating Systems Review*, 1998, Vol. 32, no. 4, ACM, pp. 9–20.
15. Rohatgi, P., A Compact and Fast Hybrid Signature Scheme for Multicast Packet Authentication, in *Proceedings of 6th ACM Conference on Computer and Communication Security*, 1999.
16. Perrig, A. et al., Efficient and Secure Source Authentication for Multicast, presented at *Network and Distributed System Security Symposium, NDSS '01*, 2001.
17. Mintzer, F., Lotspiech, J., and Morimoto, N., Safeguarding digital library contents and users. Digital watermarking. *D-Lib on-line Mag.*, 1997, http://www.dlib.org.
18. Anderson, R. and Petitcolas, F., Information Hiding: An Annotated Bibliography, http://www.cl.cam.ac.uk/~fapp2/steganography/bibliography/.
19. Petitcolas, F., Anderson, R., and Kuhn, M., Attacks on Copyright Marking Systems, *Second Workshop on Information Hiding, Lecture Notes in Computer Science*, Aucsmith, D., Ed., 1998, Vol. 1525, pp. 218–238.

20. Petitcolas, F., Weakness of existing watermarking schemes. stirmark — samples, http://www.petitcolas.net/fabien/watermarking/stirmark31/samples.html.
21. Herrigel, A., An Image Security Solution for JPEG 2000, presented at *Seminar on Imaging Security and JPEG2000*, Vancouver, 1999.
22. Grosbois, R., Gerbelot, P., and Ebrahimi, T., Authentication and Access Control in the JPEG 2000 Compressed Domain, *Applications of Digital Image Processing XXIV*, *SPIE 46th Annual Meeting Proceedings*, San Diego, July 29–August 3, Vol. 4472, SPIE, 2001, pp. 95–104.
23. JPEG 2000 Related Publications, http://jj2000.epfl.ch/jj_publications/index.html.
24. Taubman, D. et al., Embedded Block Coding in JPEG2000, in *Proceedings of the IEEE International Conference on Image Processing (ICIP)*, September 2000, Vol. 2, pp. 33–36.
25. Taubman, D., High performance scalable image compression with EBCOT, *IEEE Trans. Image Process.*, 9(7), 1151–1170, 2000.
26. Houchin, J. and Singer, D., File format technology in JPEG 2000 enables flexible use of still and motion sequences, *Signal Process.: Image Commun.*, 17, 131–144, 2002.
27. ISO/IEC JTC 1/SC 29/WG 1, Coding of Still Pictures. ISO/IEC 15444-3 (JPEG 2000, Part 3) Committee Draft.
28. Dittmann, J., Steinmetz, A., and Steinmetz, R., Content Based Digital Signature for Motion Pictures Authentication and Content-Fragile Watermarking, in *Proceedings of the IEEE International Conference on Multimedia Computing and Systems (ICMCS)*, IEEE Computer Society, New York, 1999, Vol. II, pp. 209–213.
29. Canny, J., A computational approach to edge detection, *IEEE Trans. Pattern Anal. Mach. Intell.*, 8, 679–698, 1986.
30. Chang, S. and Schneider, M., A Robust Content Based Digital Signature for Image Authentication, presented at *IEEE International Conference on Image Processing (ICIP)*, Lausanne, 1996.
31. Lin, C. and Chang, S., Generating Robust Digital Signature for Image/Video Authentication, presented at *ACM Multimedia and Security Workshop*, Bristol, 1998.
32. Lu, C. and Liao, H., Structural Digital Signature for Image Authentication: An Incidental Distortion Resistant Scheme, presented at *ACM Multimedia Workshop*, 2000, pp. 115–118.
33. Mihçak, M. and Venkatesan, R., New Iterative Geometric Methods for Robust Perceptual Image Hashing, presented at *ACM Workshop on Security and Privacy in Digital Rights Management*, Philadelphia, 2001.
34. Mallat, S., *A Wavelet Tour of Signal Processing*, Academic Press, San Diego, CA, 1998.
35. Mallat, S. and Zhong, S., Characterization of signals from multiscale edges, *IEEE Trans. Pattern Anal. Mach. Intell.*, 14, 710–732, 1992.
36. Skraparlis, D., Methods for Safeguarding Authenticity and Integrity of Digital Image and Video during Reception, Transmission and Distribution via Communication Networks, Diploma thesis, Aristotle University of Thessaloniki, 2002 (in Greek).
37. Chaum, D. and van Heyst, E., Group Signatures, in *Advances in Cryptology*, EUROCRYPT'91, *Lecture Notes in Computer Science*, Vol. 547, Springer-Verlag, Berlin, 1991, pp. 257–265.
38. Ateniese, G. et al., A practical and provably secure coalition-resistant group signature scheme, in *Advances in Cryptology CRYPTO 2000, Lecture Notes in Computer Science*, Vol. 1880, Springer-Verlag, 2000, pp. 255–270.
39. Camenisch, J. and Damgård, I., Verifiable Encryption, Group Encryption, and Their Applications to Separable Group Signatures and Signature Sharing Schemes, presented at *Asiacrypt 2000*, 2000, pp. 331–345.
40. Eastman Kodak Whitepaper. Understanding and Integrating Kodak Picture Authentication Cameras, 2000.

41. Krawczyk, H., Simple Forward-Secure Signatures from Any Signature Scheme, presented at *ACM Conference on Computer and Communications Security*, 2000, pp. 108–115.
42. Anderson, R., Invited Lecture, presented at *Fourth Annual Conference on Computer and Communications Security*, ACM, 1997.
43. Bellare, M. and Miner, S., A Forward-Secure Digital Signature Scheme, presented at *Crypto 99*, 1999, pp. 431–448.
44. Itkis, G. and Reyzin, L., Forward-Secure Signatures with Optimal Signing and Verifying, presented at *Crypto 01*, 2001, pp. 332–354.
45. Anderson, R. and Kuhn, M., Tamper Resistance — A Cautionary Note, in *The Second USENIX Workshop on Electronic Commerce Proceedings*, Oakland, CA, 1996, pp. 1–11, http://www.usenix.org

9
Signature-Based Media Authentication

Qibin Sun and Shih-Fu Chang

In other chapters of this book, we know that (semifragile) watermarking solutions work well in protecting the integrity of multimedia content. Here, we are interested in those authentication methods that protect both content integrity and source identity. In cryptography, digital signature techniques are the natural tools for addressing data authentication issues. To date, many signature-based authentication technologies, particularly Public Key Infrastructure (PKI), have been incorporated into international standards (e.g., X.509) and state-of-the-art network protocols (e.g., SSL, Secure Socket Layer) for the purposes of data integrity and source identification. It would be great if we could extend digital signature schemes from data authentication to multimedia authentication. First, the system security of a digital signature scheme, which is a very important issue in authentication, has been well studied in cryptography. Second, the current security protocols in a network, which work for data exchange or streaming, do not need to redesign for multimedia exchange or streaming. Therefore, in this chapter, we focus on the discussion of authenticating multimedia content based on digital signature schemes, although digital watermarking techniques might be employed in some specific schemes.

Considering that the content in this chapter closely relates to the techniques from multimedia processing and analysis, security and cryptography, communication and coding, and so forth, we start by introducing the basic concepts and unifying the technical terms. More detailed descriptions on state-of-the-art signature-based authentication methods are categorized and presented in sections "Complete Authentication," "Content Authentication," and "A Unified Signature-Based Authentication Framework for JPEG2000 Images," respectively. Section "System Performance Evaluation" discusses how to evaluate the performance of multimedia authentication systems. Section "Summary and Future Work" summarizes this chapter and discusses future work.

INTRODUCTION
Basic Concepts and Definitions

Multimedia authentication is a relatively new research area compared to other "traditional" research areas such as multimedia compression. Different researchers with different research backgrounds may have different understandings of the term "authentication." For example, people from multimedia watermarking usually use the term "authentication" to refer to content integrity protection; people from biometrics may use the term to refer to source identification, verification, and so forth. To help the reader, we first introduce some concepts and definitions borrowed from cryptography [1,2], in which digital signature techniques have been well studied for traditional computer systems. We then extend them for multimedia applications.

Data Authentication. Data authentication is a process determined by the authorized receivers, and perhaps the arbiters, that the particular data was most probably sent by the authorized transmitter and has not subsequently been altered or substituted. Data authentication usually associates with data integrity and nonrepudiation (i.e., source identification) because these issues are very often related to each other: data that has been altered effectively should have a new source; and if a source cannot be determined, then the question of alteration cannot be settled (without reference to the original source).

Data Integrity. Data integrity means that the receiver can verify that the data has not been altered by even one bit during the transmission. The attacker should not be able to substitute false data for the real data.

Nonrepudiation. Nonrepudiation, also called *source identification*, means the data sender should not be able to falsely deny the fact that he sent the data.

Typical methods for providing data authentication are digital signature schemes (DSS) together with a data or message authentication code (DAC or MAC), which actually is a type of keyed one-way hash function.

One-Way Hash Function. The one-way hash function or crypto hash is a hash function that works only in one direction. A good one-way hash function should have the following requirements: (1) given a message m and a hash function H, it should be easy and fast to compute the hash $h = H(m)$; (2) given h, it is hard to compute m such that $h = H(m)$ (i.e., the hash function should be one-way); (3) given m, it is hard to find another data m' such that $H(m') = H(m)$ (i.e., collision-free). Such a crypto hash guarantees that even a one-bit change in the data will result in a totally different hash value. To differentiate it from other kinds of hash functions, we introduce a *crypto hash*, which will be used throughout this chapter. Typical crypto hash functions include MD5 (128 bits) and SHA-1 (160 bits) [1,2].

Digital Signature Schemes. The digital signature scheme (DSS) is a bit string that associates the data with some originating entity. It includes a signature generation (signing) procedure and a signature verification procedure. Public key DSS is a very common technology and has been adopted as the international standard for data authentication [1,2]. Public key DSS uses the sender's private key to generate the signature and his public key to verify to a recipient the integrity of data and identity of the sender of the data. Typical public key DSS include the well-known Rivest-Shamir-Adleman algorithm (RSA) and digital signature algorithm (DSA) [1,2]. Figure 9.1 shows the block diagram of RSA and DSA digital signature schemes. Given an arbitrary length of data, a short fixed-length hash value is obtained by a crypto hash operation (e.g., 128 bits by MD5 or 160 bits by SHA-1). The signature is generated using the sender's private key to sign on the hash value (a standard length of private key, public key, and the generated signature is 1024 bits). The original data associated with its signature is then sent to the intended recipients. Later, the recipient can verify whether his received data was altered and the data was really sent from the sender, by using the sender's public key to authenticate the validity of the attached signature. The final authentication result is then drawn from a bit-by-bit comparison between two hash values (one is decrypted from the signature and the other is obtained by rehashing the received data; refer to Figure 9.1) by the criterion: even if for one-bit difference, the received data will be deemed unauthentic.

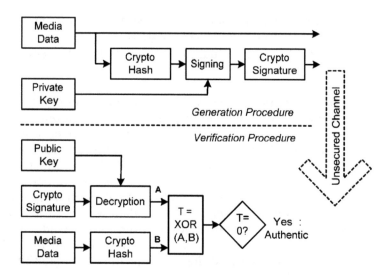

Figure 9.1. Block diagram of crypto signature schemes.

To differentiate the original public key digital signature schemes in cryptography from their modified schemes in multimedia security, we name them *crypto signatures*.

Data vs. Content. Given a specific type of multimedia (e.g., image), multimedia data refers to the exact representation (e.g., binary bit stream). Multimedia content refers to its understanding or its meaning on the same representation. For example, before and after lossy compression, multimedia data should be different while multimedia content could be the same.

Content Authentication. For content authentication, as long as the meaning of multimedia content is not changed, it should be considered authentic, because the meaning of multimedia is based on content instead of data. Such requirements come from real applications where manipulations of the data without changing the meaning of content are considered acceptable. Lossy compression and transcoding are examples. In addition to the distortions from malicious attacks, these acceptable manipulations will also introduce distortions into the multimedia content.

Incidental Distortion and Intentional Distortion. Content authentication has to deal with two types of distortion. One is the distortion introduced by malicious content modifications (e.g., content meaning alteration) from attackers (hereafter we refer this type of distortion as intentional distortion); the other is the distortion from real applications, where some manipulation of content (e.g., lossy compression or transcoding) has to be considered allowable during the process of media transmission and storage (hereafter we refer to this type of distortion as incidental distortion). Content authentication has to tolerate all incidental distortions and reject any intentional distortions.

Content-based multimedia authentication has many potential applications. Consider the case of a police station transmitting a suspect's image to its officers' mobile terminals in order to identify a criminal. The policemen need to have guarantees that the image they received was indeed from the station. The police station also wishes to ensure that the sent image was not altered during transmission. However, due to different models of mobile terminals used by the policemen and different bandwidth conditions between the station and each policeman, the authentic image will undergo some manipulations such as lossy compression or format conversion before reaching the policemen's mobile terminals. The image still needs to be securely authenticated in such a case. Therefore, we have two requirements to consider. On the one hand, the scheme must be *secure* enough to prevent any attacked content from passing the authentication test (sensitive to intentional distortions). On the other hand, the scheme also needs to be *robust* enough to accept an image that has undergone some acceptable manipulations (insensitive to incidental distortions). The authentication robustness to the incidental distortions is the main difference between data authentication and content authentication because no robustness is required for data authentication (any bit change is not allowable).

It would be interesting to put all authentication-related technologies into one graph (Figure 9.2) in terms of three functions: integrity protection, source identification, and robustness. Ideally, from a signed handwritten signature on paper we (the trained experts) could identify who is the signer even in the case that the handwritten signature varies a lot; but we cannot tell whether the signed paper content was altered or not because no link exists between his signature and the paper content he signed. Digital watermarking could achieve a good capability of integrity protection at a high robustness level, but most watermarking schemes are unable to securely identify the source (i.e., the true and undeniable watermark embedder) because a symmetric key is used for both watermark embedding and watermark extraction. Crypto signature schemes can achieve both integrity protection and source identification at a very high security level; but their robustness level is fragile (i.e., any bit change will result in a failure of authentication). Media signature for content authentication, which covers all three functions in a tunable manner, is the topic we mainly discuss in this chapter.

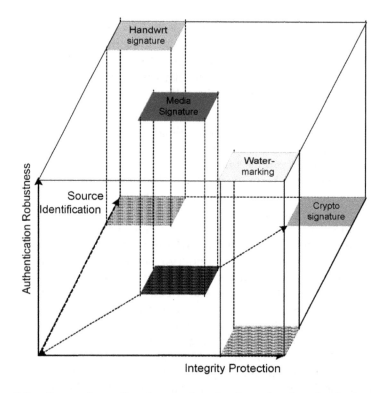

Figure 9.2.   Comparison of various authentication-related technologies.

Signature-Based Content Authentication

As we described in the previous subsection, data authentication provides the authentication result in such a way that even data changed by one bit will be claimed as unauthentic (i.e., the data to be verified is either authentic or unauthentic). Such a criterion motivated the researchers to create many crypto signature schemes whose system security level is very high and can even be proved mathematically. DSA and RSA are two good crypto signature schemes adopted by the international standards [1,2].

The requirement of a certain level of authentication robustness is the main difference between data authentication and content authentication. Such a difference makes authenticating multimedia content much more challenging and complex than authenticating multimedia data [3,4].

- A good media signature is required to be robust to *all* incidental distortions and sensitive to *any* intentional distortions. However, different incidental distortions come from different defined acceptable content manipulations. Defining acceptable content manipulations is application dependent.

- Given a specific application, it is very hard to formalize a clear boundary between incidental distortions and intentional distortions (i.e., differentiating the acceptable content manipulations clearly from the malicious content modifications). Consequently, instead of presenting the authentication result precisely as either authentic or unauthentic, content authentication may have to say "don't know" in some circumstances, as shown in Figure 9.3. It also means that a certain false acceptance rate and false rejection rate are normal in the case of content authentication.

- An existing gray area in authentication results implies that system security is not as good as data authentication, although we could argue that the portion of system security impaired by system robustness could be compensated for by the contextual property of the media content. For example, if the attacker is to modify a black pixel to the white one in a natural image, the case that its surrounding pixels are all black is more likely to be detected than that its surrounding pixels are all white pixels.

Based on the robustness level of authentication and the distortions introduced into the content during content signing, we categorize state-of-the-art techniques based on signature-based authentication as follows (Figure 9.4). Different types of signature-based authentication methods

(a) Data authentication   (b) Content authentication

Figure 9.3. Presentation of authentication results.

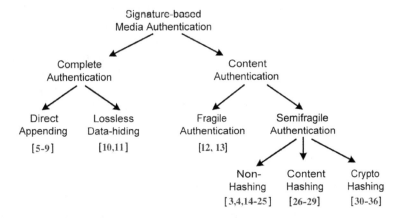

Figure 9.4. Categories of signature-based authentication.

are targeted for different applications:

Complete authentication. Complete authentication refers to directly applying the crypto signature scheme to multimedia data authentication. It works in a way that the multimedia data to be sent to the recipient is either in its original form [5–9] or is able to be exactly recovered at the receiver site [10,11]. We call it complete authentication because the case of any bit changing its original form will be deemed unauthentic. The generated signature is sent to the recipient either by appending it to the data or by inserting it into the data in a lossless way. Note that complete authentication cannot only authenticate the stable multimedia data, but also authenticate the streaming multimedia data, even slightly robust to packet loss.

Content authentication. Content authentication includes fragile authentication and semifragile (sometimes it is also called semirobust) authentication. We call it content authentication because both methods need to "distort" the multimedia data to achieve the authentication.

Fragile authentication. Fragile authentication refers to those methods that authenticate the multimedia content via modifying a small portion of multimedia content, but in a fragile way (i.e., any bit changing in the protected multimedia content is not allowed). Typical solutions are to embed the generated signature into the content via fragile watermarking [12,13]. In other words, it does not have any authentication robustness, although it still needs to modify the multimedia data.

Semifragile authentication. Semifragile authentication refers to those methods that are robust to predefined content manipulations such as lossy compression or transcoding. To achieve a certain level of robustness, the actual data to be authenticated is a "distorted" version of the original multimedia data (e.g., the extracted feature). Its typical approaches include nonhashing methods (i.e., crypto hashing is not applicable for those methods) [3,4,14–25], content hashing methods (i.e., some proprietary methods mapping the content into a short data sequence) [26–29], and crypto hashing methods [30–36].

COMPLETE AUTHENTICATION

Complete authentication refers to directly applying the crypto signature scheme to multimedia data authentication, as shown in Figure 9.1. A detailed description of how to generate and verify the crypto signature can be found in Reference 2 (chap. 8).

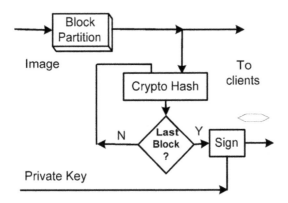

Figure 9.5. Signature generation by successively hashing blocks.

Friedman first proposed to incorporate the crypto signature scheme into digital cameras to make the captured images authentic [5]: the trustworthy digital camera. Later, Quisquater et al. proposed an improved solution by partitioning the image into a number of blocks and then signing on the last hash value obtained by successively crypto hashing block by block [6], as shown in Figure 9.5. It brings some authentication flexibilities for imaging applications such as image editing.

In the direction of increasing authentication flexibility, Gennaro and Rohatgi extend crypto signature schemes from signing static data to signing streaming data and proposed a tree-based authentication structure to increase the efficiency of signature generation [7]. Yu [8] further extended the schemes in Reference 7 to the applications of scalable multimedia streaming. Again, all of these methods do not have any robustness; that is, they cannot tolerate any single bit loss, for authentication. In order to tolerate packet loss, which frequently occurs during data transmission especially over an unreliable channel, Park et al. proposed an interesting authentication work based on the concept of Error Correcting Coding (ECC) [9]. Their basic idea is illustrated in Figure 9.6. Naturally, a MAC has to be appended to its corresponding packet for stream authentication, as shown in the upper part of Figure 9.6. The authentication can be executed after receiving the last packet. Such a scheme cannot deal with packet loss during the transmission because the signature was generated based on all hash values from all packets. To overcome this problem, a straightforward solution is to add some redundancies by attaching several hashes from other packets into the current transmitting packet. If the current packet (e.g., N) is lost, its hash still can be obtained from other packets (e.g., $N+m$). The verification of the whole stream can still be

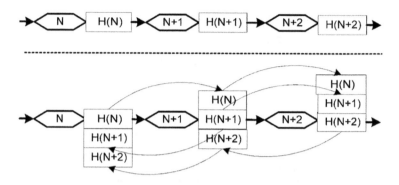

Figure 9.6.   Data streaming authentication robust to packet loss.

executed. Obviously, such solutions obtain a certain robustness by paying for the extra transmission cost. In Reference 9, they proposed an optimized solution that balances the robustness and transmission cost. Although it achieves a certain robustness, we still classify it as complete authentication because all of the received data cannot tolerate any bit errors.

Instead of storing and transmitting the generated signature separately, the generated signature can also be inserted back into the multimedia content via lossless data hiding [10,11]. The basic procedure is as follows:

Signing:

- Generate the crypto signature from the whole set of multimedia data.
- Embed the signature back into the multimedia content in a lossless way (watermarking).
- Send this watermarked multimedia content to the recipient.

Verifying:

- Receive the watermarked content from the sender.
- Extract the signature and recover the original form of the multimedia content.
- Verify the original form of the multimedia content based on the crypto signature scheme.

One example of lossless watermarking is to compress the least significant bit (LSB) portion of the multimedia data by a lossless data compression algorithm such as ZIP and then insert the signature into the free space earned by this lossless data compression algorithm.

CONTENT AUTHENTICATION

Content authentication includes fragile authentication and semifragile (sometimes it is called semirobust) authentication. We call it content authentication because both methods need to modify the multimedia data to achieve the authentication, although the meaning of "modification" is different for fragile and semifragile authentication. For fragile authentication, the content needs to be chopped in portions to store the signatures; for semifragile authentication, the content needs to be abstracted to a level that will tolerate the incidental distortions.

Fragile Authentication

Fragile authentication refers to those methods that authenticate the multimedia content via modifying a small portion of multimedia content, but in a fragile way (i.e., any bit changing in the protected multimedia content is not allowed). Typical solutions can be depicted as follows [12,13].

Signing:

- Set all LSB portions to zero to obtain the protected data.
- Generate the crypto signature by signing on the whole set of protected data.
- Store the signature into the LSB portion to obtain the watermarked multimedia content.
- Send this watermarked multimedia content to the recipient.

Verifying:

- Receive the watermarked content from the sender.
- Extract the signature from the LSB portion of the received multimedia content.
- Regenerate the protected data by setting all LSB portions to zero.
- Verify the protected data based on the selected crypto signature scheme.

Both complete authentication and fragile authentication work on the fragile level; that is, they do not allow any bit change in their protected data. However, complete authentication protects the whole set of multimedia data (i.e., the authentication process will not distort any multimedia data and the users can obtain the original form of their wanted multimedia data), whereas, fragile authentication only protects the multimedia data, excluding the LSB watermarked portion (i.e., the authentication process will distort a small portion of multimedia data permanently and the users can only obtain the watermarked version of the original multimedia data, although the introduced distortion is invisible).

Semifragile Authentication

Semifragile authentication refers to those methods that are robust to pre-defined content manipulations such as lossy compression or transcoding. Usually, it authenticates an abstracted version of the original multimedia data to achieve a certain degree of robustness. Its typical approaches include nonhashing methods (i.e., crypto hashing is not applicable for those methods) [3,4,14–25], content hashing methods (i.e., some proprietary methods mapping the content into a short data sequence) [26–29], and crypto hashing methods (i.e., crypto hashing is incorporated into the scheme) [30–36].

Nonhashing. Originating from the ideas of crypto signature schemes as described earlier, Schneider and Chang [14] and other researchers proposed using some typical content-based measures as the selected features for generating content signature, by assuming that those features are insensitive to incidental distortions but sensitive to intentional distortions. Those features include the histogram map [14], the edge or corner map [16,17], moments [19], a compressed version of the content, and more [20–25]. Considering that applying a lossy compression such as JPEG should be deemed an acceptable manipulation in most applications, Lin and Chang [15] discovered a mathematically invariant relationship between two coefficients in a block pair before and after JPEG compression and used it as the selected feature. Similarly, Lu and Liao [18] presented a structural signature solution for image authentication by identifying the stable relationship of a parent–child pair of coefficients in the wavelet domain.

Referring to Figure 9.7, we can see that the module of the "crypto hash" in Figure 9.1 has been replaced with the module of "feature extraction" here in order to tolerate some incidental distortions. The replacement is applied because the acceptable manipulations will cause changes to the content features, although the changes may be small compared to content-altering attacks. Such "allowable" changes to the content features make the features non-crypto-hashing. (Any minor changes to the features may cause a significant difference in the hashed code due to the nature of the crypto hashing methods such as MD5 and SHA-1.) Accordingly, as a result of the incompatibility with crypto hashing, the generated signature size is proportional to the size of the content, which is usually very large. In typical digital signature algorithms, signature signing is more computational than signature verifying; this will also result in a time-consuming signing process because the size of the formed signature is much greater than 1024 bits [1,2] and it has to be broken into small pieces (less than 1024 bits) for signing. On the other hand, no crypto hashing on selected features will make the decision of authenticity, which is usually based on

278

Figure 9.7. **Semifragile signature-based authentication (non-crypto-hashing).**

comparison of the feature distance (between the original one decrypted from the signature and the one extracted from the received image) against a threshold value, which is hard to determine in practice and brings some potential security risks.

Content Hashing. Because directly applying crypto hashing to images (features) seems infeasible and feature-based correlation approaches still do not resolve issues such as signature size and security risks, other researchers have been working on designing their own hash functions: *robust hash* or *content hash* (see Figure 9.8). Differing from crypto hash functions, content hashing aims to generate two hash codes with a short Hamming distance if one image is a corrupted version of another image by incidental distortions. In other words, if two images or two image blocks are visually similar, their corresponding hash codes should be close in terms of Hamming distance. For example, in the Fridrich–Goljan [26] solution, the hash function is designed to return 50 bits for each 64×64 image block by projecting this 64×64 image block onto a set of 50 orthogonal random patterns with the same size (i.e., 64×64) generated by a secret key. The final hash value of the image is then obtained by concatenating the hash codes from all 64×64 image blocks.

Xie et al. [27] proposed a content hash solution for image authentication called Approximate Message Authentication Codes (AMACs). The AMAC is actually a probabilistic checksum calculated by applying a series of random XOR operations followed by two rounds of majority

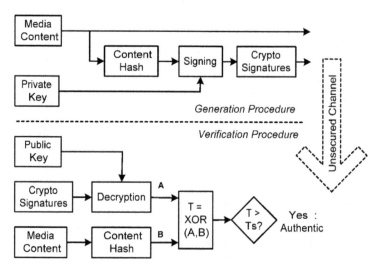

Figure 9.8. Semifragile signature-based authentication (content hashing).

voting to a given message. The similarity between two messages can be measured by the Hamming distance of their AMACs. The length of an AMAC is typically around 80 to 400 bits. Venkatesan et al. [28] also proposed a solution for generating content hash for an image. First, the image is randomly tiled and the wavelet transform is applied to each tile independently. Some statistics measures such as mean and variance are calculated in each wavelet domain. Second, those obtained measures are quantized using a random quantizer (i.e., the quantization step size is random) to increase security against attacks. Third, the quantized statistics measures in each tile are decoded by a predefined error correction coding scheme. Finally, the content hash value of the image is obtained by concatenating the ECC decoder outputs of all tiles. Kailasanathan et al. [29] proposed another compression-tolerant discrete cosine transform (DCT)-based image hash method, which is robust to lossy compression (e.g., JPEG). Conceptually, they obtained the hash value by an intersection of all subsets compressed with different JPEG quality factors.

However, some limitations also exist for this type of content-hash-based scheme. Due to a short representation of generated content hash, it is very hard for content hash to differentiate incidental distortions from intentional distortions, especially when the intentional distortions are the result of attacks to only part of the image. Consequently, it is very difficult to set a proper threshold for making the authentication decision. Furthermore, this scheme also lacks the ability to locate the content modifications if the authentication fails.

Crypto Hashing. After studying the non-crypto-hashing and content-hashing signature schemes for semifragile multimedia authentication, we can summarize here that a good semifragile digital signature scheme should satisfy the following requirements. First, the size of the signature signed by a semifragile scheme should be small enough to reduce the computational complexity. Ideally, the size is comparable to or the same as that which is signed by a crypto signature scheme. Second, such a scheme should be able to locate the attacked portion of the image because that would easily prove the authentication result. Finally, and most importantly, a proper content-based invariant feature measure should be selected in such a way that it is sensitive to malicious attacks (intentional distortions) and robust to acceptable manipulations (incidental distortions). In addition, the feature should be able to characterize the local property of an image because most attacks only act on part of the image (e.g., only changing the digits in a check image, not the whole image); feature selection is obviously application dependent because different applications have different definitions of incidental distortions as well as intentional distortions. Therefore, defining acceptable manipulations and unallowable modifications of the image content is the first step in designing a good semifragile authentication system.

To achieve the requirements described, another type of signature-based approach is proposed [30–35]. Crypto hashing was incorporated into the proposed approach to fix the length of the generated signature and enhance system security. Figure 9.9 illustrates the whole framework, which consists of three main modules. Signature

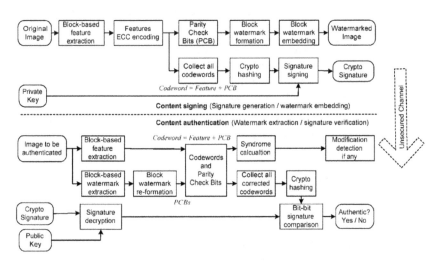

Figure 9.9. Crypto-hashing signature-based semifragile authentication.

generation and verification modules are mainly employed for the role of content signing and authentication. Watermark embedding and extraction modules are only used for storing signatures. ECC is employed to tackle the incidental distortions.

The procedure of content signing (the upper part in Figure 9.9) can be depicted as follows. The input original image is first partitioned into nonoverlapping blocks. A transform such as DCT is usually needed for each block. Block-based invariant features are then extracted and mapped onto binary values if the subsequent ECC scheme is binary. After ECC encoding, their corresponding parity check bits (PCBs) of each block-based feature set can be obtained, taking PCBs as the seed of a watermark to form the block-based watermark. One necessary condition in selecting a watermarking scheme is that the embedded watermark should be robust enough for extraction from received images under acceptable manipulations. Therefore, a simple method for generating watermark data is to use ECC again: PCBs are encoded by another ECC scheme and then the ECC-encoded output is embedded as watermark data. The watermark data for each block is embedded either into the same block or into a different block. In the meantime, all codewords (features together with their corresponding PCBs) are concatenated and hashed by a typical cryptographic hashing function such as MD5. Finally, the content owner's private key is used to sign the hashed value to generate the robust crypto signature.

The content signing algorithm is further described as follows.

System setup:

- Content owner requests a pair of keys (private key and public key) from the PKI authority.

- Select an adequate ECC scheme (N, K, D) given domain-specific acceptable manipulations. Here, N is the length of output encoded message, K is the length of original message, and D is the error correction capability.

- Select another ECC scheme (N', K', D') for watermark formation as described above (optional).

Input:

Original image to be signed I_o

Begin:

- Partition image into nonoverlapping blocks $(1, \ldots, B)$.

- For block 1 **to** block B, Do:

    Conduct block-based transform such as DCT.

Extract invariant feature.

Map each feature set into one or more binary messages, each of which has length K.

ECC encode each binary vector to obtain its codeword W (N bits) and PCBs ($N–K$ bits).

1. Take PCBs is used as watermark.
   Embed watermark into selected block.
   Inverse transform to obtain watermarked image I_w.

2. Collect codewords from all blocks W (1...B).
   Concatenate them to form a single-bit sequence Z.

End

Hash the concatenated codeword sequence Z to obtain $H(Z)$.

Sign on $H(Z)$ by the owner's private key to obtain the signature S.

End

Output:

- Watermarked image I_w

- Content-based crypto signature S

As described earlier, only the PCBs are embedded as watermarks and are used later in the verification stage for correcting potential changes in the signatures (i.e., content features). As shown in the example ECC in Table 9.1, we can see that the first four bits in a codeword are from the original message bits. Assume that we want to protect the message 0001; its corresponding codeword is 0001111. We only need to

Table 9.1. (7, 4) Hamming Code

Message	Codeword		Message	Codeword	
	Message	PCB		Message	PCB
0 0 0 0	0 0 0 0	0 0 0	1 0 0 0	1 0 0 0	0 1 1
0 0 0 1	0 0 0 1	1 1 1	1 0 0 1	1 0 0 1	1 0 0
0 0 1 0	0 0 1 0	1 1 0	1 0 1 0	1 0 1 0	1 0 1
0 0 1 1	0 0 1 1	0 0 1	1 0 1 1	1 0 1 1	0 1 0
0 1 0 0	0 1 0 0	1 0 1	1 1 0 0	1 1 0 0	1 1 0
0 1 0 1	0 1 0 1	0 1 0	1 1 0 1	1 1 0 1	0 0 1
0 1 1 0	0 1 1 0	0 1 1	1 1 1 0	1 1 1 0	0 0 0
0 1 1 1	0 1 1 1	1 0 0	1 1 1 1	1 1 1 1	1 1 1

use the last three bits (PCBs) to form the MAC and use it as watermark data. Later, assume that we receive a message like 0011 (one-bit change compared to the original message 0001). By checking with its original parity check value 111, we can detect and correct the code 0011 back to 0001 and obtain its correct corresponding codeword 0001111 again. It is clear that by using a simple ECC scheme, the system robustness is improved. It is likely that minor changes caused by acceptable manipulations (e.g., lossy compression or codec implementation variation) can be corrected by the ECC method. However, the use of ECC also raises some security concerns. Because the mapping from messages to PCBs is a multi-to-one mapping, the reverse mapping is not unique. In the example shown in Table 9.1, one PCB is shared by two messages. It results in some security problems. For example, given the original message 0001, its PCB is 111. We can replace the original message with a faked one: 1111; its corresponding PCB also is not affected — still 111. This case will become worse in practice, as the length of the message (i.e., extracted feature) usually is much longer than that of PCBs. Such a security problem is solved by cryptographically hashing all codewords instead of only hashing message bits or PCBs. Let us recheck Table 9.1. We can see that, although given one PCB, there are multiple messages sharing the PCB. However, their corresponding codewords are different (0001111 and 1111111, respectively). In other words, each syndrome (message and PCB) is uniquely defined. Any change in the message or the PCBs will make the syndrome different. Given the uniquely defined concatenated codeword sequence, we can apply cryptographic hashing (e.g., MD5) to the codeword sequence and form a much shorter output (about a few hundreds bits).

Refer to Figure 9.9 (lower part) to authenticate a received image content; in addition to the image itself, two other pieces of information are needed: the signature associated with the image (transmitted through external channels or as embedded watermarks) and the content owner's public key. The image is processed in the same way as feature generation: decompose image into blocks, to extract features for each block, to form finite-length messages. From the embedded watermarks, we also extract the PCBs corresponding to messages of each block. Note that messages are computed from the received image content, whereas the PCBs are recovered from the watermarks that are generated and embedded at the source site. After we combine the messages and the corresponding PCBs to form codewords, the whole authentication decision could be made orderly. First, we calculate the syndrome block by block to see whether there exist any blocks whose codewords are uncorrectable. If yes, then we could claim that the image is unauthentic. Second, we assume that all codewords are correctable, and replace those erroneous codewords with their corrected ones.

Then, we repeat the same process at the source site: concatenate all corrected codewords into a global sequence and cryptographically hash the result sequence. By using the owner's public key, the authenticator can decrypt the hashed value that is generated at the source site. The final authentication result is then concluded by bit-by-bit comparison between these two hashed sets: if there is any single bit different, the authenticator will report that the image is unacceptable ("unauthentic").

It is interesting and important to understand the interplay between the decision based on the block-based syndrome calculation and the crypto signature. The syndrome can be used to detect any unrecoverable changes in a block. However, because we do not transmit the entire codeword, there exist changes of a block that cannot be detected (as for the case 0001111 vs. 1111111 discussed earlier) because of their normal syndrome calculation. However, such changes will be detected by the crypto signature, because the hashed value is generated by using the entire codewords, not just the PCBs. Therefore, there exist such possibilities: the image is deemed unauthentic because of inconsistence between hashed sets while we are unable to indicate the locations of attacks because there are no uncorrectable codewords found. In such a case, we still claim that the image is unauthentic, although we are not able to indicate the exact alteration locations.

The above-described framework has been successfully applied to JPEG authentication [31,35], JPEG2000 authentication [32], MPEG-4 object [33], MPEG-1/2 [34], and so forth. Their defined acceptable manipulations, selected features, and watermarking methods are summarized in Table 9.2.

It is interesting to revisit the issue of authentication robust to packet loss here. Recall that such an issue could be solved by complete authentication [9]. Figure 9.10 illustrates the typical procedure of image transmission over a lossy channel (i.e., some data will be lost during transmission). The original image is encoded together with some error-resilient techniques, block by block. The compressed bit stream is then packetized for transmission. Assume that the transmission channel is unreliable; some data packets will be lost before reaching the receiver (e.g., packets corresponding to block 5). Such loss will be known at the receiver end either by the transmission protocols (e.g., Real-Time Protocol [RTP]) or by content-based error detection techniques. The corrupted image could be approximately recovered by error concealment techniques before displaying or further processing. Refer to Figure 9.10 at the receiver end; the authentication could be done either at point X or point Y, depending on applications. If we want to authenticate the corrupted image without error concealment, then we should conduct

Table 9.2. Crypto-Hashing-Based Semifragile Signature Schemes

Media	Acceptable Manipulations	Malicious Attacks	Features	Watermarking
JPEG [31]	Lossy compression, transcoding	Content copy–paste and cutting, etc.	DCT DC/AC coefficients	DCT quantization
JPEG2000 [32]	Lossy compression, rate transcoding	Content copy–paste and cutting, etc.	Wavelet coefficients	Bitplane modification
MPEG-4/object [33]	Lossy compression, object translation/scaling/rotation, segmentation errors	Background or object replacement, partial object modification, etc.	MPEG-7 object descriptor	FFT grouping and labeling
MPEG-1/2 [34]	Lossy compression, frame resizing, and frame dropping	New frame insertion, content modification within frame, etc.	DCT DC/AC coefficients	DCT grouping and quantization
JPEG [35]	Lossy compression, noise, packet loss	Content copy–paste and cutting, etc.	Preprocessed DCT DC/AC coefficients	DCT quantization

Figure 9.10. Image transmission over an unreliable channel.

the authentication at point X, which has been achieved by complete authentication [9]; otherwise, we should select point Y for authentication. The advantage of authenticating at point Y is that the concealed image is still securely reusable for other applications without redoing error concealment.

The solution of authenticating at point Y was proposed in Reference 35. Figure 9.11 presents some test examples done in Reference 35. Figure 9.11a is the original image with a size of 768×512. Figure 9.11b is the signed watermarked image compressed with JPEG QF (quality factor) 8; the robustness of authentication and watermarking is set to JPEG QF 7. Note that the QF for authentication robustness is lower than the QF for compression. Figure 9.11c is the damaged image of Figure 9.11b due to packet loss. (The bit error rate [BER] is 3×10^{-4}.) It can still pass the authentication after concealing the errors. Figure 9.11d is the attacked image on the damaged image in Figure 9.11c (one window in the image center was filled with its surrounding image content). Figure 9.11e is the recovered image obtained by applying the error concealment techniques in Figure 9.11d. It cannot pass the authentication, and Figure 9.11f shows the detected attacked location. Due to packet loss and its subsequent error concealment, some false detected locations occur and are shown in Figure 9.11f.

A UNIFIED SIGNATURE-BASED AUTHENTICATION FRAMEWORK FOR JPEG2000 IMAGES

In this section, we describe a signature-based authentication framework for JPEG2000 images [36]. The proposed framework integrates complete authentication and semifragile authentication together to form a scalable authentication scheme, targeting various applications because different applications may have different requirements for authentication robustness.

Recently, the Joint Photographic Experts Group issued a new still-image compression standard called JPEG2000 [37]. Compared to JPEG compression based on DCT, this new standard adopts the wavelet

(a) Original image

(b) Signed watermarked image

(c) Damaged image due to packet loss

(d) Attacked image (one window is removed)

(e) Recovered image by error concealment

(f) Detected attacks

Figure 9.11. Authentication examples robust to packet loss.

transform (WT) to obtain better energy compaction for the image. Therefore, it can achieve improved compression efficiency, especially for a bitrate compression lower than 0.25 bpp (bits per pixel). By adopting a multiple-resolution representation and an embedded bit stream, decoding can be flexibly achieved in two progressive ways: resolution scalability and signal-to-noise (SNR) scalability. Some other rich features provided by JPEG2000 include region-of-interest (ROI) coding, tiling, error resilience, random codestream access, and so forth. Figure 9.12

Figure 9.12.   A brief diagram of JPEG2000 encoding.

illustrates the main encoding procedure of JPEG2000. Given a color image, after forward multicomponent transformation (i.e., color transformation), it will be decomposed into different resolution levels and subbands by forward wavelet transformation. It is then quantized by a uniform scalar quantizer (Standard Part I). An adaptive binary arithmetic coder will start encoding all quantized WT coefficients from the most-significant-bit (MSB) bitplane to the least-significiant-bit (LSB) bitplane. The final bit stream will depend on the predefined compression bitrate and the progression order. The last two steps are also called EBCOT (Embedded Block Coding with Optimized Truncation). Through EBCOT, the user can quantitatively define the intended compression ratio for his images in terms of the bitrate.

Because of the novel features in JPEG2000, JPEG2000 has received significant attention and support from various applications such as mobile communication, medical imaging, digital photography, digital library, e-commerce, and so forth. Such applications demand content-integrity protection and source identification (i.e., a secure and robust authentication solution for JPEG2000-compatible images). However, flexible and efficient coding strategies for JPEG2000 also pose some new challenges. For example, JPEG2000 is known as "encode once and decode many times." This means that once a JPEG2000 codestream is formed at a given compression bitrate, any other new codestream whose bitrate is lower than the given compression bitrate can be simply obtained by just truncating this formed codestream from its end. Furthermore, JPEG2000 is the first international image standard that integrates lossy and lossless compression into one codestream. Hence, it requires that the proposed authentication solution be able to align with these flexibilities.

Some potential applications of such JPEG2000 authentication framework could be:

- *Content streaming*: protecting the integrity of the streamed content under a given authentication bitrate. The streaming could be done in several ways, such as streaming the content into a buffer with bitrate A, later streaming it into the client with bitrate B, and so on. As long as all of the streamed bitrates in terms of the original file size are greater than the said authentication bitrate, the streamed content should be protected against unauthorized modifications.

- *Content transformation in different domains*: given the authentication bitrate, the content to be protected may undergo some practical transformations among different domains, such as digital-to-analog and analog-to-digital. By using the ECC scheme, the transformed content should be protected against unauthorized modifications as long as the bitrate of the transformed content remains greater than the authentication bitrate.

Based on these JPEG2000 targeting applications, we identify a list of acceptable manipulations for the proposed solution, which may not be complete:

- *Multicycle compression*. Typically, this involves reencoding a compressed image to a lower bitrate. The reencoding can be repeated multiple times. In practice, there is a minimal requirement for image quality. Thus, one can set a minimal acceptable bitrate beyond which the image will be considered unauthentic. Such manipulations will unavoidably introduce some incidental distortions. Assume that we want a 1-bpp JPEG2000 compressed image. One example is that the original image repeatedly undergoes JPEG2000 compression; that is, compressing the original image into 1 bpp and decompressing it to an 8-bit raw image (one cycle), compressing it again and again at 1 bpp. Furthermore, we know that JPEG2000 provides much flexibility in compressing an image to a targeted compression bitrate, such as directly encoding from a raw image or truncating or parsing from a compressed codestream. Another example of obtaining a 1-bpp JPEG2000 compressed image is to compress the original image with full, 4 bpp, and 2 bpp, respectively, and then truncating to the targeted bitrate of 1 bpp.
- *Format or codec variations*. Differences may exist between different implementations of JPEG2000 codec by different companies. Such differences can be due to different accuracies of representation in the domains of (quantized) WT, color transformation, and the pixel domain.
- *Watermarking*. Image data is "manipulated" when authentication feature codes are embedded back into the image. Such a manipulation should not cause the resulting image to be considered unauthentic.

In Reference 36, we proposed a unified authentication system that can protect a JPEG2000 image with different robustness modes: complete and semifragile fragile (lossy and lossless). The whole framework is compliant with PKI. After image signing, the signature together with the watermarked image is sent to the recipients. At the receiver site, the recipient can verify the authenticity of the image by using the image sender's public key and the signature. The complete authentication mode is straightforward by employing the traditional crypto signature scheme. Lossy and lossless modes are robust against predefined image manipulations such as image format conversion or transcoding. In addition, lossy and lossless modes can allocate the attacked area if the image is maliciously manipulated. Moreover, the lossless mode is able to recover the original image after image verification if no incidental distortion is introduced. Finally, the authentication strength could be quantitatively specified by the parameter lowest authentication bitrate (LABR). This means that all data or content of the image above the LABR will be protected. Thus, it will offer users convenience. It is worth mentioning that the proposed solution is also compatible with other JPEG2000 features such as JPEG2000 codestream transcoding (i.e., parsing and truncation), ROI coding, and so forth. This facilitates the proposed solution for more JPEG2000 applications. Figure 9.13 is the diagram of the proposed system.

In Figure 9.13, the proposed solution can work in three modes: complete authentication mode (i.e., traditional signature scheme), semifragile authentication mode with lossy watermarking, and semifragile authentication mode with lossless watermarking. Different levels of the authentication robustness provided by the three authentication modes, together with the authentication strength, which can be quantitatively specified by the LABR parameter, form a scalable authentication scheme. In addition, the protected areas can also be defined in terms

Figure 9.13. Diagram of the proposed authentication framework for JPEG2000 images.

of component, tile, resolution, subband, layer, codeblock, and even packet (all are used for representing JPEG2000 images with different granularities).

Complete Authentication Mode

The complete authentication mode is selected for protecting JPEG2000 compressed codestreams. The signing and verifying operations are quite straightforward. Figure 9.14 shows its signing procedure. During signing, the original image is encoded as per normal. While the codestream is formulated, its protected parts, as specified by LABR and other parameters, are extracted and fed to the crypto hashing and signing operation. As result, a crypto signature is generated. The verification procedure is the inverse procedure of signing, as shown in Figure 9.15. During verifying, while the codestream is parsed during decoding, its protected part, as specified by LABR and other parameters, is extracted and fed to the traditional hashing and verifying operation, which

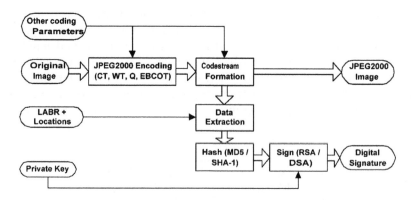

Figure 9.14. Complete authentication mode for JPEG2000 images (signing).

Figure 9.15. Complete authentication mode for JPEG2000 images (verifying).

returns the verification result; even a one-bit change in the protected part will be deemed unauthentic.

Semifragile Content Authentication (Lossy)

The semifragile content authentication (lossy) mode is usually selected for those applications demanding more robustness, such as wireless communication. It is the most robust mode of the three authentication modes.

The proposed signing procedure is shown in Figure 9.16. In the scheme, the signature generation and verification modules are mainly employed for content signing and authentication. Watermark embedding and extraction modules are only used for storing ECC check information. Instead of directly sending an original image to recipients, we only pass them the watermarked copy associated with one signed digital signature whose length is usually very short (e.g., 1024 bits if signed by DSA or RSA). In Figure 9.16, among the four inputs — original image, JPEG2000 compression bit rate (CBR) b, LABR a, and the image sender's private key — CBR is the mandatory input for compressing images into the JPEG2000 format. In addition to the original image, only two inputs are needed to generate the JPEG2000 image signature in a content-based way: the private key and the LABR a. If a JPEG2000 image signature is generated with the LABR value a, a new image with the CBR b will be authentic as long as b is greater than a and the new image is derived from defined acceptable manipulations or transcoded (by parsing or truncation) from a compressed JPEG2000 image.

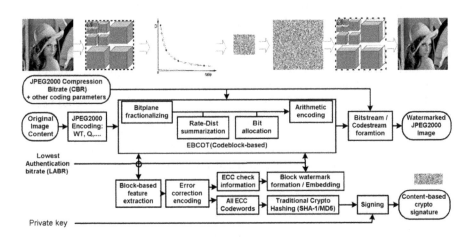

Figure 9.16. Content authentication (lossy) mode for JPEG2000 images (signing).

The original image first undergoes color transformation, wavelet transformation, and quantization, which are all basic procedures in JPEG2000 encoding [37]. EBCOT is then employed for bitplane fractionalizing or encoding and optimal bitrate control. We extract content-based features from the available fractionalized bitplanes by assuming the image is encoded above LABR. Feature values from each codeblock are thresholded and ECC coded to generate corresponding PCBs. Then, we take PCBs as the seed to form the block-based watermark. One necessary condition in watermarking is that the embedded watermark should be robust enough for extraction from received images under acceptable manipulations. Because incidental changes to the embedded watermarks might occur, we apply another ECC scheme again to encode the PCB data before it is embedded. The watermark data for each block is embedded into either the same block or a different block. The watermark embedding location is also determined based on the LABR value. Note that only the PCB data (not including the feature codes) is embedded in the above watermarking process. All codewords (features together with their corresponding PCBs) from all resolution levels and all subbands are concatenated and the resulting bit sequence is hashed by a cryptographic hashing function such as MD5 or SHA-1. The generated semi-fragile crypto hash value can then be signed using the content sender's private key to form the crypto signature. Differing from a data-based signature scheme in which the original data is sent to the recipients associated with its signature, in the proposed solution we send out the watermarked image to the recipients instead of sending the original image.

We select EBCOT [37] to generate robust content-based features based on the following considerations. First, EBCOT is the last processing unit prior to forming the final compressed bitstream in JPEG2000. It means that all possible distortions have been introduced before running EBCOT in the encoding procedure and no distortion is introduced afterward. If we are to authenticate the encoding output or output of directly truncating the compressed bitstream, the extracted features will not be distorted. Second, EBCOT expands the scalability of the image by fractionalizing the bitplane. The significant bitplanes of EBCOT represent closely the image content and, thus, it is hard to alter the image while intentionally keeping the same significant bitplanes. Third, in JPEG2000, EBCOT is the engine of bitrate control and provides exact information about specific passes of data to be included in the final bitstream given a target bitrate. Such information allows us to specify the invariant layers of data and quantitatively select an authenticable level.

EBCOT provides a finer scalability of image content resulting from multiple pass encoding of the codeblock bitplanes (i.e., fractionalizing each bitplane into three subbitplanes: significant pass, magnitude refinement pass, and cleanup pass based on predefined contextual models). The coding summaries for each codeblock after EBCOT include feasible truncation points, their corresponding compressed size (rate), and estimated distortions (rate-distortion curve). The target compression bitrate is achieved by globally scanning the contributions from all codeblocks and optimally selecting truncating points for each codeblock (using the Lagrange multiplier method). One important property is worth noting: passes included in the bit stream at one rate (say a) are always included in the bit stream at a higher rate ($\geq a$). Such a property is illustrated in Figure 9.2, in which no curves cross the curves that correspond to passes included at different compression bitrates. Such a property is important for our proposed solution in order to obtain invariant feature sets. Based on the above observation, we select two measures as invariant features directly from EBCOT: one is the state of passes (i.e., the fractionalized bitplanes) of MSBs and the other is the estimated distortion associated with each pass. The estimated distortion is a measure of the change of "1" in a given bitplane [37]. However, from the experiments [32], there are still some small perturbations introduced to the features by the defined acceptable manipulations. This is why we employ ECC to tame such distortions in order to generate stable crypto hash values and signature.

Refer to Figure 9.17. To authenticate the received image content, in addition to the image, two other pieces of information are needed: the signature associated with the image (transmitted through external channels or as embedded watermarks) and the content sender's public key. The image is processed in the same way as content signing: decompose and quantize image into blocks, to extract features for each block. (Note that here we assume that the JPEG2000 image has been decoded into a raw image and we are authenticating this raw image given LABR. If the image is still JPEG2000 compressed, the features and watermarks

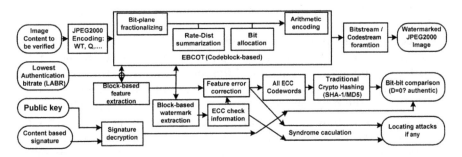

Figure 9.17. **Complete authentication (lossy) mode for JPEG2000 images (verifying).**

can also be obtained in the EBCOT domain from the JPEG2000 decoding procedure.) From these embedded watermarks, we extract the PCB data generated at the source site. Note that the features are computed from the received image, whereas the PCBs are recovered from the watermarks that are generated and embedded at the source site. After we combine the features and the corresponding PCBs to form codewords, the whole content verification decision can be made orderly. First, we calculate the syndrome of the codeword block by block to see whether any blocks exist whose codewords are uncorrectable. If yes, then we claim that the image is unauthentic and use the above ECC checking process to display alteration locations. If all codewords are correctable (i.e., errors in any feature code are correctable by its PCB), we repeat the same process at the source site: concatenate all corrected codewords into a global sequence and cryptographically hash the result sequence. The final verification result is then concluded through a bit-by-bit comparison between these two hashed sets (i.e., one is this new generated one and the other is decrypted from the associated signature by the obtained public key). If any single bit differs, the verifier will deem the image unacceptable ("unauthentic").

Semifragile Content Authentication (Lossless)

The semifragile content authentication (lossless) mode is usually selected for medical or remote-imaging-related applications where lossless recovery of the original image is required. The signing operation is very similar to the lossy signing operation (Figure 9.16). The only difference lies in the watermark embedding module. The lossless watermarking method used is novel [38]: it does not generate annoying salt-and-pepper noise, and is robust against image compression. The codeblock whose size is usually 64×64 is further divided into 8×8 blocks called patches. The coefficients in a patch are split into two subsets. Then, we calculate the difference value α, which is defined as the arithmetic average of differences of coefficients in two respective subsets. Because in a patch the coefficients are highly correlated, the difference value α is expected to be very close to zero. Furthermore, it has a certain robustness against incidental distortions because α is based on all coefficients in the patch. Each patch is embedded with one bit. If 1 is to be embedded, we shift the difference value α to the right or left beyond a threshold by adding or subtracting a fixed number from each coefficient within one subset. If 0 is to be embedded, the patch is intact. There is a chance that the value α is originally beyond the threshold and a bit of binary 0 is to be embedded. In this case, we shift the value α further beyond the threshold and rely on the ECC to correct the bit error, because the watermark bits are ECC encoded again before being embedded.

296

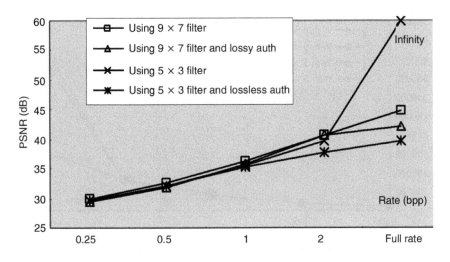

Figure 9.18.   Image quality comparison between compressed and compressed plus signed JPEG2000 images.

The verifying operation is also similar to the lossy one, with the exception of watermark extraction. The code block is divided in patches and the difference value α of each patch is calculated in the same way as lossless sign. For each patch, if value α is beyond the threshold, a bit of "1" is extracted and the difference value is shifted back to its original position, which means that the original coefficients are recovered. If the value α is inside the threshold, a bit of "0" is extracted and nothing needs to be done. Finally, an ECC correction is applied on the extracted bit sequence to get the correct watermark bits.

More detailed test results are given in Reference 36. Figure 9.18 and Figure 9.19 compare the image quality and file size before and after signing. The image is encoded with a 9×7 filter (with and without lossy watermark) and a 5×3 filter (with and without lossless watermark), respectively. We can see that the image quality drops slightly with a watermark embedded and no significant difference exists between the image sizes.

In summary, the main contributions of the proposed solution can be listed as follows:

- JPEG2000 images can be quantitatively authenticated in terms of the LABR. By utilizing the JPEG2000 coding scheme, the proposed solution can quantitatively authenticate images specified by the LABR. It will offer users more convenience and achieve a good trade-off among system robustness, security, and image quality. It is noted that to control the authentication strength, the

297

Figure 9.19. File size comparison between compressed and compressed plus signed JPEG2000 images.

state-of-the-art content-based authentication systems (signature based or watermarking based) are mainly based on the following techniques: empirical trials, (R)MSE measure associated with the human vision system (HVS), or quantization measure. Although the latter is "implicitly" related to bitrate allocation, it is still not convenient because it is not easy to set the quantization step size properly under various types of image content, especially for ordinary users. JPEG2000 images can be flexibly authenticated in three modes: complete authentication, semifragile authentication with lossy watermarking, and semifragile authentication with lossless watermarking. The image can be signed or verified with different granularities: codestream level, quantized wavelet coefficient level, and wavelet coefficient level. In addition, the protected area can be specified via different representation levels used for JPEG2000 coding, such as ROI, component, tile, resolution, subband, precinct, codeblock, and packet. All of these authentication flexibilities are well aligned with the JPEG2000 coding procedure (Part 1). ECC is employed to tame incidental distortions, which integrates the signature-based solution and the watermarking-based solution into one unified scheme in a semifragile way. Thus, we obtain only one crypto hash or signature per image, regardless of its size, in a semifragile way. As we can see later, ECC is used in a novel way in our proposed solution. ECC's message comes from the extracted features of the image. ECC's PCBs are the seeds of watermarks and will be embedded back into the image. Such novel usage of ECC will bring the system the ability to correct some possible errors in its extracted features without increasing system payload: the code-block-based watermarks (PCBs) could be used for locating malicious modifications and the final content-based signature is obtained by cryptographically hashing all corresponding codewords (message + PCB) to make sure that no catastrophic security holes exist.

- The proposed solution can be incorporated into various security protocols (symmetric and asymmetric). By using the ECC scheme on extracted features, we can obtain stable crypto hash results, thus gaining more room and flexibility in designing authentication protocols in real applications. For example, by using PKI, the content signer and content verifier can own different keys. Working under PKI will also let the proposed solution be easily incorporated into current data-based authentication platforms.

- The proposed solution is fully compatible with the JPEG2000 encoder and decoder (Part 1). Based on the description given earlier, we can see that all features are directly extracted from EBCOT and the generated watermarks are also embedded back in the procedure of EBCOT. The proposed solution is fully compatible with JPEG2000 codec and could efficiently co-work with the procedure of JPEG2000 image compression and decompression.

SYSTEM PERFORMANCE EVALUATION

The performance of a media authentication system mainly relates to system security and system robustness. For cases of complete authentication and content-based fragile authentication, which adopt traditional crypto signature schemes, system security should be equivalent to the traditional crypto signature whose security is assumed to be very secure (it cannot be broken based on the computation capability of current computers); system robustness is also the same as the traditional crypto signature schemes, which is fragile (even a one-bit change is not allowed). Therefore, our discussion in this section on system performance evaluation only focuses on semifragile content authentication.

System Security Evaluation

System security plays a vital role in an authentication system. From our previous description of noncrypto-hashing methods, content hashing methods, and crypto hashing methods, we can see that three main modules affect system security (i.e., feature extraction, hashing, and ECC). If we denote the performance of system security in terms of the probabilities of the system being crashed (i.e., given an image, the probabilities of finding another image that can pass the

Figure 9.20.   Illustration of system security analysis.

signature verification, under the same parameters). Therefore, system security can be represented by three probabilities: P_F in the feature extraction module, P_E in the ECC module, and P_C in hashing. Assume that they are mutually independent and very small; the overall system security could be drawn as

$$P = 1 - (1 - P_F)(1 - P_E)(1 - P_C) \approx P_F + P_E + P_C$$

In fact, P_F and P_E impair system security in different ways, as shown in Figure 9.20. A good feature descriptor should represent the original source as closely as possible. Differing from feature extraction, which functions by "removing" redundancy from the original source, ECC functions by "adding" redundancy in order to tolerate incidental distortions. Thus, a good feature extraction method and a proper ECC scheme are the key factors in system security. More detailed analysis is given below.

Hash. Typically, two types of hashing functions are used in a semifragile authentication system: crypto hashing and content hashing. The security of crypto hashing is known to be very secure, based on the computation capability of current computers. For example, the security of a 160-bit SHA-1 hash value is about $P_C \approx 2^{-80}$, under a birthday attack[1] assumption [1,2]. Therefore, we ignore the security risk of crypto hashing.

Usually, content hashing is very robust to acceptable manipulations. However, robust content hashing is also robust to local attacks. Analysis of the security of content hashing is a little complicated because it relates to the following issues. The first one is the feature selected for content hashing: a good feature representation is the first step in designing a secure content hashing scheme. The second one is the length of the generated content hash code because it implicitly means how detailed the content is represented, given the same feature representation. Finally

---

[1]A typical brute force attack against crypto hashing: an adversary would like to find two random messages, M and M', such that $H(M) = H(M')$. It is named the birthday attack because it is analogous to finding two people with the same birthday [1].

(a)   (b)   (c)   (d)

Figure 9.21. (a) Original image; (b) attacked image of (a). (c) Original image; (d) attacked image of (c).

and most importantly, the authentication decision of content hash is based on the (Hamming) distance between the two sets of hash codes and it is hard to differentiate the local attacks from the acceptable manipulations.

Feature Extraction. Again, the purpose of attacking an image authentication system is to make the faked image pass the verification. At the content level, the forgery should alter the image in such a way that its semantic meaning will be changed; for instance, using the face [39] shown in Figure 9.21b to pass the authentication whose signature is generated from the face image shown in Figure 9.21a. Note that the usual attacks may only try to modify parts of the image rather than take a totally different image for verification by assuming that the authentication system is appropriately designed. For example, Figure 9.21d is the attacked image in Figure 9.21c, where only parts of the image are altered.

We now evaluate some typical features selected for image authentication.

Histogram. The histogram of an image represents the relative frequency of occurrence of the various gray levels in the image. It is actually a global measure of an image and is unable to characterize the local changes in the image. Therefore, it is too robust to be used as the feature for image authentication in most cases. For example, Figure 9.22a and Figure 9.22b show the histograms of face images in Figure 9.21a and Figure 9.21b, respectively. We can see that their histograms look very similar although they are different faces. Such similarity of Figure 9.22b still fails in passing the authentication of Figure 9.22a. We can adopt a technique called "histogram warping" to further shape Figure 9.22b until it passes authentication. As a result, the face image shown in Figure 9.22c has a histogram exactly the same as that of

(a)   (b)   (c)

**Figure 9.22. The histograms of face images and the attacked image.
(a) Histogram of Figure 9.21a; (b) histogram of Figure 9.21b; (c) the modified
image of Figure 9.21b but with the same histogram as Figure 9.21a.**

(a) Original image   (b) Modified image by adding some clouds

Figure 9.23.   The extracted feature points (corner) are used for authentication.

Figure 9.21a. Therefore, the histogram alone is not suitable as the feature
for content authentication.

Edge and Corner. The corner points in an image are defined as the
maxima of absolute curvature of image edges that are above a preset
threshold value. Image corner points are usually used in computer
visions to find the correspondences between two images. Taking image
edges or corners as the features for image authentication can be found in
some publications such as References 16 and 17. It can characterize the
local significances in the image, as shown in Figure 9.23a. However, it
usually fails in detecting some gradual changes, as shown in Figure 9.23b,
where we did some modifications on Figure 9.23a by adding more
clouds on the upper-right side. From their detected corners, we can see
that their corner points are almost the same. Therefore, the edge or
corner is not suitable for authenticating those attacks, such as gradually
changing part of the image.

302

Reference image   Four original images for testing

Attacks on DCT DC coefficient based signature

Attacks on DCT AC coefficients based signature

Attacks on DCT DC+AC coefficients based signature

Figure 9.24. DCT test under attacks.

DCT Coefficients. Because a discrete cosine transform (DCT) is used for JPEG lossy compression, DCT coefficients are also considered to be the feature for image authentication, as usually lossy compression is required as acceptable for authentication. However, how to select DCT coefficients and how many DCT coefficients should be taken as the representative feature of the image still need to be carefully designed, especially when the feature needs to be embedded back to image as watermarks because the watermark capacity also affects the feature selection. Figure 9.24 presents a visual illustration of these issues.

In Figure 9.24 (first row), the image on the left is taken as the reference and the other four images on the right are taken as the attack images. Our purpose is to modify these four images until they can pass the authentication whose signature is based on the reference image. We illustrate three examples for every 8×8 DCT block: DC coefficients only (the second row), three AC coefficients (the third row), and DC plus two AC coefficients (the fourth row). Visually, DC plus AC coefficients are the best selection and, in practice, use as many DCT coefficients as possible.

303

Compressed Version of the Original Content. Some authentication systems directly employed the compressed version of the original content as the feature for authentication [22–24,32]. In such a case, we argue that the following assumption is valid:

Assumption 1: Lossy compression such as JPEG2000 is the approximate representation of its original source in terms of an optimal rate-distortion measure.

Intuitively, this implies that no security gap exists between the original source and its compressed version under a given authentication strength. Therefore, we would argue that if an authentication system could make use of all compressed information (e.g., all quantized coefficients in all blocks) as the feature, it should be deemed the same as having made use of all the original source. In other words, if an attacker intends to modify the content in the spaces between the original source and its compressed version, this attack should not be considered harmful to this content (i.e., cause the meaning of the content to change) because, eventually, the attacked content will be discarded by its lossy compression.

Note that in the proposed solution for the JPEG2000 image [36], we have used almost all compressed information (e.g., the state of significant pass and the estimated distortions among different passes) above LABR for generating hash. Therefore, we could argue that P_F [36] is negligible (small enough) under Assumption 1.

Generic Framework for System Security Evaluation. Considering the varieties of features selected for authentication, originating from the brute force attack experiences in cryptography [1,2], a similar evaluation framework for content authentication could also be drawn, as shown in Figure 9.25.

Refer to Figure 9.25; given a reference image and an attacked image, we can keep their similarity score increasing by randomly perturbing the attacked image and recording it in a discarding-keeping manner (i.e., if the trial makes the score up, then records it, and discards it otherwise). Such an evaluation framework does not need any prior knowledge of the authentication design (i.e., no information about feature selection) and has been widely used in information security and biometrics systems.

Error Correction Coding. An (N, K, D) code [40] is a code of N-bit codewords, where K is the number of message digits (the extracted feature set in this chapter) and D is the minimum distance between codewords. $N - K = P$ is the number of parity check digits (i.e., checksum or check information). It should be noted that an ECC with rate K/N can correct

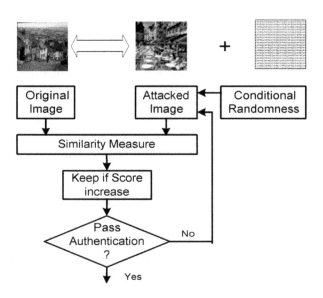

Figure 9.25. Generic framework for security evaluation.

up to $T = (D-1)/2$ errors. Here, we are only interested in binary BCH ECC (i.e., Bose–Chaudhuri–Hochquenghem code). BCH code is a multilevel, cyclic, error-correcting, variable-length digital code used to correct errors of up to approximately 25% of the total number of digits. Like other linear ECC codes, the first K-bit digits in its N-bit codeword are exactly the same as its original K-bit message bits. This is the main motivation for selecting the BCH code: in the procedure of content signing, the output (codeword) from the ECC encoder can still be separated into two parts: the original message and its corresponding PCBs. We can then embed the PCB into the image as a watermark. In the procedure of content authentication, the authenticity can be verified by checking the syndrome of the merged codeword (message comes from the feature set extracted from the image to be verified and PCB comes from the watermark extracted from the same image).

To check how the ECC scheme affects system security (i.e., P_E), we have the following lemma [32]:

Lemma 1: Let H_C be our proposed content hash scheme based on an ECC scheme (N, K, D) with error correction ability t [e.g., $t = (D-1)/2$]. For any K' that satisfies $\|N - N'\| \le t$, we have $H_C(N) = H_C(N')$. It means that in a properly selected ECC scheme, all corrupted codewords will be deemed as authentic as long as they are still within the error correction capability. Hence, a proper ECC scheme could make P_E negligible.

Clearly, ECC diminishes system security in some sense, as ECC does provide the property of fuzziness. This goes back again to the issue of how to select a proper ECC scheme to balance between system robustness and security. However, we have to accept the fact that ECC does introduce some security risk into the system. Refer to Table 9.1; for instance, if the formed codeword is 0000000, seven codes will be considered as acceptable in hash verification (1000000, 0100000, 0010000, 0001000, 0000100, 0000010, and 0000001) because they are all within the designed error correction capability (correcting 1-bit error) and will be corrected as 0000000 in the procedure of content authentication. Now the issue is whether taking these seven codes as acceptable is secure. This also requires that a well-designed application-oriented ECC scheme under predefined acceptable manipulations plays a key role in the semifragile content-based hash function.

The final concern related to security is watermarking used in References 30 to 36. In such a case, we do not need to pay more attention to watermarking security because watermarking only functions for storing part of the ECC information.

In practice, the threats from attacks are also closely related to other factors, such as the attackers' knowledge background, and some counter-measures have been addressed and proposed by researchers in cryptography but are beyond the scope in this chapter.

System Robustness Evaluation

To quantitatively evaluate system performance on robustness, two important measures used are false acceptance rate (FAR) and false rejection rate (FRR). The FRR is the percentage of failure among attempts in generating its derived signature from the authentic image, averaged over all authentic images in a population O. The FAR is the percentage of success among attempts in generating its derived signature from the forged image, averaged over all forged images in a population M. Faced with some practical difficulties when we conduct testing, such as manually forging a number of meaningful images, FAR and FRR can be measured in an alternative way; that is, the FAR and FRR can be derived based on block-based evaluation, not image-based evaluation. Given a pair of images to be tested (one is the original watermarked and the other is its fake version), assume that there are a total of N blocks in the pair of images, M blocks are modified, and O blocks remain unchanged; $N = M + O$. We then pass the pair of images (e.g., watermarked image and modified watermarked image) through various kinds of acceptable manipulation such as multiple-cycle compression, transcoding, and so forth. FAR and FRR will be derived based on checking all of these distorted images block by block. Assuming that after

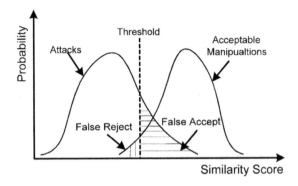

Figure 9.26. Evaluation of system robustness.

distorting the images, M' among M blocks can pass the authentication and O' among O cannot pass the authentication. FAR and FRR could be obtained as

$$\text{FRR} = \frac{O'}{O} \quad \text{and} \quad \text{FAR} = \frac{M'}{M}$$

In practice, the system performance could also be described by a receiver operating characteristic (ROC) curve indicating the operating point (threshold) for various applications with different robustness requirements, as shown in Figure 9.26.

Actually, system security and system robustness are mutually dependent. A secure authentication system may result in a low authentication robustness or a high FRR, and a robust authentication system may unavoidably have a high FAR, which means that some attacked content could pass the authentication.

Before we end this section, we tabulate all signature-based authentication methods described earlier (see Table 9.3), which is an extension of Figure 9.2 but focusing only on multimedia content.

SUMMARY AND FUTURE WORK

In this chapter, we introduced a list of state-of-the-art signature-based authentication schemes for multimedia applications. Based on whether the original multimedia data can be obtained at the receiver site, it was classified into complete authentication and content authentication. Content authentication was further classified into fragile authentication and semifragile authentication, based on the robustness of authentication. We then focused on discussing various semifragile signature-based authentication techniques. In summary, we argued that a good semifragile authentication system should not only be secure

Table 9.3. Comparison of Various Authentication Methods

	Content Integrity	Source Identification	Robustness	Signature Size	Security	Attack Localization
Complete authentication	Yes	Yes	No	1024 bits	Very strong	No
Fragile authentication	Yes	Yes	No	0	Very strong	Yes
Semifragile (watermarking)	Yes	No	Yes	0	Weak	Yes
Semifragile (nonhashing)	Yes	Yes	Yes	Very large	Some	Some
Semifragile (content hashing)	Yes	Yes	Some	Large	Some	No
Semifragile (crypto hashing)	Yes	Yes	Yes	1024 bits	Strong	Yes

enough to the malicious attacks, but also be robust enough to the acceptable manipulations. Such a good system should be application dependent.

The demands of adaptively streaming the media in a pervasive environment pose new requirements as well as new challenges for semifragile media authentication system design. A pervasive environment may contain many heterogeneous devices with varying computing resources and connected through different channels. Therefore, in such an environment, traditional security solutions, which only provide yes or no answers (i.e., either authentic or unauthentic), cannot work well because different devices and channels may have different required security levels due to their limited computing power or their targeted applications. Therefore, it requires a scalable, robust, and secure authentication framework.

REFERENCES

1. Menezes, A., Oorschot, P., and Vanstone, S., *Handbook of Applied Cryptography*, CRC Press, Boca Raton, FL, 1996.
2. Schneier, B., *Applied Cryptography*, John Wiley & Sons, New York, 1996.
3. Lin, C.-Y. and Chang, S.-F., Issues and Solutions for Authenticating MPEG Video, presented at *SPIE International Conference on Security and Watermarking of Multimedia Contents*, San Jose, 1999, Vol. 3657, pp. 54–65.
4. Wu, C.-W., On the design of content-based multimedia authentication systems, *IEEE Trans. Multimedia*, 4, 385–393, 2002.

5. Friedman, G.L., The trustworthy digital camera: restoring credibility to the photographic image, *IEEE Trans. Consumer Electron.*, 39(4), 905–910, 1993.
6. Quisquater, J.-J., Macq, B., Joye, M., Degand, N., and Bernard, A., Practical Solution to Authentication of Images with a Secure Camera, presented at *SPIE International Conference on Storage and Retrieval for Image and Video Databases V*, San Jose, 1997, Vol. 3022, pp. 290–297.
7. Gennaro, R. and Rohatgi, P., How to Sign Digital Streams, in *Proceedings of CRYPTO 97*, Santa Barbara, CA, 1997.
8. Yu, H., Scalable Multimedia Authentication, in *Proceeding of the 4th IEEE Pacific-Rim Conference on Multimedia (PCM)'03*, Singapore, 2003.
9. Park, J.M., Chong, E.K.P., and Siegel, H.J., Efficient Multicast Packet Authentication Using Signature Amortization, in *Proceedings of the IEEE Symposium on Security and Privacy*, 2002, pp. 227–240.
10. Goljan, M., Fridrich, J., and Du, R., Distortion-free Data Embedding, in *Proceedings of 4th Information Hiding Workshop*, 2001, pp. 27–41.
11. Shi, Y.Q., Chap. 7, this volume.
12. Yeung, M.M. and Mintzer, F., An Invisible Watermarking Technique for Image Verification, in *Proceedings of International Conference on Image Processing '97*, 1997.
13. Wong, P.W. and Memon, N., Secret and public key image watermarking schemes for image authentication and ownership verification, *IEEE Trans. Image Process.*, 10(10), 1593–1601, 2001.
14. Schneider, M. and Chang, S.-F., A Robust Content-based Digital Signature for Image Authentication, in *Proceedings of International Conference on Image Processing '96*, 1996.
15. Lin, C.-Y. and Chang, S.-F., A robust image authentication method distinguishing JPEG compression from malicious manipulation, *IEEE Trans. Circuits Systems Video Technol.*, 11(2), 153–168, 2001.
16. Dittmann, J., Steinmetz, A., and Steinmetz, R., Content-based Digital Signature for Motion Pictures Authentication and Content-Fragile Watermarking, in *Proceedings of the IEEE International Conference on Multimedia Computing and Systems*, 1999, Vol. II, pp. 209–213.
17. Queluz, M.P., Authentication of digital image and video: generic models and a new contribution, *Signal Process.: Image Commun.*, 16, 461–475, 2001.
18. Lu, C.S. and Liao, H.-Y.M., Structural digital signature for image authentication: an incidental distortion resistant scheme, *IEEE Trans. Multimedia*, 5(2), 161–173, 2003.
19. Tzeng, C. H. and Tsai, W.-H., A New Technique for Authentication of Image/Video for Multimedia Applications, in *Proceedings of ACM Multimedia Workshop '01*, Canada, 2001.
20. Wu, C.-P. and Kuo, C.-C.J., Comparison of Two Speech Content Authentication Approaches, presented at *SPIE International Symposium on Electronic Imaging 2002*, San Jose, CA, 2002.
21. Sun, Q., Zhong, D., Chang, S.-F., and Narasimhalu, A., VQ-based Digital Signature Scheme for Multimedia Content, presented at *SPIE International Conference on Security and Watermarking of Multimedia Contents II*, San Jose, CA, 2000, Vol. 3971, pp. 404–416.
22. Bhattacharjee, S. and Kutter, M., Compression Tolerant Image Authentication, in *Proceedings of the IEEE International Conference on Image Processing '98*, Chicago, 1998.
23. Lou, D.-C. and Liu, J.-L., Fault resilient and compression tolerant digital signature for image authentication, *IEEE Trans. Consumer Electron.*, 46(1), 31–39, 2000.
24. Chang, E.-C., Kankanhalli, M.S., Guan, X., Huang, Z., and Wu, Y., Image authentication using content based compression, *ACM Multimedia Syst.*, 9(2), 121–130, 2003.

25. Memon, N.D., Vora, P., and Yeung, M., Distortion Bound Authentication Techniques, presented at *SPIE International Conference on Security and Watermarking of Multimedia Contents II*, San Jose, CA, 2000, Vol. 3971, pp. 164–175.
26. Fridrich, J. and Goljan, M., Robust Hash Functions for Digital Watermarking, in *Proceedings of IEEE International Conference on Information Technology — Coding and Computing '00*, Las Vegas, 2000.
27. Xie, L., Arce, G.R., and Graveman, R.F., Approximate image message authentication codes, *IEEE Trans. Multimedia*, 3(2), 242–252, 2001.
28. Venkatesan, R., Koon, S.-M., Jakubowski, M.H., and Moulin, P., Robust Image Hashing, in *Proceedings of IEEE International Conference on Image Processing '00*, Vancouver, 2000.
29. Kailasanathan, C., Naini, R.S., and Ogunbona, P., Compression Tolerant DCT Based Image Hash, in *Proceedings of the 23rd International Conference on Distributed Computing Systems Workshops (ICDCSW '03)*, Rhode Island, 2003.
30. Sun, Q., Chang, S.-F., and Maeno, K., A New Semi-fragile Image Authentication Framework Combining ECC and PKI Infrastructure, in *Proceedings of International Symposium on Circuits and Systems '02*, Phoenix, 2002.
31. Sun, Q., Tian, Q., and Chang, S.-F., A Robust and Secure Media Signature Scheme for JPEG Images, in *Proceedings of Workshop on Multimedia Signal Processing '02*, Virgin Islands, 2002.
32. Sun, Q. and Chang, S.-F., A quantitative semi-fragile JPEG2000 image authentication solution, *IEEE Trans. Multimedia*, in press.
33. He, D., Sun, Q., and Tian, Q., An object based authentication system, *EURASIP J. Appl. Signal Process.*, in press.
34. Sun, Q., He, D., Zhang, Z., and Tian, Q., A Robust and Secure Approach to Scalable Video Authentication, in *Proceedings of International Conference on Multimedia and Expo '03*, 2003.
35. Sun, Q., Ye, S., Lin, C.-Y., and Chang, S.-F., A crypto signature scheme for image authentication over wireless channel, *Int. J. Image Graphics*, 5(1), 1–14, 2005.
36. Zhang, Z., Qiu, G., Sun, Q., Lin, X., Ni, Z., and Shi, Y., A unified authentication framework for JPEG2000, ISO/IEC JTC 1/SC 29/WG1, N3074, and N3107, 2003.
37. JPEG2000 Part 1: Core coding system, ISO/IEC 15444-1:2000.
38. Ni, Z. and Shi, Y.Q., A Novel Lossless Data Hiding Algorithm and Its Application in Authentication of JPEG2000 Images, Technical Report, New Jersey Institute of Technology, 2003.
39. Face database: http://www.ee.surrey.ac.uk/Research/VSSP/xm2vtsdb, 2002.
40. Lin, S. and Costello, D.J., *Error Control Coding: Fundamentals and Applications*, Prentice-Hall, Englewood Cliffs, NJ, 1983.

10
Digital Rights Management for Consumer Devices

Jeffrey Lotspiech

INTRODUCTION

The ongoing digital revolution has presented both a threat and a promise to the entertainment industry. On one hand, digital technologies promise inexpensive consumer devices, convenient distribution and duplication, and flexible new business models. On the other hand, digital copies are perfect copies, and the industry risks losing substantial revenue because of casual end-user copying and redistribution. The entertainment industry and the technology companies that service it have been attacking this problem with increasing sophistication. This chapter outlines the history of this effort and concludes with some discussion of a possible future direction.

Digital rights management in consumer electronics devices, to date, is about restricting unauthorized copies. As such, it has been the subject of much controversy and misunderstanding. "Bits want to be free" is John Perry Barlow's catchy phrase [1]; and others, even cryptographers such has Bruce Schneier, have joined the chorus. Schneier [2] argues that any technology that tries to prevent the copying of bits is doomed to failure. This is probably true, but misses the point. Bits can be freely copied, moved, and exchanged, but it is possible that the bits themselves are encrypted. The devices that have the keys necessary to decrypt the bits may be constrained by rules to refuse to decrypt the bits if they find them in the wrong place.

Therefore, modern copy protection is fundamentally about rules, not about technology. The rules may be enforced by law, but the trend has been to encode them instead in voluntary technology licenses. In other words, the manufacturer of a consumer device, wanting to allow a certain type of content to be played, signs a license to obtain the secrets (usually encryption keys) necessary to play the content. In return, the license constrains what functions that device might offer and calls out specific penalties for breaches.

Many copy protection technologies have the technical means to exclude from the system devices whose manufacturers have broken the rules they agreed to in the license. Curiously, however, licenses often have forgone this remedy, depending, instead, on legal enforcement rather than technical revocation. Technical revocation has been reserved for cases of unlicensed circumvention devices, whose makers have somehow obtained the secrets without signing the license.

"What prevents a playing device, which obviously has the decryption key, from turning around and making an unauthorized copy in the clear?" is a question cryptographers, who think they have found the fatal flaw in a given protection scheme, often ask. The answer is, "Nothing technical, but the manufacturer building such a device would be violating his license and would be liable to civil action and damages." It is the license, not the technology, that offers the fundamental protection; the technology is just the hook that provides something to license. It is no accident that, in a technology I am intimately familiar with, Content Protection for Recordable Media (CPRM), the average specification runs about 40 pages, whereas the average license plus attachments runs about 90 pages.

The rest of this chapter focuses on the technical aspects of specific content protection schemes. However, remember that these technologies are always offered in the context of a license, and the license defines the rules that ultimately shape the consumer experience.

MACROVISION™ [1]

Soon after video cassette recorders (VCRs) hit the market in the late 1970s, the race was on for a technology that would prevent consumers from simply copying prerecorded movies for their friends. As early as

[1]MacroVision is a trademark of MacroVision, Incorporated; additional information is available at http://www.macrovision.com.

1979, tapes appeared on the market that had techniques to make them difficult to copy. Unfortunately for consumers, the same techniques that made a tape difficult to copy often made it difficult to view on some televisions. In the late 1980s, John Ryan embarked on a systematic study of the differences between a VCR's input circuit and a television's tuner.

Ryan's first successful technology, which he called MacroVision, inserted a 4-μsec, high-amplitude noise pulse in the vertical blanking interval of a prerecorded tape. The vertical blanking interval is the period during each frame of a TV broadcast in which the TV swings its picture tube's guns back to the top of the picture to start the next frame. Thus, no picture data is broadcast during that interval, and the TV ignores it. On the other hand, VCRs must record the vertical blanking interval, and the automatic gain circuit of many VCRs can be thrown off by that artificially loud signal. As a result, the VCR may not correctly record hundreds of lines of valid picture data that follow the vertical blanking interval. A recording made of a MacroVision-protected program usually has an objectionable band of low intensity rolling across the picture.

Unfortunately for the movie studios, not all VCRs are sensitive to this first version of MacroVision, either coincidentally or deliberately. Also, "black boxes" have appeared on the market that strip out the noise pulse on its way to the VCR. Therefore, MacroVision, Inc. created a new technology based on modifications to the 11-cycle color burst signal that is present at the beginning of every line of the picture. The company claims that 85% of all VCRs are sensitive to the combination of MacroVision I and MacroVision II. Although this is not enormously effective, unlike the other technologies described herein, MacroVision (1) works in the analog domain and (2) requires no secrets and no device license, because it is based on the fundamental differences between TVs and VCRs.

SERIAL COPY MANAGEMENT SYSTEM

In the late 1980s, the consumer electronics industry had developed a new technology called Digital Audio Tape (DAT). DAT offered consumers the capability to make a perfect digital copy of a music compact disk (CD). It offered the music industry nothing. Prerecorded music CDs are mass produced by a lithographic process analogous to a printing press's process. No magnetic media could possibly achieve the same economy of scale, so CDs would always be preferred to DATs for releasing prerecorded music. DAT was strictly a copying technology.

313

An alarmed music industry reached a compromise with the consumer electronics industry, and this compromise was enacted into law in the United States as the Audio Home Recording Act of 1992. There were three main features of the act. First, because some uses of DAT would certainly be infringing legitimate copyrights, small royalties would be imposed on blank media, to be paid to the music industry, to compensate them for the infringement. Second, it established that it was *not* an infringement for consumers to make copies for "space shifting." In other words, it is not an infringement for consumers to make a copy of music they have purchased to play it on a different device, such as in their car. Third, it had a technical aspect: it required digital audio recording devices to implement the Serial Copy Management System (SCMS).

The Serial Copy Management System is the heart of simplicity. Two bits in a header are used to encode three states: "copy freely," "copy once," or "copy never." If a compliant device makes a copy of content marked "copy once," it must mark the copy "copy never." Of course, it cannot record "copy never" content.

As the hearings about the proposed law were being held, a third industry started to become alarmed. The computer industry, at that time worried about hard disks, felt the royalty on blank media was inherently unfair. Why should someone saving a spreadsheet, for example, end up paying the music industry for the privilege? The industry argued that computer media should be exempt from the legislation, and it won.

Since the act was passed, DAT has not been very successful, at least not in the United States; and two unanticipated computer-related technological advances have made the computer exemption, at the very least, ironic. First, effective music compression technologies, such as MP3, were invented, so that even a moderately sized hard disk could store a huge music library. Second, the cost of CD recording technology went from tens of dollars per disk to tens of cents per disk. The impact of all this on the record industry has been substantial. The Recording Industry Association of America has stated that the industry loses $4.2 billion per year due to different forms of "piracy," but this figure includes traditional sources such as counterfeit recordings and is not entirely the effect of home computers.

The Audio Home Recording Act's exemption on computer media leads to other anomalies. Consumer electronics companies have begun to offer purpose-built music CD copying devices. Because these devices are not exempt from the Audio Home Recording Act, they must use special, and more expensive, CD blank disks rather than those used by computer software to perform the same function. The price of the special blank disk includes the royalty to the music industry. Likewise, the devices honor the SCMS bits. Although some music-copying computer programs also honor SCMS bits, they are probably not legally obligated to, and doing so puts them at a competitive disadvantage.

CONTENT SCRAMBLING SYSTEM

At the end of 1994, the movie industry and the consumer electronics industry were poised to introduce a new technology, Digital Versatile Disk (DVD), which promised a superior consumer experience for prerecorded movies compared to magnetic tapes. This promise has been more than fulfilled; DVDs are the most successful new consumer technology ever introduced, in terms of rate of adoption — more successful than music CDs, more successful than cell phones.

The movie industry, of course, was concerned about rampant copying of the digital DVD movies. They had agreed with the consumer electronics industry that they would ask Congress to extend the law so that SCMS would be compulsory with the new technology. Because there is no strong "space shifting" argument with movies, the new disks could be marked "copy never" at the source. Unlike music CDs, however, DVDs were designed from the beginning to be computer compatible, so they knew that it would be necessary to get the computer industry to agree with this proposed law. They did not anticipate any problem; after all, checking a couple of bits was a trivial function in a device as powerful as a personal computer.

Universally, however, the computer companies that got involved in this issue reacted negatively to the proposal. Their arguments focused on two main problems. First, they argued that computers were general-purpose devices and designers might inadvertently provide a circumvention path while building an entirely different function. For example, imagine a medical image system using this new high-density DVD technology to store medical images. If the designers were ignorant of the movie industry and ignored the SCMS bits on the DVDs, the system could be viewed as a circumvention device, with criminal penalties to the manufacturer. Second, they argued that SCMS was a totally ineffective system on the personal computer (PC); any 12-year-old Basic programmer could figure out how to flip the SCMS bits to make copies.

Regardless of the merits of the first argument, the second argument got the attention of the movie industry. After much discussion, the three industries (movie, computer, and consumer electronics) agreed upon some basic principles that still govern content protection technologies today:

1. If content owners want their content protected, they must encrypt it at the source.

2. It is a voluntary choice whether or not a manufacturer supports that protection scheme.

3. Because the content is encrypted, it is not possible for a manufacturer to inadvertently create a circumvention device; circumvention requires overt action.

Based on these principles, in 1996 engineers from Matsushita and Toshiba designed an encryption system for DVD video they called the Content Scrambling System (CSS). Because of concerns about the United States' and especially Japan's export laws on cryptography, it was based on a 40-bit key size. Even with 1996 personal computers, a 40-bit key could be found by exhaustive search in less than a day of processing. Even worse, the encryption algorithm they chose is actually invertible, meaning it was not a true encryption algorithm. It is, like its name implied, simply a way to scramble the data. All of the weaknesses of CSS were known by insiders before the system was ever deployed. As a result, the details of the system have always been confidential. The system was deployed in time for Christmas 1996.

The Content Scrambling System works by assigning each device manufacturer a single key. There are 400 different manufacturer keys, and the disk key (the key that fundamentally protects the content on the disk) is "encrypted" by each one of them. The encryptions are placed in the lead-in area on the DVD. Each device goes to its manufacturer's particular spot in the lead-in area, then uses its manufacturer's key to decrypt the disk key. From the disk key, it can decrypt individual title keys and decrypt the content itself.

For 3 years, CSS went along swimmingly. In November 1999, however, it was reported that a 16-year-old in Norway found a global secret: one of the manufacturer's keys. Despite the glaring weaknesses in the cryptography of the system, the break was apparently achieved by reverse-engineering a poorly protected software implementation. It was also clearly helped by information that had been circulating for many months on some Linux newsgroups, apparently from anonymous employees of licensees who had access to the confidential specification. Once the break was announced and studied, the cryptographic weaknesses became apparent, and within weeks, the remaining 399 manufacturers' keys had been published on the Internet.

It is easy for cryptographers to criticize the CSS technology. Of course, it is now completely broken; a few minutes' search on the Web can get you a program that will allow you to copy DVDs. The technology certainly could have been improved, but only at the cost of missing the critical 1996 Christmas season. Had the entire deployment, and therefore the movie industry's enormous DVD revenues, been moved back a year,

I believe that the industry would have lost more money than they are ever going to lose due to the break. Because the manufacturers' keys act as global shared secrets in the system, an irrevocable break was inevitable in any event.

CONTENT PROTECTION ON RECORDABLE MEDIA[2]

Most of the people who were working on DVD copy protection in 1996 — and I was among them — agreed that the one fundamental weakness of CSS, the manufacturer's key, was unavoidable. It was recognized that if a manufacturer's key was ever compromised, and there were large numbers of devices already using the key, the system would be broken. There would be no way to revoke the compromised key without causing unacceptable consumer dissatisfaction. What else could be done? Because the system needed to play disks worldwide across all manufacturers' players and the players had to work in a disconnected mode, it seemed inevitable that the system had to be based on shared secrets.

It turned out that this intuition was wrong. A few years before, Amos Fiat and Moni Naor had written a theoretical paper [3] in which they asked the question, "Can a key management system be devised if the parties involved have only a one-way communication?" The answer was "yes," and they provided a concrete example. They were thinking of the case of broadcasting encrypted programs to many receivers, so they called their approach "broadcast encryption." It turns out that the one-way property is also essential for protecting physical media: a recorder makes a recording, and years later a player needs to play it back. There may be no opportunity for the player and recorder to get together and share a cryptographic key.

In 1997, Kevin McCurley and I at IBM became attracted to broadcast encryption, not because of its applicability to protecting physical media — we had not made the connection, either — but because it needed substantially less device overhead than public key cryptography. We devised an improvement over the Fiat–Naor method and described it to several companies. A couple of months later, Brendan Traw from Intel came back and said, "You know, this would solve the problem of DVD recording, don't you?" He was right, of course, and with that, the technology called Content Protection for Recordable Media (CPRM) was born. IBM and Intel were later joined by Matsushita and Toshiba in developing and licensing this technology.

Like any broadcast-encryption-type technology, CPRM works by having a block of data, the *media key block*,[3] prerecorded on the blank

---

[2]Additional information is available at http://www.4centity.com.
[3]Fiat and Naor called it the "session key block."

media. Every CPRM device in the world has a unique set of keys, called *device keys*. Two devices may have some keys in common, but no two devices will have exactly the same set. The devices process the media key block using their device keys. Each device follows a unique path through the media key block, but they all end up with the same answer, called the *media key*. The media key is the key that fundamentally protects the content on the media. If a circumvention device appears in the world, new media key blocks can be produced so that that particular device's path is blocked — it does not calculate the same media key as the rest of the compliant devices. It cannot be used to copy a recording if it has been made on the new media. Thus, CPRM solves the problem that plagued CSS: if a 16-year-old in Norway discovers a set of keys, the hacked program he or she produces will not work on newly released media. The value of the hack becomes less and less as time passes.

Figure 10.1 illustrates a media key block. For each type of protected media, the CPRM license agency has created a matrix of keys. The matrices are always 16 columns wide, but the number of rows depends on the type of media (from 500 to 24,000 rows). For each device, a manufacturer gets 16 device keys, one in each column, shown as small rectangles. In the meantime, the license agency is producing media key blocks for blank media. The media key blocks contain the encryption of the media key, over and over again, at each position in the matrix. The media key is picked at random and is different for each media key block.

When the device processes a media key block, it can use any of its device keys. As of early 2004, no circumvention devices had yet appeared, so any device keys would work. Eventually, however, circumvention devices may appear. The compromised keys they are using are shown as X's. Those positions in the matrix will not contain the correct encryption of the media key. If by bad luck, an innocent device may have a key or two that is compromised, it just uses one of its other keys.

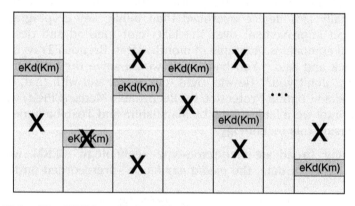

Figure 10.1.   The CPRM media key block.

Unless a large fraction of the matrix is covered with X's, an innocent device has an extremely high probability that it will have at least one uncompromised key. If that large a part of the matrix is compromised, the system will be effectively broken. This will require hundreds to tens of thousands of independent attacks, depending on the size of the matrix.

It turns out to be prohibitively expensive, for most types of media, to produce a new media key block for each piece of blank media. Instead, the media key blocks are mass produced (in the case of DVD recordable blanks, up to one million blanks can use the same media key block). However, a unique serial number has been burned into the physical media, and the devices use it as part of the cryptographic calculation. In particular, they perform a cryptographic hash, combining the media key and the serial number. The result is then treated as a key, called the *media unique key,* which, with very high probability, is unique for the particular piece of media. Even though the serial number is freely readable by any device, only compliant devices can calculate the media unique key, because only a compliant device can calculate the media key correctly.

Just like CSS, CPRM adds one more level of indirection before the actual key that encrypts the content is obtained. That key is called the *title key,* and there can be many title keys on a single piece of media. The title key is randomly picked by the recorder, which then encrypts that title key with the media unique key. It places the encrypted content and the encrypted title key on the media. A compliant player can play back the encrypted content by reversing the steps: after calculating the media unique key, the player reads and decrypts the encrypted title key. Then, using the title key, the player can decrypt and play the content itself.

The title key calculation is slightly more complicated on some types of CPRM media. Before encrypting the title key, the recorder Exclusive-ORs it with the Copy Control Information (CCI). The CCI can be as simple as our old friend, the two bits from SCMS, but it can also contain more information (e.g., the number of copies allowed). Now, if the 12-year-old Basic programmers flip the CCI bits to obtain more copy permission, it does not make it available. They can change the bits, but the compliant players will no longer calculate the title keys correctly, and the content has been rendered useless.

Content Protection on Recordable Media was intended to allow recorders to make copies that could not be further copied; it was designed for recordable media. The same principles, however, are obviously applicable to prerecorded content. An offshoot of CPRM, called Content Protection for Prerecorded Media (CPPM), has been developed by the same companies. In CPPM, the idea of having a unique serial number per piece of media has been replaced by the idea of having a serial number (called an *album ID*) for each particular release. Other than that, the two technologies are identical. CPPM is used to protect DVD audio, a successor technology to DVD video. To date, DVD audio has been a high-resolution format of interest only to audiophiles; but because of its strong copy protection capability, the music industry is looking at it as a replacement for music CDs.

Both CPRM and CPPM have been remarkably successful. As of year-end 2003, over 200 million devices had been licensed. CPRM has been employed on DVD recordables (DVD-RAM, DVD-R, and DVD-RW), on the Secure Digital Memory Card (SD Card[4]), and on secure CompactFlash.[5] To be honest, however, a great deal of the success of CPRM has been due to the success of the SD Card, and the success of the SD Card has everything to do with its price, performance, and convenient form factor, and little to do with its inherent copy protection feature.

DIVX

After examining a successful copy protection technology like CPRM, it might provide some balance to consider a copy protection scheme that failed in the market. Divx was a technology developed by Circuit City together with some Hollywood-based investors. It was an innovative idea, with some interesting consumer and distribution advantages that the company seemed singularly unable to articulate. Fundamentally, Divx was a rental replacement technology. Built on top of the DVD technology, the Divx player would allow the consumer to play the disk for a 48-h period. If the user wanted to play it again later or if he had obtained the disk from a friend who had already used the 48-h period, that was permitted, but it would require an additional payment.

Divx was implemented by requiring the player to have a phone connection to a clearinghouse and periodically to call and report usage. If the consumer blocked the phone calls, the player would eventually refuse to play disks. A consumer might be able to obtain a few weeks of free play by that trick, but it would be a one-time attack.

What were the advantages of the Divx technology? It had the potential to revolutionize the way the movie rental business works. Today, the most difficult aspect of renting movies, from the point of view of the outlet offering them, is maintaining inventory. In other words, the outlets must keep track of the returned movies. Most retail stores shy away from this complication. Divx disks, however, were designed not to be

---

[4]SD is a trademark of the SD Card Association.
[5]CompactFlash is a trademark of the CompactFlash Association.

returned. The store could manage them like any other retail item. Convenience stores were the ideal retail outlets for Divx disks.

The consumer value proposition for Divx came indirectly from the retail advantage. If the disks were available in many retail outlets, the consumer would not have to make a special trip to rent a movie, and no trip at all to return it. Because the 48-h period did not begin until the disk was inserted in the player, a consumer buying a quart of milk on Tuesday, for example, could rent a movie on impulse for Saturday night. If it turned out that she was busy that Saturday, she could play the movie the next Saturday.

The Divx company seemed unable to exploit the obvious advantages of its technology. Reasoning, presumably, that consumers would be wary of renting movies from unfamiliar sources, they focused, unsuccessfully, on traditional movie rental outlets such as Blockbuster.[6] Blockbuster must have seen Divx as a major threat. Divx also seemed unable to explain its value proposition to consumers. The San Francisco Bay Area was one of its test markets, so I observed its early advertisements. Its first advertising slogan was, "Build your movie library at $5 a disc!" Divx was many things, but it *absolutely* was not that. The $5 price was a rental fee.

Opponents of content protection technologies have often cited the failure of Divx as an example of consumer revolt against overly restrictive content protection technologies. This appears to be wishful thinking. Although Divx players were sold in only about 10% of the retail consumer electronics outlets in the United States, they accounted for 20% of the sales of DVD players. This remained true up until the moment the company went out of business. It can be argued, then, that consumers preferred Divx players two-to-one over conventional DVD players. Instead, the failure of Divx appears to be a failure to correctly exploit a good idea. Or perhaps it was an idea ahead of its time.

DIGITAL TRANSMISSION CONTENT PROTECTION[7]

Up to now, this chapter has focused on content protection for physical media. That is only part of the problem. At the same time that the industry was developing DVD video, it recognized that some of the high quality of the digital content could be lost if it had to be connected to a TV over a conventional analog coax connection. The digital bus called Firewire (IEEE 1394) was designed to carry compressed digital TV streams with perfect fidelity. If the streams were transmitted in the clear,

---

[6]Blockbuster is a trademark of Blockbuster, Inc.
[7]Additional information available at http://www.dtcp.com.

however, hackers would have an easy circumvention path to get the copy-protected movies.

Five companies (Intel, Toshiba, Sony, Hitachi, and Matsushita) developed a technology to solve this problem. Called Digital Transmission Content Protection (DTCP), it is available on Firewire, on the Universal Serial Bus, and, most recently, on any transmission technology that supports Transmission Control Protocol/Internet Protocol (TCP/IP).

Unlike physical media, transmission media allow the two devices to have a conversation. Therefore, conventional public key cryptography can be applied. Each device has a public key and its corresponding private key. It has a certificate, signed by the licensing agency, that reveals its public key. For example, let us say a DVD player wants to output to a TV over DTCP. The two devices exchange their certificates, and each device verifies that the other's certificate is correctly signed. Furthermore, they both consult a certificate revocation list (called a System Renewal Message in DTCP) to verify that other device has not been revoked.

They also agree on a cryptographic key, using a technique called the Diffie–Hellman protocol. Diffie–Hellman is perhaps the best-known public key method, and is based on two principles:

1. $(g^x)^y = (g^y)^x$.
2. There is no efficient way to calculate x if you are given the remainder of g^x after dividing by some number (such as a large prime), even if you know g. Thus, if g and x are large numbers, finding x is an intractable calculation.

All the devices in the system agree upon a number g and a prime P; these are wired in at the factory. One device picks a random x and transmits the remainder of g^x after dividing by P; the other device picks a random y and transmits the remainder of g^y after dividing by P. The first device raises g^y to the x power; the second device raises g^x to the y power. Thus, they both calculate the remainder of g^{xy} after dividing by P, and this becomes the common key in which they encrypt other keys. In effect, they have established a secret value while having a completely public conversation.

In DTCP, each device signs its Diffie–Hellman messages with the private key that corresponds to the public key in its certificate; this is called an *authenticated* Diffie–Hellman protocol. Second, the signatures in the messages and the values in the Diffie–Hellman protocol are not integers, but points on an elliptic curve. Although a discussion of this *elliptical curve cryptography* is too detailed for this chapter, it does not change the underlying Diffie–Hellman mathematical principle. Instead, it allows the calculations to use smaller numbers than would otherwise have been needed to prevent exhaustive search.

This is a very standard cryptographic approach. However, some consumer electronics companies felt that the calculations involved in public key cryptography were too onerous for their low-end devices. A compromise was reached. Devices that could only handle "copy once" content — which is to say, recorders — were allowed to establish the bus key in a simpler way, called *restricted authentication*. The argument was that "copy once" content was less valuable than "copy never" content, so its cryptographic protection did not need to be as strong. Devices that could handle "copy never" content (e.g., TVs, DVD players, set-top boxes) had to implement both types of authentication.

Once a recorder makes a recording of "copy once" content, the recording can no longer be copied. However, if the recording was marked "copy never," that would require the recorders to have the full authentication to play back the recordings they made, which was what the designers were trying to avoid. Instead, the recording is marked "copy no more," a state that is logically the same as "copy never," but one in which the receiving device does not demand full authentication.

The DTCP restricted authentication is superficially similar to CPRM's media key block. Like CPRM, it is based on a matrix of values. The license agency has produced this matrix. Each source device (player, set-top box) is given three rows from the matrix; each sink device (recorder, TV) is given three columns. As sketched in Figure 10.2, the devices are not given the actual values in their rows or columns; instead, they are given a

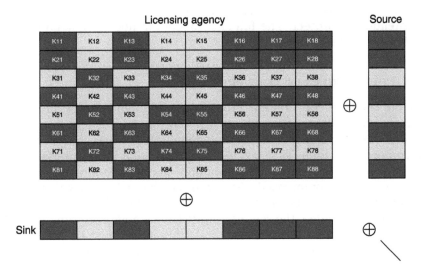

Figure 10.2. DTCP restricted authentication.

summary, which is referred to as their keys. The summary is the element-by-element Exclusive-OR of the selected rows or columns. For example, the source device is given a key for each row in the matrix, and that value is the Exclusive-OR of its selected columns at that row.

A source and a sink agree upon a common key as follows. The source device tells the sink which columns it is using. Because the sink device has a key for every column, it selects the keys from the three sink columns and Exclusive-ORs them together. Concurrently, the sink device tells the source which rows it is using. The source device Exclusive-ORs the three keys that correspond to those rows. In effect, each device is calculating the Exclusive-OR of the nine values they have in common, shown in black, although they are each doing it in a different way and neither of them knows the actual nine values. That result of the calculation is then the common key for the two devices.

The amount of revocation that can be achieved with such a system is limited, even though there are two matrices, one for "copy once" transfers and one for "copy no more" transfers. The DTCP matrix is 12×12; this means that there are only 220 possibilities each for source devices and sink devices. If a particular set of rows or columns needs to be revoked, there will be many innocent devices that are using the same set. Also, each compromised set gives the attackers an equation in 3 unknowns; and after 12 such compromises, they will have 12 equations in 12 unknowns and be able to calculate the entire matrix. The well-publicized "break" of DTCP was nothing more than an observation of this obvious truth, which had been long admitted by the designers of the system. The restricted authentication mode of DTCP is weak, but it is arguably sufficient for the lower-value content that it is intended to protect. The full authentication mode is a sound public-key-based system.

HIGH DEFINITION CONTENT PROTECTION[8]

Digital Transmission Content Protection was intended to protect compressed video data, especially on the Firewire bus. There is a second digital bus in common use on high-definition televisions that conveys uncompressed video. That bus is called the Digital Video Interface (DVI) and was originally designed for computer monitors. Points in the system that contain uncompressed video are substantially less vulnerable to attack than points that contain compressed data. In order to record uncompressed video, the recorder must have a huge recording capacity, both in terms of bandwidth and total storage, or must be prepared to compress on-the-fly. Either solution has its problems and costs.

[8]Additional information available at http://www.digital-cp.com.

Nonetheless, there were concerns about the DVI bus not having any protection. In 1999, Intel defined the High Definition Content Protection (HDCP) technology to protect the DVI bus. HDCP's keys use the same scheme used in DTCP's restricted authentication mode. Also, the scheme uses scrambling, not encryption, to actually protect the data. So, HDCP is not a particularly strong protection scheme, but the data it is protecting is not particularly vulnerable. Because HDCP can be inexpensively implemented in the device, it appears as though the designers have achieved a reasonable balance.

BROADCAST FLAG

As was alluded to earlier, the licenses for the technologies we have described are often more involved than the specifications. The licenses contain numerous rules describing what the manufacturers can and cannot do. These are called *compliance rules*. However, they also contain rules that constrain how the content owners can use the technology. These are *encoding rules*. The consumer electronics and computer companies that develop these technologies make more money the more copying that is allowed, up to a point. After all, the companies make recorders, hard disks, computers, and so forth that are used for copying. However, it is in no one's interest, not even consumers', if the content owners' worst fears are realized, and rampant copying destroys the entertainment industry.

The encoding rules in the DTCP license, which are also mimicked in the other licenses that want to be compatible, are consumer oriented:

1. Over-the-air digital broadcasts must be marked "copy freely."
2. Cable-only programs may be marked no more restrictive than "copy once." However, if a cable signal is also part of an over-the-air broadcast, it must be marked "copy freely." For example, 99% of the cable viewers in the United States receive WTBS through their cable system; however, the signal is broadcast over-the-air in Atlanta, so it must be "copy freely."
3. Pay-per-view or video-on-demand programs may be marked "copy never."
4. Temporarily recording a program (called a "transient image") for implementing consumer convenience functions such as rewind and fast forward does not count as a copy; even a "copy never" program can be recorded for this purpose. The content owners control how long the transient image can exist, but they cannot set the period to less than 90 min.

These rules were basically acceptable to television and movie studios. However, they had some real concerns about the "copy freely" content remaining in the clear, where it could be widely redistributed on the Internet. They were concerned that in the new high-bandwidth world, consumers might stream a digital over-the-air broadcast out over the Internet in real-time. This could destroy the value of regional advertisements, which are a substantial source of revenue for local television stations. They were also concerned that file-sharing networks or casual personal Web sites might save all of the programs from a popular television series as they are broadcast, destroying the value of the reruns of the series in syndication.

The studios were willing to accept DTCP's relatively liberal encoding rules if the technology companies could solve the problem of Internet redistribution for them. The DTCP group came up with the idea called Encryption Plus Non-assertion (EPN). The video content is marked "copy freely," but it is also encrypted. The compliance rules of the DTCP license prohibit devices from putting such content on the Internet. Of course, they are also prohibited from releasing the content in the clear so that downstream, noncompliant devices could put it on the Internet for them.

Incidentally, EPN gave those of us working on CPRM fits. Although DTCP had separate bits for encryption and copy control information, we did not; we had made the simplifying assumption for DVD video recording that encryption was synonymous with "copy no more." So technically, EPN content in CPRM is marked "copy no more." However, there is an 8-byte field in the content itself that says, in effect, "I don't really mean that; it is actually 'copy freely'." This 8-byte value is a cryptographic value called a Message Authentication Code (MAC) and is different for each piece of content and media. It can only be correctly calculated by a device that can calculate the media unique key. In other words, it can only be calculated by a compliant device.

Concurrently with the work being done by the various content protection technology groups, the Motion Pictures Expert Group (MPEG) had defined a field, called the *broadcast flag*, which could be used to denote that a given digital broadcast should have EPN protection. The content companies asked the Federal Communications Commission (FCC) to pass a rule requiring digital tuners to respond to the broadcast flag with an approved content protection scheme. Observe that this approach is completely at odds with the agreements that had been hammered out in the original DVD discussions: content should be protected at the source, and downstream participation should be strictly voluntary. However, to apply this principle in this case would require the public airwaves to carry encrypted signals. This is a political hot potato that few wanted to touch.

In November 2003, the FCC passed a rule requiring digital receivers manufactured after July 2005 to respond correctly to the broadcast flag.

This rule has been controversial. At least some of the opposition, however, seems to be coming from consumer rights groups who are under the misapprehension that the broadcast flag somehow restricts copying. EPN allows unlimited physical copies; if there is any doubt, ask anyone in the CPRM group about the hoops they had to jump through to make that possible. The broadcast flag and EPN are strictly about restricting the Internet redistribution of digital television broadcasts.

ADVANCED BROADCAST ENCRYPTION

Compared to public key cryptography, broadcast encryption is a younger technology, and remarkable strides have been made in recent years. The original Fiat–Naor and the later CPRM matrix approaches have the property that they have only a finite amount of revocation. Although this finite number may be quite large and, therefore, the chance of defeating the system by running out of revocation capability is negligible, this theoretical limitation has been overcome. In 1997 and 1998, two independent groups, one led by Debbie Wallner [4] and one led by C.K. Wong [5], devised a scheme based on a tree of keys instead of a matrix. The tree approach allowed unlimited revocation.

The tree approach also solved a problem that we in CPRM called the "evil manufacturer problem." If a fraudulent manufacturer signs a license and begins using keys to build circumvention devices, he does substantially more damage to CPRM's revocation capability than a hacker compromising individual devices, despite a clever key assignment algorithm to mitigate this exact problem. In a tree, it is no more expensive to revoke an entire branch (i.e., an entire manufacturer) than it is to revoke an individual device.

With the invention of the tree approach, the state of the art of broadcast encryption had advanced so that it had equivalent revocation capability to public key cryptography, but it still required substantially more space to convey that information. In other words, the two-way handshake of public key cryptography allowed a concise encoding of the revocation information, whereas the one-way transfer of broadcast encryption needed a much larger media key block (e.g., $100\times$ larger) to achieve the same amount of revocation. In 2001, however, Dalit Naor and Moni Naor (among others) at IBM broke through this barrier and invented a tree-based scheme [6] that was equivalent in space to a public key certificate revocation list.

In the Naor–Naor scheme, which they called *subset difference*, each device has almost every key in the tree. The tree is carefully designed so it is always possible for you to find a single key that every device in the system knows, except the device you are trying to revoke. What if you are trying to revoke two devices? The answer is that there is not a single tree. There are literally billions of different independent trees. Thus, revoking a list of devices in the subset-difference scheme requires you to first identify the trees you want to use (the "subsets") and then identify the single device being revoked in each tree (the "differences"). You then encrypt the media key repeatedly in the keys that the revoked devices do not know. Like a public key certificate revocation list, the amount of data that needs to be transmitted is proportional to the number of devices you are revoking and, unlike all previous broadcast encryption schemes, independent of the total number of devices in the system.

This description of the subset-difference scheme so far has implied that the device needs billions of keys — clearly impractical. However, an earlier paper by Canetti and others [7] had provided an answer: it is not necessary for the keys to be truly independent. If the keys that are closer to the leaves of the trees are one-way functions of the keys that are closer to the root, devices can calculate almost all the keys they need on-the-fly, from a few keys they have stored. With this principle, subset-difference devices need to store only hundreds of keys, instead of billions. Although storing 250 keys, for example, is eminently practical, it requires noticeably more storage than the 16 keys that the original CPRM technology required. In 2001, however, Havely and Shamir observed [8] that subset-difference's "independent" trees could, in fact, be related to each other in a similar way to the way the keys within the tree were. They called their modification *layered subset difference*; and with that improvement, the number of keys required in the device was comparable to the previous schemes that required much larger media key blocks.

So, the state of the art of broadcast encryption has advanced remarkably in the 10 years since it was invented. These advances stand ready to protect the new generation of high-definition DVDs, which will probably hit the market in late 2005. With effectively infinite revocation capability, those new disks will not be at the mercy of the first 16-year-old who discovers a key. However, the promise of broadcast encryption is even greater. Essential for applications like physical media that require its one-way property, broadcast encryption no longer pays any penalty in two-way applications compared to public key cryptography. Because it has some interesting consumer advantages compared to public key cryptography, which is discussed in the next section, it seems inevitable that more and more content protection schemes will be based on broadcast encryption.

PERSONAL DIGITAL DOMAIN

The technologies we have discussed so far are focused on restricting the number of physical copies that can be made from a given media source. Even the transmission-oriented technologies such as DTCP and HDCP have this as their end goal; they provide a secure way in which the copy restrictions can be communicated and restrict the transfer of content to compliant devices. Recently, however, a different approach has gotten the attention of both industry and consumer groups: instead of restricting the number of physical copies of a particular content item, it restricts the number of devices that are allowed to play the item. This idea has come to be called the *personal digital domain.*[9] The idea is that each household's extended devices — not just the devices actually in the home, but in-car devices, portable devices, and perhaps even office personal workstations — would comprise the household's personal digital domain.

The consumer promise of the personal digital domain is enticing. Freed from having to count copies, consumers could make unlimited copies for backup and for the convenience of playback at various places and times. However, this promise could be lost if setting up the personal digital domain is an administrative headache or perceived to be an intrusion on privacy. Those working on this concept in IBM, including myself, became convinced that for the personal digital domain to succeed, it must be essentially "plug and play." Devices must form a personal digital domain simply by being connected, and they must do this autonomously, without external registration, except under the most unusual circumstances.

There are several technical approaches being proposed for the personal digital domain. None has yet been adopted by the consumer electronics industry. Basically, the technical problem resolves itself into having a group of devices agree upon a common cryptographic key. This is a classic application of public key cryptography, and all the solutions, save one, have used public key techniques. The one exception is the one with which I am involved. In 2001, Florian Pestoni, Dalit Naor, and I, buoyed by the recent substantial improvements in broadcast encryption, devised a personal digital domain scheme based on broadcast encryption. We called our solution the *xCP Cluster Protocol.*[10]

Broadcast encryption brings with it several desirable properties, not the least of which is that it needs substantially less device overhead than public key cryptography. However, it also turns out to be the ideal cryptographic primitive when you are building a system that works autonomously and anonymously. Public key cryptography is fundamentally based on *identity*. Parties first exchange their certificates and then enter a protocol in which they each prove that they have the private key that corresponds to the public key in that certificate. In broadcast

---

[9]Also called the "authorized domain" in some circles.

[10]From Extensible Content Protection, our name for a family of content protection technologies based on broadcast encryption, including CPRM and CPPM.

encryption, identity is irrelevant. A device can safely encrypt content based on a media key block, never knowing which device might finally end up decrypting it. However, the first device is confident that this unknown second device is compliant, because it must be to correctly process the media key block.

The fundamental property of any content protection is compliance, not identity. A content protection scheme needs to guarantee that all the devices are playing by the rules. If the scheme is based on public key cryptography, it achieves compliance as a side effect of determining identity. There is a list of those devices that are not playing by the rules, and the scheme needs the identity of the devices in the system to make sure that none of them are on the list. In effect, there is a level of indirection in achieving compliance. A broadcast-encryption-based scheme is more direct: the media key block enables compliant devices explicitly, by allowing them, and no one else, to calculate the key.

What does this all mean for the personal digital domain? At the risk of overgeneralizing, the public key approach suggests systems that are based on the registration and administration of devices, whereas the broadcast-encryption approach suggests systems where the devices, freed from the task of having to explicitly establish the compliance of the whole system, self-organize into personal digital domains. That is not a hard and fast rule; in both cases, one could design a system that bucks this trend.

Assuming that registration of devices with an external authorization center would lead to an awkward and intrusive consumer experience, what other alternatives are there? Basically, there are two: the personal digital domain can be based on physical proximity or the domain can be approximated simply by limiting the number of devices that can be in a single domain. Using physical proximity has both technical and philosophical problems. Technically, network protocols like TCP/IP are deliberately designed to be transparent to distance. They work the same if the devices are around the room or around the world. Philosophically, should your vacation home not be part of the same personal domain as your main home?

That leaves limitations on the number of devices as the best technique for establishing the personal domain. As long as there is an easy exception mechanism (undoubtedly requiring an external connection) to handle those gadget-happy homes that have far more than the normal number of devices, I think this approach is eminently workable. However, it almost immediately suggests attacks where the attackers try to fool the autonomous devices into creating an artificially large domain. Most of the attacks resolve themselves into the attack I call the "dormitory snowball."

330

In this attack, the attackers form a domain of two devices and then separate them. To each, they introduce one more device. The domain now contains four devices, but no single device knows about more than two others. The process is repeated with the new devices. The domain ends up with many more devices than it should, perhaps even an unlimited number, depending on how devices are allowed to leave the domain.

This attack is thwarted in the xCP protocol by making the domain key be based, in part,[11] on the list of devices in the domain. xCP calls this list the *authorization table*, and each device has its own copy of it. If two devices have a different authorization table, they cannot successfully share content. Thus, in the dormitory attack, the different overlapped clusters effectively operate as different domains. Of course, it is possible for two devices to have different authorization tables for perfectly benign reasons; for example, a device was powered off or disconnected when a new device joined the domain. In the benign case, however, one authorization table is always a subset of the other, whereas in the attack scenario, they must remain disjoint (or else the number of devices in the table gets too large). It is easy for compliant devices to detect and automatically update their authorization table in the benign case.

To maintain this important superset and subset property, devices leaving the cluster are not simply deleted from the authorization table. They remain in the table, but they are marked as deleted. Furthermore, they must acknowledge that they have been deleted. The rule is that a deleted device can no longer play any content in the domain. Because all devices are compliant, they play by that rule.

What if the user prevents the device from learning that it has left the domain? Then, it continues to count as one of the devices the domain. Suppose a consumer wants to sell a device on eBay,[12] together with his library of content, but retain a copy of his library for his own use. In effect, he is selling unauthorized copies of his content. There is nothing in our protocol that absolutely prevents this. However, the sold device cannot be deleted from the seller's domain, or else the content would be useless. Therefore, the device must be sold together with an authorization table that contains all of the other seller's devices. This can greatly reduce the value of the device to the buyer. The buyer, to use the content, must have his other devices join this domain, which is artificially large. If, as a result, he needs an external authorization to successfully build the new domain, the authorization center can observe that the

---

[11]The other values that are used to calculate the domain key are a domain identifier and, of course, a media key from a media key block. The latter guarantees that only compliant devices can calculate the domain key.

[12]eBay is a trademark of eBay Inc.

domain has an unusually large number of devices that are not active, and guess what has happened. At that point, the center has several possible courses of action, including refusing to allow the domain to grow. I recommend, however, that the center should offer the consumer in this state the chance to make things right in a way that is not too onerous to the consumer.

Note also that attacks of this type are inherently self-limiting. After one or two such attacks, the size of the authorization tables becomes a serious problem to the attackers. However, we allow the possibility of these attacks because we want normal consumers, who are not attempting to traffic in unauthorized content, to have a completely seamless experience. Ideally, personal digital domain content protection should be completely transparent to the average consumer.

CONCLUSIONS

In this chapter, I have sketched a history of content protection on consumer electronics devices, together with a brief description of each. Over time, improvements in the underlying cryptography have made the content protection schemes increasingly effective. Perhaps fortuitously, the same underlying cryptographic improvements also offer the consumer the promise of increased privacy, transparency, and flexibility. Rather than cloaking the consumer in a content protection straightjacket, it seems that the newest technologies have the opposite potential: the consumer should be able to do more things with entertainment content than he or she has ever been able to do in the past. This flexibility can be achieved without substantial inroads to the entertainment industry's business. In fact, the new digital modes, offering new business opportunities and new consumer value, can be a boon to the industry.

REFERENCES

1. Barlow, J.P., The economy of ideas, *Wired*, Vol. 203, March 1994.
2. Schneier, B., The Futility of Digital Copy Prevention, http://schneier.com, May 15, 2001.
3. Fiat, A. and Naor, M., Broadcast encryption, in *Advances in Cryptology — Crypto '93, Lecture Notes in Computer Science*, Vol. 773, Springer-Verlag, Berlin, 1994, pp. 480–491.
4. Wallner, D.M., Harder, H.J., and Agee, R.C., Key Management for Multicast: Issues and Architectures, IETF Draft Wallner-Key, July 1997. ftp://ftp.ietf.org/internet-drafts/draft-wallner-key-arch-01.txt.
5. Wong, C.K., Gouda, M., and Lam, S., Secure Group Communications Using Key Graphs, in *Proceedings of ACM SIGCOMM '98*, 1998, p. 68.
6. Naor, D., Naor M., and Lotspiech, J., Revocation and Tracing Routines for Stateless Receivers, in *Advances in Cryptology — Crypto '2001, Lecture Notes in Computer Science*, Vol. 2139, Springer-Verlag, Berlin, 2001, p. 41.

7. Canetti, R. et al., Multicast Security: A Taxonomy and Some Efficient Constructions, in *Proceedings of IEEE INFOCOMM '99*, 1999, Vol. 2, p. 708.
8. Halevy, D. and Shamir, A., The LSD Broadcast Encryption Scheme, in *Advances in Cryptology — Crypto '2002, Lecture Notes in Computer Science*, Springer-Verlag, Berlin, 2002.

11
Adult Image Filtering for Internet Safety

Huicheng Zheng, Mohamed Daoudi,
Christophe Tombelle, and Chabane Djeraba

INTRODUCTION

Internet filters allow schools, libraries, companies, and personal computer users to manage the information that final users can access. Filters may be needed for legal, ethical, or productivity reasons. In the context of legal reason, many new laws require schools and libraries to enforce the policy of Internet safety that protects against minors and adults accessing visual content that is obscene or harmful to minors, and child pornography. More generally:

- Parents can check their home computer for evidence of inappropriate usage by children, as well as protect their children from files that may exist there already.
- Teachers can use the content filters to make sure no improper documents have compromised school and university computer systems. So, schools need to limit access to Web sites so children will not be exposed to objectionable or inappropriate documents.
- Companies can use the content filters to make sure their systems are not contaminated with adult or otherwise unsuitable documents and to determine if files were downloaded during office hours.

Internet surfing can cut into a company's productivity and place a strain on network services. That is why a company may want to filter access to sites that employees might visit during working hours, like Amazon and certain magazine publisher sites. Technical staff can track down the reasons for excess Internet bandwidth and hard drive usage.

To deal with content filtering, three notions are necessary: image information retrieval, text categorization, and image categorization. Even though these three notions are important to efficient content filtering, we will focus in this chapter on image content filtering. We plan to consider all of these notions in future experiments.

Why Is Content Filtering a Multimedia Information Retrieval Notion?

Multimedia information retrieval [1] deals with the representation, storage, organization of, and access to multimedia information ingredients. The representation and organization of multimedia information ingredients should provide the user with easy access to the information in which he is interested. Unfortunately, characterization of the user information requirement is not a simple problem. Consider, for instance, the following hypothetical user information need in the context of the World Wide Web (or just the Web): find all multimedia documents containing visual descriptions of research that are maintained by a country, and participate in a European project. To be relevant, result documents [2] must include Web pages, including images and video of research and the coordinates of the research team head.

Clearly, this full description of user visual information need cannot be used directly to request information using the current interfaces of Web search engines. Instead, the user must first adapt this visual information need into a query that can be processed by the search engine. In its most common form, this adaptation meets a set of keywords, which summarizes the description of the user's visual information need. Given the user query, the key goal of a multimedia information retrieval system is to retrieve information that might be useful or relevant to the user.

When people refer to filtering, they often really mean information retrieval. The filtering corresponds to the Boolean filter in multimedia information retrieval [3]. So, decisions would concern every multimedia document regarding whether or not to visualize it to the user who is searching the information. Initially, a profile describing the user's information [4] needs is set up to facilitate such decision making; this profile may be modified over the long term through the use of user models. These models are based on a person's behavior — decisions, reading behaviors, and so on — which may change the original profile. Both information retrieval and information filtering attempt to maximize the good material

336

that a person sees (that which is likely to be appropriate to the information need at hand) and minimize the bad material.

The difference between multimedia information retrieval and multimedia information filtering is that multimedia information retrieval is intended to support users who are actively searching for multimedia information, as in Internet searching. Multimedia information retrieval typically assumes a dynamic or relatively active behavior of users, because they interact with the search engine by specifying queries. On the basis of the first results, users interact again with the search engine on the basis of his feedback that are useful for the further queries. By contrast, multimedia information filtering supports users in passively monitoring the desired information. It is typically understood to be concerned with an active incoming stream of information objects.

In content filtering, we deal with the same problems as in multimedia information retrieval. For example, in the online side of multimedia information retrieval, the accurate specification of the queries is not simple and rough, because users look for information they do not know, and it is probably inappropriate to ask them to specify accurately what they do not know. The representation of multimedia information content requires interpretations [5] by a human or machine indexer. The problem is that anyone's interpretation of a particular text or medium is likely to be different from that of another indexer, and even different for the same indexer at different times. As our state of knowledge or problems change, our understanding of a text and medium changes. Everyone has experienced the situation of finding a document not relevant at some point but highly relevant later on, perhaps for a different problem or perhaps because we are different. Studies showed that when people are asked to represent an information ingredient, even if they are highly trained in using the same indexing language, they might achieve as much as only 60 to 70% consistency in tasks such as assigning descriptors. We will never achieve "ideal" information retrieval — that is, all the relevant documents and only the relevant documents, or precisely that one thing that a person wants. Because of these roughs, the retrieval process is also inherently rough and probabilistic.

The understanding of soft- and hard-porn Web sites is subjective, and, therefore, representation is necessarily inconsistent. Algorithms for representing images do give consistent representations. However, they give one interpretation of the text and image, out of a great variety of possible meanings, depending on the interpreter. Language is ambiguous in many ways: polysemy, synonymity, and so on, and the context matters greatly in the interpretation.

The meta-language used to describe information objects, or linguistic objects, often is construed to be exactly the same as the textual language.

However, they are not the same. The similarity of the two languages has led to some confusion. In information retrieval, it has led to the idea that the words in the text represent the important concepts and, therefore, can be used to represent what the text is about. The confusion extends to image retrieval, because images can be ambiguous in at least as many ways as language. Furthermore, there is no universal meta-language for describing images. People who are interested in images for advertising purposes have different ways to talk and think about them than do art historians, even though they may be searching for the same images. The lack of a common meta-language for images means that we need to think of special terms for images in special circumstances.

In attempting to prevent children from getting harmful material, it is possible to make approximations and give helpful direction. However, in the end, that is the most that we can hope for. It is not a question of preventing someone from getting inappropriate material but, rather, of supporting the person in not getting it. At least part of the public policy concern is children who are actively trying to get pornography, and it is unreasonable to suppose that information retrieval techniques will be useful in achieving the goal of preventing them from doing so.

There are a variety of users. The user might be a concerned parent or manager who suspects that something bad is happening. However, mistakes are inevitable and we need to figure out some way to deal with that. It is difficult to tell what anything means, and usually we get it wrong. Generally, we want to design the tools so that getting it wrong is not as much of a nuisance as it otherwise might be.

Why Is Content Filtering a Text Categorization Notion?

Categorization is a problem that cognitive psychologists have dealt with for many years [6]. In the process of categorization of electronic documents, categories are typically used as a means of organizing and getting an overview of the information in a collection of several documents. Text categorization is the sorting of text into groups, such as pornography, hate speech, violence, and unobjectionable content. A text categorizer looks at a Web page and decides into which of these groups a piece of text should fall.

Automatic categorization of electronic documents is dependent on the structure of the documents — documents can be partitioned into categories based on, for example, differences in their layouts [7]. Keywords or phrases are often very useful for categorizing electronic documents, but only to a certain degree. The physical appearance of a document is not enough for a good categorization of the document; the documents in one domain (e.g., the domain "tax forms") may have a well-known and predefined structure, whereas in other domains (e.g., e-mail letters), they may have less structure and, as is typical for e-mail, be more "anarchic" by nature.

Content filtering is a categorization task because the categories are decisions, such as "allow," "allow but warn," or "block." We either want to allow access to a Web page, allow access but also give a warning, or block access. Another way to frame the problem is to say that the categories are different types of content, such as news, sex education, pornography, or home pages. Depending on which category we put the page in, we will take different actions. For example, we want to block pornography and give access to news.

There are two general and basic principles for creating categories: cognitive economy and perceived world structure [6]. The principle of cognitive economy means that the function of categories is to provide maximum information with the least cognitive effort. The principle of perceived world structure means that the perceived world is not an unstructured set of arbitrary or unpredictable attributes. The attributes that an individual will perceive and thus use for categorization are determined by the needs of the individual. These needs change over time and with the physical and social environment. In other words, a system for automatic text categorization should in some way "know" both the type of text and the type of user. The maximum information with least cognitive effort is achieved if categories map the perceived world structure as closely as possible [6].

Searching and retrieving information can be treated as a process in which query information is mapped onto the categories (the structure of the filing system) in order to retrieve a specific document. Relatively unstructured documents, as in the case of e-mail letters, and unstructured queries might require some transformation on the query information.

One of the goals in the authors' current research is to find a means for automatically measuring something similar to the typicality of an electronic document (images), so that the typicality can be used for measuring dissimilarity between a pair of documents or between a document and a summary of category members. The typicality of a letter has to be defined — a combination of information retrieval and simple natural language processing techniques may be feasible to use to extract important information from letters.

Text categorization can be seen as the basis for organization and retrieval of information. Automatic categorization may be used to organize relatively unstructured documents and make it easier to use other methods of creating and presenting the documents (e.g., associative methods such as hypertext, which are more natural to a user) [8].

Adding something like measurement of typicality to an individual letter may give e-mail a new "sense." This might make the (manual or automatic) categorization of letters easier, hopefully more natural, and also more like categorization of letters in traditional postal mail.

Why Is Content Filtering an Image Categorization Notion?

In the problem of image categorization, we assume that a fixed set of classes or categories has been defined and that each image belongs to one category. We are given a set of training images whose category membership is known. In addition, we have a set of unlabeled images and we want to assign each of these images into one of the categories. For an automatic approach to this problem to be feasible, one needs to assume that images that are in some way similar will fall into the same category, and that this underlying notion of similarity can be captured automatically using a suitable representation of images and some learning algorithm. In addition, before applying machine learning techniques to images in order to learn models, we need to represent images with structures with which known machine learning algorithms can actually work. Thus, the problem of image categorization bears a strong relationship to image retrieval, where the notions of representation and similarity are also of great importance. One way of applying results from image retrieval to the problem of image categorization would be to take image descriptors, such as histograms or autocorrelograms, and use any of the numerous machine learning techniques that can work with image descriptors. Alternatively, one could take an arbitrary similarity measure from image retrieval, no matter what the underlying representation, and use it in combination with a machine learning algorithm that can work with arbitrary similarity or distance measures, such as nearest neighbors or, possibly, the generalized kernel variety of support vector machines [9].

Determining whether a picture is pornographic is difficult for several reasons. First, an image looks different from different angles and in different lights. When color and texture change, images look different. People can change their appearance by moving their heads around. So, we apparently have different images, but these images support the same semantic.

The approach we propose is situated in continuity of image categorization.

Multimedia Filtering Approaches

It is important to note that no filtering method is perfect. The Web changes minute by minute. Web URLs are fleeting. Companies buy and sell domain names. Web hosting companies are bought by other companies. URLs that previously pointed to safe content can now point to different content. Filtering products need to be constantly updated or they lose their effectiveness. Nothing can replace proper training and adult supervision. The following are some of the methods that are used to restrict access to Web files:

- *Restrict access by file types.* Do not allow viewing of graphics, sound, or movie files. Browsers can be set not to display these types of files. Some browsers do not allow the viewing of these file types.

- *Restrict access based on words found on the page.* If restricted words are found on the page, access to the page will be blocked. A problem with this method is that the word patterns used to block questionable sites also end up blocking sites that probably should not be blocked.

- *Restrict access to Web sites by blocking IP addresses.* Questionable URLs (Internet Protocol [IP] addresses) are added to a list or database. The blocking can be to deny access or only allow access if the URL is in the database or list. Rating services and some blocking software use this method. Some software offers updates to their list of questionable sites for a yearly renewal fee. The problem with this type is that a third party decides what should or should not be filtered. Many of these companies do not fully share their blocking criteria.

- *Restrict access to Web pages using a rating system.* Rating systems provide a method of assigning values to page content. The system would allow the content to be rated suitable or unsuitable for children. These systems depend on webmasters embedding certain meta-tags in their Web pages. In this way, the content is rated by the content creator. The process is usually handled by the webmaster answering questions on a Web page and the rating system site e-mails the appropriate meta-tags to the webmaster, who then inserts the meta-tags into his Web pages. Some common rating systems are RSACi (http://www.rsac.org/homepage.asp), ICRA, Weburbia, and SafeSurf. The greatest drawback to this system is the number of sites that have voluntarily rated their Web pages. Although these rated sites number in the hundreds of thousands, there are millions of Web sites that have not adopted any self-rating system. Many educational institutions have thousands of Web pages they would have to rate. The labor costs associated with applying a rating to each Web page makes it a huge investment of educational resources. Access can be restricted using a PICSRules file (http://www.w3.org/PICS/). A PICSRules file is a text file that uses PICS rules to define what sites can be viewed by a browser. ICRA provides a free template for building your own filter. Project Interconnect has a PICSRules file you can download and change to suit your needs. PICSRules files have an extension of .prf (profile). The downside of this method is as the file grows larger, it takes more time to look up addresses and slows down the Web responses. It is not that easy for novices to figure out how to allow or block sites.

- *Restrict access by redirecting requests to a local Hosts file*. A Hosts file resides on many computer platforms (Mac, Windows, Linux) and can be used by the computer to resolve a Web address. A Web address like www.yahoo.com needs to be resolved to its IP number. If the IP number is found in your Hosts file, your computer stops looking and goes to the site listed in your Hosts file. If it is not in the Hosts file, a DNS (domain name server) computer is queried and your request is sent to that IP address. Because the Hosts file is checked first, it provides a method that can be used to block sites that have objectionable content, or are used for advertisements, or any other site that you choose to block. A drawback is if the URL is already an IP number, the Hosts file is not queried and the URL cannot be blocked by the Hosts file. Like the PICSRules file, as the Hosts file gets larger, Web response slows down.

Paper Objective

This chapter is aimed at the detection of adult images appearing on the Internet. Indeed, images are an essential part of today's World Wide Web. The statistics of more than 4 million HTML Web pages reveal that 70.1% of Web pages contain images and that on average there are about 18.8% images per HTML Web page [10]. These images are mostly used to make attractive Web contents or to add graphical items to mostly textual content, such as navigational arrows.

However, images are also contributing to harmful (e.g., pornographic) or even illegal (e.g., pedophilic) Internet content. Therefore, effective filtering of images is of paramount importance in an Internet filtering solution.

Protecting children from harmful content on the Internet, such as pornography and violence, is increasingly a research topic of concern. Fleck et al. [11] have detected naked people with an algorithm involving a skin filter and a human figure grouper. The WIPE system [12] uses Daubechies wavelets, moment analysis, and histogram indexing to provide semantically meaningful feature vector matching. Jones and Rehg [13] propose techniques for skin color detection and simple features for adult image detection. Bosson et al. [14] propose a pornographic image detection system that is also based on skin detection and the multilayer perception (MLP) classifier.

In our adult image filter, the first step is skin detection. We build a model with Maximum Entropy Modeling (MaxEnt) for the skin distribution of the input color image. This model imposes constraints on color gradients of neighboring pixels. We use the Bethe tree approximation to eradicate the parameter estimation and the Belief Propagation (BP) algorithm to obtain an exact and fast solution. Our model outperforms the baseline model in Reference 13 in terms of pixel classification performance. Based on the output of skin detection, features including global ones and local ones are extracted. We train an MLP classifier on 5084 patterns from the training set. In the testing phase, the MLP classifier takes a quick decision on the pattern in one pass. The adult image filter takes 0.08 sec for an inquiry 256×256 image. Compared with 6 min in Reference 11 and 10 sec per image in Reference 12, our system is more practical. Plenty of experimental results on 5084 photographs show stimulating performance.

The chapter is organized as follows. In section "The Structure of the System," we give a brief overview of the system. An adult image filter is presented in sections "Skin Detection" and "Adult Image Detection." Section "Experimental Results" presents the results obtained by our adult image detector. Section "Conclusion" summarizes the chapter.

THE STRUCTURE OF THE SYSTEM

Our object is blocking images that are objectionable, including adult images and harmful symbols. The system structure is shown in Figure 11.1. After an unknown image is captured, it is first classified by a classifier discriminating natural images from artificial images. If an image is classified as a natural image, it is passed to an adult image filter or a symbol filter. In this chapter, we present our adult image filter.

SKIN DETECTION

Methodology and Notations

Skin detection is of paramount importance in the detection of adult images. We build a MaxEnt model for this task. MaxEnt is a method for inferring models from a dataset. See Reference 15 for the underlying philosophy. It works as follows: (1) choose relevant features, (2) compute their histograms on the training set, (3) write down the MaxEnt model within the ones that have the feature histograms as observed on the training set, (4) estimate the parameters of the model, and (5) use the model for classification. This plan has been successfully completed for several tasks related to speech recognition and language processing. See, for example, Reference 16 and the references therein. In these

Figure 11.1.   The structure of the system.

applications, the underlying graph of the model is a line graph or even a tree, but in all cases it has no loops. When working with images, the graph is the pixel lattice. It, indeed, has many loops.

A breakthrough appeared with the work in Reference 17 on texture simulation where steps 1 to 4 were performed for images and step 5 was replaced by simulation.

We adapt to skin detection as follows: in step 1, we specialize in colors for two adjacent pixels given "skinness."

We choose RGB color space in our approach. In practice, we know from References 13 and 14 that the choice of color space is not critical given a histogram-based representation of the color distribution and enough training data. In step 2, we compute the histogram of these features in the Compaq manually segmented database. Models for step 3 are then easily obtained. In step 4, we use the Bethe tree approximation; see Reference 18. It consists of approximating locally the pixel lattice by a tree. The parameters of the MaxEnt models are then expressed analytically as functions of the histograms of the features. This is a particularity of our features. In step 5, we pursue the approximation in step 4: we use the BP algorithm (see Reference 19), which is exact in a tree graph but only approximate in loopy graphs.

344

Indeed, one of us had already witnessed in a different context that a tree approximation to loopy graph might lead to effective algorithms; see Reference 20.

Let us fix the notations. The set of pixels of an image is S. Let $C = \{0, \ldots, 255\}^3$. The color of a pixel $s \in S$ is x_s, $x_s \in C$. The "skinness" of a pixel s is y_s, with $y_s = 1$ if s is a skin pixel and $y_s = 0$ if not. The set of neighbors of s is denoted as $v(s)$. $\langle s, t \rangle$ denotes a pair of neighboring pixels. We use a four-neighbor system here. The color image, which is the vector of color pixels, is denoted by x and the binary image made up of the y_s's is denoted by y.

From the user's point of view, the useful information is contained in the one-pixel marginal of the posterior; that is, for each pixel, the quantity $p(y_s = 1 | x)$, quantifying the belief of skinness at pixel s. Bayesian analysis tells us that whatever cost function the user might think of, all that is needed is the joint distribution $p(x, y)$. In practice, $p(x, y)$ is unknown. Instead, we have to model the segmented Compaq Database [13]. It is a collection of samples

$$\{(x^1, y^1), \ldots, (x^n, y^n)\}$$

where, for each $1 \leq i \leq n$, x^i is a color image and y^i is the associated binary skinness image. We assume that the samples are independent of each other with distribution $p(x, y)$. The collection of samples is referred to later as the training data. Probabilities are estimated using classical empirical estimators and are denoted with the letter q.

First-Order Model

Our MaxEnt model respects the two-pixel marginal of the joint distribution. We define the following constraints:

$$C: \forall\, s \in S, \forall \in V(s), x_s \in C, \forall x_t \in C,$$

$$\forall y_s \in \{0, 1\}, \forall y_t \in \{0, 1\}$$

$$p(x_s, x_t, y_s, y_t) = q(x_s, x_t, y_s, y_t)$$

The quantity $q(x_s, x_t, y_s, y_t)$ is the proportion of times we observe the values (x_s, x_t, y_s, y_t) for a couple of neighboring pixels, regardless of the orientation of the pixels s and t in the training set.

Using Lagrange multipliers, the solution to the MaxEnt problem under $C(x)$ is then the following Gibbs distribution:

$$p(x, y) \approx \prod_{\langle s, t \rangle} \lambda(x_s, x_t, y_s, y_t)$$

Figure 11.2. **The output of skin detection is a gray-scale skin map with the gray level indicating the probability of skin.**

where $\lambda(x_s, x_t, y_s, y_t) > 0$ are parameters that should be set up to satisfy the constraints. This model is referred as the first-order model (FOM). Parameter estimation in the context of MaxEnt is still an active research subject, especially in situations where the likelihood function cannot be computed for a given value of the parameters. This is the case here. We use the Bethe tree approximation to deal with parameter estimation and build a model TFOM (tree approximation of FOM). We use the BP algorithm to obtain an exact and fast solution. The detailed description can be found in our previous work [21].

Our TFOM model outperforms the baseline model in Reference 13, as shown in Reference 21 in the context of skin pixel detection rate and false-positive rate. The output of skin detection is a *skin map* indicating the probabilities of skin on pixels. In Figure 11.2, skin maps of different kinds of people are shown.

Vezhnevets et al. [22] recently compared some most widely used skin detection techniques and concluded that our skin detection algorithm [21] gives the best performance in terms of pixel classification rates.

ADULT IMAGE DETECTION

There are propositions for high-level features based on groupings of skin regions [11], but the actual application needs a high-speed solution; therefore, along with References 12 and 13, we are interested in trying simpler features. We calculate two fit ellipses for each skin map: the global fit ellipse (GFE) and the local fit ellipse (LFE). The GFE is computed on the whole skin map, whereas the LFE only on the largest skin region in the skin map (see Figure 11.3).

We extract nine features from the input image, most of them based on fit ellipses. The first three features are global; they are (1) the average skin probability of the whole image, (2) the average skin probability inside the GFE, and (3) the number of skin regions in the image. The other

Figure 11.3. **The original input image (left); the global fit ellipse on the skin map (middle); and the local fit ellipse on the skin map (right).**

six features are computed on the largest skin region of the input image: (1) distance from the centroid of the largest skin region to the center of the image, (2) angle of the major axis of the LFE from the horizontal axis, (3) ratio of the minor axis to the major axis of the LFE, (4) ratio of the area of the LFE to that of the image, (5) average skin probability inside the LFE, and (6) average skin probability outside the LFE.

Evidence from Reference 14 shows that the MLP classifier offers a statistically significant performance over several other approaches, such as the generalized linear model, the k-nearest-neighbor classifier, and the support vector machine. In this chapter, we adopt the MLP classifier. We train the MLP classifier on 5084 patterns from the training set. In the testing phase, the MLP classifier intakes a quick decision on the pattern in one pass, and the output is a number $o_p \in [0, 1]$, corresponding to the degree of adult. One can set a proper threshold to get the binary decision.

EXPERIMENTAL RESULTS

All experiments are made using the following protocol. The database contains 10,168 photographs, which are imported from the Compaq Database and the Poesia Database. It is split into two equal parts randomly, with 1297 adult photographs and 3787 other photographs in each part. One part is used as the training set and the other one, the test set, is left aside for the receiver operating characteristics curve computation. The performance figures are initially correlated into a confusion matrix (Table 11.1), where the letters are defined as follows:

- A: harmless URLs that represent URLs that have been judged harmless by the end user
- B: harmful URLs that represent URLs that have been judged harmful by the end user

Table 11.1. Evaluation Confusion Matrix

Actual	Predicted		
	Harmless (Accepted) Pages	Harmful (Blocked) Pages	Total
Harmless pages	a	b	A
Harmful pages	c	d	B
Total	C	D	

- C: accepted URLs that represent URLs that have been judged harmless by the POESIA filter
- D: blocked URLs that represent URLs that have been judged harmful by the POESIA filter

Calculation of Evaluation Measures

The results will be presented using the standard measure from Information Retrieval: Precision, Recall, and F-Measure:

- **Precision** is the proportion of pages predicted correctly, given the total number of pages predicted in that category.
- **Recall** is the proportion of pages predicted correctly, given the total number of pages belonging to that category.
- **F-Measure** is the most commonly used measure for balancing precision and recall. In the standard used here, it provides equal importance to Precision and Recall and is calculated as $(2 \times \text{Precision} \times \text{Recall})/(\text{Precision} + \text{Recall})$. For harmless pages, Precision $= a/C$ and Recall $= a/A$; for harmful pages, Precision $= d/D$ and Recall $= d/B$.

Blocking Effectiveness and Overblocking

In terms of filtering, the simplest interpretation of the performance of the POESIA system can be seen in terms of:

- *Effectiveness at blocking harmful pages* (i.e., maximizing the number of harmful pages that are blocked). This is indicated by the Recall value for harmful pages (i.e., d/B).
- *Overblocking of harmless pages* (i.e., minimizing the number of harmless pages that are blocked). This is indicated by a high Recall measure for harmless pages. The overblocking value is generally represented as the inverse of the Recall value for harmless pages [i.e., $1 - (a/A)$].

Graphical Interpretation (ROC)

For image filtering, an ROC (receiver operating characteristic) curve is also used to show its performance as a trade-off between the true-positive rate (i.e., effectiveness or Recall value for harmful pages) and the false-positive rate (i.e., overblocking or Recall measure for harmless pages).

One part of image collection is used for the ROC curve computation. In Figure 11.4, we can observe that if we accept 20% of false positives, then we can detect around 91% of pornographic images. In this case, we obtain the results in Table 11.2.

The image filter for the identification of pornographic images provides an effectiveness of 0.91 with an overblocking value of 0.2. These values are worse than those seen in the text filters; however, the image filter is only categorizing a single image rather than all of the image content found on a given Web page.

Figure 11.4.   ROC curve of adult detection.

Table 11.2.   Results Using Harmful Filter

Actual	Predicted		Total
	Harmful	**Harmless**	
Harmful	910	90	1000
Harmless	200	800	1000
Total	1110	890	2000
Precision	0.82	0.90	
Recall	0.91	0.80	
F-Measure	0.86	0.85	

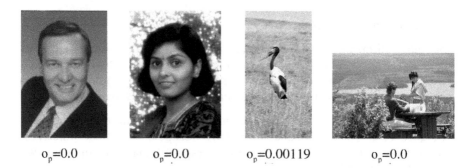

$o_p=0.0$ $o_p=0.0$ $o_p=0.00119$ $o_p=0.0$

Figure 11.5. **Experimental results on non-adult images. Below the images are the associated outputs of the MLP.**

Figure 11.6. **Misclassified images and the associated outputs of the MLP.**

The elapsed time of image filtering is about 0.18 sec per image. Compared with 6 min in Reference 11 and 10 sec per image in Reference 12, our system is more practical. Figure 11.5 shows some examples of non-adult images with the corresponding output neural networks.

However, there are also some cases where this detector does not work well. In Figure 11.6, several such examples are presented. The first adult image is not detected because the skin appears almost white due to overexposure. We see that most of the skin is not detected on the skin map. The second adult image contains two connected large frames. The LFE of this image will then be very large, and the average skin probability inside this LFE will be very small. The third image is benign, but it is detected adult because the toy dog takes a skinlike color and the average skin probabilities inside the GFE and the LFE are very high. The fourth image is a portrait but decidedly adult because it exposes a lot of skin and even the hair and the clothes take skinlike colors. We believe that skin detection based solely on color information cannot do much more, so perhaps some other types of information are needed to improve the adult image detection performance. For example, some kind of face detector could be implemented to improve the results. However, generally, adult images in Web pages tend to appear together and are surrounded by text, which could be an important clue for the adult content detector.

CONCLUSION

This work aims at filtering objectionable images appearing on the Internet. Our main contributions are as follows:

1. In skin detection, build an FOM that introduces constraints on color gradients of neighboring pixels and use the Bethe tree approximation to eradicate parameter estimation. The BP algorithm is used to accelerate the process. This model improves the performance in a previous work [13].
2. By using simple features based on skin map output by skin detection and MLP classifier, our adult image filter can give a promising performance.
3. Our adult image filter is more practical compared with those in References 11 and 12 in terms of processing speed.

To improve the performance of our filters, we can use a face detector in the adult image filter. Research in face detection has progressed significantly. The best systems recognize 90% of faces, with about 5% false positives. This is good performance and getting much better. In 3 to 5 years, the computer vision community will have many good face-detection methods. This might help in identifying pornography, because skin with a face is currently more of a problem than skin without a face. Face-detection technology probably can be applied to very specific body parts; text and image data and connectivity information also will help. However, distinguishing semantic concepts such as hard-core from soft-core pornography will remain difficult. These terms are rough, and the relationships between visual features of images and these semantic concepts are not evident. In general, images tend to appear together and are surrounded by text in Web pages, so combining with text analysis could improve the performance of our image filters.

REFERENCES

1. Van Rijsbergen. C.J., *Information Retrieval,* Butterworths, Stoneham, MA, 1979.
2. Salton G. and McGill, M.J., *Introduction to Modern Information Retrieval*, McGraw-Hill, New York, 1983.
3. Frakes, W.B. and Baeza-Yates, R., *Information Retrieval: Data Structures & Algorithms*, Prentice-Hall, Englewood Cliffs, NJ, 1992.
4. Lesk, M., *Books, Bytes, and Bucks*, Morgan Kaufmann, San Francisco, 1997.
5. Strzalkowski, T., Ed., *Natural Language Information Retrieval*, Kluwer Academic, Boston, 1999.
6. Rosch, E., Principles of categorization, in *Cognition and Categorization*, Rosch, E. and Lloyd, B. B., Eds., Lawrence Erlbaum Associates, Hillsdale, NJ, 1978, pp. 27–48.
7. Spitz, L. and Dengel, A., Eds., *Document Analysis Systems*, World Scientific, Singapore, 1995.
8. Jonassen, D.H., Semantic network elicitation: tools for structuring hypertext, in *Hypertext: State of the Art*, McAleese, R. and Green, C., Eds., Intellect Limited, Oxford, 1990.

9. Mangasarian, O.L., Generalized support vector machines, in *Advances in Large Margin Classifiers*, Smola, A.J., Bartlett, P.J., Schölkopf, B., and Schuurmans, D. Eds., MIT Press, Cambridge, MA, 2000, pp. 135–146.

10. Starynkevitch, B. et al., POESIA Software Architecture Definition Document, http:// www.poesia-filter.org/pdf/Deliverable 3 1.pdf, Deliverable 3.1:7–9, 2002.

11. Fleck, M.M. et al, Finding Naked People, in *Proceedings of the European Conference on Computer Vision*, Buxton, B. and Cipolla, R., Eds., Springer-Verlag, Berlin, 1996, Vol. 2, pp. 593–602.

12. Wang, J.Z. et al., System for screening objectionable images, *Computer Commun.*, (21)15, 1355–1360, 1998.

13. Jones, M.J. and Rehg, J.M., Statistical Color Models with Application to Skin Detection, in *Proceedings of the Conference on Computer Vision and Pattern Recognition*, 1999, Vol. 1, pp. 1274–1280.

14. Bosson, A., Cawley, G.C., Chian, Y., and Harvey, R., Non-retrieval: Blocking Pornographic Images, in *Proceedings of the International Conference on the Challenge of Image and Video Retrieval, Lecture Notes in Computer Science*, Vol. 2383, Springer-Verlag, London, 2002, pp. 50–60.

15. Jaynes, E., Probability Theory: The Logic of Science, http://omega.albany.edu:8008/ JaynesBook, 1995.

16. Berger, A., Pietra, S.D., and Pietra, V.D., A maximum entropy approach to natural language processing, *Comput. Linguist.*, 22, 39–71, 1996.

17. Zhu, S., Wu, Y., and Mumford, D., Filters, Random fields and maximum entropy (Frame): towards a unified theory for texture modeling, *Int. J. Computer Vis.*, 27(2), 107–126, 1998.

18. Wu, C. and Doerschuk, P.C., Tree approximations to Markov random fields, *IEEE Trans. Pattern Anal.*, 17, 391–402, 1995.

19. Yedida, J.S., Freeman, W.T., and Weiss, Y., Understanding Belief Propagation and its Generalisations, Technical Report TR-2001-22, Mitsubishi Research Laboratories, 2002.

20. Geman, D. and Jedynak, B., An active testing model for tracking roads in satellite images, *IEEE Trans. Pattern Anal.*, 18(1), 1–14, 1996.

21. Jedynak, B., Zheng, H., and Daoudi, M., Statistical Models for Skin Detection, presented at *IEEE Workshop on Statistical Analysis in Computer Vision*, in conjunction with *CVPR 2003*, Madison, WI, 2003.

22. Vezjnevets, V., Sazonov, V., and Andreeva, A., A Survey on Pixel-Based Skin Color Detection Techniques, presented at *Graphicon 2003, 13th International Conference on the Computer Graphics and Vision*, Moscow, 2003.

12
Digital Rights Management Issues for Video

Sabu Emmanuel and Mohan S. Kankanhalli

INTRODUCTION

A huge amount of digital assets involving media such as text, audio, video, and so forth is being created these days. Digital asset management involves the creation, transfer, storage, and consumption of these assets. It is chiefly in the transfer function context that Digital Rights Management (DRM) becomes a major issue. The term *DRM* refers to a set of technologies and approaches that establish a trust relationship among the parties involved in digital asset creation and transaction. The creator creates a digital asset and the owner owns the digital asset. The creators need not be owners of a digital asset, as in the case of employees creating a digital asset for their company. In this case, although the employees are the creators, the ownership of the digital asset can reside with the company. The digital asset needs to be transferred from the owner to the consumer, usually through a hierarchy of distributors. Therefore, the parties involved in digital asset creation and transaction are creators, owners, distributors, and consumers. Each of these parties has its own rights; namely creators have *creator rights*, owners have *owner rights*, distributors have *distributor rights*, and consumers have *consumer rights*. We lay down the requirements of these rights in section "Digital Rights Requirements." A true DRM system should be able to support all of these rights. It is to be noted that there can be multiple creators jointly creating a digital asset and, likewise, multiple owners jointly owning a digital asset. There can also be a hierarchy of distributors and also distributorships allocated by geographic regions or time segments. The consumer can also be either an individual or a group of individuals or a corporate entity. Tackling DRM issues in this multiparty, multilevel scenario is a very challenging problem. We continually point out challenges in this chapter that can be the bases for further research.

Digital rights requirements vary with the kind of digital asset being transferred. Digital assets can possess different transaction values. Some can be free, whereas others can be of high value (digital cinema, high-valued digital arts). Some can be truly invaluable, especially archival and historical photographs, audios, and videos. The creation or production cost of a digital asset is different from the transaction value. The transaction value is most often assigned by the owner (which is usually higher than the production cost). The transaction cost consists of the distribution cost and the cost of setting up the DRM (DRM cost). Designing an economically viable DRM system is particularly challenging for low-valued digital assets.

The framework of DRM consists of technical, business, social, and legal components [1–4]. The business aspect of DRM involves new business models such as a free evaluation copy for a few days, followed by a full permission or a downloadable stream for immediate use followed by a digital versatile disk (DVD) copy in the mail. The social angle of DRM is governed by societal norms concerning fair use, privacy management, and the education of consumers so as to inform them of the risks associated with using pirated content. The legal aspect deals with the laws of the license jurisdiction and includes legislation, compliance, investigation, and enforcement. The technical DRM perspective deals with the technical standards and infrastructure, which consist of protection mechanisms, trading protocols, and rights language. In this chapter, we will discuss the business, social, legal, and technical aspects of DRM in detail.

Consider a digital commerce transaction completed over the Internet for DVDs. In such a transaction, usually the consumer and the seller are geographically far apart and possess scant knowledge of each other. To initiate the transaction, the consumer browses the Web for DVDs. In this scenario, a few typical issues are raised. Can the consumer trust that the online stores are legitimate and possess the right to distribute the copyrighted DVDs? Can the consumer be guaranteed that the payment information and order information are secure? Can the consumer trust that the digital content he is about to download is authentic, untampered material from the original author, owner, or distributor? Can the consumer trust that the content will work on his usage devices and whether he can give the content to his friend? Can the consumer trust that his privacy regarding his buying behavior is secured? The questions that the legitimate online DVD seller would ask are as follows: Can I trust the consumer that he will not create unauthorized copies and redistribute? In the event of a copyright violation, can I identify and trace the consumer who did it so as to bring him to justice? Without proper DRM, answers to most of these questions are negative.

Let us look at the example of a new business model where a consumer wants to buy a DVD over the Web. E-mail could straightaway stream out the video to the consumer, which could be watched on the personal computer (PC) or sent to the liquid crystal display (LCD) projectors of the home theater system immediately and a physical DVD could be dispatched for viewing and possession. However, the rights usage of the streamed version should be limited. The stream should be allowed to play on the machines indicated by the consumer and also may be allowed to be diverted to systems as specified by the user. Also, the DVD should be allowed to play as and when required and on any machine. The DRM system should support these usage requirements. We discuss various usage requirements in section "Digital Asset Usage Controls."

Already, products and services are available that support DRM. However, these products are often not interoperable, do not support newer business models, and support only limited digital rights of parties. The current DRM systems are quite primitive, as they tie the content to a particular playback device. The content is not allowed to be played on any other device or to be diverted to another device. The DRM system depends on strong encryption schemes and ties the decryption to the device on which it is decrypted [5]. Often, these DRM products only support the digital rights of owners; they do not address false implication, fair use, and the privacy concerns of consumers. Therefore, these DRM solutions are not widely used. Consequently, not many high-valued copyrighted or archival digital contents are available on the Web due to piracy, or recreation and reuse concerns. It must be noted that there are digital delivery channels, such as satellite, cable broadcasts, and so on, other than the Internet. They, too, need to address piracy and reuse concerns. We discuss various delivery techniques in section "Digital Video Asset Management."

Although digital assets fall into various categories such as text, audio, image, and video, in this chapter we concentrate on the DRM issues for digital video. The challenges in solving DRM for digital video are multifaceted. Video files are large and require significant storage space. Therefore, to reduce the storage requirement, videos are compressed before being stored. For example, a typical 2-h, 35-mm feature film scanned at a standard high-quality resolution of 1920×1080 pixels, 1 byte per color, and 24 frames per second would, in its uncompressed form, require $120 \times 1920 \times 1080 \times 3 \times 24 = 17{,}915{,}904{,}000$ bytes of disk space. Assuming a compression ratio of $30:1$, the disk space requirement becomes more manageable. These requirements are going to go up as the high-resolution 4000×4000-pixel scanners (Kodak Cineon and Quantel Domino) gain widespread use [6]. Therefore, compressed video would be preferred over uncompressed video. Again, the large size of the video compels the owners and distributors to broadcast the video to multiple receivers rather than to unicast to individual receivers. Broadcasting reduces the channel bandwidth requirement and also the transmission costs. Therefore, the preferred transmission technique for the digital video is broadcast. For DRM, compressed domain processing and broadcast-type transmission make matters more complex. Essentially, DRM is a one-to-one contract whereby rights of both the parties are to be defined, complied with, monitored, and enforced. However, broadcast is a one-to-all transmission scenario, where every receiver in the broadcast region receives the video. How to satisfy these seemingly contradictory requirements is a challenging problem for DRM in the broadcasting environment.

Past decades might have seen tremendous achievements in the creation, processing, and delivery of multimedia data. However, growth of digital commerce of these digital objects over the Internet or other digital delivery mechanisms has been somewhat slow, due to the major concerns regarding DRM.

Section "Digital Video Asset Management" to section "Digital Rights Requirements" concentrate on the environments and requirements for achieving the DRM. Particularly, section "Digital Video Asset Management" discusses digital video asset management, section "Digital Asset Usage Controls" presents digital usage controls, and section "Digital Rights Requirements" discusses digital rights requirements. Section "Business Aspects of DRM" to section "Technical Aspects of DRM" elaborate on the various components of DRM. Specifically, section "Business Aspects of DRM" discusses the business aspects, section "Social Aspects of DRM" presents social aspects, section "Legal Aspects of DRM" describes the legal aspects, and section "Technical Aspects of DRM" elaborates on the technical aspects.

DIGITAL VIDEO ASSET MANAGEMENT

After creating the digital asset, storage and delivery functions need to be addressed as part of digital asset management [2]. We discuss storage and delivery mechanisms in this section.

Storage

Digital video is usually compressed. The open compression standards from ISO/IEC, Moving Pictures Experts Group (MPEG) are MPEG-1, MPEG-2, and MPEG-4 [7]. The MPEG-1 standard is used for the video compact disk (VCD). The DVD, digital video broadcasts (digital TV transmissions), and high-definition television (HDTV) transmissions currently use the MPEG-2 standard. The MPEG-4 is a newer standard intended for low-bitrate (wireless, mobile video applications) and high-bitrate applications. There are other open standards such as H.261 and H.263 from ITU primarily for videoconferencing over telephone lines. Apart from the open standards, there are proprietary compression standards from Real Networks, Apple, Microsoft, and so forth. In addition to compression, the digital assets are to be wrapped in metadata to declare the structure and composition of the digital asset, to describe the contents, to identify the contents, and to express the digital rights. We discuss the declarations, descriptions, and identifiers in section "Content Declarations, Descriptors, and Identifiers."

Digital Video Delivery

E-shops on the World Wide Web (WWW) typically offer downloading or streaming modes for delivering the video. The downloading mode employs a unicast type of transmission technique, whereas the streaming mode can use either a unicast or broadcast type of transmission. Digital TV transmissions usually use the broadcast channel. The most popular medium of digital TV transmission is terrestrial digital TV transmission. Other popular mediums are satellite and cable transmissions. Direct to home satellite transmissions are becoming more and more popular due to their ease of deployment. Stored media such as DVD and VCD are other means of distributing digital video.

Digital cinema is a system to deliver motion pictures and "cinema-quality" programs to theaters throughout the world using digital technology. The digital cinema system delivers digitized or mastered, compressed, and encrypted motion pictures to theaters using either physical media distribution (such as DVD-ROMs) or electronic transmission methods such as the Internet as well as satellite broadcast methods. Theaters receive digitized programs and store them in hard-disk storage while still encrypted and compressed. At each showing, the digitized information is retrieved via a local area network from the hard-disk storage, and is then decrypted, decompressed, and displayed using cinema-quality electronic projectors.

As we can see, digital TV, digital cinema, and Internet streaming services use the broadcasting technique, whereas the Internet downloading service uses the unicast technique for transmission. In all of the above delivery methods except in stored media such as DVD and VCD delivery for home segments, a return channel (other than the content and control signal delivery channel from the owner or distributor to the consumer) is provided for communication from the consumer to the distributors or the owner for DRM implementation. The return path need not be always online, as in the case of certain prepaid digital pay TVs for which the communication is at certain intervals of time.

DIGITAL ASSET USAGE CONTROLS

Owners often want usage controls to be associated with the digital asset. These controls essentially specify the various ways the digital asset can be used; for example, whether the digital asset can be copied or not, and if allowed to copy, the number of times that the digital asset can be copied. Currently, DRM systems are being designed with no copy, one-time copy, and many-times copy features [5,8,9]. The controls can specify whether the digital asset is allowed for usage activities such as play, copy, or reuse. If allowed, additional controls based on count, time, time period, and territory can also be placed [2,10].

The count parameter will support a service such as "pay-per-usage" (i.e., if the video is allowed to copy once, after making a copy once, no further copying of the original video is allowed). A new video needs to be purchased to make another copy. The time-period parameter supports "pay-per-view-per-time period" programs (i.e., the billing can be for the period of time the video program is viewed). Another application may be to have a differential billing scheme based on the time of the day. The territory parameter may support differential billing for different geographic regions. The reuse control specifies whether the digital asset can be reused. If reuse is allowed, new digital assets can be created from the digital asset. For example, consider the creation of a home music VCD album where the music is from different VCDs, or the creation of a new VCD with new characters replacing the original characters. These controls support new business models.

DIGITAL RIGHTS REQUIREMENTS

The digital asset creation and delivery chain consists of creators, owners, distributors, and consumers. Each of these parties has its own rights and we call these the digital rights. The DRM system is expected to build trust among the parties by meeting the digital rights of each party. It must be

Creators

Owners

Level 1
distributors

Level 2
distributors

⋮

Level n
consumers

──▶ Flow of digital asset   ·····▷ Flow of fees

Figure 12.1.   Digital asset creation and delivery chain.

noted that in this chain, the created digital asset moves from the creator
to the consumer through the owner and distributors. Also, the fee for the
digital asset flows from the consumer to the creator through owner and
distributors. This can be seen in Figure 12.1. Often, the owner already
pays the fee for the creation of the digital asset to the creators, as in the
case of the employee–employer relationship. Therefore, the owner is the
one concerned about the loss of revenue due to piracy and unauthorized
usage. The owners can directly deliver the digital asset to the consumers
or they may use a hierarchy of distributors. This can be seen in
Figure 12.1. The hierarchy of distributors is preferred to deal with the
business scalability and viability. Each of the distributors may have its
own already-existing consumer bases and infrastructure, which can easily
be tapped into by the owners to deliver their digital asset to the
consumers. When there is a hierarchy of distributors, building trust
relationships between the owner and the distributor, and the distributor
and the subdistributor, becomes more complex. This is because whereas
the owner is concerned about the revenue loss due to malpractices of the
distributors and also of the end consumer, the distributors would be
concerned about the false framing by the owners and also would be
concerned about the revenue loss due to the malpractices of the
subdistributors and the end consumer. Because the consumer is at the
end of the distribution chain, he would be concerned about the digital
asset, its quality and integrity, and also false framing by the distributor or
owner [11]. There should also be a trust relationship built between the

359

consumer and the distributor or the owner. We now elaborate on the digital rights requirements of each party for various application scenarios.

Digital Rights of Creators

A digital asset may be jointly created by one or more creators. All participating creators would expect that their participation be provable to any party. This requires that a jointly created mark be placed on the digital asset or individually created marks be individually placed on the digital asset. In either case, the idea is to establish the right of creatorship. The mark should be robust so that no one can remove it except the concerned creator himself. The mark also should be robust against collusion removal attacks. For example, a few creators may collude and remove the creatorship information of another creator from the digital asset, which should not be allowed. Only a few researchers have addressed this problem. The marking technique should be scalable with an increase in the number of creators, and the mark should not cause considerable perceptual degradation of the digital asset.

The creators may be paid a royalty by the owner for every copy of the digital asset made, as in the case of publishing books. In this case, the creators would need to track the number of copies made. The typical scenario in digital movie and video creations is that the creators are the employees of the production house and, hence, no such tracking of the number of copies is needed.

Digital Rights of Owners

Video distribution can either be subscription-based distribution or free. In both of these cases, the owner would like to specify how the distributors and consumers should use the digital asset. This is primarily specified through usage controls. Often, the copyright-protected videos are distributed using subscription-based schemes. In these subscription-based schemes, the owners may want to associate various usage controls on viewing, copying, playback device in use, and reuse. The usage control can vary from one-time view to many-times view, no copy to many times copy, play back on dedicated device to any device, and conditional to unconditional reuse.

The free-distribution mode can fall into two categories: one that can be reused as well as modified and the other in which the asset cannot be tampered with. An example of free distribution that cannot be tampered with is archival material with historical importance. In this case, usage control needs to specify whether the digital video can be reused or not. Also, the other usage control parameters are of little

360

importance because distribution is free. These usage controls essentially constrain the usage of digital assets by consumers and distributors.

We list the owner's requirements for subscription-based distribution:

- Needs to specify the usage controls
- Needs the consumer/distributor to be authenticated
- Needs the ability to trace the consumer/distributor who has violated the DRM contract
- Needs to declare the ownership of the digital asset
- Needs to distinguish consumers from non-consumers
- Needs a payment protocol to handle the fees

The authentication of consumers or distributors is needed to reliably identify the consumer or distributor. In the event of DRM contract violation, the violating consumer or distributor can be identified. This can be implemented using authentication protocols. In order to trace the DRM-contract-violating consumer or distributor and to declare the ownership of the digital asset, digital watermarking techniques can be used. The digital watermarking technique should be robust against attacks and also noninvertible to prove the ownership of the digital asset. Because the distribution is subscription based, only the consumers (who have paid the subscription fee) should get a clear video for viewing, whereas the non-consumers should not get a clear video for viewing. This requirement is the confidentiality requirement and can be implemented using encryption techniques.

Next, we list the owner's requirements of free distribution with archival importance:

- Needs to specify the reuse policy (essentially no tampering allowed)
- Needs the consumer or distributor to be authenticated
- Needs to detect any tampering of the content
- Needs the ability to trace the consumer or distributor who has tampered with the video
- Needs to declare the ownership of the video

For tamper detection, one can employ fragile watermarks. For tracing the consumer or distributor who has tampered with the video and also to declare the ownership of the video, noninvertible robust watermarking techniques can be used. Authentication can be implemented using authentication protocols.

For free distribution with no archival importance, there need not be any rights associated, as the digital asset is free to use in whichever way the consumer desires.

Digital Rights of Distributors

It can be seen from the digital asset delivery chain that the distributors act as middlemen. The owners fall at the upper end, the distributors are at the middle part, and the consumers fall at the lower end of the delivery chain. To the owners or upstream distributors, the downstream distributors are consumers with the same or less restrictions on usage compared to end consumers. For example, usage control on viewing or playing on any device may be unimportant, whereas usage control on copying and reuse would be important. As far as trust-building measures between the downstream distributor and the owner or upstream distributor, the downstream distributor will have the following concerns for both subscription-based and free distribution with archival importance:

- Needs to address false implication by the owner or upstream distributor
- Needs the owner or upstream distributor to be authenticated
- Needs proof of ownership or distributorship of the video
- Needs the integrity of video to be proved
- Needs a payment protocol to handle the subscription fee (for subscription-based schemes only)

The above requirements apply to both subscription-based and free distributions with archival importance. The false implication concern is that often the fingerprinting mark for tracing the copyright violator is placed by the owner or upstream distributor alone [11]. It is possible that the owner or upstream distributor may knowingly or unknowingly create a second fingerprinted copy with the same mark, which had been already used for someone else, and distribute the second copy to a second party. Later, the owner or upstream distributor can sue the first legal recipient for the copy with the second recipient. This false implication by sellers is a major concern for downstream distributors and end consumers. As a trust-building measure between the upstream distributor and downstream distributor or end consumer, the following requirements of upstream distributors should be addressed:

- Needs to specify the usage controls (this can be a subset of what the owner has specified)
- Needs the consumer or downstream distributor to be authenticated
- Needs to trace the consumer or downstream distributor who has violated the DRM contract
- Needs to distinguish consumers or downstream distributors from non-consumers or non-downstream distributors (for subscription-based schemes only)

- Needs to detect the tampering (for free distribution with archival importance only)
- Needs a payment protocol to handle the subscription fee (for subscription-based schemes only)

Digital Rights of Consumers

The consumers are at the lower end of the delivery chain. The following concerns of the consumers should be addressed:

- Needs to address false implication by the owner or distributor
- Needs the owner or distributor to be authenticated
- Needs proof of ownership or distributorship of the video
- Needs the integrity of video to be proved
- Needs a payment protocol to handle the subscription fee (for subscription-based schemes only)
- Needs to address fair use and privacy concerns

The digital rights requirements such as authentication of parties; confidentiality against the non-consumers and non-distributors; proving the integrity, ownership, or distributorship of the video; and payment protocols can be implemented using cryptographic and watermarking techniques in the DRM system. However, incorporating techniques to deal with false implication concerns, DRM contract violator tracing, fair use [12,13], and privacy management [14–16] into the designed DRM is a challenging task. Some of the requirements are seemingly contradictory (e.g., authentication and privacy management). In a broadcasting environment, how to implement DRM contract violator tracing is another problem. The false implication concern can be dealt with using nonrepudiation techniques, and how to integrate this into the DRM system is another challenging problem. How to support the fair use requirement is a major concern. How to design invisible multiple watermarking technique for tracing a DRM contract violator in a multilevel delivery chain is another challenge.

Next, we discuss various components of DRM, such as business aspects, social aspects, legal aspects, and technical aspects of DRM.

BUSINESS ASPECTS OF DRM

The Internet and broadcast channels (such as satellite, cable, and terrestrial) act as low-cost (compared to hardcopy transport) and quick transmission channels for the distribution of video data. These channels often transcend geographic and national boundaries connecting owners, distributors, and consumers. Various new business models leverage on the anywhere connectivity, quickness, and low-cost properties of these channels [17–19].

Some of the new business models are as follows:

- *Preview and purchase.* The preview is through quick and low-cost channels; the purchased version can be a hard copy or soft copy with fewer constraints on the usage compared to the preview version.
- *Pay-per-usage.* The usage can be viewing, copying, or reusing. As an example, the pay-per-view programs of TV channels belong to this category. In the pay-per-view TV program, the payment is for a single program feature as desired, which could be prebooked or impulsive.
- *Pay-per-usage-per-usage constrained.* The usage constraints can be count, time, time period, territory, device, and so forth. The constraint time is for supporting differential pricing schemes based on peak hour, nonpeak hour, and so forth.
- *Subscription based.* An example for this business model is pay TV.

Some of the business models make use of dedicated transmission channels (cable, satellite link, etc.) and end-rendering hardware (set-top box, etc.) and software. Some other business models make use of open networks such as the Internet and general rendering software (Microsoft's media player, Apple's quick time, etc.), and general hardware such as computers.

Designing a DRM solution for the dedicated setup is easier compared to the open and general setups, because the owner or distributor is connected to the consumer through a dedicated transmission channel and rendering hardware and software. Designing DRM solutions for this open or general setup is challenging for the following reasons. The Internet service providers (ISPs) do not belong to the owner or distributor category. ISPs merely provide bit pipes and switching mechanisms for transferring the data from one party to the other. However, they often implement caching and other temporary storages, which can cause stale or multiple copies to reach the consumers. In the DRM solutions, if we use DRM-aware, general-purpose, third-party rendering software and hardware, the third party that is providing the software and hardware also should be part of the DRM agreements. This is because the third party can act as an intruder. For example, third-party software and hardware can keep track of the transactions between the owner or distributor and the customer (maybe for market analysis). This problem is especially important when the client is a corporate entity. Designing a DRM-compliant computer would restrict the usefulness of the computer. To the contrary, if the copyrighted materials cannot be played or used on the computer, the charm of the computer is lost.

New revenue models are being contemplated to make DRM viable. One is to recover the cost of the copyrighted material by allowing third-party advertisers to advertise their wares along with the video. In return, they share the cost of the video. This makes the cost of video that is to be borne by the consumers nominal and makes piracy unattractive. Another model proposes making the ISPs the retailers, which makes the DRM more implementable [19]. Yet another model proposes some ticket-based system for free or low-cost digital videos. Escrow-services-based systems propose an architecture that uses economic incentives instead of tamper resistance to motivate users to keep the digital asset within the subscription community [20].

SOCIAL ASPECTS OF DRM

The social angle of DRM is governed by societal norms of fair use, such as institutions that are not for profit being allowed to use the material free of cost and make any number of copies, but those institutions and organizations that run on a profit basis need to pay for it. Other fair use problems are how the DRM supports the act of giving gifts, loaning a digital video to a friend, making a backup copy for oneself, and so forth. How to support DRM in a library scenario where loaning is a major function is another problem. Guaranteeing privacy regarding consumer buying practices is another social aspect of DRM. The social aspect includes also the education of consumers, such as to inform them of the risks associated with using the pirated content. Education involves disseminating proper norms on how copyrighted material is to be used, in addition to information on the penalties associated with the breaking of a copyright agreement.

LEGAL ASPECTS OF DRM

A proper legal framework is necessary for successful implementation of the (DRM) system [18,21–25]. The framework primarily involves enacting new legislation that supports DRM issues such as compliance, investigation, and enforcement. DRM compliance lays out rules for the hardware and software manufacturers, service providers, owners, distributors, and consumers — what each one of them should do in order to be DRM compliant. In the event of DRM agreement violations, how do we track the violations and prove the culpability of the violators? How do we enforce DRM-related laws, and also what are the penalties or compensations for DRM agreement violations? These are some of the issues tackled in the legal aspects of DRM. One of the major concerns is how the legal aspects of DRM work across the national boundaries. Often, different countries have their own DRM-related laws and the digital asset transactions often take place beyond national boundaries. Another major concern is how the fair use issue is to be tackled in DRM laws.

The United States, the European Union, and Australia have already enacted laws to support DRM. The Digital Millennium Copyright Act (DMCA), passed in 1998, is an American law implementing the 1996 World Intellectual Property Organization (WIPO) Copyright Treaty (WCT) and the WIPO Performances and Phonograms Treaty (WPPT). In 2001, the European Union enacted the European Union Copyright Directive (EUCD), which also implements the WIPO treaties. Both of these acts of law make it compulsory to outlaw any attempt to circumvent a technical copyright protection. Both also outlaw the creation and distribution of DRM circumvention tools. Whereas the DMCA allows fair use such as using digital content for research and teaching, with the exception of distance learning, the EUCD does not allow fair use. Fair use also allows the consumer to resell what he bought or make a backup copy for personal use. However, there are no clear rules defining fair use, which is usually decided by a judge on a case-by-case basis. The Australian Copyright Amendment (digital agenda) Act 2000 (DACA) is similar to the DMCA. A new act called the Consumer Broadband Digital Television Promotion Act (CBDTPA) was introduced to the U.S. Senate in 2002. The CBDTPA mandates that anyone selling, creating, or distributing "digital media devices" must include government-approved security to prevent illegal copying of protected data. The devices include CD and DVD devices and desktop PCs. This act might restrict the deployment of open-source products such as Linux and also would limit the usefulness of the desktop PC.

TECHNICAL ASPECTS OF DRM

The technical aspects of DRM include defining the technical standards and infrastructure needed to support DRM in new business models, fair use, and privacy issues of the social aspects of DRM, and provability and traceability requirements of the legal aspects of DRM [2,18]. The technical infrastructure consists of the hardware and software protection mechanisms that use cryptographic and watermarking techniques, trading protocols, rights language, and content descriptors and identifiers. We further elaborate on these technical infrastructures in this section. We also discuss the standardization efforts by various bodies such as MPEG, IETF, W3C, SMPTE, and so forth, and also current DRM techniques and tools in digital video broadcasts, stored media such as DVD, and digital cinema.

Cryptographic Techniques

Cryptographic techniques provide confidentiality, authentication, data integrity, and nonrepudiation functions. They are also designed for traitor tracing. However, in the DRM world, cryptographic techniques are primarily used for providing media confidentiality, trading party authentication, and trading protocol nonrepudiation. There are well-established party authentication protocols such as Kerberos, X.509, and so forth. Some of these are based on a symmetric key cryptosystem, whereas others are based on public key infrastructure. They authenticate the parties involved and also, if necessary, hand over secrets such as keys for confidential communication. The confidential communication may be intended to transfer payment information and also may be the medium in transaction. Free video with tracing requirement and pay video need confidentiality to be implemented. Conditional access (CA) systems, which implement confidentiality through a scrambling technique, are used in most subscription-based video systems [26,27]. The nonrepudiation function provides for nonrepudiation of the trading agreement. It is easy to combine the party authentication, trading agreement nonrepudiation, and payment function into a trading protocol, as they are usually one-to-one protocols and take place before the delivery of media.

Confidentiality of media against nonintended receivers is achieved by scrambling the media under the control of a scrambling key. The descrambling key is distributed only to the intended receivers. Various traitor-tracing schemes have been proposed by the researchers in cryptography [11,28]. Some of the works focus on fingerprinting the descrambling key; thus, each intended receiver possesses and uses a different descrambling key. Therefore, by looking at the descrambling key used in the pirate decoder, the traitor receiver who has leaked out the descrambling key can be identified. These schemes make certain assumptions, such as the video being of a large size, so it is easy for traitors to hand over the descrambling key, which is small in size in comparison to the descrambled video. Thus, in these schemes, traitor tracing cannot be performed from the descrambled video because all descrambled videos are identical. With today's distribution networks, such as copy and distribute over the Internet or through CDs, the above schemes would not be effective in combating piracy.

There are other cryptographic schemes that employ fingerprinting the video for traitor tracing. Fingerprinting of video takes place while descrambling. Combining confidentiality and video fingerprinting for traitor tracing is a challenging problem due to the following reasons. Video data being large sized, broadcast transmission techniques are preferred over unicast transmission, which reduces the transmission bandwidth requirement. Thus, a single scrambled copy of video is broadcasted to the receivers. Also, video data would be compressed before transmission. The compression scheme used is often a lossy scheme. Hence, the scrambling needs to be performed after the compression and the descrambling needs to be performed before the decompression. However, if fingerprinting is done along with descrambling, the fingerprints can be considered as bit errors occurring during transit. Especially in coding schemes, which employ interframe coding techniques, the errors can propagate into other frames and cause drifts. Thus, designing a scrambling technique that would simultaneously perform fingerprinting while descrambling with no adverse effects is a challenging problem [29].

Although it is desirable to have the fingerprinting and the descrambling processes combined into one atomic process to force the pirate to exert more effort to get an unfingerprinted clear video for piracy, they are often implemented as two separate processes. This allows the pirate to turn off the control bits for the fingerprinting process or bypass the fingerprinting process completely and thus obtain an unfingerprinted but descrambled video [11].

Media data integrity can be ensured through digital signature schemes or by using hashing functions. However, these techniques may not survive benign processing that might happen while in transit. However, for media data integrity, watermarking is preferred because watermarking techniques can be designed to survive processing such as compression, transcoding, and so forth. For traitor tracing, watermarking techniques are preferred because the watermarks can survive various benign or hostile operations.

In a multiparty distribution network (such as owner, distributor, consumer), implementing a trading protocol consisting of party authentication, trading agreement nonrepudiation, and payment function is easy, as it is essentially a one-to-one protocol (between owner and distributor, distributor and subdistributor, subdistributor and consumer, etc.). However, in order to trace the traitor along the distribution channel, owner → distributor → consumer, at every level (owner → distributor one level, distributor → subdistributor another level, and subdistributor → consumer another level) of the distribution channel in order to differentiate and identify the recipient of the media in that level, the media needs to be fingerprinted. Thus, for an n-level distribution channel, the end consumer would get media with n fingerprints in it. Multiple fingerprints can cause them to be visible and can lead to the deterioration of video quality. The multiple fingerprinting technique is a challenging problem, and one that needs to be addressed by the research community.

Watermarking Techniques

Watermarking techniques are usually preferred for copyright owner-ship declaration, creator or authorship declaration, copyright violation detection (fingerprinting function), copyright violation deterrence, copy control, media authentication, and media data integrity functions. They are also devised for variety of media (viz., text, digital audio, digital image, and digital video). A digital watermark is an embedded piece of information either visible or invisible (audible or inaudible, in the case of audio) [30]. In the case of visible watermarking [31,32], the watermarks are embedded in a way that is perceptible to a human viewer. Hence, the watermarks convey an immediate claim of ownership or authorship, providing credit to the owner or author, and also deter copyright violations. In the case of invisible watermarking [33,34], the watermarks are embedded in an imperceptible manner. The invisible watermarks can be fragile or robust. Fragile invisible watermarks [35] attempt to achieve data integrity (tamper-proofing). The fragile invis-ible watermarks must be invisible to the human observers, altered by the application of most common image processing techniques, and should be able to be quickly extracted by authorized persons. The extracted watermark indicates where the alterations have taken place. Sometimes, it is necessary that the marks remain detectable after legitimate tampering and fail to provide content authentication for illegitimate operations. These watermarks are referred to as semifragile watermarks. The desired properties for robust invisible watermarks are that they must be invisible to a human observer and that the watermarks should be detectable or extractable by an authorized person even after the media object is subjected to common signal processing techniques or after digital-to-analog and analog-to-digital conversions. A robust invisible watermarking technique is suitable for copyright ownership declaration, creator or authorship declaration, copyright violation detection (fingerprinting function), copyright violation deter-rence, and copy control. Many watermark algorithms have been proposed in the literature [36,37]. Some techniques modify spatial and temporal data samples, whereas others modify transform coefficients [29]. To be robust, the watermark must be placed in perceptually significant regions [33].

The input to a watermark embedding system is usually original data, watermark information, and a secret embedding key; the output of a watermark embedding system is watermarked data. The watermarking system can also be classified based on the watermark detection scheme in use. If original data or watermark information is needed along with watermarked data and the secret key, the system is called a *private watermarking* system [33,37–40]. If neither the original data nor the watermark information is needed for detection, the watermarking scheme is known as a *public watermarking* scheme or a *blind watermarking* scheme [29,34]. The original data and the watermark information in certain applications are to be kept secret even at the time of detection. Therefore, in these applications, blind watermarking schemes are preferred. Sometimes, during a dispute, the author has to prove the existence of a watermark to a third party. However, divulging the original data or watermark information or the key may not be desirable. The *zero knowledge watermark detection* schemes [41,42] are designed for this purpose. *Asymmetric watermarking* schemes [43,44] make use of another key for the detection rather than the embedding key.

Various types of attack on watermarking techniques have been described in References 30 and 45 to 47. There are several software tools available for benchmark watermarking techniques (e.g., Stirmark, Checkmark, and Optimark). These tools primarily support benchmarking of image watermarking techniques, but Checkmark also supports benchmarking of video watermarking techniques.

Trading Protocols

The Internet Engineering Task Force (IETF) Trade Working Group is designing a trading protocol framework for Internet commerce under the title "Internet Open Trading Protocol (IOTP)" [48]. IOTP provides an interoperable framework for Internet commerce. IOTP tries to provide a virtual capability that safely replicates the real world — the paper-based, traditional, understood, accepted methods of trading, buying, selling, and value exchanging that have existed for many years. The negotiation of who will be the parties to the trade, how it will be conducted, the presentment of an offer, the method of payment, the provision of a payment receipt, the delivery of goods, and the receipt of goods are the events that would be taken care of in the IOTP. IOTP messages are eXtensible Markup Language (XML) documents that are physically sent between the different organizations taking part in a trade. IOTP v2 (version 2) is intended to extend IOTP v1 (version 1). IOTP v2 will provide optional authentication via standards-based XML digital signatures; however, neither IOTP v1 nor v2 provides any confidentiality mechanism. Both depend on the security mechanisms of the payment system (such as Secure Electronic Transaction [SET], CyberCash, etc.) used in conjunction with them to secure payments, and both require the use of secure channels such as those provided by Secure Sockets Layer and Transport Layer Security (SSL/TLS) or Internet Protocol Security (IPsec) for confidentiality. Electronic commerce frequently requires a substantial exchange of information in order to complete a purchase or other transaction, especially the first time the parties communicate. Electronic Commerce Modeling Language (ECML) provides a set of hierarchical payment-oriented data structures (in an XML syntax) that will enable wallet software to automate the task of supplying and querying the needed information to complete a purchase or other transaction. IOTP is also designed to support the use of ECML.

The World Wide Web Consortium (W3C) is also developing standards for e-commerce on the Web. The W3C has actively contributed in developing an XML signature, XML encryption, XML protocol, micropayment, and platform for Privacy Preferences Project (P3P) standards [49]. The XML signature provides a mechanism for signing documents and metadata in order to establish who made the statement. XML encryption specifies a process for encrypting or decrypting digital content and an XML syntax used to represent the encrypted content and information that enables an intended recipient to decrypt it. The XML protocol is aimed at developing technologies that allow two or more peers to communicate in a distributed environment, using XML as its encapsulation language, allowing automated negotiations. The Platform for Privacy Preferences Project (P3P) provides communication about data privacy practices between consumers and merchant sites on the Web as well as enhanced user control over the use and disclosure of personal information. The micropayment initiative specifies how to provide in a Web page all of the information necessary to initialize a micropayment and transfer this information to the wallet for processing.

The IOTP and W3C standards for e-commerce do not address the DRM issues explicitly. However, there is a proposal for a digital Rights Management System (RMS) that is integrated into IOTP for electronic commerce applications and services [50]. It introduces a rights insertion phase and a rights verification phase for IOTP. In the proposed framework, digital watermarking plays a very important role in facilitating DRM.

Rights Languages

In order to manage the rights of the parties, the rights are to be specified in a machine-understandable way [1,51–53]. For this purpose, a rights data dictionary of allowed words and allowed constructs of these words is defined. The allowed constructs are often defined using the XML scheme, which forms the rights language. One of the rights languages is eXtensible rights Markup Language (XrML) defined by ContentGuard Inc., and another is Open Digital Rights Language (ODRL) from IPR Systems Pvt Ltd. Both have their own rights data dictionary and vocabulary for the language. These languages express the terms and conditions over any content, including permissions, constraints, obligations, offers, and agreements with rights holders. XrML is designed to be used in either single-tier or multi-tier channels of distribution with the downstream rights and conditions assigned at any level. The MPEG-21 Rights Expression Language (REL) is using XrML as the base language. In addition, the OASIS (Organization for the Advancement of Structured Information Standards) Rights Language Technical Committee and the Open eBook Forum (OeBF) are using XrML as the base for their rights language specification. The Open Mobile Alliance (OMA) accepted ODRL as the standard rights expression language for mobile content [54].

Content Declarations, Descriptors, and Identifiers

A digital content may comprise many subcontents. The makeup, structure, and organization of the content or subcontent can be specified using XML-based declaration techniques. Metadata can be used to describe the contents or subcontents (by specifying the media type, playback requirements, etc.). In order to specify the digital rights information associated with the contents or subcontents, they need to be identifiable. For example, in a video, the visual, audio, and text streams each can be considered as subcontents. Another example, an audio CD, may contain different audio tracks and each track can be considered as individual subcontents. In the first example, the types of subcontent are different; however, for the second example, the types of subcontent are the same. Several identifier codes are already defined and can be seen in Table 12.1. Except for the DOI and URI, all of the others are content-type-specific (e.g., ISBN for books, ISMN for printed music, etc.) [49,51]. MPEG-21 uses URIs to identify digital items and their parts.

Table 12.1. List of Identifier Codes and Type of Content for Which It Is Intended

Identifier Codes	Type of Content
BICI (Book Item and Component Identifier)	Book content
SICI (Serial Item and Contribution Identifier)	Serial content
DOI (Digital Object Identifier)	Any creation
URI (Uniform Resource Identifier)	Any creation
ISAN (International Standard Audiovisual Number)	Audiovisual programs
ISBN (International Standard Book Number)	Books
ISMN (International Standard Music Number)	Printed music
ISRC (International Standard Recording Code)	Sound recordings
ISSN (International Standard Serial Number)	Serials
ISWC (International Standard Musical Works Number)	Musical works
UMID (Unique Material Identifier)	Audiovisual content

MPEG and Digital Rights Management

The MPEG standards MPEG-2, MPEG-4, MPEG-7, and MPEG-21 address the DRM issues. The MPEG's specific term for DRM is "Intellectual Property Management and Protection" (IPMP) [38,55–58].

The MPEG-2 Intellectual Property Management and Protection (IPMP) standard [57] provides placeholders for sending the information about whether the packet is scrambled, the information about which conditional access system (CAS) is used, control messages such as the encryption control message (ECM) and the encryption management message (EMM), and the copyright identifier of 32 bits, which identifies the type of work (like ISBN, ISSN, etc.). The IPMP specification only addresses confidentiality and watermarking. However, IPMP-X (Intellectual Property Management and Protection – eXtension) includes an authentication function, along with the confidentiality and watermarking functions. This standard, however, does not specify the algorithms to be used for confidentiality, watermarking, or authentication.

The MPEG-4 IPMP "Hooks" covers identification of content, automated monitoring and tracking of creations, prevention of illegal copying, tracking object manipulation and modification history, and supporting transactions among users, media distributors, and rights holders [58]. The more recent call for proposal IPMP-X (extensions) stresses the interoperability of the solution to IPMP, renewability of the security, flexible expression of different business models or rules, protection of user privacy, user rights, and mobility of terminal and content. The IPMP–Descriptors (IPMP-Ds) and IPMP–Elementary Streams (IPMP-ESs) provide a communication mechanism between the IPMP system and the MPEG-4 terminal. IPMP-Ds are part of the MPEG-4 object descriptors that describe how an object can be accessed and decoded. These IPMP-Ds are used to denote which of the IPMP systems was used to encrypt the object and, consequently, at the decoder, which IPMP system is to be used for decrypting the object. IPMP-ESs are special elementary streams that are used to specify IPMP-specific data, which can be used to deliver cryptographic keys, to deliver key update information, and to initiate rekeying protocols. The IPMP-Ds and IPMP-ESs are the inputs to the IPMP system at the MPEG-4 decoder, and the IPMP system decides where to apply the IPMP control in the MPEG-4 decoder, depending on the inputs. Watermarking technology is also envisaged for sending the IPMP information. There are mainly three scenarios in which the watermarking technologies are envisaged: broadcast monitoring, watermarking-based copy control, and fingerprinting. For broadcast monitoring purposes, the MPEG-4 decoder need not contain the watermark detectors, as the required monitoring can be done after rendering. The copy control systems require that the IPMP system inside the MPEG-4 decoder implements the watermark retrieval algorithm; and for fingerprinting, the IPMP system inside the MPEG-4 decoder must implement the watermark embedding algorithm.

MPEG-7 is a content description standard for content management [7]. The descriptions can be used for searching and retrieval of the content. The description consists of a description scheme (DS), descriptors (Ds), and a binary streamable representation of DSs and Ds called the binary format for MPEG-7 (BiM). Because MPEG-7 is for descriptions, the IPMP manages, protects, and authenticates these descriptions. MPEG-7 does not manage and protect the contents; however, it will accommodate and provide a mechanism for pointing to the content rights. MPEG-7 will provide the usage rules, usage history, identification of contents, and identification of contents in descriptions.

The vision of MPEG-21 is to define a multimedia framework to enable transparent and augmented use of multimedia resources across a wide range of networks and devices used by the different sectors [38,56]. The MPEG-21 multimedia framework will identify and define the key elements needed to support the multimedia value and delivery chain, the relation between them, and the operations supported by these elements. There are seven key elements that have been identified for supporting inter-operability and one of them is IPMP. In the IPMP area, MPEG-21's aim is to provide a uniform framework that enables all users to express their rights and interests in agreements related to digital objects and to have assurance that those rights, interests, and agreements will be persistently and reliably managed and protected across a wide range of networks and devices. The MPEG IPMP extensions are designed so that they can be applied to any MPEG multimedia representation (MPEG-2, MPEG-4, MPEG-7, and MPEG-21).

Digital Video Broadcasts and DRM

There are three popular digital TV broadcasting standards: the American Advanced Television Systems Committee (ATSC) standard, the European Digital Video Broadcasting (DVB) standard, and the Japanese Integrated Services Digital Broadcasting–Terrestrial (ISDB-T) standard. These broadcasting standards use MPEG-2 for video coding. The pay channels of digital video broadcasts require that a confidentiality requirement be implemented against the nonsubscribers. Hence, current pay channels employ a conditional access system (CAS) for this purpose. Primarily, the CAS uses a scrambling technique for providing the confidentiality [11,22,26,27,59,60]. The broadcaster scrambles the video data using a control word (CW) and broadcasts the scrambled video data. The sub-scribers use the same CW to descramble the received scrambled video data to obtain clear video. The Data Encryption Standard (DES) is used in ATSC, and the digital video broadcasting common scrambling algorithm

(DVB-CSA) [59] is used in DVB. The DVB supports the Simulcrypt and Multicrypt standards, whereas ATSC supports only the Simulcrypt standard [59,60]. The Simulcrypt standard allows the coexistence of more than one CAS, simultaneously addressing different consumer bases in one transmission. In the case of Multicrypt, no program is available through more than one CAS.

The current CAS only supports confidentiality against nonsubscribers; it does not implement any fingerprinting technique to trace the copyright violator. Because the broadcasting requires a single copy to be transmitted and the copyright violator identification requires individual subscribers copy to be unique, the fingerprinting for copyright violator identification should be performed at each subscriber end. This means that current CASs, at the subscriber end, have to implement the fingerprinting process for copyright violator identification in addition to the descrambling process. It is more secure if the fingerprinting and descrambling processes can be combined into a single atomic process. However, it is hard to combine the existing descrambling process and the fingerprinting process into a single atomic process. It is even more challenging to support confidentiality and copyright violator identification in a compressed (MPEG-2) domain broadcast. The challenges are due to the quantization step, which is lossy, and interframe coding, which makes use of motion-compensated predictions. Thus, DRM in digital video broadcasts currently implements only the confidentiality requirement against nonsubscribers.

Stored Media (DVD) and DRM

The DVD Copy Control Association (DVD CCA) licenses Content Scrambling System (CSS) to the owners and manufacturers of DVD disks with video contents and manufacturers of DVD players, DVD recorders, and DVD-ROM drives [8,9,61]. CSS is a data encryption and authentication scheme intended to prevent copying video files directly from prerecorded (read-only) DVD video disks. CSS was developed primarily by Matsushita and Toshiba. The information on the DVD video disk is CSS encrypted. DVD players have CSS circuitry that decrypts the data before being decoded and displayed. Computer DVD decoder hardware and software would include a CSS decryption module, and the DVD-ROM drive would have extra firmware to exchange authentication and decryption keys with the CSS decryption module in the computer. The CSS license is extremely restrictive, in an attempt to keep the CSS algorithm and keys secret. However, this CSS algorithm was broken and posted on the Internet.

Content Protection for Prerecorded Media (CPPM) is for DVD audio, which performs the same function as that of CSS. A disk may contain both CSS and CPPM content if it is a hybrid DVD video/DVD audio disk. Content Protection for Recordable Media (CPRM) protects the exchange of entertainment content recorded on portable or removable storage media such as DVD-RAM, DVD-R, DVD-RW, and secure compact flash. The companies responsible for CPPM and CPRM are Intel, IBM, MEI, and Toshiba. CSS, CPPM, and CPRM are not designed to protect against copying through the analog output port. However, Macrovision's DVD copy protection system supports protection against such analog copying. Macrovision's Copy Generation Management System (CGMS) can accommodate fair-use copying by allowing an unlimited number of first-generation copies, but prohibiting those copies from being recorded again. The CGMS works by storing 2 bits of CGMS copy control information (CCI) in the header of each disk sector. The CGMS is CGMS-A for analog output and CGMS-D for digital output. Verance developed a DVD audio watermarking technique (which uses CGMS CCI) to guard against copying through audio analog output. The Watermark Review Panel (WaRP) under the DVD Copy Protection Working Group (CPTWG) is working on video watermarking proposals from the Galaxy Group (IBM, NEC, Pioneer, Hitachi, and Sony) and the Millennium Group (Macrovision, Digimarc, and Philips) to choose one standard technique for DVD content protection. The minimum watermark payload expected is of three states (never copy, no more copying, and copy once) and an additional 2 bits for triggering an analog protection system.

Digital Transmission Content Protection (DTCP) safeguards data streams transmitted over digital interfaces like IEEE-1394 and USB. DTCP was developed by Intel, Sony, Hitachi, Matsushita, and Toshiba, and the Digital Transmission Licensing Administrator (DTLA) issues licenses to use DTCP. DTCP can be used to protect DVD content only if it has already been encrypted by CSS, CPRM, or CPPM. DTCP also uses 2-bit CCI to signal "copy one generation," "copy freely," "copy never," and "no more copies."

Digital Cinema and DRM

Cinemas also are not out of the compulsions of the digital age [6,62–65]. The digital cinema system delivers motion pictures that have been digitized or mastered, compressed, and encrypted to theaters using either physical media distribution (such as DVD-ROMs) or electronic transmission methods, such as via Internet and satellite multicast methods. Although today's digital cinema quality is not as good as that of film-based cinema, the digital cinema has many compelling factors in its favor. One of the advantages is that although the quality is currently not as good, the quality of the digital cinema is preserved over repeated shows; whereas in the film-based cinema, the quality deteriorates after multiple viewings. Another advantage is that the distribution cost is low for digital cinema, as it can be transmitted to cinema halls through electronic transmission methods or through stored media such as DVDs, which are much more manageable than the bulkier and heavier film reels. Making copies of film reels for distributing to cinema halls is an enormous task compared to making copies in the digital domain. In addition, digital cinema can incorporate advanced theatrical experiences such as moving seats and so forth through the use of metadata.

Usually, movies are mastered on film and then digitized to obtain the digital version. However, with the introduction of high-definition digital camcorders, motion pictures are mastered directly in the digital domain. This digital movie is then compressed, encrypted, and delivered to the cinema halls. At the cinema hall, the digital movie is temporarily stored, decrypted, decompressed, and projected or played back. The cinema halls are equipped with a storage system and a projector system. There are two models for the secure storage and playback of digital cinema content: the broadcast server model and the data server model. In the broadcast server model, the storage system provides for temporary storage, decryption decompression, and local encryption. The projector system implements local decryption, and playback. As far as security is concerned, the storage system and the projector system need to be physically secured, and the communication between the projector system and the storage system needs to be secured through local encryption. However, in the data server model, the storage system needs only temporary storage and the projection system implements decryption, decompression, and playback. In this model, only the projector system needs to be physically protected. The audio stream and other advanced-feature control streams are routed to the relevant processor and played back after decryption and demultiplexing by the storage or playback system. The producer should employ a strong encryption scheme and the key needs to be transmitted through a secure channel to the security manager in the cinema hall. Usually for enhanced security and control, producers or distributors apply the encryption in such a way that it can be decrypted only in a designated storage or projector system and they can also control the playback schedules or revoke the playback if the storage or playback system is found compromised or the exhibitor is found aiding in piracy.

In a film-based cinema system, pirates can make a pirate copy by taking possession of film reels and digitizing the content. This is possible because the reel content is not encrypted. In the case of digital cinema, because the digital cinema content is transferred in an encrypted mode, it would be difficult for the pirates to break the encryption scheme to make a pirated copy. Another technique for making a pirated copy is by directly videographing off the screen during the show. In order to trace and control this kind of piracy in digital cinema systems, digital watermarking techniques can be employed. None of the current digital cinema systems explicitly mention the use of any schemes for tracing piracy. The current systems only provide conditional access using an encryption scheme. Thus, much work remains to be done in this area.

The Society for Motion Picture and Television Engineers (SMPTE) of the United States has constituted the DC28 Digital Cinema Technology Committee, a working group to discuss the various issues that face the full deployment of digital cinema. DC28 is divided into seven study groups: mastering, compression, conditional access, transport and delivery, audio, theater systems, and projection. The European counterpart of the SMPTE is the European Digital Cinema Forum (EDCF), where study groups from different European countries share their information on digital cinema and the "technical module" is where all of the security research is being performed.

CONCLUSION

This chapter discussed the rights requirements of each party involved over the life cycle of the digital video. It also discussed various requirements for DRM stemming from asset management and usage controls needs. In addition, the requirements and constraints of DRM, and the business, legal, and social aspects of DRM were also presented. The technical aspect of DRM elaborated on the technologies used for obtaining DRM; techniques and tools for obtaining DRM in digital video broadcasts, stored video such as DVDs, and digital cinema; and standardization efforts by bodies such as MPEG, IETF, W3C, SMPTE, and so forth.

Most of the current DRM systems support confidentiality against non-consumers. Some of the systems implement copy protection and control mechanisms. Some envisage the use of fingerprinting mechanisms for tracing piracy. These systems are essentially intended to mitigate the concerns of owners. Although the trading protocols and rights languages are being designed with the intention of supporting consumer concerns, the supporting cryptographic and watermarking techniques and protocols have yet to be designed. A full-fledged DRM system should be capable of supporting the rights of all parties (creators, owners, distributors, and consumers) involved in digital asset creation and transaction. DRM in its broadest sense is end-to-end management of digital trust. Therefore, tremendous research challenges abound in this vital area of information security.

REFERENCES

1. The Open Digital Rights Language, http://odrl.net/, 2002.
2. Iannella, R., Digital rights management (DRM) architectures, *D-Lib Mag.*, 7(6), 2001.

3. Löytynoja, M., Seppänen, T., and Cvejic, N., Experimental DRM Architecture Using Watermarking and PKI, presented at *First International Mobile IPR Workshop: Rights Management of Information Products on the Mobile Internet*, Helsinki, 2003.
4. Mooney, S., Interoperability: Digital rights management and the emerging ebook environment, *D-Lib Mag.*, 7(1), 2001.
5. Linnartz, J.P., Depovere, G., and Kalker, T., *Philips Electronics Response to Call for Proposals Issued by the Data Hiding SubGroup Copy Protection Technical Working Group*, July 1997.
6. Peinado, M., Petitcolas, F.A.P., and Kirovski, D., Digital rights management for digital cinema, *Multimedia Syst.*, 9, 228–238, 2003.
7. The MPEG Home Page, http://www.chiariglione.org/mpeg/.
8. The Copy Protection Technical Working Group, http://www.cptwg.org/.
9. DVD, The DVD Copy Control Association, http://www.dvdcca.org/.
10. Park, J. and Sandhu, R., Towards Usage Control Models: Beyond Traditional Access Control, in *Proceedings of 7th ACM Symposium on Access Control Models and Technologies*, 2002, pp 57–64.
11. Emmanuel, S. and Kankanhalli, M.S., A digital rights management scheme for broadcast video, Multimedia Syst., 8(6), pp. 444–458, 2003.
12. Erickson, J.S., Fair Use, DRM, and trusted computing, *Commun. ACM*, 46(4), 34–39, 2003.
13. Fox, B.L. and LaMacchia B.A., Encouraging recognition of fair uses in DRM systems, *Commun. ACM*, 46(4), 61–63, 2003.
14. Cohen, J.E., DRM and privacy, *Commun. ACM*, 46(4), 47–49, 2003.
15. Korba, L. and Kenny, S., Towards Meeting the Privacy Challenge: Adapting DRM, in *Proceedings of ACM Workshop on Digital Rights Management*, 2002.
16. Durfee, G. and Franklin, M., Distribution Chain Security, in *Proceedings of the 7th ACM Conference on Computer and Communications Security*, Athens, ACM Press, New York, 2000, pp. 63–70.
17. DRM Business Models, http://www.microsoft.com/windows/windowsmedia/wm7/drm/scenarios.aspx.
18. Liu, Q., Safavi-Naini, R., and Sheppard, N.P., Digital Rights Management for Content Distribution, presented at *Australasian Information Security Workshop*, Adelaide, 2003.
19. Sobel, L.S., DRM as an Enabler of Business Models: ISPs as Digital Retailers, presented at *Digital Rights Management Conference*, The Berkeley Center for Law and Technology, February, 2003.
20. Horne, B., Pinkas, B., and Sander, T., Escrow Services and Incentives in Peer-to-Peer Networks, presented at *3rd ACM Conference on Electronic Commerce*, 2001.
21. Clark, D., Future of Intellectual Property: How Copyright Became Controversial, in *Proceedings of the 12th Annual Conference on Computers, Freedom and Privacy*, 2002.
22. Clayson, P.L. and Dallard, N.S., Systems Issues in the Implementation of DVB Simulcrypt Conditional Access, presented at *International Broadcasting Convention*, 1997, pp. 470–475.
23. Rosnay, M.D., Digital Right Management Systems toward European Law: Between Copyright Protection and Access Control, in *Proceedings of the 2nd International Conference on WEB Delivering of Music*, 2002.
24. Samuelson, P., Encoding the law into digital libraries, *Commun. ACM*, 41(4), 13–18, 1998.
25. Williams, J., IT Architecture meets the real (legal) world, *IT Prof.*, 3(5), 65–68, 2001.
26. Mooij, W., Advances in Conditional Access Technology, presented at *International Broadcasting Convention*, 1997, pp. 461–464.
27. Zeng, W. and Lei, S., Efficient Frequency Domain Digital Video Scrambling for Content Access Control, presented at *ACM Multimedia '99 Proceedings*, Orlando, FL, 1999.

28. Anderson, R. and Manifavas, C., Chameleon—A New Kind of Stream Cipher, in *Proceedings of the 4th Workshop on Fast Software Encryption*, Haifa, 1997.
29. Emmanuel, S. and Kankanhalli, M.S., Copyright Protection for MPEG-2 Compressed Broadcast Video, in *Proceedings of the IEEE International Conference on Multimedia and Expo (ICME 2001)*, Tokyo, 2001.
30. Hartung, F. and Kutter, M., Multimedia watermarking techniques, *Proc. IEEE*, 87(7), 1079–1107, 1999.
31. Braudaway, G.W., Magerlein, K.A., and Mintzer, F., Protecting Publicly Available Images with a Visible Image Watermark, presented at *International Conference on Image Processing*, 1997, Vol. 1, pp. 524–527.
32. Meng, J. and Chang, S.F., Embedding Visible Video Watermarks in the Compressed Domain, presented at *International Conference on Image Processing*, 1998, Vol. 1, pp. 474–477.
33. Cox, I.J., Killian, J., Leighton, T., and Shamoon, T., Secured spread spectrum watermarking for multimedia, *IEEE Trans. Image Process.*, 6(12), 1673–1687, 1997.
34. Hartung, F. and Girod, B., Watermarking of uncompressed and compressed video, *Signal Process.*, 66(3), 283–301, 1998.
35. Kundur, D. and Hatzinakos, D., Digital Watermarking Using Multiresolution Wavelet Decomposition, in *Proceedings of IEEE International Conference on Acoustics, Speech, and Signal Processing*, 1998, Vol. 5, pp. 2969–2972.
36. Barni, M., Bartolini, F., Cappellini, V., and Piva, A., A DCT domain system for robust image watermarking, *Signal Process.*, 66(3), 357–372.
37. Podilchuk, C.I. and Zeng, W., Digital image watermarking using visual models, in *Proceedings of the IS&T/SPIE Conference on Human Vision and Electronic Imaging II*, San Jose, CA, B.E. Rogowitz and T.N. Pappas, Eds., IS&T and SPIE, 1997, pp. 100–111.
38. Bormans, J., Gelissen, J., and Perkis, A., *MPEG-21*: The 21st century multimedia framework, *IEEE Signal Process. Mag.*, 20(2), 53–62, 2003.
39. Piva, A., Barni, M., Bartolini, F., and Cappellini, V., DCT-based Watermark Recovering without Resorting to the Uncorrupted Original Image, presented at *International Conference on Image Processing*, 1997, Vol. 1, pp. 520–523.
40. Wolfgang, R.B. and Delp, E.J., A Watermarking Technique for Digital Imagery: Further Studies, in *Proceedings of IEEE International Conference on Imaging, Systems, and Technology*, Las Vegas, 1997, pp. 279–287.
41. Adelsbach, A. and Sadeghi, A.R., Zero-Knowledge Watermark Detection and Proof of Ownership, in *Proceedings of Fourth Information Hiding Workshop, IHW2001*, Pittsburgh, 2001.
42. Craver, S., Zero Knowledge Watermark Detection, in *Proceedings of the Third International Workshop on Information Hiding, Lecture Notes in Computer Science*, Vol. 1768, Springer-Verlag, Berlin, 2000, pp. 101–116.
43. Eggers, J.J., Su, J.K., and Girod, B., Asymmetric Watermarking Schemes, in *Proceedings of Sicherheit in Mediendaten*, Berlin, September 2000, Springer-Verlag, Berlin, 2000.
44. Pfitzmann, B. and Schunter, M., Asymmetric fingerprinting (extended abstract), in *Advances in Cryptology — EUROCRYPT '96*, Maurer, U., Ed., *Lecture Notes in Computer Science*, Vol. 1070, Springer-Verlag, Berlin, 1996, pp. 84–95.
45. Langelaar, G.C., Lagendijk, R.L., and Biemond, J., Removing Spatial Spread Spectrum Watermarks, presented at *European Signal Processing Conference (EUSIPCO'98)*, Rhodes, Greece, 1998.
46. Cox, I.J. and Linnartz, J.P., Some general methods for tampering with watermarks, *IEEE J. Selected Areas Commun.*, 16(4), 587–593, 1998.

47. Craver, S., Memon, N., Yeo, B., and Yeung, M.M., Resolving rightful ownerships with invisible watermarking techniques: Limitations, attacks and implications, *IEEE J. Selected Areas Commun.*, 16(4), 573–586, 1998.

48. Internet Open Trading Protocol (trade), http://www.ietf.org/html.charters/trade-charter.html.

49. The W3C Trading Protocols, http://www.w3.org/Help/siteindex.

50. Kwok, S.H., Cheung, S.C., Wong, K.C., Tsang, K.F., Lui, S.M., and Tam, K.Y., Integration of digital rights management into Internet Open Trading Protocol (IOTP), *Dec. Support Syst.*, 34(4), 413–425, (2003).

51. The Extensible rights Markup Language, http://www.xrml.org.

52. Mulligan D. and Burstein A., Implementing Copyright Limitations in Rights Expression, in *Languages Proceedings of ACM Workshop on Digital Rights Management*, 2002.

53. Wang, X., Lao, G., DeMartini, T., Reddy, H., Nguyen, M., and Valenzuela, E., XrML — Extensible rights Markup Language, in *Proceedings of the 2002 ACM Workshop on XML Security*, 2002, pp. 71–79.

54. Messerges, T.S. and Dabbish, E.A., Digital Rights management in a 3G Mobile Phone and Beyond, in *Proceedings of ACM Workshop on Digital Rights Management*, 2003.

55. Hartung, F. and Ramme, F., Digital rights management and watermarking of multimedia content for M-commerce applications, *IEEE Commun. Mag.*, 38(11), 78–84, 2000.

56. ISO/IEC TC JTC1/SC 29/WG11/N 6269: Information Technology — Multimedia Framework (MPEG-21) – Part 1: Vision, Technology and Strategy.

57. ISO/IEC 13818-1: Generic Coding of Moving Pictures and Associated Audio: Systems. (MPEG-2 Systems).

58. ISO/IEC 14496-1: Coding of Audiovisual Objects: Systems (MPEG-4 Systems).

59. Cutts, D.J., *DVB conditional access, Electron., Commn., Engi. J.*, 9(1), pp. 21–27, 1997.

60. ATSC Standard A/70: Conditional Access System for Terrestrial Broadcast with Amendment, http://www.atsc.org/standards.html, 2004.

61. Simitopoulos, D., Zissis, N., Georgiadis, P., Emmanouilidis, V., and Strintzis, M.G., Encryption and watermarking for the secure distribution of copyrighted MPEG video on DVD, *Multimedia Syst.*, 9(3), 217–227, 2003.

62. Byers, S., Cranor, L., Cronin, E., Kormann, D., and McDaniel, P., Analysis of Security Vulnerabilities in the Movie Production and Distribution Process, in *Proceedings of ACM Workshop on Digital Rights Management*, 2003.

63. The Motion Picture Association's Role in Digital Cinema, http://www.mpaa.org/dcinema.

64. Korris, J. and Macedonia, M., The end of celluloid: digital cinema emerges, *Computer*, 35(4), 96–98, 2002.

65. Lubell, P.D., A coming attraction: digital cinema, *IEEE Spectrum*, 37(3), 72–78, 2000.

66. Camp, L.J., DRM: Doesn't Really Mean Digital Copyright Management, in *Proceedinss of the 9th ACM Conference on Computers and Communications Security*, 2002, pp. 78–87.

67. The Digital Object Identifiers, http://www.doi.org/.

Index

Index